Mountain Biking
New York

by
Michael Margulis

FALCON™

HELENA, MONTANA

A FALCON GUIDE

Falcon Press Publishing is continually expanding its list of recreational guidebooks. All books include detailed descriptions, accurate maps, and all the information necessary for enjoyable trips. You can order extra copies of this book and get information and prices for other Falcon guidebooks by writing Falcon, P.O. Box 1718, Helena, MT 59624, or calling toll-free 1-800-582-2665. Also, please ask for a free copy of our current catalog. Visit our web site at http:\\www.falconguide.com.

© 1997 by Michael Margulis
All rights reserved
Printed in Canada.
Published by Falcon Press Publishing Co., Inc.
First edition, first printing
10 9 8 7 6 5 4 3 2 1

Library of Congress Cataloging-in-Publication Data

Margulis, Michael.
    Mountain biking New York / Michael Margulis ; Foreword,
    introduction, and afterword by Dennis Coello.—1st ed.
       p.   cm.—
    ISBN 1-56044-534-3 (pbk.)
    1. All terrain cycling—New York (State)—Guidebooks. 2. Trails—New York (State)—Guidebooks. 3. New York (State)—Guidebooks.
I. Title.
GV1045.5.N7M37   1997
796.6'3'09747—dc21   97-593
                                                                    CIP

Photos by the author unless otherwise credited
Maps by Brian Taylor
Cover photo by Barbara Margulis

Falcon Press Publishing Co., Inc.
P.O. Box 1718
Helena, Montana 59624

♻ Text pages printed on recycled paper

CAUTION
Outdoor recreation activities are by their very nature potentially hazardous. All participants in such activities must assume the responsibility for their own actions and safety. The information contained in this guidebook cannot replace sound judgment and good decision-making skills, which help reduce risk exposure, nor does the scope of this book allow for disclosure of all the potential hazards and risks involved in such activities. Learn as much as possible about the outdoor recreation activities in which you participate in, prepare for the unexpected, and be cautious. The reward will be a safer and more enjoyable experience.

To my dad

"I go to nature to be soothed and healed and to have my senses put in tune once more."

John Burroughs

Table of Contents

List of Maps

MAP LEGEND

Ride trailhead

Primary bike trail

Direction of travel

Optional bike trail and trailhead

Other trail

Hiking Only trail

Interstate highways (with exit no.)

U.S. routes

State routes

Other paved roads
Jeffers Rd.

Unpaved, gravel or dirt roads (may be 4WD only)

U.S. Forest Service roads

Cities
New York City

Towns or settlements
Scarborough
Cold Spring

Lake
Dam

Intermittent stream

Perennial stream

0 1/2 1
MILES

Approximate scale in miles

True North

CLARENCE FAHNESTOCK MEMORIAL STATE PARK

Public Lands*

State Border

✈ Airport

🏛 Fire tower or lookout

Observatory

Archeological or historical site

Falls or rapids

Park office or ranger station

Boat ramp

Food

Picnic area

▲ Campground (CG)

Gate

Power line or pipeline

Cattle guard

House or cabin

Restrooms

Cemetery or gravesite

Lodging

Spring

Church

Mountain or butte

Stable, corral or ranch

Cliff, escarpment or outcropping

Mountain pass

Swimming Area

Drinking water

△ Mountain summit
3312 (elevation in feet)

Transmission towers

✕ Mine or quarry

Tunnel or bridge

Remember, private property exists in and around our National Forests.

Acknowledgments

While writing this book, I had much help from a few special people. I would like first to mention my dad, Charles Margulis, who first introduced me to my two-wheeled adventures.

Special thanks go to my lovely wife, Barbara, for making all those sustaining peanut-butter sandwiches, filling my thermos with French cafe, and hiding a Milky Way in my gear bag. And then there were all those times she accompanied me on one of those "I wonder what this trail is like" trips, and all we would do for two hours is carry our bikes on our shoulders. Her understanding and support during the past year were priceless.

My inspiration: My father on his WW II mission—running payroll to the troops in the Philippines in 1942.

Thanks to my little pumpkin Alize, who withstood all those countless bumps in the road in the bike trailer I towed behind. As long as she had Mr. Moose and Bear, a couple of raisins, and a banana, she never complained.

I would like to thank my mom for having the intuition to spot a good trail and for coming with me on my more technical rides. Well, rather than actually ride the demanding trails, she opted to watch my daughter, who complained of too many bumps on the last ride.

I would like to express my gratitude to MARIN Mountain Bikes in Marin County, California, for providing me with their agile, well-crafted, and well-designed "Pine Mountain" mountain bike for my research. My bike was hit by a tree while I was maneuvering down a steep hill and was severely trashed. Fortunately, and as a rule, I was wearing helmet protection. In addition, Joannou Cycle in Northvale, New Jersey, supplied my wife with a Jamis mountain bike, a high-performance piece of equipment that provided her with a safe and superior ride.

Many thanks go out to my good friend, David Moin, for his advice and assistance on the text.

And last but not least, I can't forget my faithful companion, Shogun, our Norwegian Elkhound, who accompanied me on many of my excursions, keeping pace and frequently sniffing out the direction to take on some of the more poorly marked trails.

Michael Margulis

Foreword

This series is designed to provide all-terrain bikers with the information they need to find and ride the very best trails everywhere in the mainland United States. Whether you're new to the sport and don't know where to pedal, or an experienced mountain biker who wants to learn the classic trails in another region, this series is for you. Drop a few bucks for the book, spend an hour with the detailed maps and route descriptions, and you're prepared for the finest in off-road cycling.

My role as editor of this series was simple: First, find a mountain biker who knows the area and loves to ride. Second, ask that person to spend a year researching the most popular and very best rides around. And third, have that rider describe each trail in terms of difficulty, scenery, condition, elevation change, and all other categories of information that are important to trail riders. "Pretend you've just completed a ride and met up with fellow mountain bikers at the trailhead," I told each author. "Imagine their questions, be clear in your answers."

As I said, the *editorial* process—that of sending out riders and reading the submitted chapters—is a snap. But the work involved in finding, riding, and writing about each trail is enormous. In some instances our authors' tasks are made easier by the information contributed by local bike shops or cycling clubs, or even by the writers of local "where-to" guides. Credit for these contributions is provided, when appropriate, in each chapter, and our sincere thanks goes to all who have helped.

But the overwhelming majority of trails are discovered and pedaled by our authors themselves, then compared with dozens of other routes to determine if they qualify as "classic"—that area's best in scenery and cycling fun. If you've ever had the experience of pioneering a route from outdated topographic maps, or entering a bike shop to request information from local riders who would much prefer to keep their favorite trails secret, or know how it is to double- and triple-check data to be positive your trail info is correct, then you have an idea of how each of our authors has labored to bring about these books. You and I, and all the mountain bikers of America, are the richer for their efforts.

You'll get more out of this book if you take a moment to read the Introduction explaining how to read the trail listings. The "Topographic Maps" section will help you understand how useful topos will be on a ride, and will also tell you where to get them. And though this is a "where-to," not a "how-to" guide, those of you who have not traveled the backcountry might find "Hitting the Trail" of particular value.

In addition to the material above, newcomers to mountain biking might want to spend a minute with the glossary, page 408, so that terms like *hardpack, single-track,* and *water bars* won't throw you when you come across them in the text.

Finally, the tips in the Afterword on mountain biking etiquette and the land-use controversy might help us all enjoy the trails a little more.

All the best.

Dennis Coello
St. Louis

Preface

The key to surviving in the city is to discover nature. I discovered the great outdoors at an early age. My father took our family on trips into upstate New York, luring us to the wilderness, compelled as he was to escape the pressures of urban life, the stress of commuting to work, and the strains of working a long week. This fostered a sense of adventure and appealed to our sensibilities. Time and again we would return to the peace and tranquility of nature. As a child, I didn't sense my father's compulsion, yet I was absorbed in the grand scheme to escape to the country. On the ride up, even before we arrived, I felt that sense of adventure when my father pulled off to the side of the road to take in some panoramic vista. We felt his appreciation as he photographed or painted these panoramas.

We would always learn something from our excursions. We learned a lot about what made us feel good and what we enjoyed, and about the beauty of the environment.

Decades later, I have continued the family tradition. I understand why my father brought us into nature and away from all the responsibilities associated with urban living.

Just as he was compelled to escape and seek peace of mind in nature's quiet setting, I am compelled to do the same and share with you my outdoor discoveries through mountain biking.

One of the major challenges of this sport is determining where to ride. Typically, we take the trails that are closest or most familiar to us. This is particularly true with those who are not members of mountain bike clubs. The pleasures of mountain biking are greatly enhanced if our choice of trails can be expanded. This is the premise for my book.

There is a myriad of trails for mountain bikers even within a 100-mile radius of New York City. The last 200 years have left a network of logging, mining, carriage, and old forest routes within the Highland, Ramapo, Shawangunk, and Catskill Mountains as well as the pine barrens of Long Island. My excursions through wilderness tracts have uncovered many great routes of exceptional beauty off the beaten path.

My mountain bike odyssey was enriched as I ventured into woods unknown and found traces and historical remnants of the original trailblazers of hundreds of years before. I rode on dirt roads used by stage coaches and hunting routes of Native Americans and along escape routes used by the military forces in the American Revolutionary War. Imagine all the purposes these routes served through the centuries for farming, mining, logging, warfare, and hunting. Now this historical network of forested trails provides a great opportunity for mountain biking.

It is surprising that mountain biking is not more popular, considering the region's wealth of wilderness and the soulful high of silently gliding on these pristine trails. It's a thrill finding a new path. The ride becomes a fountain of energy. The day belongs to you.

This book should provide inspiration and enlightenment for those living and working in the metropolitan area and far beyond. It covers a wide variety of trails suitable for riders of all abilities. Mountain biking has provided us with a vehicle to enjoy and explore nature. We must work to preserve nature not only for ourselves, but for our families and for the generations to come.

During the writing of this book, my father passed away. However, I was fortunate to spend hours chatting with him about my riding experiences, which triggered his memories of carrying U.S. Army Payroll during World War II. He spent three years motorcycling the jungle trails of New Guinea, all the while dodging the enemy. Though we lived in different times, we shared the same philosophy of life: to get the most out of life, to get out and go, and to get others going. My father always used to say "Let's take a ride." With those words, I knew we were in for a day of adventure. He would be proud to know his message will be imparted to so many others and that this book will give others a taste of the outdoors he savored.

Michael Margulis

Mountain Biking
New York

Introduction

TRAIL DESCRIPTION OUTLINE

Information on each trail in this book begins with a general description that includes length, configuration, scenery, highlights, trail conditions, and difficulty. Additional description is contained in eleven individual categories. The following will help you to understand all of the information provided.

Trail name: Trail names are as designated on United States Geological Survey (USGS) or Forest Service or other maps, and/or by local custom.
Length: The overall length of a trail is described in miles, unless stated otherwise.
Configuration: This is a description of the shape of each trail—whether the trail is a loop, out-and-back (that is, along the same route), figure eight . . . or if it connects with another trail described in the book.
Scenery: Here you will find a general description of the natural surroundings during the seasons most riders pedal the trail, and a suggestion of what is to be found at special times (like great fall foliage or cactus in bloom).
Highlights: Towns, major water crossings, historical sites, etc., are listed.
Trail conditions: Trails are described in terms of being paved, unpaved, sandy, hard-packed, washboarded, two- or four-wheel-drive, single-track or double-track. All terms that might be unfamiliar to the first-time mountain biker are defined in the Glossary.
Difficulty: This provides at a glance a description of the degree of physical exertion required to complete the ride, and the technical skill required to pedal it. Authors were asked to keep in mind the fact that all riders are not equal, and thus to gauge the trail in terms of how the middle-of-the-road rider—someone between the newcomer and Ned Overend—could handle the route. Comments about the trail's length, condition, and elevation change will also assist you in determining the difficulty of any trail relative to your own abilities.

General location: This category describes where the trail is located in reference to a nearby town or other landmark.
Elevation change: Unless stated otherwise, the figure provided is the total gain and loss of elevation along the trail. In regions where the elevation variation is not extreme, the route is simply described as flat, rolling, or possessing short steep climbs or descents.

1

Season: This is the best time of year to pedal the route, taking into account trail conditions (for example, when it will not be muddy), riding comfort (when the weather is too hot, cold, or wet), and local hunting seasons.

Note: Because the exact opening and closing dates of deer, elk, moose, and antelope seasons often change from year to year, riders should check with the local Fish and Game department, or call a sporting goods store (or any place that sells hunting licenses) in a nearby town before heading out. Wear bright clothes in fall, and don't wear suede jackets while in the saddle. Hunter's-orange tape on the helmet is also a good idea.

Services: This category is of primary importance in guides for paved-road tourers, but is far less crucial to most mountain bike trail descriptions because there are usually no services whatsoever to be found. Authors have noted when water is available on desert or long mountain routes, and have listed the availability of food, lodging, campgrounds, and bike shops. If all these services are present, you will find only the words "All services available in . . . ."

Hazards: Special hazards like steep cliffs, great amounts of deadfall, or barbed-wire fences very close to the trail are noted here.

Rescue index: Determining how far one is from help on any particular trail can be difficult due to the backcountry nature of most mountain bike rides. Authors therefore state the proximity of homes or Forest Service outposts, nearby roads where one might hitch a ride, or the likelihood of other bikers being encountered on the trail. Phone numbers of local sheriff departments or hospitals have not been provided because phones are almost never available. If you are able to reach a phone, the local operator will connect you with emergency services.

Land status: This category provides information regarding whether the trail crosses land operated by the Forest Service, Bureau of Land Management, a city, state, or national park, whether it crosses private land whose owner (at the time the author did the research) has allowed mountain bikers right of passage, and so on.

Note: Authors have been extremely careful to offer only those routes that are open to bikers and are legal to ride. However, because land ownership changes over time, and because the land-use controversy created by mountain bikes still has not completely subsided, it is the duty of each cyclist to look for and to heed signs warning against trail use. Don't expect this book to get you off the hook when you're facing some small-town judge for pedaling past a "Biking Prohibited" sign erected the day before. Look for these signs, read them, and heed the advice. And remember there's always another trail.

Maps: The maps in this book have been produced with great care, and, in conjunction with the trail-following suggestions, will help you stay on course. But as every experienced mountain biker knows, things can get tricky in the backcountry. It is therefore strongly suggested that you avail yourself of the detailed information found in the 7.5 minute series USGS (United States Geological Survey) topographic maps. In some cases, authors have found that specific Forest Service or other maps may be more useful than the USGS quads, and tell how to obtain them.

Finding the trail: Detailed information on how to reach the trailhead, and where to park your car is provided here.

Sources of additional information: Here you will find the address and/or phone number of a bike shop, governmental agency, or other source from which trail information can be obtained.

Notes on the trail: This is where you are guided carefully through any portions of the trail that are particularly difficult to follow. The author also may add information about the route that does not fit easily in the other categories. This category will not be present for those rides where the route is easy to follow.

ABBREVIATIONS

The following road-designation abbreviations are used:

CR	County Road
FR	Farm Route
FS	Forest Service road
I-	Interstate
IR	Indian Route
US	United States highway

State highways are designated with the appropriate two-letter state abbreviation, followed by the road number. *Example:* UT 6 = Utah State Highway 6.

Postal Service two-letter state codes:

AL	Alabama		IA	Iowa
AK	Alaska		KS	Kansas
AZ	Arizona		KY	Kentucky
AR	Arkansas		LA	Louisiana
CA	California		ME	Maine
CO	Colorado		MD	Maryland
CT	Connecticut		MA	Massachusetts
DE	Delaware		MI	Michigan
DC	District of Columbia		MN	Minnesota
FL	Florida		MS	Mississippi
GA	Georgia		MO	Missouri
HI	Hawaii		MT	Montana
ID	Idaho		NE	Nebraska
IL	Illinois		NV	Nevada
IN	Indiana		NH	New Hampshire

NJ	New Jersey	SD	South Dakota
NM	New Mexico	TN	Tennessee
NY	New York	TX	Texas
NC	North Carolina	UT	Utah
ND	North Dakota	VT	Vermont
OH	Ohio	VA	Virginia
OK	Oklahoma	WA	Washington
OR	Oregon	WV	West Virginia
PA	Pennsylvania	WI	Wisconsin
RI	Rhode Island	WY	Wyoming
SC	South Carolina		

TOPOGRAPHIC MAPS

The maps in this book, when used in conjunction with the route directions present in each chapter, will in most instances be sufficient to get you to the trail and keep you on it. However, you will find superior detail and valuable information in the 7.5 minute series United States Geological Survey (USGS) topographic maps. Recognizing how indispensable these are to bikers and hikers alike, many bike shops and sporting goods stores now carry topos of the local area.

But if you're brand new to mountain biking you might be wondering "What's a topographic map?" In short, these differ from standard "flat" maps in that they indicate not only linear distance, but elevation as well. One glance at a "topo" will show you the difference, for "contour lines" are spread across the map like dozens of intricate spider webs. Each contour line represents a particular elevation, and at the base of each topo a particular "contour interval" designation is given. Yes, it sounds confusing if you're new to the lingo, but it truly is a simple and wonderfully helpful system. Keep reading.

Let's assume that the 7.5 minute series topo before us says "Contour Interval 40 feet," that the short trail we'll be pedaling is two inches in length on the map, and that it crosses five contour lines from its beginning to end. What do we know? Well, because the linear scale of this series is 2,000 feet to the inch (roughly 2 ¾ inches representing 1 mile), we know our trail is approximately ⅘ of a mile long (2 inches × 2,000 feet). But we also know we'll be climbing or descending 200 vertical feet (5 contour lines × 40 feet each) over that distance. And the elevation designations written on occasional contour lines will tell us if we're heading up or down.

The authors of this series warn their readers of upcoming terrain, but only a detailed topo gives you the information you need to pinpoint your position exactly on a map, steer yourself toward optional trails and roads nearby, plus let you know at a glance if you'll be pedaling hard to take them. It's a lot of information for a very low cost. In fact, the only drawback with topos is their size—several feet square. I've tried rolling them into tubes, folding them carefully, even cutting them into blocks and photocopying the pieces. Any of these systems is a pain, but no matter how you pack the maps you'll be happy they're along. And you'll be even happier if you pack a compass as well.

In addition to local bike shops and sporting goods stores, you'll find topos at major universities and some public libraries where you might try photocopying the ones you need to avoid the cost of buying them. But if you want your own and can't find them locally, write to:

USGS Map Sales
Box 25286
Denver, CO 80225

Ask for an index while you're at it, plus a price list and a copy of the booklet *Topographic Maps*. In minutes you'll be reading them like a pro.

A second excellent series of maps available to mountain bikers is that put out by the United States Forest Service. If your trail runs through an area designated as a national forest, look in the phone book (white pages) under the United States Government listings, find the Department of Agriculture heading, and then run your finger down that section until you find the Forest Service. Give them a call and they'll provide the address of the regional Forest Service office, from which you can obtain the appropriate map.

TRAIL ETIQUETTE

Pick up almost any mountain bike magazine these days and you'll find articles and letters to the editor about trail conflict. For example, you'll find hikers' tales of being blindsided by speeding mountain bikers, complaints from mountain bikers about being blamed for trail damage that was really caused by horse or cattle traffic, and cries from bikers about those "kamikaze" riders who through their antics threaten to close even more trails to all of us.

The authors of this series have been very careful to guide you to only those trails that are open to mountain biking (or at least were open at the time of their research), and without exception have warned of the damage done to our sport through injudicious riding. My personal views on this matter appear in the Afterword, but all of us can benefit from glancing over the following International Mountain Bicycling Association (IMBA) Rules of the Trail before saddling up.

1. *Ride on open trails only.* Respect trail and road closures (ask if not sure), avoid possible trespass on private land, obtain permits and authorization as may be required. Federal and State wilderness areas are closed to cycling.

2. *Leave no trace.* Be sensitive to the dirt beneath you. Even on open trails, you should not ride under conditions where you will leave evidence of your passing, such as on certain soils shortly after rain. Observe the different types of soils and trail construction; practice low-impact cycling. This also means staying on the trail and not creating any new ones. Be sure to pack out at least as much as you pack in.

3. *Control your bicycle!* Inattention for even a second can cause disaster. Excessive speed can maim and threaten people; there is no excuse for it!

4. *Always yield the trail.* Make known your approach well in advance. A friendly greeting (or a bell) is considerate and works well; startling someone may cause loss of trail access. Show your respect when passing others by slowing to a walk or even stopping. Anticipate that other trail users may be around corners or in blind spots.

5. *Never spook animals.* All animals are startled by an unannounced approach, a sudden movement, or a loud noise. This can be dangerous for you, for others, and for the animals. Give animals extra room and time to adjust to you. In passing, use special care and follow the directions of horseback riders (ask if uncertain). Running cattle and disturbing wild animals is a serious offense. Leave gates as you found them, or as marked.

6. *Plan ahead.* Know your equipment, your ability, and the area in which you are riding—and prepare accordingly. Be self-sufficient at all times. Wear a helmet, keep your machine in good condition, and carry necessary supplies for changes in weather or other conditions. A well-executed trip is a satisfaction to you and not a burden or offense to others.

For more information, contact IMBA, P.O. Box 412043, Los Angeles, CA 90041, (818) 792-8830.

HITTING THE TRAIL

Once again, because this is a "where-to," not a "how-to" guide, the following will be brief. If you're a veteran trail rider these suggestions might serve to remind you of something you've forgotten to pack. If you're a newcomer, they might convince you to think twice before hitting the backcountry unprepared. **Water:** I've heard the questions dozens of times. "How much is enough? One bottle? Two? Three?! But think of all that extra weight!" Well, one simple physiological fact should convince you to err on the side of excess when it comes to deciding how much water to pack: a human working hard in 90-degree temperature needs approximately ten quarts of fluids every day. Ten quarts. That's two and a half gallons—*12* large water bottles, or *16* small ones. And, with water weighing in at approximately eight pounds per gallon, a one-day supply comes to a whopping 20 pounds.

In other words, pack along two or three bottles even for short rides. And make sure you can purify the water found along the trail on longer routes. When writing of those routes where this could be of critical importance, each author has provided information on where water can be found near the trail—if it can be found at all. But drink it untreated and you run the risk of disease. (See *Giardia* in the Glossary.)

One sure way to kill both the bacteria and viruses in water is to bring it to a "furious boil." Right. That's just how you want to spend your time on a bike ride. Besides, who wants to carry a stove, or denude the countryside stoking bonfires to boil water?

Luckily, there is a better way. Many riders pack along the effective, inexpensive, and only slightly distasteful tetraglycine hydroperiodide tablets (sold under the names Potable Aqua, Globaline, and Coughlan's, among others). Some invest in portable, lightweight purifiers that filter out the crud. Yes, purifying water with tablets or filters is a bother. But catch a case of giardiasis sometime and you'll understand why it's worth the trouble.

Tools: Ever since my first cross-country tour in 1965 I've been kidded about the number of tools I pack on the trail. And so I will exit entirely from this discussion by providing a list compiled by two mechanic (and mountain biker) friends of mine. After all, since they make their livings fixing bikes, and get their kicks by riding them, who could be a better source?

These two suggest the following as an absolute minimum:

    tire levers
    spare tube and patch kit
    air pump
    allen wrenches (3, 4, 5, and 6 mm)
    six-inch crescent (adjustable-end) wrench
    small flat-blade screwdriver
    chain rivet tool
    spoke wrench

But, while they're on the trail, their personal tool pouches contain these additional items:

    channel locks (small)
    air gauge
    tire valve cap (the metal kind, with a valve-stem remover)
    baling wire (ten or so inches, for temporary repairs)
    duct tape (small roll for temporary repairs or tire boot)

boot material (small piece of old tire or a large tube patch)
spare chain link
rear derailleur pulley
spare nuts and bolts
paper towel and tube of waterless hand cleaner

First-Aid Kit: My personal kit contains the following, sealed inside double Ziploc bags:

sunscreen
aspirin
butterfly-closure bandages
Band-Aids
gauze compress pads (a half-dozen 4" × 4")
gauze (one roll)
ace bandages or Spenco joint wraps
Benadryl (an antihistamine, in case of allergic reactions)
water purification tablets
Moleskin/Spenco "Second Skin"
hydrogen peroxide, iodine, or Mercurochrome (some kind of antiseptic)
snakebite kit

Final Considerations: The authors of this series have done a good job in suggesting that specific items be packed for certain trails—raingear in particular seasons, a hat and gloves for mountain passes, or shades for desert jaunts. Heed their warnings, and think ahead. Good luck.

Dennis Coello

Long Island Tours

With its proximity to New York City and density of developed towns, Long Island is unlikely grounds for mountain biking. Yet there are 13 remarkable trail systems that range from easy cruising to technically demanding single-tracks. The broad spectrum of riding explores the North Shore regions or "Gold Coast," an area of twentieth-century estates and rolling hills, south to the flat meadows and beaches of Long Island's southern shore.

The topography of Long Island shapes the character and quality of the trails and was created over the last million years by several glacial advances. Each glacier sculpted the topography by eroding bedrock and transporting boulders, cobbles, gravel, and sand. The last glacial period, which occurred about 18,000 years ago, settled the 1,000-foot Wisconsin glacier over the region, compressing, transporting, depositing, and reshaping as it advanced and retreated, profoundly affecting the land. During the Ice Age of that same period, much of northern Europe and the northern United States, as well as most of Canada, had been covered by great ice sheets. Geologic features characteristic of glaciation are distinctly different from the features formed by running water. Once recognized, they lead one to appreciate the great extent of glaciation during the Ice Age. From the Matterhorn in Switzerland to the north shore of Long Island, glaciation has left its mark. When the Wisconsin glacier began to melt, it left behind enormous hills of morainal debris, most of it scoured out of northern New England. Bedrock found in Connecticut is scattered on the North Shore of Long Island as rocks and pebbles. The rides described here wind through and atop this hilly landscape.

Long Island is essentially a 120-mile-long pile of glacial debris representing the southern reach of the last glaciation in the New York/New England region. It is a rich topographical museum of end-glacier features like terminal and recessional moraines, outwash deposits, erratic boulders and knob-and-kettle terrain. Long Island is not much more than a ridge, or blanket, of direct glacial outwash sediments that almost completely conceal the underlying sedimentary bedrock. The Fire Island tour explores the dynamic shoreline of Long Island, where catastrophic changes are visible with each blink of the eye. Dunes and sandbars are continually swept away and rebuilt from the coastal storms that brew in the Atlantic Ocean.

Long Island's special terrain offers a variety of riding for riders of all levels. Throughout the tours, you will be challenged by the hills, charmed by the scenery, invigorated by the wilderness, and soothed by the solitude.

Trains to the trails: Transportation service to the towns where the trails reside can be found on the commuter trains of the Long Island Railroad (LIRR). Traveling on the trains with a bicycle requires a $5 bike pass plus the obligatory passenger fare. The bike pass, by the way, is good for life. To acquire a pass, call (718) 558-8228. Train service schedules can be found at most train stations, or you can request one by calling (718) 217-LIRR.

Various restrictions apply for individuals portaging bikes on the trains.

There are specific weekend restrictions between Memorial Day and Labor Day. Bikes are prohibited on trains departing from Penn Station between 7:30 A.M. and 10 A.M.; Saturday arrivals into Penn Station between 8 A.M. and 10 A.M.; Sunday and Monday holiday arrivals into Penn Station between 4 P.M. and 6 P.M. On the Montauk trains, which service the Hamptons, restrictions apply for arrivals between 3 P.M. and 10 P.M.

Weekday restrictions apply during the rush-hour commuting periods. No bikes are allowed on departing trains from Penn Station between 7 A.M. and 9 A.M. and 3 P.M. and 8 P.M. No bikes are allowed on arriving trains into Penn Station between 6 A.M. and 10 A.M. and 4 P.M. and 7 P.M. For all other questions call the LIRR.

RIDE 1 *FOREST PARK*

Within the urban sprawl is a woodland oasis in Forest Park that provides some serious off-road opportunities for novice and intermediate mountain bikers. There is something for everyone on more than 13 miles of hard-packed single-track and wide bridle paths that crisscross the park's 538 acres, 413 of which are wooded. Seven miles of bridle paths provide an abundance of unique cruising experiences, and there are enough tight turns and hills in the single-track section to satisfy the average hammerhead. The trails traverse an ancient glacial ridge deposited by a retreating glacier over 10,000 years ago. Forest Park, located on top of a glacial moraine, consists of rounded pebbles, stones, boulders, sand, and clay, and runs northeast to southwest. The direction of this moraine is consistent with the hilly backbone of the north shore of Long Island. As you travel through the park, you will notice many small depressions, boulders, and rocky terrain. They're all clues to Forest Park's glacial past.

These small depressions or gullies formed when glaciers retreat are "kettles." Large ice blocks tumble off and become partially buried by sand and gravel. A depression in the ground results when the ice blocks melt. Scattered throughout the park are several of these kettles. If a kettle is so deep that its bottom is below the groundwater level, it can become a kettle pond or lake. Small kettle ponds once dotted the landscape of this park.

The single-track trails traverse small isolated hills or knobs that are prominent in the forest. Many large boulders mark the entrance to some of the trails. They are "erratics" and were left behind by the glaciers, which rounded and

smoothed the surface of these huge stones. The mile-high, glacial ice sheets polished and dragged the boulders along the ground. These landmarks are reminders of the glacier's immense size.

Throughout your ride you will be passing through an oak forest with some trees over 150 years old. There are also dogwoods, Virginia creeper, black birch, pignut hickory, tulip trees, red oaks, and a few black walnuts.

If you ride between April and May you might catch one of the 100 species of migrating birds that use Forest Park as a stopover along their coastal migratory route. The park offers prime feeding for these transitory birds. There are approximately 35 breeding birds including pheasant, woodpeckers, and many others. The gully and East Waterhole are popular birdwatching spots.

General location: Forest Hills, Queens.
Elevation change: Riding consists of small hills and level bridle paths.
Season: Year-round except during extremely wet weather, when the bridle paths get very muddy.
Services: Austin Street near Queens Boulevard in Forest Hills offers great cafes and restaurants.
Hazards: The park is beautiful, popular, and shared with hikers and equestrians. Be careful with horses; try not to spook them by riding close or fast from either direction on the trail. The current policy of trail usage is managed by the individual, and for now the people involved in these activities coexist and respect each other's rights to use this special park. As mountain bikers, we need to be sensitive while riding here. Let's keep up a responsible image. By employing commonsense etiquette and respect for other users we will assure our place on these trails.
Rescue index: The park is surrounded by urban development and you are never farther than a half-mile from major civilization.
Land status: City of New York Parks and Recreation.
Maps: City of New York Parks and Recreation supplies the *Forest Park Guide,* which comprehensively describes the park and includes a small park map.
Finding the trail: Bikes can be taken on the subway. From New York City, take the E or F train to 71st/Continental Avenue. Exit onto Queens Boulevard and turn south on Continental Avenue, proceeding through charming Forest Hills Gardens. If you are coming from New York City by car, take Queens Boulevard (east) and turn right (south) on Continental Avenue (71st Avenue). Park on the north side of Queens Boulevard near the complexes of apartment buildings, where parking is free. The streets in Forest Hills Gardens are private and parking is prohibited. Booting cars, an unpopular practice for motorists, results in a $180 fine to remove the boot.

Pedal south on Continental Avenue to the intersection of Continental Avenue and Union Turnpike. Facing the park, you will see a small playground to your right. The trail begins on the bridle path that appears just left of this little playground.

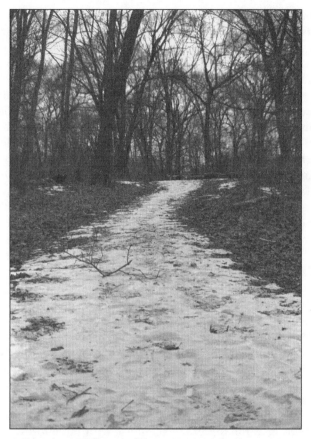

Off-road possibilities in frozen Forest Park.

Sources of additional information:

Queens Borough Office (The Overlook)
80-30 Park Lane
Kew Gardens, New York 11415
(718) 520-5900

Forest Park Administrator's Office (The Clubhouse)
1 Forest Park
Woodhaven, New York 11421-1166
(718) 235-0684

Notes on the trail: There are 3 color-marked single-track trails available for riding. Their wide, hard-packed surface makes it a pleasure to ride. The map I have supplied describes their general location. The red and yellow trails explore the northeast section. The red trail starts at the Buddy Monument and loops around the lower half of the Northern Forest. The yellow trail begins at the Overlook and eventually parallels the railroad, taking you to the southeast side. The blue trail begins at Woodhaven Boulevard and East Main Drive and takes you through the Gully. The main bridle path trail is described below. As a courtesy and safety measure, please pull to the side for equestrian riders so you won't scare the horses.

The bridle path trail begins at the end of 71st Avenue (Continental Avenue) at its intersection with Union Turnpike. Look south in the direction of a small playground. The bridle-path trail begins immediately to the left. The trail parallels Union Turnpike for a short distance and then ducks beneath an overpass through a small tunnel as it enters the park. Proceed straight past the 2 smaller paths that intersect from both sides. These were old paved walking paths with lantern poles along them.

Continue straight to a large fork and bear left onto a wide, flat bridle path. You enter a clearing in .6 mile. Take the right fork down a short hill. Another clearing appears in .3 mile. Continue straight onto the East Main Drive, a park road. Turn right onto the park road as it crosses a bridge that spans some railroad tracks. After the bridge, you will have a choice of 2 double-track paths on your right. Turn right onto the second path, which is the bridle path, and go beyond a group of wooden pilings that gate the trail. On a tree, a white marker with a red horse in the middle marks the trail. This flat path parallels East Main Road for a tenth of a mile. You will pass a red-blazed single-track that leads off to your right. You may want to come back and try that later. At the next clearing, fork right through a barrier of 2 large stones and remain on the wide, smooth horse path. Fork left in .3 mile and proceed down a small hill. Continue straight on the rolling bridle path and ignore the next intersection that includes a trail leading off to your right. You will soon come to a clearing at the top of the small hill with three forks. The left fork loops around to where the right fork ends, and the center single-track path is part of the blue trail. Take the right fork and continue for a short distance through an old woodland. As you approach a small clearing, notice the wide hardpack that enters from your right. Take a sharp right and head back toward the direction you were just traveling. This section of the trail is flat and wide, and it traverses moderately hilly terrain. Notice the small pine trees planted in clearings. These plantings were the effort of the Parks Department, which, through these regrowth programs, is trying to preserve this primitive wilderness. This section of Forest Park has been left to its own devices, and attempts at these new plantings are a kind of assurance and hopefully will preserve this unique environment.

Continue straight through the next clearing, which is filled with large, tall oaks in the middle. After .4 mile, bear left at the next intersection past some log barriers. The trail switches to single-track at this point. Continue straight through the next 4-way intersection and bear right to pedal up a small hill. Bear left and, at the top of the hill, bear right and then make a quick left. Continue straight on this red-marked trail to the **T** intersection with the bridle path. East Main Road is directly beyond the bridle path. Turn left on the bridle path, which will lead you back over the railroad tracks. Make a quick left into the woods after the bridge. You are now on the path which you had taken earlier. Continue straight to complete the loop.

RIDE 2 NASSAU–SUFFOLK GREENBELT TRAIL

In real estate and retailing, location is practically everything. It's what brings up the value and popularity. In some ways, the same can be said about this moderately challenging, 16-mile (8 miles one way), out-and-back tour. It makes a straight course through a wooded, protected wilderness corridor in the middle of Long Island, making it quite accessible for most of the local mountain biker enthusiasts.

This special designated mountain bike path is part of the larger 22-mile Nassau–Suffolk Greenbelt trail that practically spans the width of Long Island from Massapequa Preserve on the South Shore to Cold Spring Harbor on the North Shore. The trail offers a refreshing diversity and a welcome contrast to the heavily populated areas it traverses. It parallels the Nassau–Suffolk hiking trail and shares the same rich plant and animal habitat. The trail is in great shape, is generally not too crowded, and provides a great opportunity to sample a variety of terrain. The ride doesn't offer the twists and turns of the Stillwell Woods spaghetti track, but it allows the confident novice to try something more challenging. The length of the ride and the occasional rocks and conspiring roots supply enough gnarls for the average dirthead.

The type of riding and the variety of terrain found on Long Island is closely tied to the region's recent glacial past and the titanic forces associated with the Ice Age. The ride begins in the hilly, wooded northern shore of Long Island at an elevation close to 200 feet. It continues southward, traversing a glacial plain that slopes gently to the broader, flatter, sea-level farmland plains that are characteristic of the southern shore of Long Island. The plain consists mainly of outwash sediments mixed with till and clay that were deposited after the last major glacial period, about 10,000 years ago.

The wilderness corridor you will be traveling remains the home to many types of animals, plants, and trees. As you silently glide through this forested land, try to catch a glimpse of the local wildlife, and I don't mean the helmeted type. The habitat is home to hawks and the elusive fox. If you are lucky, you may spot them along the way. As you travel from north to south, notice the hardwood stands of oak, red maple, and beech. These are typically found on the North Shore and differ from the softer conifers of pines found in the pine-barren sections typical of the South Shore. The hardwoods can

To
Cold Spring
Harbor

STILLWELL WOODS
COUNTY PRESERVE

To
25A

N

0   1/2   1
MILES

To
Woodbury

Jericho Turnpike

25

To
Jericho

Woodbury Rd.

To
N.Y.C.

Washington Ave.

495

135

To Eastern
Long Island

Seaford Oyster Bay Expwy.

NY

To
Suffolk County

Old Country Rd.

To
Hicksville

To
Southern State
Parkway

To
Southern Section of
The Nassau–Suffolk Greenbelt Trail

BETHPAGE
STATE PARK

survive in rockier terrain with less water. The pines grow better in the sandy, moist soils of the South Shore.

The Long Island Greenbelt Trail Conference, which has helped establish and protect these wilderness corridors, is committed to working with mountain bikers. They work with C.L.I.M.B. (Concerned Long Island Mountain Bicyclists) in a coalition that has created and continues to maintain a system of parallel trails that allows hikers and bikers to enjoy these protected wilderness corridors. Thanks to the success of these organizations, we have the opportunity to share the rich forest and animal habitat, a rare commodity in highly populated communities.

General location: On the Nassau–Suffolk border on Long Island. The trail begins on Jericho Turnpike on the North Shore of Long Island and reaches south into Bethpage State Park.

Elevation change: The trail traverses the typically hilly terrain of Long Island's North Shore area, so expect some minor ascents and descents. Farther south, the trail levels out as it passes through some old overgrown farmlands.

Season: Year-round usage is available, but keep the trails from eroding too fast by staying off them during wet conditions.

Services: The parking area where you will launch your adventure has a tailgate bike repair stand, and if you wear out your tread they even sell tires. A mall located on Jericho Turnpike just before you reach the parking area provides food services. Often on weekends a refreshment truck parks and dispenses the valuable food stuffs. Bicycle Planet at 540 Jericho Turnpike in Syosset offers service and equipment to mountain bikers.

Hazards: This trail tends to be more congested on weekends. Since the usage on the trail is bi-directional (riders travel in both directions), one ought to pay special attention when coming around a blind turn. Erosion and good wholesome use have exposed some roots and rocks, and a few sections of the trail will require minor technical skills. The best times to go are early in the morning or for a sunset ride after dinner.

Rescue index: The trails for hikers and mountain bikers are heavily used and sometimes help may be only arm's-length away.

Land status: The Long Island Greenbelt was opened in 1978 as a National Recreational Trail and connects state, county, and town parkland.

Maps: The Long Island Greenbelt Trail Conference provides a membership for hikers that includes a full set of maps and a quarterly newspaper.

Finding the trail: Take the Long Island Expressway or Northern State Parkway to the Seaford Oyster Bay Expressway (North) NY 135 to Exit 14 East. You will exit onto Jericho Turnpike. Proceed about half a mile east on Jericho Turnpike, past a shopping mall on your left and past a condominium complex known as Woodbury Village. Begin looking for a parking area on your left. There are usually other cars unloading riders and bikes, so it is hard to miss. Turn into the parking lot. The trail begins directly across from the parking area, which faces south across Jericho Turnpike, and can be recognized as a dirt path through some trees.

Sources of additional information:

Long Island Greenbelt Trail Conference
23 Deer Path Road
Central Islip, New York 11722
(516) 360-0753

Bicycle Planet
540 Jericho Turnpike
Syosset, New York 11791
(516) 364-4434

C.L.I.M.B.
P.O. Box 203
Woodbury, New York 11797
(516) 262-0909

Notes on the trail: The trail is well maintained and the hardpack surface of this single-track makes for a challenging but not too technically difficult trail experience. The path is practically straight and passes through a variety of forest habitats, from hardwoods to pines. You will pass a hillside covered in young oak and go through a dark fern-covered forest floor, and as you go farther south you will pass through the overgrown meadows of abandoned farms.

From the parking area, cross Jericho Turnpike and head south on the single-track that leads through a small clearing. Whoever is leading the ride should pay attention to what may lie ahead, since this is a bidirectional trail. Shout or use a bell when going around blind turns.

Continue onto the trail through a mixed hardwood forest over moderately hilly terrain. After about .6 mile you will approach a large, steep hill with tracks leading directly up it. Bear left at the trail that crosses the paved Woodbury Road. The trail picks up on the other side of the road. On the top of the hill, which is actually a high ledge, is an old cemetery of early Dutch and English settlers, and some limestone headstones date back to 1803. After some riding you will arrive at a wider dirt road coming from the left. Bear right onto this road. You will come out on the right side of a bridge onto a 2-lane roadway. Turn left, cross the bridge, and turn left back into the forest cover as the ubiquitous white-painted blazed trail picks up farther ahead. This is the Nassau–Suffolk Greenbelt Trail. White plastic rectangular blazes on the trees mark the trail after this point. The trail heads into this forest for a short stretch, crosses another paved highway ramp, and leads back into the woods on a small descent over some small, wooden erosion-prevention logs.

Bruce Horowitz picks his line on the rolling single-track
of the Nassau–Suffolk Greenbelt.

After 3.8 miles, bear to your right and proceed through an underpass
beneath the Long Island Expressway. This barren area resembles the deserted,
abandoned-car landscape from the set of *Road Warrior,* from which civilization had disappeared. I kept expecting to see some riders wearing steel armor,
riding black mountain bikes with gun turrets. As you emerge from the underpass, continue straight on the main wide path. You will see many tire tracks
leading toward the familiar white trail blazes. At the intersection with a paved
road, cross and pick up the trail beyond the Interstate 495 sign. Soon you will
cross another roadway where the trail picks up across the road, beyond a
sparsely treed grassy knoll alongside an overgrown farm meadow. You will
soon emerge into a cul-de-sac where the trail wraps back into wooded farm
meadow. Proceed along this meadow for a short way and then cross another
roadway. By now the terrain has changed from the rolling hilly terrain that is

characteristically North Shore to the flatter farmland of the South Shore. At about 6.9 miles you will come into a large, 4-way trail clearing. Bear to the right in a southwesterly direction where the triangular white plastic blazes mark the trail's continuation. You will now be entering Bethpage State Park and can hook up with the Bethpage State Park mountain bike network. The trail is fairly straightforward as you must return the way you came.

RIDE 3   *STILLWELL SPAGHETTI*

The little-known Stillwell Woods County Park contains a prime, grade-A mountain bike path and provides many a weekend workout for Long Island's hammerheads and recent converts. Ranked as one of the best single-tracks in the East, this custom, well-maintained five-mile work of art was built by the Long Island mountain bike club C.L.I.M.B., or Concerned Long Island Mountain Bikers. The one-way single-track loop traverses a hilly wooded landscape on the North Shore of Long Island, which owes its challenging riding to retreating glaciers 10,000 years ago. The park resides on top of an ancient glacial ridge built up from the deposits left behind when the glacier stalled and melted. The result is one gnarly, rocky landscape with many small depressions, gullies, and small hills. As you zip along this trail, climbing in and out of the many gullies, take a moment to look back and ponder the climb and how all this came to be.

From the beginning, the trail unravels through an abandoned, regrown farm field and soon takes you through a deep forest of many twists, turns, and miniature loops. The trail has been developed to take full advantage of the hilly terrain and varied woodland that characterizes the North Shore of Long Island. To ride it, you need to nurse the front wheel around the tight corners. Shift back and float over roots and branches. Then spin hard down a gully with enough power to ramp up the opposite side. Here's the typical pattern of the trail: Go up 30 feet, down 20, stay flat for 50, and get ready for the next roll. The trails consist mostly of hard-packed single-track instead of the softer, sandier soils that make up many of the trails in the pine-barren sections of Long Island's southern and eastern woodlands. Serious off-road riding opportunities exist and good bike-handling skills are required throughout the loop. Quick descents and climbs through the many gullies and sections of tight turning constitute hammerhead heaven and demand some adroit handling. The Stillwell Woods County Park trail system also completes the northern end of the Nassau–Suffolk hiking trail and mountain bike path. Sharing the same rich forest and animal habitat, the rider is immersed in the type of primitive wilderness that is a rare sight on the highly populated Long Island.

Note: *More trails exist in this area
than can be shown on this map.*

General location: Near the towns of Woodbury and Syosset, Long Island.

Elevation change: The trail was designed to take full advantage of the moderately hilly terrain. It traverses many gullies and ascends many small hills. There are very few elevations exceeding 200', but the amount of vertical feet gained during the ride accumulates rapidly.

Season: Year-round except during wet weather periods. There are signs at the beginning of the ride that advise bikers not to ride if the trail is wet.

Services: Bicycle Planet at 540 Jericho Turnpike in Syosset offers service and equipment to mountain bikers. Their phone number is (516) 364-4434.

Hazards: Remember that the trail is a one-way loop. These popular trails are heavily used during the weekends, and the one-way direction prevents many of the hammerheads from hammering their heads together. With collisions out of the way, the next item to pay attention to is the tight twists and turns through trees that are sometimes little more than one handlebar wide. There are some steep sections which you might wish to blast through and ride like a roller coaster. Overall, the main hazard is not having the sufficient skills to handle this great track.

Rescue index: You are never more than half a mile from major civilization and there is usually some mountain biker passing by every fifteen minutes on the weekends.

My appreciation and respect go out to the members and volunteers of the Concerned Long Island Mountain Bicyclists Club (C.L.I.M.B.) for building and maintaining many of the trails on Long Island. Their work parties clean up, repair, and improve the conditions of the trails and develop methods to fight erosion on special sections along the routes. They and all the work party teams that build and maintain the myriad of trails described in this book deserve special acknowledgment for the work they are doing to accommodate and minimize the ecological impact of the growing number of mountain bikers. These organizations interface and open up channels of communication between trail users and land management agencies, and they need our support and deserve our cooperation.

Land status: Nassau County Park.

Maps: The Long Island Greenbelt Trail Conference provides a membership for hikers that includes a full set of maps and a quarterly newspaper. Unfortunately these maps do not provide the fine detail you might expect on a USGS topo series map, but the trail is so well marked that it is virtually impossible to get lost if you follow the white triangular markers.

Finding the trail: Take the Southern State Parkway east and take Route 135, Seaford Oyster Bay Expressway, north to Exit 14 East. You will exit onto Jericho Turnpike. Continue about half a mile and turn left (north) on South Woods Road. Look for the entrance to the Stillwell Woods County Park, approximately 1.2 miles on your right. Turn into the parking lot. The trail begins past a wooden sign detailing the rules of the mountain bike trail. By

Miles of single-track snake through the dense forest of Stillwell Woods.

train, take the Long Island Railroad to Cold Spring Harbor and proceed north on Route 108 and west on Stillwell Lane.

Sources of additional information:

Long Island Greenbelt Trail Conference
23 Deer Path Road
Central Islip, New York 11722
(516) 360-0753

Bicycle Planet
540 Jericho Turnpike
Syosset, New York 11791
(516) 364-4434

C.L.I.M.B.
P.O. Box 203
Woodbury, New York 11797
(516) 262-0909

Notes on the trail: The trail is blazed by white plastic triangular markers that are serially numbered based on your progress into the trail and will guide you quite easily through the loop. I will detail the ride below, but it is much easier to just follow the numbered white triangular markers than to keep glancing at this set of instructions for every turn.

Pedal to the south end of the parking area, past the baseball diamonds, and onto a gated gravelly utility road. You will soon see a brown wooden sign marking the Stillwell Woods Mountain Bike Trail. The trail has been created and is currently maintained by C.L.I.M.B. A list of courtesy rules includes always wear a helmet, yield to horses and hikers, stay on the trail, follow white markers, and don't ride when trail is wet.

The hard-packed single-track begins through an old grown-in abandoned farm field traversing about half a mile and soon enters a wooded area, where it zigzags around some mature white pine trees. You will soon pass a trail leading in from your left. Ignore this trail and continue straight on the well-worn single-track. When in doubt, as a rule, you are in good hands if you stay on the more worn trails. Bear left at the next fork and soon you will come to another fork with a large white pine bearing the trail's white triangular markers. Bear right at this tree and enter into a denser wooded forest. As you come into a clearing, make a left at the **T** intersection and take the first right into another wooded area, picking up the number 7 marker. You will know you are on the right trail when the white triangular markers attached to the trails appear soon after a questionable intersection.

Ride through a large forest of oak trees and exit into another open field, remaining on the well-worn track. At a wooden post with an arrow pointing to the right, turn right into the woods and follow the single-track. The trail spirals downhill to another **T** intersection where you must turn right. Notice the number 12 marker. Bear left at the next fork, which is tagged with the number 13. The trail then climbs steeply through a dry stream gully; bear left at the top where the trail snakes for another half a mile. Bear left at the next 2 forks. At marker number 27, bear right. You soon will descend into a deep gully; if you are good, let it rip and channel that momentum to get back up the other side. Before you have time to catch your breath, you will start another descent to a 5-way intersection with a clearing in the middle. Look for marker number 35 in a westerly direction; it should lead you straight ahead and up the trail. You should encounter marker number 36. If you do not, pedal back to the intersection and try again.

At marker number 45, you **T**-intersect with another trail. Turn right here and continue straight through the next intersection up a small, steep hill, where you will encounter marker 47. After riding on the plateau for 10 minutes or so, you go down and up another gully and smile at marker number 53. Another gully follows and then the trail levels out and empties into another clearing. Take the leftmost fork, which is tagged with marker number 58, and hug the left trail that takes you back into the woods. Ascend a short hill and come into another clearing. Take the middle fork that is labeled number 61 down and up another gully, and continue straight, ignoring the white painted marker to your right and continuing on the trail marked by white triangles. Even though it may feel like more, at this point you have only gone 3.5 miles.

The trail ends at a wide utility road. Turn left and make a quick right, proceeding through an old abandoned farm field in a westerly direction. At the end of the field bear left and then turn right at the first right turnoff. Descend for about 500', bearing left at an abandoned car, and turn right at the next intersection onto the single-track and up a small hill. You will soon encounter trail marker 84. You will travel through a mature cypress grove that is quite dark and then descend to another intersection and turn right, following the white triangles. You cannot become lost on these well-marked trails. At 5 miles you exit where you began, by the wooden sign.

RIDE 4   *GLACIER 8 TRAIL*

This new single-track has been recently created for the Long Island hammerhead crowd. It is relatively unknown, but it is grade-A material. The Long Island mountain bike club C.L.I.M.B. designed, built, and now maintains the five-mile trail. The trail, which consists of two loops, ranks as one of the newest, most artistically groomed mountain bike trails on Long Island. This trail is a must-do for anyone searching for an easy yet moderately challenging mountain bike experience. The wide single-track is not technically challenging and its smoothness, good condition, and gentle, rolling grade facilitate the freedom to have a great ride without much effort. The pine needle path twists and turns along a gently rolling terrain populated with dense forests of large white pine and oak trees commonly seen along the northern shore of Long Island. The mature stands of conifers and hardwoods provide a canopy for shade that's great for summer riding. This path seems like a small oasis of attractive woodland, particularly after crossing over from one of the paved roadways.

My appreciation and respect go out to the members and volunteers of the Concerned Long Island Mountain Bicyclists Club (C.L.I.M.B.) for building and maintaining many of the trails on Long Island. Their work parties clean up, repair, and improve the conditions of the trails and develop methods to fight erosion on special sections along the routes. They and all the work party teams that build and maintain the myriad of trails described in this book

RIDE 4 *GLACIER 8 TRAIL*

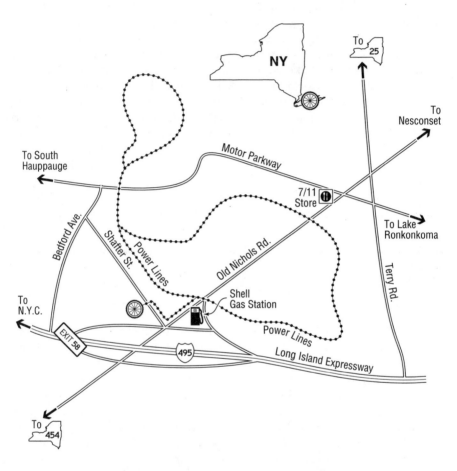

Note: *Map not drawn to scale; total distance of this ride is 5 miles.*

deserve special acknowledgment for the work they are doing to accommodate and minimize the ecological impact of the growing number of mountain bikers. These organizations interface and open up channels of communication between trail users and land management agencies, and they need our support and deserve our cooperation.

General location: Near Hauppauge, Long Island, approximately 42 miles from New York City and just north of Connetquot River State Park.

Elevation change: The tour is sectioned into 2 loops: A southern loop that is relatively level and a northern loop designed to traverse in spaghetti loops and take advantage of the moderately hilly terrain, dropping into gullies and ascending small hills.

Season: This tour has year-round potential. Try to stay off the trails after heavy rains or when they are defrosting from occasional winter storms.

Services: Bicycle Planet at 540 Jericho Turnpike in Syosset offers service and equipment to mountain bikers. Their phone number is (516) 364-4434.

Hazards: Remember that the trail is a one-way loop. These popular trails are heavily used during the weekends and the one-way direction prevents many hammerheads from hammering their heads together. The next item to pay attention to is the busy paved roads. Look both ways when coming out of the woods to cross Old Nichols Road and Motor Parkway.

Rescue index: The land this ride traverses is surrounded by residential areas and crisscrossed by 2 major roadways. Help can easily be flagged down, if needed.

Land status: New York State.

Maps: Unfortunately there are no USGS topo series maps that provide the fine detail you might expect. There are many small twists, turns, and loops that are difficult to map but great to ride. The map I have supplied will give you the general flow and direction of the route and an idea where things are located. The trail is well marked, and if you follow the white markers you can't get lost.

Finding the trail: Take the Long Island Expressway east and exit at 58, Old Nichols Road. Proceed to the end of the exit ramp and turn left at the light onto Nichols Road. Make a left at the next light (Shafter St.), following the green Park and Ride signs into the parking area. Commuters park here and the area is available for you, too.

Sources of additional information:

Long Island Greenbelt Trail Conference
23 Deer Path Road
Central Islip, New York 11722
(516) 360-0753

Bicycle Planet
540 Jericho Turnpike
Syosset, New York 11791
(516) 364-4434

C.L.I.M.B.
P.O. Box 203
Woodbury, New York 11797
(516) 262-0909

Shogun searching for a Long Island Iditarod at the Glacier 8 Trail.

Notes on the trail: Continue out of the Park and Ride parking area and proceed on Shafter Street, turning left (east) on Old Nichols Road. The trail crosses the road about 200' ahead, immediately past a Shell gas station. The trail begins beyond 2 metal poles with a metal barrier across them. The trail will parallel the power lines, heading in an easterly direction. After the third solid-structure utility pole, you pass another metal barrier. Look for a single-track trail leading into the woods on your left, in a northerly direction, about 100' past this barrier.

Proceed on this single-track going east for about 500' and past some dirt mounds that are used as jumps. Bear left at the next fork, in a northerly direction, and continue past a housing development on your right. You will begin to pick up the white paint blazes on the trees and the mountain bike trail's white triangle. At .9 mile you will cross the paved Old Nichols Road.

Cross the road and continue through a young forest of hardwoods. Continue on the single-track as it winds through a forest of oak and pine. After

.3 mile of easy single-track, you arrive at a clearing. Bear left at the green sign with a white arrow pointing in a southwesterly direction. Continue for a short distance through thick shrubs and then ascend a short, steep hill. The trail levels out and terminates at the wide, grassy power line strip. Turn right and go up another hill. At the top, you terminate at the paved Motor Parkway. Cross and pick up the trail on the other side, bearing right in the direction of the sign painted green with a white arrow. White triangles mark the trail also. The trail soon turns into a double-track and descends along a gully through an oak and pine forest. After your descent, the trail traverses a few spaghetti loops, going up and down the hillside. At about 3 miles into the ride, you begin the ascent out of this pasta palace and reach the top of a hill marked by an old fire tower.

Continue following the white triangles. The trail terminates right next to your entry point into this loop, on Motor Parkway. Continue across the road, proceeding in the same direction you came from before. Go down the grassy slope in a southeasterly direction alongside the power lines until you come to paved Old Nichols Road. Turn right on Old Nichols Road and right onto Shafter Street to the Park and Ride parking lot.

RIDE 5   *PANDORA'S BOX*

With its close proximity to New York City and density of surrounding towns, one might question the availability of high-quality mountain bike paths in dense townships in this part of Long Island. But in beautiful Bethpage State Park there are many single-track surprises locked in the web of trails. This five-mile loop proves that it's not necessary to travel far to sample some of the best mountain bike adventures in the East.

Bethpage State Park is the deluxe urban playground for the Long Island mountain biker. Only 40 miles from New York City, this 1,475-acre state park offers the mountain biker an endless repertoire of single- and double-track trails. Most of the smooth, hard-packed trails include fire roads, bridle paths, and woodland single-tracks. These trails wind through a dense, hilly landscape of oak and maple woodland. You can construct numerous riding configurations through this hilly park along a seemingly endless network of paths. The hard, compact conditions of the trails make a pleasant yet challenging ride for advanced beginners. There are plenty of obstacles, as in the specially placed logs and large earthen hump jumps which challenge the advanced wheelhead seeking more technical thrills. C.L.I.M.B. helps maintain and blaze some of the single-tracks, using special erosion-control techniques.

As in most of Long Island, much of the hilly terrain and challenging riding of these trails are products of retreating glaciers 10,000 years ago. The park

RIDE 5 *PANDORA'S BOX*

resides on top of an ancient glacial ridge built up from the deposits left behind when the glacier stalled and melted. The result is one gnarly landscape with many small depressions, gullies, and small hills.

This park's reputation is spreading. Long Island mountain bikers are discovering its intriguing and challenging trails.

General location: Near Farmingdale, Long Island.
Elevation change: There are some minor hills to negotiate, but nothing too strenuous. The terrain is a mixed bag of hills and flat woodlands.

Season: Riding opportunities exist year-round, except during wet weather periods, when it is advisable to remain off the trails. We can help save the trails from further erosion by staying off them during these periods. Wait for them to dry out and then ride. In the fall, one of the better times to ride, the colors are laid on with a bold hand and the dense woodland glows.

Services: This is a great place to have a picnic and do some riding. Those who might not be ready for a single-track through the woods have the opportunity to ride on an excellent, well-made, 2-way paved path. It winds through the park and provides a smooth path for rollerblading, jogging, or just strolling. In the large picnic area, you can have a picnic or just throw out a blanket and read a book. Broadway provides loads of shops and is within riding distance of the park. Playfields and tennis courts are also available.

Hazards: Since usage on the trail is bidirectional, one ought to pay special attention when coming around a blind turn. When it is hard to see around the next turn, take extra care to slow down and signal ahead with a whistle, or just say "Rider approaching."

Riding at Bethpage State Park is a little like a trip to Las Vegas, except here the commodity gambled is time, not money. Many of the trails and intersections are unmarked, so there is a gamble at every turn. In most cases, instinct, common sense, and careful following of the route description will suffice to see you through.

The park is beautiful and quite popular and is shared by other users. Occasionally, you will encounter horses and hikers on some of the trails. The current policy of trail usage is managed by the individual, and for now the people involved in these activities coexist and respect each other's rights to use this special park. We, as mountain bikers, need to be sensitive while riding here. Let's display a mutual respect and courtesy for each other, and this beautiful park will remain a recreation area for all to enjoy. In my experience a passing hello has always been met with one in return from equestrians and hikers. They are glad to see you enjoying the park also.

Rescue index: The park is a fairly lively one and help is never far away. I found that other mountain bikers in the park were always willing to lend a hand when I asked for directions or even a patch kit. Most of the bikers I have encountered are very friendly. While you may feel this park is easy to become disoriented in, it is, in fact, hard to get lost. Residential homes surround the park, whose perimeter is usually no more than 1 or 2 miles away.

My appreciation and respect go out to the members and volunteers of the Concerned Long Island Mountain Bicyclists Club (C.L.I.M.B.) for building and maintaining many of the trails on Long Island. Their work parties clean up, repair, and improve the conditions of the trails and develop methods to fight erosion on special sections along the routes. They and all the work party teams that build and maintain the myriad of trails described in this book deserve special acknowledgment for the work they are doing to accommodate and minimize the ecological impact of the growing number of mountain bikers. These organizations interface and open up channels of communication between trail users and land management agencies, and they need our support and deserve our cooperation.

Land status: New York state park.

Maps: A general park map is provided for you at the entrance, or you can mail away for one. This map unfortunately does not detail the mountain bike route. There are also no USGS topo series maps that provide the fine detail you might expect. The many small twists, turns, and loops are difficult to map but great to ride. The map I have supplied will give you the general flow and direction of the route and an idea of where things are located. The trail is well marked, and if you follow the white triangular markers, you can't get lost.

Finding the trail: Take the Southern State Parkway east to Exit 31 North/ Linden Street and take the left fork for the Bethpage State Parkway. Take this road all the way to the Bethpage State Park Picnic Area. There is a $3 fee for parking. You can take the Long Island Railroad to Bethpage and, from the station, ride east on Powell Avenue into Bethpage State Park.

Sources of additional information:

Bethpage State Park
Farmingdale, New York 11735
(516) 249-0701

Long Island State Park Region
Belmont Lake State Park
P.O. Box 247
Babylon, New York 11702
(516) 669-1000

Bicycle Planet
540 Jericho Turnpike
Syosset, New York 11791
(516) 364-4434

C.L.I.M.B.
P.O. Box 203
Woodbury, New York 11797
(516) 262-0909

Notes on the trail: The trail begins in the southwest corner of the large Bethpage State Park Picnic Area parking lot. It is a little tricky to find. Stand with the picnic area behind you and notice the well-worn single-track that diagonally leads into the trees, to the left of the tollbooth. The trail is marked with the white triangle that is used to signify the mountain bike trail. The single-track goes into the woods immediately before the large sign reading "No Pets, No Alcohol, Park Closes at Sunset."

A desolate Bethpage State Park on a snowy January afternoon.

Climb a short hill and follow along the hard-packed single-track as it winds through a dense forest of oak. The trail straightens out as it travels along some power lines in a northeasterly direction. At .3 mile, the trail turns left into the woods, and you will come to a large oak tree with white triangular markers. Bear right at this intersection and follow some more winding track. A few earthen humps have been shaped and positioned for a quick technical tango, but you can go around them as well. At .7 mile, you come to another intersection. Turn right and notice the red paint blazed on the trees with the white triangular markers. You will be heading in a northwesterly direction. After another 500', fork right at a tree with 2 white triangles. Keep bearing right, ignoring the red blazed trail. The trail ends in about .2 mile at a wide, hard-packed maintenance road. Turn right on this road, following the white triangles. In this section you are sharing the bridle path, which is marked with a yellow rectangle and black arrows.

You will soon come to a large wooden piling in the ground placed at the junction of two forks. The bridle path continues along the left fork, but you should take the right fork. After cresting the small hill, the trail crosses the bridle path again and continues past a large oak tree. Bear left at the next fork, as the right fork leads to a paved road, and then turn right at the next T intersection.

This section of the trail is an old semipaved, broken-up path that takes you along the perimeter of the park. After about .2 mile, you come to a large tree. Bear right, following the white triangle–marked semipaved path to descend to the wide bridle path. Turn left and head in a southwesterly direction. Following the white triangles, bear right at the next large fork. In perhaps another 1,000', bear right again, as the bridle path forks left. After another .1 mile, bear left onto a flat, dirt double-track. Very soon you will come to a large clearing with trails leading out from all directions. Continue straight through and then turn right onto the wide bridle path. Soon after, notice a pine tree on your left with painted white blazes on it. Turn left onto the single-track as it enters the woods and ascends a short hill in an easterly direction. You will pick up the white triangles again. After cresting the top of the hill, you will be riding alongside the picnic area to your left. After about a minute of riding, the trail turns right and descends back down into the woods, away from the picnic area. Cross a bridle path and continue through some dense oak and pine woods. The white triangles are well spaced and easy to follow. Turn right at the next wide dirt road and then make a quick left into the forest. Ascend a short hill for 300' and fork left, following the triangles. You will be riding along a ridge that is overlooking a small gully to your left. The ridge is also parallel to NY 135 on your right, and you will be able to hear the sounds of the cars. Ride along this ridge for about 10 minutes. Descend off the ridge and bear left at a small fork onto the bridle path; notice the white triangles ahead. Continue straight and bear right at the next fork, following the white triangles. Soon after you will come to a piling with the number 13 marked on it. Go past the second piling and up a small hill in a southeasterly direction. Proceed up the small hill and go straight for about half a mile, where the trail terminates at the paved bike path. Turn left and take this path down into the parking area.

RIDE 6 *ROCKY POINT*

Cross-country skiers can pretty much ski anywhere, providing there is the minimum snow ground cover. A well-groomed track can do wonders for a skier's technique, rhythm, and efficiency in covering the distance. Once in the skier's groove, so to speak, there's an enormous sense of freedom to move and enjoy the beauty of the passing scenery, a freedom we mountain bikers share here in warmer weather. Rocky Point Natural Resources Management Area offers a well-planned, 13-mile, groomed, single-track loop that snakes through an incredibly versatile forest filled with pine barrens, hardwoods, and swamps. If Leonardo Da Vinci was a mountain biker, he would have been proud of the overall design and layout of this trail system. This trail is a work of art. The hard, compact single-track, sometimes covered with a bed of soft pine needles, has been laid out over 5,000 acres of plains and woodlands. The track's layout is designed to provide the mountain biker with great scenery

RIDE 6 *ROCKY POINT*

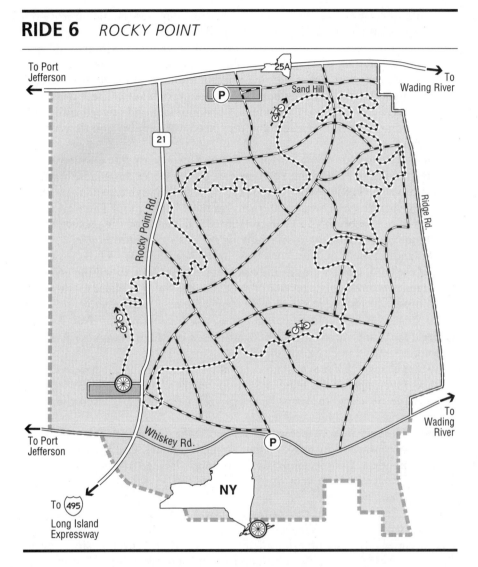

and action-packed technical hurdles that really put your skills to the test. A network of woodland roads crisscrosses the sandy, wooded pine area and provides ample biking trails. All access is prohibited on Rocky Point lands except under permit from the Department of Environmental Conservation or from the Navy Department.

The development of the trail was made possible by C.L.I.M.B., which is on a mission to preserve and maintain existing paths. My appreciation and respect go out to the members and volunteers of the Concerned Long Island Mountain Bicyclists Club (C.L.I.M.B.) for building and maintaining many of the trails on Long Island. Their work parties clean up, repair, and improve the conditions of the trails and develop methods to fight erosion on special sections along the routes. They and all the work party teams that build and maintain the myriad of trails described in this book deserve special acknowledgment for the work they are doing to accommodate and minimize the ecological impact of the growing number of mountain bikers. These organizations interface and open up channels of communication between trail users and land management agencies, and they need our support and deserve our cooperation.

There are rules for riding in Rocky Point. Riders must stay on the yellow-marked mountain bike trails. You may ride on the larger dirt roads, but their condition in the sandy terrain may vary and is not always dependable. There is a satisfying range of twists and turns on the 13-mile loop. The trail is one way, so once you begin you have committed. Helmets and eye protection are also required. Bicycling on marked hiking trails is strictly prohibited.

The land was sold to New York State in the late 1970s for $1. RCA, which owned the land, owed so much in back taxes that it chose to sell the property for practically nothing to get out of debt. On the trail you'll see many fallen radio towers straddling the steel cables that once held them erect.

General location: Approximately 55 miles east of Manhattan, near Port Jefferson on Long Island's North Shore.
Elevation change: It's mostly flat riding, although the trail has been developed to take advantage of the many variations in the landscape. Several gnarly spaghetti loops carve through the moderately hilly terrain, descending and ascending many small hills and gullies.
Season: Hunters may be present from September 15 to April 16, with the highest concentration from November through January. Call the Department of Environmental Conservation (DEC) for more detailed information.
Services: Rocky Point Cycle on 664 Route 25A in Rocky Point provides sales, repairs, and equipment.
Hazards: Remember that the trail is a one-way loop. These popular trails are heavily used during the weekends, and the one-way direction prevents many hammerheads from hammering their heads together. With collisions out of the way, the next item to pay attention to is the tight twists and turns through trees that are sometimes little more than one handlebar wide. Then there are some steep sections you might wish to blast through and ride like a roller coaster. Overall, the main hazard is not having the sufficient skills to handle this great track.

Watch for ticks during the summer months. It is also advisable to call the Fish and Wildlife clerk at (516) 444-0273 for the January deer season dates. Pine needles cover the ground and trails, so be careful about brush fires; they can be easily started.

Smooth, fast-paced, rolling single-track at Rocky Point.

Rescue index: These trails see their fair share of traffic, and there is usually another rider passing by every 15 minutes or so. It is hard to become lost since the trail is a loop and will eventually end where it began. As long as you stay on the trail, you will have no problem. You are never more than 2 miles from major civilization.

Land status: New York State Department of Environmental Conservation. A permit is required for access into the preserve. Call to find out details for acquiring the permit. Work parties are an important component in keeping the Rocky Point trail open and are conducted through C.L.I.M.B. Trail maintenance is the responsibility of the trail users. This means you!

Maps: New York State Department of Environmental Conservation will supply you with a trail map when you send away for the required permit. The mountain bike trail is well marked with square yellow mountain bike signs. They are posted quite frequently and you will probably never have to look at a map to find your way.

Finding the trail: Take the Long Island Expressway to Exit 66/Sills Road, Yaphank. Make a left on Count Road 101 North and continue straight toward Yaphank. At the stoplight bear right in the direction of Route 21. You will pass Upper Lake on your left, a small body of water which feeds into Carmans River. There is a convenience store across from it. At the next light bear left and continue on Route 21. After the intersection with Whiskey Road you will see a New York State Department of Environmental Conservation,

Rocky Point Natural Resource Area sign. Turn left into the parking area. Park your vehicle and make sure your permit is in the window. The trail begins beyond the wooden kiosk sign. A park ranger is usually parked in the parking area and will provide extra assistance if needed.

Sources of additional information:

New York State Department of Environmental Conservation
SUNY Building 40
Stony Brook, New York 11790-2356
(516) 444-0273/444-0310

C.L.I.M.B.
P.O. Box 203
Woodbury, New York 11797
(516) 262-0909

Rocky Point Cycle
664 Route 25A
Rocky Point, New York 11778
(516) 744-5372

Notes on the trail: The directions are simple. The trail is well marked with yellow blazes and it is virtually impossible to get lost. These yellow markers on the trees guide you for the entire 13-mile loop. This trail has been developed to challenge and satisfy any gonzo dirthead. There are numerous twists and turns and miniature loops that take advantage of the varied, hilly terrain. All you have to do is get on and not get off. If you cannot complete the entire loop, there are bail-out points indicated on the map. You may return by following the yellow markers back to the Rocky Point Road parking lot.

RIDE 7   *EDGEWOOD OAK BRUSH PLAINS PRESERVE*

For an easy morning or afternoon ride, set your wheels down on this relatively unknown 3,000-acre preserve. It offers a four-mile loop-and-other mixture of wide, hard-packed, old abandoned dirt roads and some single-tracks. Set in the middle of suburban sprawl, this large piece of land offers basic, no-frills riding and some semblance of solitude—a few trees and not too many people, other than a few members of a dog club who train and clock their Labradors in the act of retrieving fallen game. This may not be a mecca for mountain bikers, but the terrain contains sufficient woodland for some basic off-road riding opportunities. The trails traverse a generally flat, pine-barren forest with spacious fields. The riding provides the novice with a good lesson in basic handling of the bike and offers the average rider some

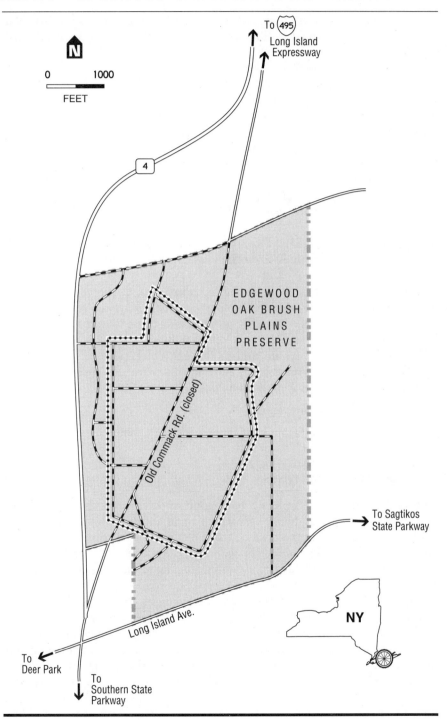

fast-paced double-track. Most trails are wide, smooth, and easy to ride. All access is prohibited on the Edgewood Oak Brush Plains Preserve lands, except under permit from the Department of Environmental Conservation or special permit from the Navy Department.

General location: Suffolk County, Exit 52 on the Long Island Expressway, near the town of Edgewood.

Elevation change: Negligible. Generally flat terrain.

Season: Year-round riding is available.

Services: Most services are along Jericho Turnpike. Proceed north on Commack Road until it intersects with Jericho Turnpike in about 7 miles.

Hazards: Watch for ticks during the summer months.

Rescue index: Suburbia surrounds the preserve, and help is never more than a mile away.

Land status: New York State Department of Environmental Conservation. A permit is required for access into the preserve. Call to find out details for acquiring the permit.

Maps: New York State Department of Environmental Conservation will supply you with a trail map when you send away for the required permit.

Finding the trail: Take the Long Island Expressway east to Exit 52/Commack Road, County Road 4. Go south on Commack Road (CR 4) for about 4 miles and on your left you will see an entrance through a metal fence. It is unmarked, but there is a parking area directly beyond this entrance. Turn in here and make sure your permit is in your window.

Source of additional information:

New York State Department of Environmental Conservation
SUNY Building 40
Stony Brook, New York 11790-2356
(516) 444-0273/444-0310

Notes on the trail: The trail is a basic loop trail with blue blazes marking most of the way. It may be tricky because there are several other woodland roads that intersect with the main course. For this trail description, follow the blue-marked trails. Go beyond the wooden pole barrier. The trail begins on your left as a wide sandy dirt road between a row of old trees that appear to have been planted long ago to line the road. This road veers to your right as it approaches the edge of the large plain on your right. Proceed straight ahead in a northerly direction after the turn and onto a grass-covered lane, passing between some low bushes. Turn right at the next intersection and pick up the first blue trail marker on a tree. The blue markers will be your guide for the remainder of the trip. Proceed down a corridor of white pines. You are now in a pine-barren forest. Make the left at the next 4-trail intersection going in a northerly direction, and after a short distance you will see a small break in the trees and a blue marker. Turn right here and go through some dense cover, but

"I think we need to discuss frame size." Three-year-old Alize Margulis offers her expertise.

remain on the trail. You will soon come onto an old abandoned paved road. This is Old Commack Road and you may cruise up and down for some additional leisurely riding. Turn right onto the road and notice the blue markers on the utility poles. After a short distance, there will be another break in the trees on your left, with a blue trail marker near that entrance. You will come to a dirt road. Make a right, and you will see the continuation of the blue markers on the trees. Continue past a field on your left and make a right and then a quick left back into the forest, where the blue markers pick up again. Continue for about a mile and look for a break in the trees on your right. Turn right, where the blue trail markers appear on the trees. This will take you in a northerly direction. You will come out into a trail intersection of dirt roads. Bear right and pick up the blue trail on your left. Turn left and pedal back to the parking area.

RIDE 8 *SOUTHAVEN COUNTY PARK*

Southaven County Park is an interesting package. This Suffolk County park consists of a typical eastern Long Island pine-barren habitat. The dense oak woodlands are interspersed with open fields and picnic areas. The wide,

scenic Carmans River forms one of the park's borders. As an extra bonus, over ten miles of dirt road provide a full supply of off-road opportunities. All that's necessary for enjoyment on this eight-mile loop is a good picnic lunch and a bike that rides. There is enough variety for the beginning rider to learn some basic handling and endurance skills and get an excellent introduction to the sport. There's also some fast double-track for the more experienced biker. Seasoned riders can relax and enjoy some easy cruising along a network of secluded bridle paths and wide, hard-pack, unimproved dirt roads. Equestrians, walkers, and bike riders gladly share the trails.

Carmans River establishes the eastern park border, hosts many migrating birds, and is a favorite spot for canoeists. Several paths lead you down to the shore. Park your bikes and cool your heels and wheels at the river's edge. Take a moment just to sit by the sandy shore and watch the waterfowl.

During the high season, between Memorial Day and Labor Day weekends, the bridle paths tends to become chopped up. These trail sections have a sandy consistency and are less stable and resistant to usage. After completing this loop, you'll find a great ride along the scenic Carmans River where it's perfect to stop by the water and have lunch. Bordered on one side by Carmans River, Southaven Park provides fine opportunities for viewing wildlife and reflective moments for gazing at a beautiful river. For the more hardy, a brisk morning ride in the off-season is invigorating. Share the park with a few other polar bikers.

The demands for this ride are simple. A drive to the park, some sandwiches and snacks, a couple of bikes and friends or family, mix for a few hours and *voila*, a recipe for some great fun.

General location: Exit 68 off the Long Island Expressway, near the town of Shirley.
Elevation change: The terrain is generally flat with a few modest hills that climb and descend an ear-popping 40'.
Season: If there is no snow on the ground this is potentially 4-season territory. The trails get muddy and unmanageable for riding during wet periods, but it is a great place to get away from the crowds during the off-seasons. During the colder winter months, providing there is no snow on the trails, this park provides a great opportunity to enjoy some solitude and have these popular trails all to yourself. During the summer and warmer months, check your clothing and socks for ticks. Before I head out, I usually spray some bug repellent on my socks. The little rascals seem to stay away, but I'm not sure it's because of the spray . . . .
Services: Most services can be found in the towns of Southaven and Shirley.
Hazards: The park sees an increase in usability from Memorial Day to Labor Day weekends. Pay extra attention and ride responsibly during these busy times. The park is beautiful and popular and is shared by hikers and equestrians. The current policy of trail usage is managed by the individual, and for now

the people involved in these activities coexist and respect each other's rights to use this special park. We, as mountain bikers, need to be sensitive while riding here. Let's maintain a responsible image. By using commonsense etiquette and having respect for other users, we will assure our place on these trails.

Rescue index: Suburban sprawl surrounds the park, and you will probably bump into someone else riding, hiking, or running on the trails. Park maintenance vehicles use the trails as well and are always helpful. Most of the trails are within a mile of Victory and Gerard roads that border the park.

Land status: Suffolk County Parks Department manages Southhaven County Park.

Maps: USGS, 7.5 minute series, Bellport quadrangle provides good detail for these unimproved dirt roads.

Finding the trail: Take the Long Island Expressway east to Exit 68 and go south on William Floyd Parkway; just before Sunrise Highway, turn right on Victory Avenue. Turn right at the park entrance sign to gain access into the park. There is a parking area on your right.

Sources of additional information:

Southaven County Park
Brookhaven, New York
(516) 854-1414

Suffolk County Parks
P.O. Box 144
West Sayville, New York 11796
(516) 854-4949

Notes on the trail: The ride in Southaven Park can be put together as one basic loop. Begin at the park entrance, go past the park maintenance buildings, and bear left onto the wide, well-surfaced, dirt park road through a stand of white pine. In just under a mile, you will come to a sign that says "Field Trial Area Large Upper Picnic Area 17–22." Straight ahead is a horse path that travels along the eastern perimeter of the park, paralleling Gerard Road. This trail begins past 2 wooden pilings with a metal pole going across them. For the shorter loop, turn right and go past several picnic areas. At a fork in the road, you have 2 choices. The left fork takes you north along a wide horse path past several open fields and leads you back to the parking area in 2 miles. The right fork takes you back to the parking area in just over a mile.

For the wider loop, continue straight through the 2 wooden pilings and travel through a mixed hardwood forest for 1.5 miles. Turn right and continue south on a dirt unimproved road. Follow it for .7 mile. A spur trail to your left leads in a northeasterly direction down to Carmans River. In just under a .5 mile turn right, in a westerly direction, onto another spur for a quick 1.5-mile loop. If you choose not to, then just ignore the spur, the fun,

My wife Barbara and daughter Alize by the western shore of Carmans River.

the adventure, and continue straight, where in just under a mile you will arrive at the park maintenance buildings. Another less-defined path runs along the western shore of Carmans River. This trail can be reached from the parking area. Just ride to the river and travel north along a sandy, hard-pack double-track for about 1 mile.

RIDE 9 *FIRE ISLAND NATIONAL SEASHORE*

Mountain biking along this flat, hard-packed, unimproved jeep sand trail gives you access to one of Long Island's finest beaches and charming beach communities lining the eastern portion of Fire Island. As another reward, stop along the way, providing the weather is warm, park the bike, throw out a towel, and cool off in the Atlantic Ocean. There are over 14 miles of riding available along this portion of Fire Island.

Generally, mountain biking is associated with cruising along old country roads past farm fields or descending from a mountain on single-track. Riding a mountain bike along one of the flattest sections of Long Island, the beaches can qualify as a first-rate off-road experience too. Novice riders will find the flat road an excellent introduction to the sport and will experience the sense

To Point o' Woods

Ocean Bay Park

Seaview

Ocean Beach

Robins Rest

Atlantique

Lonelyville

Atlantique Beach

GREAT SOUTH BAY

Fairharbor

ATLANTIC OCEAN

Saltaire

Kismet

Jeep Trail

Lighthouse

To Robert Moses St. Park and Causeway

Wooden barrier before trailhead

NY

N

0   1/4   1/2

MILES

of discovery that accompanies mountain biking, while the seasoned rider can relax and enjoy some easy, pleasant cruising.

Fire Island is a funny place. It's a thin, long strip of land with an incredibly diverse population; depending on the community, it's a summertime mecca for gays, singles, nude bathers, and families. Thousands of Manhattanites arrive by ferries to spend a weekend away from the asphalt jungles of Manhattan. After a weekend, there's a mass exodus of sunburned faces heading back to the city to start another week of work.

There is another side to Fire Island that few consider, but that lends itself to a pleasurable and meaningful coastal habitat ride. The trail goes past the 1858 Fire Island Lighthouse that overlooks the Great South Bay and Atlantic Ocean. Stop by the lighthouse visitor center for a history of Fire Island, including true stories about life-saving rescues in the ocean and its maritime traditions. Folklore suggests that land-based pirates built fires at night to lure cargo ships onto shore.

Fire Island is a barrier formed as the glaciers began to melt and recede and currents carried rocks and sediment and deposited them in an east-west direction. Along the ride, you will notice the natural sand dunes that create a barrier against the Atlantic Ocean. Through the centuries, the island has been bombarded by storms off the ocean. Dunes have been destroyed, creating inlets connecting the Great South Bay to the north with the ocean. About 10,000 waves a day pound and wash away the sand and dunes. Currents drift from the east and carry sands from offshore sandbars and easterly beaches, replenishing the beaches. The dunes begin to grow again as grasses seed the small growing dunes. Notice the small grasses growing on top of and around the dunes. A cycle begins as the dunes become seeded by birds and animals attracted by the grasses; they carry and deposit other seeds. Larger shrub-type plants begin to take hold, building new soil. They are then replaced by thickets and then by forests of holly, hardwoods, and pines. Along the trail, the stages of this cycle are visible. Without the anchoring roots of beach grasses there would be no dunes; without sheltering dunes there would be no forests; and without this precious balance, there would be no island. The island's wealth of seafood, waterfowl, and plants attracted the original Native American settlers and later, the European settlers.

Farther along the route are the beach communities of Kismet, Saltaire, and Fair Harbor. These towns have many interesting little roads and paths that crisscross through attractive, charming summer cottages.

General location: South Shore of Long Island near Robert Moses State Park.
Elevation change: It is negligible along the flat terrain of the beaches.
Season: Mountain biking along this route can be year-round, except during wet periods when the sandy, hard-packed roads turn into a mush mixture. Winter provides an excellent opportunity to get outside for a few hours and enjoy the solitude of this popular area.

Services: Food stands, picnic areas, and beaches are found in the Field 5 parking area, where you will park your car and begin your ride. The towns of Kismet and Saltaire have village markets and convenience stores as well as some outdoor restaurants.

Hazards: Do not tread on the dunes, since they are the primary method for fighting beach erosion. Stay out of tall grasses, since Fire Island has a large population of deer and, as follows, the infamous deer tick. During the winter the deer can be seen grazing near the dunes around the thickets and low grasses. Wear sunscreen during the summer months and watch out for poison ivy, with its 3 leaflets. Mosquitoes are abundant in summer, so come prepared with bug repellent. Do not speed through the beach communities; there may be walkers heading down to the beach, other bikes, or a car once in a blue moon. All riders are required to carry a bell and a light on their bikes when traveling any of the roads. Other than that, it is paradise to many.

Rescue index: It is very easy to find help as you travel through these busy beach communities. Other people use these roads and there are many homes in the area. In case of emergency, you can always knock on a cottage door.

Land status: The road is used by permit-holding residents of the eastern towns, but it can be used as a bike path as well. The beginning of the ride takes you through National Park Service U.S. Department of the Interior land. You then ride through the beach communities of Kismet, Saltaire, Fair Harbor, Lonelyville, Atlantique, Robins Rest, Ocean Beach, Seaview, Ocean Bay Park, and Point o' Woods. Ocean Beach does not permit bikes on its roads and paths from Memorial Day to Labor Day weekend.

Maps: Call the National Park Service Headquarters and ask them to send the "Fire Island National Seashore" official map and guide. The USGS, 7.5 minute series, Bay Shore East quadrangle provides good detail of this portion of Fire Island.

Finding the trail: This thin, 32-mile-long island can be reached by taking the Southern State Parkway east; exit where you see signs for Robert Moses State Park and Captree State Park. Travel south on Sagtikos State Parkway, which then turns into the Robert Moses Causeway and bridges over the Great South Bay. Go around the rotary and head in the direction of the Field 5 parking area. There is a $4 parking fee, and after you park you will have to walk your bike along the roadway about 1,000' in the direction of the very visible, black-and-white lighthouse. The road begins here. You will see a sign posted, "Warning, No Vehicles beyond this Point without Federal Permit." Go right in. It is open to bicycles.

Sources of additional information:

> Fire Island Lighthouse
> Burma Road
> Fire Island, New York 11706
> (516) 661-4876

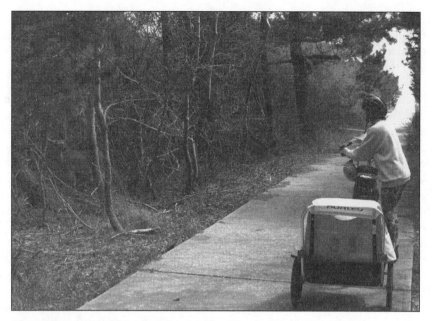

The omnipresent white-tailed deer on Fire Island.

National Park Service Headquarters
120 Laurel Street
Patchogue, New York 11772-3596
(516) 289-4810
(516) 661-2556

Notes on the trail: There is a lot to explore. You can ride for 6 miles from the lighthouse in one direction through the towns of Kismet, Saltaire, Fair Harbor, Lonelyville, Atlantique, Robins Rest, Ocean Beach, Seaview, Ocean Bay Park, and Point o' Woods. How far you penetrate into the island depends on the condition of the trail and the distance you wish to cover. Since it is a hard-packed sand trail, it may degrade from storms and extra usage and become difficult to ride on. After 1 mile you reach the town of Saltaire, where the trail traverses along a wooden boardwalk. From Saltaire to Fair Harbor, the next .7 mile is part wooden boardwalk and part semipaved. After Fair Harbor, you will ride on a jeep trail for about 1.5 miles until you get to the town of Ocean Beach, where again the trail becomes a semipaved road. From Ocean Beach it's another 2 miles until you reach Point o' Woods. The town of Ocean Beach restricts bike riding of any kind during the summer months, from Memorial Day to Labor Day weekend, due to the large crowds of people using the same roads and paths.

About a mile after the lighthouse, past the dunes, turn left on the second street. At the time of this writing, it was unmarked. You'll travel alongside the

Great South Bay and through the small town of Kismet. At the end of the road, turn right and notice the convenience store and restaurant. During the summer you may dine outside, but in the winter both may be closed. Continue through town on the wooden boardwalk, which is characteristic of the roads in these towns. Proceed past a tiny boat basin on your left, turn right at the end, and proceed up the paved road to the dirt road. Turn left on the dirt road, heading in the direction of Saltaire. There is a sign posted welcoming you in and providing a list of rules you must follow when you are visiting. The 6'-wide wooden boardwalks crisscrossing throughout the town of Saltaire are a lot of fun to explore. Turn left onto Surf Street and pass by some beautiful cottages. Head in the direction of the Great South Bay, and at the end of the path turn right onto Bay Street, which parallels the Great South Bay. Open views of the Robert Moses and Captree bridges and the bay can be seen from this street. Continue along this street past several boardwalk avenues. There is a village market on Broadway that is generally closed during the winter months. Turn right on Pacific and then left on Lighthouse Road. This will take you toward Fair Harbor. Continue straight through Fair Harbor, although you may wish to explore the tiny streets that crisscross through town. The road will change into a jeep trail after Lonelyville. As you pass through the town of Atlantique, visit some stunning beaches half a mile away along the Atlantic Ocean side. Park and lock your bike and walk a couple of blocks to the ocean on your right. After Atlantique, the jeep trail swings north into Robins Rest. Stay on the main jeep trail in an easterly direction. In about a quarter mile, you approach the town of Ocean Beach. At the time of this writing the roads were semipaved. Continue through Ocean Beach and take the last right after the town of Seaview. Make the second left, going east, and then the third right. Turn left at the next path and continue straight through the town of Ocean Bay Park and end your journey in Point o' Woods. Return the way you came to your parking via Lighthouse Street. If you become disoriented by all the roads, just remember to keep heading west.

RIDE 10 NAVY COOPERATIVE AREA TRAILS

The remote, multiuse Navy Cooperative Area is an extremely popular spot for local hunters. For mountain bikers who do not live in the neighborhood, this little-known area offers an interesting assortment of trail options. The easy riding enables the rider to explore an attractive pine-barren woodscape in a portion of Long Island off the beaten path. Only 60 miles east of New York City, the 1,657 acres of forested land include over 13 miles of wide, sandy, four-wheel-drive dirt roads. The fairly level riding does not require any special technical skills, enabling beginners to get into some secluded woods and test their emerging skills without being too technically engaged. The more experienced can get in some fast riding and blast along the double-track.

The hard-packed paths weave throughout a mixed habitat of typical eastern Long Island pine barrens and oak woodlands. There are several attractive ponds and lakes in the area along the trail. There is no formal entrance, but a multitude of roadside parking areas provide easy access.

All access is prohibited on the Navy Cooperative Area lands except under permit from the Department of Environmental Conservation. Mail away for the permit application. It costs $6 and is valid for three years. The area is open to hunters during designated seasons. Call the Department of Environmental Conservation (DEC) at (516) 444-0273 or 444-0310 to find out dates. During this period, you should try riding elsewhere, or your mountain bike bar-ends could wind up mounted next to some trophy antlers.

General location: Manorville, Suffolk County, Exit 69 of the Long Island Expressway.
Elevation change: Negligible.
Season: Hunters may be present from September 15 to April 16, with the highest concentration from November through January. Call the DEC for more detailed information.
Services: At Exit 70, south on Route 111, there is a service station and some restaurants with great munchies. My favorite is Graces.
Hazards: The hunting season is usually from November 1 through December 31 and parts of January into February. Call the DEC for more detailed information. A few paved-road links require care when traveling on them.
Rescue index: The park is surrounded by well-traveled roads and you are never farther than half a mile from help from passing vehicles.
Land status: New York State Department of Environmental Conservation. A permit is required for access into the preserve. Call to find out details for acquiring the permit.
Maps: The DEC will supply you with a map when you apply for a permit.
Finding the trail: Take the Long Island Expressway east to Exit 69/Center Moriches and Wading River Road. Continue north on Center Moriches Road. Go past the intersection with North Street and bear right onto Schultz-Wading River Road and look for parking area 4 on your left. There are several parking areas on your right and left, but the ride begins beyond parking area 4.

Source of additional information:

New York State Department of Environmental Conservation
SUNY Building 40
Stony Brook, New York 11790-2356
(516) 444-0273/444-0310

Notes on the trail: Take the wide, sandy, hard-packed four-wheel-drive path beyond the wooden barrier as it leads through a narrow meadow bordered by

0   1/2   1
MILES

Swan Pond Rd.

To
Connecticut Ave.

NY

To Eastern
Long Island

Long Island Expressway 495

111

Note: *All trails are double-track.*

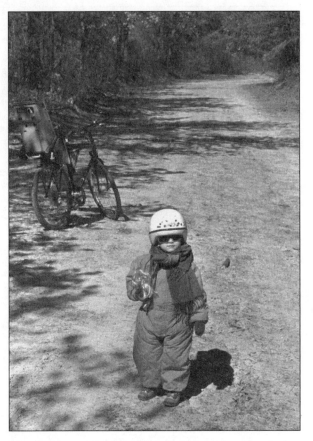

My daughter Alize is well prepared for a winter's day sojourn at the Navy Cooperative Area.

stands of white pine. In about half a mile you will come to a 4-way intersection. Turn right and pass by Sandy and Duck ponds. Right after you pass Sandy Pond and before you reach Duck Pond there will be a dirt road leading off to the right in an easterly direction. This will lead into Schultz Road, where you may return to your parking area by turning right—that is if you parked at area 4. You may link to another set of interior roads by turning left, heading north onto Schultz Road. Look for parking area 2 on your left and the wooden barrier directly across on the right side of Schultz Road. Go beyond the barrier as the road continues straight past some overgrown open fields. The condition of this road is a lot less sandy and you can rely on more dependable cruising. At about .2 mile you will come to a four-way intersection. You will return via the road on your left, but to begin this loop continue straight ahead. Keep to the right at the next fork, bear right at the following fork, and continue straight until you get to Linus Pond. At Linus Pond look for a road heading in a northerly direction. Continue along this road for about 1 mile until it reaches a 2-lane paved road. Turn left and make a left at the next paved-road intersection. On your right you will pass a fenced-in property. Continue until you see a parking area on your left using a large wooden pole as a gate. Turn in here and continue along some fields. Turn right at the next intersection, where you will connect with the road that you started on from parking area 2.

Across from parking area 6, on the east side of Schultz Road, is a 2-mile out-and-back (1-mile one-way) road. It is worth checking out, so head down for a short spell. Go beyond the wooden barrier and bear left. There is a short circular dirt road on your right. Try it. After you have completed the tiny loop, look for a road on your left heading in an easterly direction. This 4'-wide hard-pack trail leads first through a pine forest; you will notice more hardwoods as you get closer to the swamp, where the trail ends. Some single-track paths leading off to your left in a northerly direction may be worth exploring if you have the time. Return to Schultz Road along this path.

RIDE 11 SURF AND TURF

Mountain biking at Hither Hills is a mixed bag through an endless network of trails. Situated between Amagansett and Montauk on far eastern Long Island, the number of off-road opportunities makes up for the long drive it may require to get there. It's 90 miles from the New York City line. The riding includes everything from easy cruising on old, abandoned, semipaved roads and smooth, gentle, grassy double-tracks, to tight, twisting, roller-coaster single-track. Hither Hills is 1,700 acres of playland for hikers, equestrians, mountain bikers, and bathers. A public beach nearby is part of the park and provides a great opportunity to cool off in some surf after hard work in the turf. The hilly terrain of the park stands out in the flat landscape of the agricultural plains of the surrounding countryside and offers epic adventures through its variety of terrain.

A winding single-track from a dense oak and pine forest skirts the long line of bluffs facing Napeague Bay, offering wide panoramic vistas. Pause a moment and consider the impression this primeval wilderness might have made on the Native Americans who first discovered it or the first European person who landed on these shores years later.

These bluffs and the surrounding hilly landscape of the park owe their convoluted formation to the glacial moraine that was left behind by the retreating glaciers of the last Ice Age thousands of years ago. The flat land, which was formed by the melting waters of the glaciers, provides a good contrast to the hills. They mark where the glaciers paused and released their huge boulders

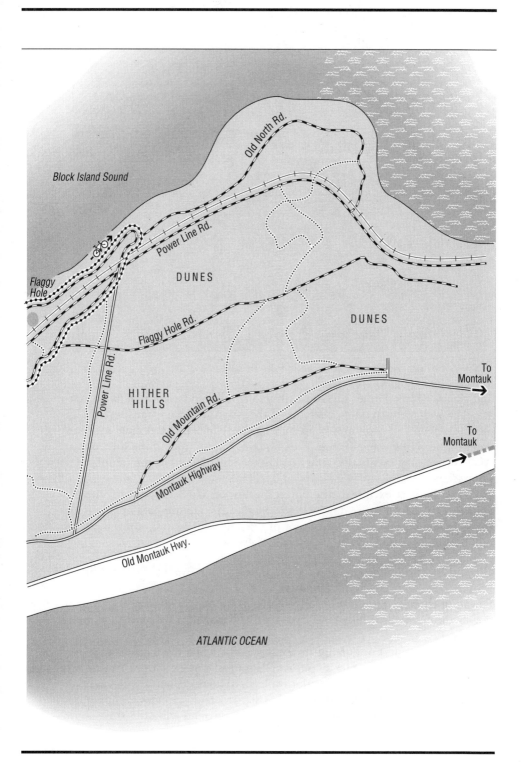

Block Island Sound

Old North Rd.

Power Line Rd.

DUNES

Flaggy
Hole

Flaggy Hole Rd.

DUNES

Power Line Rd.

To
Montauk

HITHER
HILLS

Old Mountain Rd.

To
Montauk

Montauk Highway

Old Montauk Hwy.

ATLANTIC OCEAN

View of Napeague Bay at Hither Hills State Park.

and glacial debris. Hither Hills was originally an island separated by an open sea. The westward-trending currents of the Atlantic Ocean transported sediments eroded from Montauk Point. A long sleeve of sand extending westward from Hither Hills was built up. This body of land points in the direction of Amagansett that eventually attached Hither Hills Island to the mainland of Long Island.

The scenery is excellent, the riding is fun yet challenging, and there is enough to fill up an entire day. Water is on all sides. Do not pass up an opportunity to combine a hard, sweaty tour of the hills with a cool, refreshing swim in the Atlantic Ocean. What more could there be?

General location: Eastern tip of Long Island, after Amagansett and before Montauk Point on Montauk Highway.

Elevation change: Elevations rarely exceed 100', but there are many ups and downs throughout the hilly landscape that will challenge the hardy and give a good workout.

Season: Year-round opportunities exist, except when the trails are covered with snow. Don't let winter's cold stop you; just put on more clothing and enjoy the solitude of having popular trails all to yourself.

Services: This state park is a multiple-use area and provides camping and swimming at the adjacent public beach. A campground with 165 sites, showers, restrooms, and telephones is located along the Atlantic Ocean in the park off Old Montauk Highway. There are some great surf-and-turf restaurants along Montauk Highway just west of the park entrance.

Hazards: Some of the single-track travels through low underbrush, so if you are wearing shorts and riding during the warmer seasons, give yourself a once-over for ticks. While riding along the route, stay on the trail to prevent tire punctures due to the park's many thorn bushes.

Rescue index: You are never far from major paved roads.

Land status: New York State Park.

Maps: Pick up a trail map at the park's gatehouse when entering the park on Old Montauk Highway.

Finding the trail: Take the Long Island Expressway east for about 65 miles to Exit 70/Manorville. Proceed south on County Road 111 and then go east on Sunrise Highway, NY 27, toward Montauk. Continue through Southampton, Bridgehampton, East Hampton, and Amagansett. The highway splits and forks right onto Old Montauk Highway, where you'll find the campground and beach section of Hither Hills State Park. The left fork takes the direct route into Montauk. Fork left and after the sign reading "Overlook 1200 feet," turn off Montauk Highway into the parking area on the left.

Sources of additional information:

> Cycle Path Bike Store
> P.O. Box 7074
> Main Street
> Amagansett, New York 11930
> (516) 267-6313

> Hither Hills State Park
> Old Montauk Highway
> Montauk, New York 11954
> (516) 668-2461

> New York State Park Office
> Recreation and Historic Preservation
> Long Island Region
> Belmont Lake State Park
> P.O. Box 247
> Babylon, New York 11702
> (516) 669-1000

Notes on the trail: Standing in the overlook parking area, face the park sign. To your left in a northwest direction lies a small, single-track path leading down a small hill. Proceed straight through a 3-way fork and then descend a steep hill through a dense wood of small oak trees. The single-track ends at a sandy, double-track dirt road. Turn right and bear left through some large boulders that block another double-track. You will pass by some bird houses and then end on Old Tar Road in a little over a mile. You can recognize Old Tar Road because it was originally paved but now is quite broken up. Turn right and then make a quick left over the railroad tracks. Make sure you look for trains. Proceed into a small opening in the woods on the other side of the tracks. Once you have entered the forest, make the first right onto a single-track path that runs parallel to the railroad tracks. This portion of the trail is quite pleasant; you can do some nice cruising over rolling, grass-covered single-track.

After about a mile, you will come to a group of 4 boulders with a white painted blaze marked on one. Proceed through and make the right onto the dirt road that soon comes to a T intersection. Continue straight across the wide road onto the single-track directly in front of you that leads up a small embankment. You will cover some nice rolling terrain through a heavily wooded forest and may catch glances of Napeague Bay to your left. After a steep descent this trail will merge with another from the left. Continue straight where the trail leads to the bay, and make a right after you come out to it. Ride along the trail as it proceeds between wooden stakes with white paint on them. The bay is on your left. You will eventually head back into the forest and climb 2 steep, sandy hills, one right after another. You have one choice: walk your bike. Farther ahead, a steep downhill will take your breath away, and you will end at a T intersection. Turn right to cross over the railroad tracks. From the 4 boulders you have covered approximately 2.5 miles. Look for a short, narrow, uphill trail to the left of a birdhouse; take this and it will empty you onto the double-track, Old North Road. Take Old North Road for a little over 3 miles. Continue all the way to a T intersection. Turn left onto Montauk Highway, which lies just east of the overlook parking area.

RIDE 12 *NORTHWEST BY NORTHWEST*

This manicured, four-mile, out-and-back single-track is a must-do for anyone who travels out to the Hamptons. Located just north of East Hampton off a quiet road, the pine needle path twists and turns along a gently rolling terrain. The area is populated with dense forests of large white pine and oak, which is characteristic of the northern section of the South Fork of Long Island. These mature stands of conifers and hardwoods provide a high canopy providing much-needed shade during the hot summer months. The lack of the thick, low-lying shrubbery that is so prevalent in these forests gives a sense of space, visibility, and freedom for a cerebral experience in the pure pleasures of back-country bike riding. A different, less pastoral reality returns when you cross a paved road.

The wide single-track is not technically challenging, and its smoothness, good condition, and gentle, rolling grade facilitates a sort of out-of-saddle experience. On this trail, you do not have to try hard to feel great and ride the perfect line. The out-and-back path leads through a thick, primeval forest, and as the pace sets in, as you get into that groove, the maneuvering around the many twists and turns produces a Zen-like sensation, a feeling that's difficult to describe or pinpoint. There's no overbraking and no oversteering, and the tires are carving like skates. You come out of corners with just enough momentum, and it almost feels as though the trail is controlling the bike and you are just along for the ride.

General location: Approximately 90 miles from Manhattan, just north of East Hampton, Long Island.

Elevation change: Small rolling hills take you through elevations of less than 100'.

Season: Year-round riding opportunities exist, except when the trails are covered by snow. Do not let winter's cold stop you though; just put on more clothing and enjoy the solitude and satisfaction of having popular trails all to yourself.

Services: Most services can be found along Montauk Highway, NY 27. The village of East Hampton has it all and provides food, window shopping, ice cream, movie theaters, and a busy sidewalk strip of white-shorts and sneakers-clad summer vacationers.

Hazards: Although you are not scraping past low undergrowth shrubbery, it is always a good idea to check yourself for ticks. Low pine branches overhang and you may need to duck under them, so keep your eyes in front of your helmeted head.

Rescue index: Suburban and vacation communities surround the area. Help is never more than half a mile away.

Land status: The trail follows the Northwest Path, which traverses the northwest area in the town of East Hampton.

Maps: For $2, the town of East Hampton Chamber of Commerce will mail you the "Northwest Area Trails Map," which details Northwest County through which the path traverses.

Finding the trail: Take the Long Island Expressway east for about 65 miles to Exit 70/Manorville. Proceed south on County Road 111 and then go east on Sunrise Highway, NY 27, for approximately 27 miles, until you reach the Village of East Hampton. After you pass signs for the Village of East Hampton, make a left (north) onto Stephen Hands Path. After 2 miles, turn left onto Bull Path and head north. The trail appears on your right as a small dirt path leading through some trees, about 1.5 miles north of your turnoff from Stephen Hands Path. The trailhead begins directly across from address 100 and just before a sign for Fielers Close. A small turnout up ahead from the trailhead provides some parking.

RIDE 12 NORTHWEST BY NORTHWEST

Great Swamp

Northwest Rd.

Old Northwest Rd.

To Montauk Hwy. and East Hampton Village

Wilsons Grove

Closed

Bull Path

New Landing Rd.

Crooked Hwy.

Two Holes of Water Rd.

Northwest Creek

Swamp Rd.

Russells Neck Rd.

To Sag Harbor

To Wainscott

63

Prime single-track weaves its way through the Northwest Path.

By train: Take the Long Island Railroad to East Hampton. Turn right onto Railroad Avenue, right onto Cooper, and left onto Newtown Lane. Proceed for about 1.5 miles, where the road name changes to Long Lane. Turn right onto Stephen Hands Path and take the next left onto Bull Path. Follow the remaining directions in the section above.

Source of additional information:

Town of East Hampton Chamber of Commerce
37 Main Street
East Hampton, New York 11937
(516) 324-0362

Notes on the trail: Yellow triangles posted on trees mark this well-groomed trail. The trail is straight and fairly easy to follow, with few spur trails to confuse you.

The ride begins through a predominantly conifer forest mixed with oak. You will soon come to a detour that was posted to direct mountain bikers to the left. The section of the path that leads off to your right has been temporarily closed due to its crossing private land and a request by the landowners that the mountain bike traffic bypass their properties. So respectfully, we must bear left. Soon bear right onto a wider double-track path that leads you out onto paved N.W. Landing Road. Due to the current closing of the prior section of the path, you will be able to reconnect with the Northwest Path by turning right onto N.W. Landing Road. Pass Highland Lane on your left and then bear right at the next fork to proceed onto Old Northwest Road. After passing Cattle Walk Road on your right, you will come to another intersection. This is where you pick up the Northwest Path that leads diagonally between the two intersecting roads on your left to the north. The half-mile of rolling single-track ends at a **T** intersection. After a quick right, make a left and follow the single-track to another **T** intersection. Make a left onto the double-track at this intersection and continue straight. Turn right and return to Bull Path on the same single-track trail you were on before.

RIDE 13 *CAUMSETT STATE PARK*

Seeking a long day of easy riding? Set your wheels down on the secluded former estate of the Marshall Field family for an eight-mile loop. Over 15 miles of hard-packed wide dirt roads and bridle paths form an interesting network on 1,500 acres of rolling terrain. Located at Lloyd Neck in the town of Huntington, the land was purchased in 1921 by Marshall Field III, grandson of the famous department store pioneer. Field built a self-sufficient English-style rural estate that was a combination country club, hunting preserve, and home. Establishing a herd of 80 head of prize cattle, a complete dairy farm, and vegetable gardens, his self-sufficient, self-contained community had its own water and electrical supply. Wood products came from the estate's own stands of oak, pine, dogwood, and locust. Caumsett was originally in the hands of the Long Island Matinecock Indians and is translated as "place by a sharp rock." Situated on a scenic peninsula extending into the Long Island Sound, the state park is bordered by towering bluffs and a sandy pebble beach extending to the water's edge. Several paths lead to the shore, where you can park your bike, jump in the sound, and cool off or just sit on the pebbly beach and watch the boats drift by.

Caumsett State Park has a full spectrum of rides for everybody. Most trails are well maintained, wide, smooth, and a joy to ride. There is enough variety for the beginner to learn some basic handling and endurance skills, and the more experienced rider will find some fast double-track. Woodland roads and

Long Island Sound

Salt Marsh

Freshwater Pond

Marshall Field House

CAUMSETT STATE PARK

Large Meadow

Dairy Farm

CAUMSETT PARK

Park Entrance

Dead End

West Neck/Lloyd Harbor Rd.

To Huntington

Lloyd Harbor

NY

N

0   1200

FEET

bridle paths are all available and provide for some great cruising through the park's woodlands, meadows, and salt marshes. This tour consists of an eight-mile loop that will introduce you to the park. Equestrians, walkers, and bike riders gladly share the trails, and only when there is a special equestrian event do the park rangers expect the mountain bikes to stay off the race trails.

General location: Lloyd Neck, town of Huntington.

Elevation change: The paths meander over fairly level ground with some minor hills. The only climbs are when you ascend away from the shoreline to the level of the bluffs, which represent the overall level of the park land.

Season: Year-round could almost be guaranteed if not for the occasional blanket of snow, which makes the area ideal for cross-country skiers.

Services: Huntington provides all the services you might need along NY 25A.

Hazards: You will encounter horses and hikers on the same trails, so display a mutual respect and courtesy for them and this beautiful park will remain a recreation area for all to enjoy. The ticks like mountain bikers too, and will cling to your clothing or skin regardless of whether they know you or not. There is a large population of ticks, common throughout Long Island. Signs throughout the park indicate this little bugger's presence.

Be careful not to get too close to the 100' bluffs that overlook the sound. They continually erode, become extremely unstable, and crash down to the shore.

Rescue index: The park is well traveled, and you are never more than 1 or 2 miles from the parking area. Just find a paved road and take it in any direction, and it will soon lead to one of the estate's buildings or the park office.

Land status: Long Island Region of the New York State Office of Parks, Recreation, and Historic Preservation.

Maps: A well-defined and detailed map is provided at the park entrance before you arrive at the parking area.

Finding the trail: Take Northern State Parkway east to the NY106/107 exit. Go north on NY 106 and turn right on NY 25A (Northern Boulevard). Take NY 25A past the town of Cold Spring Harbor and turn left (north) on West Neck Road at the light; go for approximately 4 miles. Travel over a narrow strip of land that has Oyster Bay on your left and part of Lloyd Harbor to your right. The road will curve to the right, and you should look for the park sign in about a quarter-mile. Turn left into the park. The park is open from 8 A.M. to 4:30 P.M. daily. There is an entrance fee of $4 per vehicle from Memorial Day through Labor Day.

Source of additional information:

Caumsett State Park
West Neck Road
Lloyd Neck, New York 11743
(516) 423-1770

High bluffs overlook Long Island Sound at Caumsett State Park.

Notes on the trail: Turn right from the parking area. Proceed past the sign, "Authorized vehicles only beyond this point," and a mall kiosk with Caumsett State Park information on it, and turn left onto the cobblestone road that passes between the dairy farm and some maintenance garages.

At the end of the road you have 2 choices. To the left you may take the Fishing Drive for 2 miles north until it reaches the shore of the Long Island Sound. From the shore you can connect with another road that will take you back in a southerly direction to explore the eastern half of the park.

Making a right turn on the trail, after the dairy barn, leads you through the eastern portion of the park. There are several loops worth exploring to your left as you head down the paved road. The park map lays out the basic trail network, and you can just pick out an area and explore it. The trail description I have outlined below is an 8-mile loop and will take you on a grand tour of the park.

At the end of the dairy barn road, turn left where you see the sign for Fishing Drive. The name is derived from the route all the local fishermen take to the shoreline to fish. Continue past open meadows on your left and right and soon the road curves north, and you gently descend a flat, hard-pack, dirt road for 1.6 miles to the Long Island Sound. The road begins a small climb into a wooded area of beech and oak. You will soon emerge and pass another large meadow on your right. Several bridle paths lead off this main road. They are clearly marked with white signs with a horse in the center. For this grand tour, continue straight on the wide road and enter a dense woodland of vine-enshrouded mature oaks. In half a mile, the salt marsh will begin appearing to your left. Stop at the fine lookout point overlooking the marsh before you begin the last descent to the shore. The road ends at the fishermen's parking area. There is an interesting trail to your left beyond a metal fenced gate. You'll ride along a narrow, raised, sandy road that traverses above a marsh and includes tremendous open views of the Long Island Sound to the right. Notice small, sand-colored shore birds, called Piping Plovers, which scurry along the beach. These tiny birds once nested and thrived along the sandy beaches of the entire Atlantic coast. Human demands for these areas have won the competition for suitable habitat and squeezed out these tiny birds. The road ends in .75 mile at a small harbor.

Return along this road to the fishermen's parking area. Notice the tall bluffs and huge boulders dotting the shoreline. Before the glaciers arrived during the last Ice Age, the Long Island Sound was actually a large valley with a stream flowing to the east in it. Glaciation scooped out the river valley and dumped the debris on the surface of the island, building the bluffs and gently sloping land.

Once in the parking area, notice the "Do not enter" sign straight ahead in an easterly direction. Proceed in that direction, ascending away from the beach up a short, steep hill. The trail levels off in .3 mile and you'll see a small road leading to a bluff overlooking the sound. Be careful not to get too close, as these bluffs continually erode and crash down to the shore.

The riding levels out and passes through a vine-covered forest. After about .4 mile, you arrive at a fork. Bear left onto the four-wheel-drive jeep road. This connects you to a quadrant of bridle paths. Ironically, you will see a sign reading "No horseback riding beyond this point." You soon arrive at a 3-pronged fork. Take the middle one. (The left fork leads you down to the beach and the right fork takes you into the bridle paths.) The road turns grassy and curves to your right. Continue straight for about .7 mile through a gentle, rolling, forested landscape. You arrive at an intersection with a well-paved road. Continue over that road and straight down another bridle path. Take this to its end and turn left onto another four-wheel-drive road. Ride alongside a large field for about 1,600', and at the end of the field you will arrive at a clearing and an intersection with a paved road. Turn right onto the paved road and take another quick left to descend another bridle path. At the next fork, bear right up a gentle slope ending in a short, steep climb. You will come out on a paved road. Turn left on the paved road, continue past 2 intersections, and arrive back at the parking area.

Harriman State Park Tours

Harriman State Park, on the west side of the Hudson River, approximately one hour north of Manhattan, is a treasure of backcountry mountain bike trails. These wonderful routes are actually remnants of nineteenth-century industry and the Revolutionary and Civil wars. The park's 52,000 acres are crisscrossed by miles of old mining and logging roads. Exploring them is like taking a fast trek through history across lands that were key strategic routes for the American colonial armies. The forest and bedrock provided invaluable resources for the Civil War and other burgeoning nineteenth-century industries. Over 200 years of history are wrapped around these trails.

Ponds and small lakes throughout the park are vestiges of the last ice age. These lake and pond basins were created by glacial plucking of rocks from the ground, or abrasion, and they then were filled with glacial meltwater. Over thousands of years, the streams draining these basins cut their channels deeper, lowering the water levels; thus, basins that once held lakes or ponds became swamps and have been gradually filled with vegetation.

Harriman and Bear Mountain State Parks are a part of the Ramapo Mountains, which stretch from northern New Jersey into Rockland and Orange counties. The Ice Age has scraped and polished much of the metamorphosed sediments that were deposited here over a billion years ago by ancient seas, establishing these rocks as among the oldest on the continent. Huge erratics, strewn throughout the parks, were left behind by receding glaciers 10,000 years ago.

The parks were created at Bear Mountain in 1908, when Mrs. Edward H. Harriman, widow of a railroad tycoon, donated 10,000 acres of a personal estate to the Palisades Interstate Park Commission. In return, plans for a prison were aborted, and the state initiated an ambitious project involving road building and park restoration. The project was extended to 51,000 acres through additional gifts and purchases. The numerous lakes found throughout the parks were enlarged and damned, preserving and enhancing this beautiful and unique historical region. During the Depression, the Civilian Conservation Corps was created, providing labor to build dams and lakes in the park.

At the time of this writing, the current mountain biking policy in Harriman State Park restricts any riding on hiking trails. (Contact officials for current policies.) Some sections of the following trails are designated for hiking only, and riders are required to portage their bikes. The majority of the paths described in this region, however, traverse abandoned, old, unpaved roads which walkers and hikers occasionally use for connections with their trails, which means that we, as mountain bikers, need to be especially sensitive when riding. When you approach a person or group of people from behind, let them know you are there before you get too near, and do not forget to smile and say hello, too. Courteous and responsible conduct along these old forest roads will help assure the mountain biker's presence in this rare and pristine park. Helmets are required.

RIDE 14 *THE DOODLETOWN TOUR*

Dunderberg and West mountains, in Harriman State Park, form a natural amphitheater around the prerevolutionary settlement of Doodletown. Dutch trading vessels that sailed up the Hudson River in the late seventeenth century spotted the dark, forbidding valley and named it Doodel, which meant "Dood" (for dead) and "del" (for dale or hollow). Legend has it that the valley had a dark, forbidding appearance. Hence the name Dooddel or Dead Hollow. "Town" was added later.

This tour explores the winding grass- and vine-covered old roads that once made up the town's passageways. Trees have advanced on the old town and reclaimed much land. You'll pass the remnants of old house foundations, steps, and apple orchards that were once planted and thrived. Over ten miles of hard-packed double-track and old pavement lead to and around abandoned Doodletown. There's an entire day's cruising through this densely wooded landscape. One loop is described in this chapter, but there are other opportunities to explore along the network of roads that crisscross and intersect in the Doodletown area.

This trail system consists of hard-packed, old country roads built to lead individuals into and around Doodletown. The roads pass through a moderately hilly landscape that does not require any special technical skills, but gives an experienced mountain biker a good workout. In addition, it's great for novices who feel ready to try something more demanding than a flat trail and are eager to test their endurance on more hilly terrain.

It's not just a trail through the woods. It's a tour through history. At any point in the ride take a moment to imagine the American Revolution and historic events that unfolded along these trails. Early in the fall of 1777, the British marched through West Mountain Pass between Dunderberg and West mountains, along what is now known as Pleasant Valley Road. Before World War II, several families moved into Doodletown to work at an ammunition factory and warehouse on Iona Island. After World War II, the government gave Iona Island to the Palisades Park Commission, thereby closing the factory and causing Doodletown's population to dwindle. In the early 1960s, the Palisades Park Commission bought Doodletown, and the last resident left in 1965. Doodletown is now a ghost town. The sounds and sights of a

thriving town have been replaced by the chatter of wildlife and a return to the natural solitude of the area. The miles of old wood roads left behind from this bygone era provide an opportunity to experience a historical, pristine, and enchanting forest environment.

General location: The trail is in Harriman Park near Bear Mountain, approximately 40 miles north of Manhattan.

Elevation change: The terrain consists of short climbs and descents except for a half-mile climb out of Doodletown. The general slope of the terrain ranges from a 700' elevation at the Seven Lakes Drive trailhead to 100' at the end, near the NY 9W trailhead.

Season: All seasons are great to explore the dramatic landscape and historical trails. The park is crowded between Memorial Day and Labor Day weekends, but the rest of the months are wide open for great fun, discovery, and even solitude. If there is no snow on the ground, do not let winter's cold stop you; just put on more clothing and enjoy the solitude and satisfaction of having a popular park all to yourself.

Services: Food services can be found all year at the Bear Mountain Inn on NY 9. The Park Visitor Center, located on the Palisades Interstate Parkway about a mile before the Long Mountain Circle, sells trail maps, books, guides, snacks, and coffee.

Hazards: Some descents require feathering the rear brake, but most of the rolling terrain does not require any special technical skills. Only a few sections of the trails have eroded. Exposed roots and rocks gnarl the surface, and if in doubt you should not hesitate to dismount.

Rescue index: You are at most 1.5 miles from Seven Lakes Drive or NY 9W. There are some sections where you can hear the vehicles on Seven Lakes Drive. Do not worry; it's hard to become lost. You can equate the shape of the road you are on with what is on the map.

Land status: The trail is within the Harriman Bear Mountain State Park and is managed by the Palisades Interstate Park Commission.

Maps: The New York–New Jersey Trail Conference "Harriman Bear Mountain Trails," Trail Map 4, "Harriman Park North Half," is a waterproof and tearproof map that provides the best detail. It can be found at most outdoor-type stores for $6.95 or can be bought at the Park Visitor Center on the Palisades Interstate Parkway.

Finding the trail: Take the Palisades Interstate Parkway north. Exit at 19/US 6 East, Bear Mountain. After the exit ramp, you will merge with US 6 East, and about 1,000' ahead on the right, you'll turn onto a small paved road. (You have gone too far if you see the sign for Perkins Memorial Drive.) Park here, pedal back to the road, and make a right. After about 200', there will be 2 short metal posts with a green steel rod set between them. There is also a sign that states, "For Your Safety, Camping-Picnicking, Fires Permitted only at Designated Areas."

Sources of additional information:

Palisades Interstate Park Commission (PIPC)
Bear Mountain State Park
Bear Mountain, New York 10911-0427
(914) 786-2701

New York–New Jersey Trail Conference (NY–NJTC)
GPO Box 2250
New York, New York 10016
(212) 685-9699

Notes on the trail: The tour begins directly beyond the green pole barrier. Start down the hard-packed jeep trail. This route joins an old paved road that is designated as the 1777 historic trail used by the British Army enroute to capture Fort Clinton and Montgomery down by the Hudson River.

Within 300' you will approach a fork in the dirt road. The left fork is your return route, so bear right and ascend a gentle hill, passing through a mature growth of hemlocks. These stands are rare. Almost all the hemlock trees from these forests north to the Catskill Mountains were cut down for the use of their bark in the tanning of leather products. Many of the leather holsters, belts, and boots for the Civil War were tanned from these trees.

Descending, notice the red and white markers on the trees. This indicates that the red trail (Fawn trail) and white trail (Appalachian trail) are sharing this road and are one at these points. Stay to your left as you see the red trail turn off to your right. Ascend a small hill on the white trail. There is a small switchback that bears left as the trail descends. You may see more red markers on the trees. Continue on this path over several stream crossings. These are the West Mountain drainage streams that flow into Doodletown Lake. The road descends a steep incline over a loose rock surface. If you do not feel confident going down a hill like this, dismount and walk your bike. Special care should be taken. Feathering the rear brake will carry you down with minimal end-overs.

Continuing, notice on your right 2 stonework constructions—a short wall and a circular one. This section along the route was the location of the Doodletown mines. There are several depressions in the ground along the path, filled up now with dirt and leaves, that were once the excavation holes. There are some swampy ponds on your left, so bring bug repellent in June and July or ride fast. At the fork, bear left. The inviting trail on your right is the continuance of the Suffern Bear Mountain Trail (yellow markers). This is a hiking trail and you are unauthorized to travel on it. Continue to your left and pass through another mature stand of hemlocks. These tall evergreens create a canopy that always gives some forest trail a tranquil feel.

There are 3 options when you arrive perpendicular to a semipaved gravel road known as Pleasant Valley Road. The trail that leads directly across from you descends to NY 9W in 1.5 miles. It's good for emergencies when you need to get to a major road. The British Army came from the right, which is the southerly direction of Pleasant Valley Road. To the left is the direction they went and the direction we want to take after a short trip along the "southern" half of Pleasant Valley Road. Turn right and soon views open up to your right of West Mountain. A little farther along, at the clearing to your left, 1,100' Bald Mountain can be seen. The abandoned Cornell iron mine is at the top of West Mountain. As you approach 2 large spruces, there is a small driveway with overgrowth and nearby an old stone house foundation. You will notice first the clearing on your left with a stone shelter, another abandoned house foundation, and a stone chimney still standing. Directly in front of you is a small wooden bridge which is optional. It ascends quite steeply over a rougher trail requiring you to dismount and push or portage your bike. For now let's turn around at this point and return up Pleasant Valley Road.

Proceeding north of the point on Pleasant Valley Road where you originally came in from, notice a small dirt road that will lead you to the original Doodletown cemetery. The trees shadow the tombstones, with some of the readable ones dating back to the 1830s. At this point, you cannot go any farther. Return to Pleasant Valley Road and turn right. Continue to the right for about 500' past the entrance to the cemetery and notice on your left some steps that once led to another abandoned Doodletown home. Walk up the steps and in front of you are large maple and spruce trees. These trees stand out among the surrounding overgrowth and were part of the owners' original landscaping design 75 years ago. Continuing along Pleasant Valley Road, you will approach the intersection with Doodletown Road. There are no street signs, but straight ahead is another rectangular ski sign with the orange number 7 on it.

Turn right for a short trip to the reservoir. At the fork there are 2 options:

The fork to the right runs along the west shore of Doodletown Lake (reservoir) and to another cemetery. This cemetery has fewer gravestones and only dates back to the 1870s, but the spot overlooking the lake is quite tranquil. Park your bike and walk down to the shore and take in the view. Doodletown Lake was formed by the damning of the Doodletown Brook. In a northeasterly direction you can make out the dam and the rooftop of a small water treatment plant. Beyond that, Doodletown Brook descends into the Hudson River. Iona Island, which was once a submerged river delta, was created from this same Doodletown Brook, a glacial stream flowing into the much larger and deeper Hudson River. The brook carried and deposited thousands of tons of silt and lead to the creation of the submerged river delta. After the glacial meltwaters slowed and the water levels dropped, this delta was exposed and became Iona Island.

The fork to the left runs along the north shore of Doodletown Lake and descends to NY 9W in less than a mile. You will have to ascend back up the long hill in the direction you came from, returning to Doodletown Road.

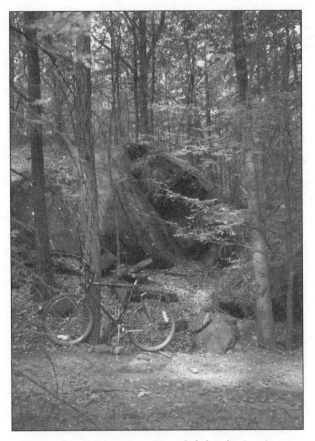

Large rocks, known as erratics, left by the Ice Age are
scattered throughout Harriman State Park.

Proceeding east and beginning your half-mile ascent of Doodletown Road,
you will pass many overgrown and abandoned driveways, crumbling fieldstone walls, and fallen chimneys. Apple, spruce, and maple trees can be seen
in overgrown clearings, evidence of the old Doodletown landscaping. These
trees are somewhat larger than the smaller overgrowth trees, since the land
was cleared and then replanted in the early days of Doodletown.

Bear right at the 3-fork intersection at the top of the hill. The leftmost path
was the 1777 west route the British forces followed north after dividing their
forces in Doodletown. The attack took place at noon, with British ships join-
ing the battle at 3 P.M. Both forts fell shortly after 5 P.M. with heavy casualties.

Continue along the rightmost double-track path and traverse a small escarpment. Some sections of the trail may be overgrown, so have faith and pedal
through to reconnect to the first fork you encountered on the trail.

RIDE 15 *LAKE MASSAWIPPA*

Although it's only four miles in length—two miles out and two miles back—this hard-packed trail earns a high rating. It passes through an area that reveals some of the Harriman Park's diverse history and creation. During the Depression in the 1930s, the Civilian Conservation Corps (CCC) was organized to provide work for the unemployed. Their enormous accomplishments in trail building, park restoration, and improvement projects have left a legacy of well-marked hiking trails throughout the United States. Most of the trails in the Catskill Mountains were constructed by the CCC.

The trail begins on the east side of Lake Massawippa and enters into an attractive woodscape, following the drainage basin that is a trough between two mountains. Views of the 1,100-foot Brooks Mountain to the northwest and Howell Mountain, roughly the same height, to the southeast, can be seen from the trail, which traverses the hollow formed between these two hilly ridges. Lake Massawippa was created when the corps dammed the stream flowing into the southern end of the lake. Due to the extent of this project, a base camp was established and built in Brooks Hollow. The beginning of the ride passes by the ruins of an old boy scout camp set along the attractive, wooded shores of the lake. Another short trail on the west shore of Lake Massawippa makes for some excellent picnic spots.

Novices will find this trail easy. More experienced riders can use the ride as a warm up before attempting the park's myriad trails in its extensive mountain bike system.

General location: The trailhead is located approximately 5.7 miles north of Long Mountain Circle on Long Mountain Parkway (US 6 West). Long Mountain Circle is the termination of the Palisades Interstate Parkway.

Elevation change: The ride is fairly level, with a beginning elevation of 830' that gradually descends to about 700' in the hollow.

Season: The best season is the period from Labor Day to Memorial Day. The summer months are very busy in Harriman State Park. If there is no snow cover on the trails, do not let winter's cold stop you; just put on more clothing and enjoy the solitude and satisfaction of having popular trails all to yourself.

Services: Food services can be found all year at the Bear Mountain Inn on NY 9. A Park Visitor Center, located on the Palisades Interstate Parkway about a mile before the Long Mountain Circle, sells trail maps, books, guides, snacks, and coffee.

Hazards: The biggest danger on this trail is trespassing. Do not go beyond the Harriman Park boundary at the end of the trail. It proceeds into the private property of the West Point Military Reservation. You will see No Trespassing signs.

RIDE 15 *LAKE MASSAWIPPA*

Rescue index: You are at most 2 miles from Long Mountain Parkway (US 6 West). Do not worry about getting lost. The trail is straight in and straight out.
Land status: The trail is within Harriman Bear Mountain State Park and is managed by the Palisades Interstate Park Commission.
Maps: The New York–New Jersey Trail Conference "Harriman Bear Mountain Trails," Trail Map 4, "Harriman Park North Half," is a waterproof and tearproof map that provides the best detail. It can be found at most outdoor-type stores for $6.95 or can be purchased at the Park Visitor Center on the Palisades Interstate Parkway.

Wooded shores of Lake Massawippa.

Finding the trail: Take the Palisades Interstate Parkway north to the Long Mountain Circle. Take Long Mountain Parkway (US 6 West) for about 5.7 miles. You will pass one lake on your left set back from the roadway, and directly opposite on your right begins a paved road which is the beginning of the trail. The tour begins from Long Mountain Parkway and runs close to the east shore of Lake Massawippa.

Sources of additional information:

Palisades Interstate Park Commission (PIPC)
Bear Mountain State Park
Bear Mountain, New York 10911-0427
(914) 786-2701

New York–New Jersey Trail Conference (NY–NJTC)
GPO Box 2250
New York, New York 10016
(212) 685-9699

Notes on the trail: After leaving Long Mountain Parkway follow the camp road northeast past Lake Massawippa (Lake "Heroine") on your left, and descend gently into Brooks Hollow. You will be riding in a "hollow" or shallow valley. To your east is Howell Mountain and to your west, Brooks Mountain. A hiking path known as the Long Path (blue markers) descends from Howell Mountain (elevation 1,000'), intercepting the trail you are on, and then ascends to Brooks Mountain (elevation 1,100'). Continuing northeast on the trail, you will pass a long narrow pond 1 mile into the ride. In another .8 mile, you will arrive at the end of the ride, which terminates at the boundary of the park and the adjoining private property of the West Point Military Reservation. This is private land, so do not trespass. Turn around at this point and head back up the trail.

RIDE 16 *LAKE STAHAHE TRAIL*

This easy-to-moderate eight-mile loop takes you through two million years of glacial geologic history along an old wood road. The ride begins in an open, rolling meadow whose hilly, topographic features are the result of sedimentation from the retreating glaciers that scoured this land over 10,000 years ago. As the route proceeds into the woods, you are thrust into a landscape that, during the Ice Ages, was hidden beneath huge masses of ice and snow, reaching depths of thousands of feet. The snow accumulated and fed the thickness of the glaciers. The extreme weight forced the glaciers to move across the terrain, scraping, gouging, and plucking apart the land. When the ice melted, it left a landscape dotted with huge boulders, lakes, ponds, swamps, and valleys. The road's condition varies from smooth to rocky, can be fast and challenging, and is composed of a fair share of short climbs and descents. It's a full-course meal. You will be served hills that will be heavy breathers, along with intriguing scenery and invigorating riding.

Along the trail, let your mind wander into the past and imagine a very different world than what appears today. The ride concludes at Lake Stahahe, a rare natural lake created from a large basin the glaciers scooped out. Water filled this basin when one end of the lake was filled with debris, thereby creating a natural dam. It has survived the millennia while most natural lakes in the region have disappeared. During the thousands of years since, the basins and dammed valleys have been gradually filling with vegetation and rock waste. The streams that flow out from these lakes, known as outlet streams, have been cutting their channels deeper and lowering the lake's water levels. Many basins and dammed valleys that once held lakes or ponds have become swamps. During the 1930s, the Civilian Conservation Corps constructed many dams and converted the numerous swamps into lakes again. Such is the story of large bodies of water like Lake Sebago, Welch, Tiorati, and Pine Meadow.

General location: Near the northwest portion of Harriman State Park.
Elevation change: The tour is punctuated with minor hill climbs, but generally follows an elevation of 800'.

RIDE 16 *LAKE STAHAHE TRAIL*

Season: The best season is the period from Labor Day to Memorial Day. The summer months are very busy in Harriman State Park. If there is no snow cover on the trails, do not let winter's cold stop you; just put on more clothing and enjoy the solitude and satisfaction of having popular trails all to yourself.

Services: Food services can be found all year at the Bear Mountain Inn on NY 9. A Park Visitor Center, located on the Palisades Interstate Parkway about a mile before the Long Mountain Circle, sells trail maps, books, guides, snacks, and coffee. Other services can be found along NY 17 nearby.

Hazards: If you go swimming in Lake Stahahe, do not swim alone since there is no posted lifeguard on duty. A small section of this tour rides along the paved Old Route 210. Be careful of the few cars that travel on it. You should not become lost. The route is well defined and easy to follow in the woods.

Rescue index: The trail is not too far from the well-traveled Old Route 210.

Land status: The trail is within the Harriman Bear Mountain State Park and is managed by the Palisades Interstate Park Commission.

Maps: The New York–New Jersey Trail Conference "Harriman Bear Mountain Trails," Trail Map 4, "Harriman Park North Half," is a waterproof and tearproof map that provides the best detail. It can be found at most outdoor-type stores for $6.95 or can be purchased at the Park Visitor Center on the Palisades Interstate Parkway.

Finding the trail: Take the Palisades Interstate Parkway north to Exit 14A/ Lake Welch Drive, and then onward to Tiorati Circle. During the winter when this road is closed, take Seven Lakes Drive from Long Mountain Circle to Tiorati Circle.

From the Tiorati Circle rotary take Arden Road for 4.7 miles and look for the posted sign, "Hiker Trailhead Parking." Turn in and park. Arden Road from Tiorati Circle is closed in the winter, so you will have to enter Arden Road from NY 17. The trailhead begins toward the south end of the parking area. A wide, wood road leads down from the west side of the parking area toward the New York State Thruway. A few trails lead from the parking area. To make sure you are on the right one, go to the southern end of the parking area and face the New York State Thruway. You will see the trail I am describing here.

Sources of additional information:

Palisades Interstate Park Commission (PIPC)
Bear Mountain State Park
Bear Mountain, New York 10911-0427
(914) 786-2701

New York–New Jersey Trail Conference (NY–NJTC)
GPO Box 2250
New York, New York 10016
(212) 685-9699

Notes on the trail: After leaving the parking area, the trail descends a small embankment and travels along a wide, four-wheel-drive road through an attractive open meadow. Bear left at the next two forks and head into the forest. As you get closer you will see some tall white pine trees. Turn right at the **T** intersection onto the old wood road. This road serves as a utility road for park maintenance vehicles and is well maintained and more obvious than the one that goes through the meadow. The road runs past a large hemlock forest on your left and the open fields on your right. Cross a small wooden bridge spanning a deep gully, and after approximately 300' notice a trail merging from the left. Turn left onto this trail and ascend a short hill. At the **T** intersection, make a left. The road now leads away from the New York State Thruway into a dense hemlock forest and follows a gently rolling landscape. After a small ascent, you will soon make a transition from the cool conifer forests into an open, hardwood forest of beech and oak. At 1.8 miles you will **T** intersect with a wider, gravelly, semipaved road. Turn left and continue past summer camps, boat docks, and some great views of Lake Stahahe. This road ends at Old Route 210. Turn right and descend the winding road. After a mile, turn right onto the next small road on your right. Turn in and make a quick left onto a wide, grassy, four-wheel-drive road in a westerly direction. This road descends for the most part all the way to the parking area. Nice reward!

RIDE 17 *ISLAND POND TRAIL*

This moderately difficult, eight-mile (four miles one way), out-and-back, double-track trail leads through a rugged and primitive-looking woodscape filled with rock gardens and jagged cliffs. The route follows an old grass-covered forest road that gently ascends through a changing forest of hardwoods and conifers. Plenty of small hills and lively double-track challenge the average hammerhead. There is also plenty of cruising material to go around for the less technically inclined, making this a pleasant mountain biking experience for riders of all levels. The landscape seems remote and the forests change dramatically to mature hemlock woods as you descend from the drier and rockier hardwood plateaus into the small, cooler valleys.

One of the major highlights of this tour is the large and picturesque Island Pond, accessed by a short spur trail. You'll see an abandoned stone ranger cabin, constructed in 1927 on the rocky shores of the lake, but a fire in 1960 destroyed a good portion of it.

Island Pond is an attractive and rare natural lake. When the mile-high glaciers from the Ice Age bulldozed the landscape, they gouged out great depressions in the land, plucking out boulders and leaving ice in its place. As these ice sheets melted and retreated, their meltwaters created a landscape dotted with lakes and ponds. Water quickly filled these deep basins and remained through the millennia, long after many of the other regional lakes dried up.

The shores of Island Pond are mostly stone, and a small island can be seen midway along the eastern shore, giving the lake its name. An outlet stream at the north end of the lake drains into Echo Lake on private land. Island Pond is surrounded to the west by Green Pond Mountain and to the northeast by Island Pond Mountain. The pond and surrounding mountains were once part of an estate owned by an iron mine developer. The Harriman family purchased it in 1885 and held onto it until 1927, when they donated 10,000 acres to the park.

General location: Near the western portion of Harriman State Park.
Elevation change: There is not much elevation change since the trailhead begins at about 900' and climbs to 1,000' in the beginning of the ride. After that, the trail gently ascends at a gradual pace, and you do not even feel it. The return ride is a blast since it is predominantly downhill.
Season: The best season is the period from Labor Day to Memorial Day. The summer months are very busy in Harriman State Park. If there is no snow cover on the trails, do not let winter's cold stop you; just put on more clothing and enjoy the solitude and satisfaction of having popular trails all to yourself. The trail is overgrown with grass and tends not to get muddy.

RIDE 17 *ISLAND POND TRAIL*

Services: During the summer you can always head up to Tiorati Circle for some refreshments. You will find a rest room, vending machines, picnic tables, telephones, barbecue pits, and some lakes to cool off in. Food services can also be found all year at the Bear Mountain Inn on NY 9. A Park Visitor Center, located on the Palisades Interstate Parkway about a mile before the Long Mountain Circle, sells trail maps, books, guides, snacks, and coffee. Other services can be found along NY 17 nearby.

Hazards: These can be popular trails during the summer months and fall, so drive cautiously; when returning downhill, check your speed and be prepared to stop. This area is a little farther away from the telephones and refreshments at Tiorati Circle, so be prepared for the season you are riding in.

Rescue index: The trail begins on Old Route 210, which is well traveled and can bring you back to telephones near Tiorati Circle. You are never more than 1.5 miles from either Old Route 210 at the beginning of the ride or Arden Road near the end of the ride.

Land status: The trail is within the Harriman Bear Mountain State Park and is managed by the Palisades Interstate Park Commission.

Maps: The New York–New Jersey Trail Conference "Harriman Bear Mountain Trails," Trail Map 4, "Harriman Park North Half," is a waterproof and tearproof map that provides the best detail. It can be found at most outdoor-type stores for $6.95 or can be purchased at the Park Visitor Center on the Palisades Interstate Parkway.

Finding the trail: Take the Palisades Interstate Parkway north to Exit 14A/ Lake Welch Drive. During the winter when this road is closed, use Seven Lakes Drive to Tiorati Circle.

Take Lake Welch Drive to Kanawauke Circle and go in the direction of Old Route 210. Stay on Old Route 210 for 2.8 miles. You will pass Kanawauke Lake on the right and then Little Long Pond on your left. Look for a semi-circular parking area on your left with a sign reading, "Hiker Trailhead Parking." Park here and then take your bike back onto Old Route 210 and turn left for about 300'. You will see 2 metal green posts with a metal barrier. The trailhead begins there.

Sources of additional information:

Palisades Interstate Park Commission (PIPC)
Bear Mountain State Park
Bear Mountain, New York 10911-0427
(914) 786-2701

New York–New Jersey Trail Conference (NY–NJTC)
GPO Box 2250
New York, New York 10016
(212) 685-9699

Notes on the trail: At the beginning of the trail, you will encounter the only major uphill climb and will begin a gradual ascent over a wide, rocky, forest road. At about 100', bear left and keep going up the hill. Although the trail is unmarked, it is very well defined, obvious as an old wood road. After that, be prepared for some fine double-track cruising. As things begin to level out, the trail gently rolls along through an open maple and oak forest. You will soon see yellow trail blazes on the trees as the road shares the yellow-marked Dunning Trail for a short distance. As you crest the top of a small hill, the Dunning Trail forks to the right. Bear left and remain on the wide forest road. The trail descends into a mature forest of hemlock, rare since much of the hemlock was cut during the late nineteenth century for leather tanning purposes. The transition from the hardwood forest to conifer forest and back to hardwood is well marked and impressionable. As you reach the bottom of the descent, notice the rocks on a hillside to your right. This is the vicinity of what remains of Boston Mine, which was closed in 1880.

At about 1.5 miles the Appalachian Trail that is marked with little red triangles on white paint blazes crosses the road. After that, you will soon come to a fork. The right fork takes you on a short spur trail that leads down to the southern shore of Island Pond, where an abandoned, stone ranger cabin remains. This is a great spot for a quick rest and some great views of the scenic Island Pond.

Pine needles blanket the trail to Island Pond.

The left fork leads down to a swampy area and traverses a ravine with Green Pond Mountain on your west and Island Pond on your east. The trail leads out to Arden Valley Road in about 1.2 miles, at which point you can turn around and return the way you just came. This will take you back to the parking area.

RIDE 18 *BAILEYTOWN PIKE*

A small eighteenth-century country road leads past some overgrown farms that were once owned by the Bailey and Lewis families. A small cemetery 1.5 miles up the road from the trailhead bears family names dating back to 1886. Riding through this terrain, one can muse on life back then and what it was like to build homes in these wild woods. The Baileys and Lewises inhabited the woods. There were many marriages between the Baileys and Lewises, and this road was constructed to provide access in and around the family lands. The riding is moderately easy and makes an ideal tour for those beginners who would like to get their knobbies off the perfect hard-pack stuff and onto some less-than-perfect double-track and into the woods. For the more adventurous, a shelter is available for camping should a sleep out in the woods be desired. The shelter is reached by a short spur trail off the main

RIDE 18   *BAILEYTOWN PIKE*

Lake Massawippa

To Long Mountain Circle

0   1/4   1/2

MILES

6

Lake Teata

Lower Twin Lake

To 87
New York State Thruway

Upper Twin Lake

NY

Summit Lake

Unmarked Trail overgrown

Baileytown Pike

Private Land

Lean-to

Note: *Ride is double-track forest roads.*

trail route, described in this tour. This pleasant four-mile loop passes between the attractive Lake Teata and Lower Twin Lake and past summer camps that are usually closed during the fall and winter. Paths around the lake make for small diversions. Take a moment, sit a spell, and munch a snack. The terrain is more secluded deeper in the woods past the camp areas.

General location: The trailhead is approximately 6 miles on Long Mountain Parkway (US 6 West) from the Long Mountain Circle in the northwest portion of Harriman State Park. The Long Mountain Circle is the conclusion of the Palisades Interstate Parkway.

Elevation change: The elevation of the area is approximately 862'. There are some easy-to-moderate hills, but nothing requiring major stamina.

Season: The best season is the period from Labor Day to Memorial Day. The summer months are very busy in Harriman State Park. If there is no snow cover on the trails, do not let winter's cold stop you; just put on more clothing and enjoy the solitude.

Services: Food services can be found all year at the Bear Mountain Inn on NY 9. A Park Visitor Center, located on the Palisades Interstate Parkway about a mile before the Long Mountain Circle, sells trail maps, books, guides, snacks, and coffee. Other services can be found farther west on US 6 about 3.5 miles away.

Hazards: The biggest danger on this trail is trespassing onto private lands. Do not go beyond the Harriman Park boundary at the end of the trail. The other risk is the possibility of acquiring ticks in the warmer months. It's a good idea to spray bug repellent around your ankles and legs before heading out into the woods. Bring a compass with you, because there is a .1-mile section of the path that is very overgrown, and you must head in a northwesterly direction to pick up the trail again after this section.

Rescue index: You are never farther than 2 miles from the well-traveled Long Mountain Parkway (US 6 West).

Land status: The trail is within the Harriman Bear Mountain State Park and is managed by the Palisades Interstate Park Commission.

Maps: The New York–New Jersey Trail Conference "Harriman Bear Mountain Trails," Trail Map 4, "Harriman Park North Half," is a waterproof and tearproof map that provides the best detail. It can be found at most outdoor-type stores for $6.95 or can be purchased at the Park Visitor Center on the Palisades Interstate Parkway. The USGS, 7.5 minute series, Popolopen Lake quadrangle also provides detail.

Finding the trail: Take the Palisades Interstate Parkway north to Long Mountain Circle. Take Long Mountain Parkway (US 6 West) for about 6 miles. Traveling along the parkway, you will pass between Lake Teata on your left and Lake Massawippa on your right. Parking is just ahead on your right. Pedal back out to US 6 and turn left. Baileytown Pike begins as a paved road on your right immediately after you pass Lake Teata and beyond the camp sign, "UT Camp 7 & 8 Te Ata."

Sources of additional information:

Palisades Interstate Park Commission (PIPC)
Bear Mountain State Park
Bear Mountain, New York 10911-0427
(914) 786-2701

New York–New Jersey Trail Conference (NY–NJTC)
GPO Box 2250
New York, New York 10016
(212) 685-9699

Notes on the trail: After leaving Long Mountain Parkway (US 6), the Baileytown Pike Trail will pass between Lake Teata and Lower Twin Lake. You will be riding on a paved camp road that runs close to the northeast shore of Lake Teata for about 1 mile. Keep bearing left as you pass many entrances to summer camps. Continue to the end, where you will see a one-way sign leading vehicles to the right. Stay to your left to pass a small, brown, wooden cabin where the paved road ends and turns into a jeep road after the last camp building. The cemetery bearing the names of the Baileys and Lewises will come up on your left. The stone wall on the right was the old boundary of the park before Mary Bailey sold her farm in 1925. The stone walls above the brook belong to the Baileys' farm. At 1.8 miles an unmarked trail leads off in an easterly direction. This is the Nawahunta Trail, which leads to Lake Nawahunta and the site of the Lewis farms. You will see a sign on a tree to your right indicating that the shelter is in the same direction. The Baileytown Pike Trail ends at the gate of the Harriman estate soon after. The Baileytown Pike continues on for another 4 miles, but unfortunately it is on private lands, and trespassing is prohibited.

At the time of this writing, there was a small overgrown double-track, barely visible, leading off the right in a northerly direction, once you reached the Harriman estate gate. Bring a compass with you because if the road is not too overgrown, there is a small .1-mile section that sort of disappears, and you need the compass to lead you in a north-northwest direction. The north shore of Summit Lake is reached in about .6 mile. If you choose not to head to Summit Lake, you may turn around and pedal out the way you just came in, making this ride an out-and-back.

After you have reached Summit Lake, fork right and proceed to Long Mountain Parkway (US 6) for about .7 mile. Turn right on US 6 and in 1 mile you will reach your parking area.

RIDE 19 *TOUR DES BOIS*

Three interconnected, old wood roads pass through boulder-strewn valleys and attractive hardwood forests. There is something for everyone. The combination of scenery, good riding, two scenic lakes to lunch at and pass an hour in solitude, and 14 miles of nontechnical single- and double-track makes for a well-rounded day. By studying the map, several loops can be constructed from the three roads: Pine Meadow Road, Conklin Road, and Woodtown Road.

Refer to the tour, listed below, that encompasses all three and requires the better part of a day to complete.

Woodtown Road is a very old route where several families of woodcutters in the early nineteenth century lived. A family of mountain people called the Conklins lived for generations on a farm at Pine Meadow, but they left in 1935. During the Depression, the Civilian Conservation Corps used the area to set up base camps. Woodtown Road was utilized for hauling the machinery in the construction of the Pine Meadow and Wanoksink lakes.

This easy-to-moderate 14-mile network glides through two million years of glacial geologic history. Here, the past was very different than the present. The route proceeds through a landscape that was hidden beneath huge masses of ice and snow thousands of feet deep. As the snow accumulated and fed the thickness of the glaciers, the glaciers began to move across the terrain, scraping, gouging, and plucking apart the land. The last ice age peaked 18,000 years ago, and when the ice melted it left a landscape dotted with huge boulders, lakes, ponds, swamps, and valleys. During your ride, notice the randomly spaced large rocks, some as big as a house. Assuming they were not left by man, and since there are no cliffs nearby from which they could have fallen, it's reasonable to conclude that these rocks were put in their place by the mammoth glaciers that covered the region, moving everything in sight. Large boulders of gray and red sandstone came from the Schunemunk Mountains, and white conglomerate or quartzite came from the Shawangunks. These rock fragments, known as erratics, were transported from mountains far away and scattered throughout this landscape. Fast-moving streams and rivers sprang from the rapid-melting glaciers. They carried rocks and tumbled them onto each other in valley bottoms, so thick that they completely hid the soil and bedrock beneath. On rides throughout Harriman State Park, you will pass some or all of these geologic phenomena.

General location: The trailhead begins approximately 7.7 miles from Long Mountain Circle, on Seven Lakes Drive in the middle portion of Harriman State Park. The Long Mountain Circle is the conclusion of the Palisades Interstate Parkway.

Elevation change: Pine Meadow Lake and Lake Wanoksink reside on a plateau. Their elevations are 972' and 1,082' respectively and require a one-mile moderate ascent from the trailhead on Seven Lakes Drive at the elevation of 800'. The terrain varies moderately, with elevation maxing out at 1,100'. After reaching the plateau, most of the riding is level with some low hills.

Season: The best season is the period from Labor Day to Memorial Day. The summer months are very busy in Harriman State Park. If there is no snow cover on the trails, do not let winter's cold stop you; just put on more clothing and enjoy the satisfaction of having popular trails all to yourself.

Services: Tiorati Circle is only 3 miles away. Telephones, beverage machines, and a swimming beach can be found there. Nearby Sloatsburg on NY 17 is

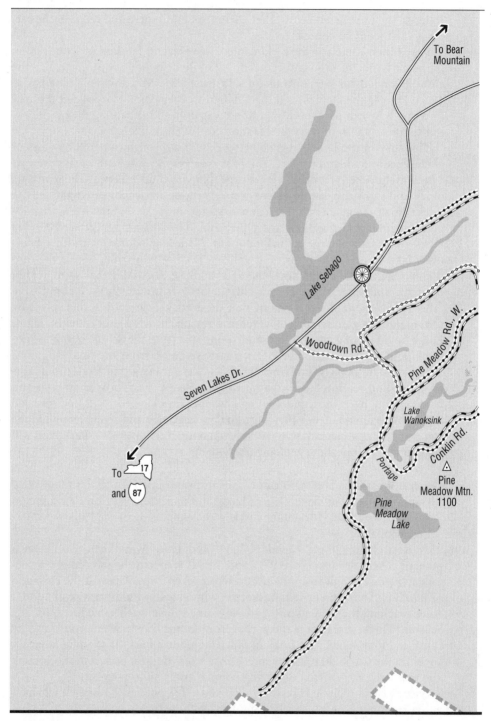

To Bear
Mountain

Lake Sebago

Woodtown Rd.

Pine Meadow Rd. W.

Seven Lakes Dr.

Lake
Wanoksink

Conklin Rd.

Portage

To 17
and 87

Pine
Meadow Mtn.
1100

Pine
Meadow
Lake

To Palisades
Interstate Pkwy.

Lake Welch Dr.

First
Reservoir

Second
Reservoir

Cranberry Mountain

Third
Reservoir

Breakneck
Pond

Breakneck
Mtn.
△ 1200

Woodtown Rd.

Minsi
Swamp

Big Green
Swamp

Pine Meadow Rd.

N

0   1/2   1
MILES

NY

only 4 miles away and offers a well-stocked health food store with food, maps, and many interesting books. If you continue southwest on Seven Lakes Drive for 4 miles, turn left and go south on NY 17. The stores are found along NY 17 just after this intersection.

Hazards: If you are bombing down any of the trails, mind the rocks that stud the eroded sections of the roads. On many of the descents or, for that matter, ascents, depending on which way you are heading, runoff from rains has eroded much soil from the roadbeds, leaving many rocks exposed along the way. Ride courteously and defensively. These trails are shared by hikers and other mountain bikers; be sure to check with park officials for current trail status.

Rescue index: The trail begins on Seven Lakes Drive. This well-traveled park road will bring you back to telephones near Tiorati Circle, 3 miles away, or nearby Sloatsburg, which is only 4 miles southwest of the trailhead.

Land status: The trail is within the Harriman Bear Mountain State Park and is managed by the Palisades Interstate Park Commission.

Maps: The New York–New Jersey Trail Conference "Harriman Bear Mountain Trails," Trail Map 3, "Harriman Park South Half," is a waterproof and tearproof map that provides the best detail. It can be found at most outdoor-type stores for $6.95 or can be purchased at the Park Visitor Center on the Palisades Interstate Parkway. The USGS, 7.5 minute series, Sloatsburg and Thiells quadrangles also provide good detail.

Finding the trail: Take the Palisades Interstate Parkway north and exit at the Lake Welch sign. During the winter, this road is usually closed. In this case, continue on toward Long Mountain Circle to get on Seven Lakes Drive. From Lake Welch Drive, continue toward Seven Lakes Drive. Do not make the first right and head north on Seven Lakes Drive to Tiorati, but go around the rotary and continue south on Seven Lakes Drive. The turnoff for a large parking area will be on your right along Seven Lakes Drive, approximately 1.25 miles south of this rotary.

Sources of additional information:

Palisades Interstate Park Commission (PIPC)
Bear Mountain State Park
Bear Mountain, New York 10911-0427
(914) 786-2701

New York–New Jersey Trail Conference (NY–NJTC)
GPO Box 2250
New York, New York 10016
(212) 685-9699

Notes on the trail: Leave the parking area and turn left on Seven Lakes Drive. The trail begins about 900' on your right, beyond a green-and-white metal

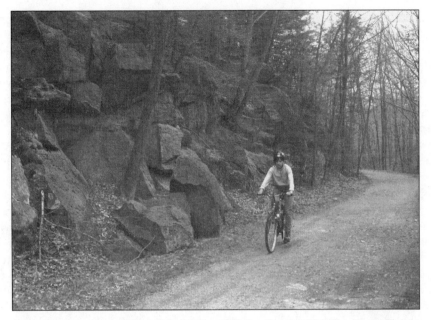

Large blocks of rock, fallen from higher cliffs, border the Old Woodtown Road.

barrier. Begin a gradual ascent for .75 mile, at which point you will see two trails. One trail continues straight beyond five large boulders. If you continue straight you can reach the northeast end of Breakneck Pond in 1.75 miles and return to your parking area by taking Lake Welch Drive to Seven Lakes Drive. However, there is plenty of great riding ahead, so bear right and follow the wide, rocky road in an easterly direction. The ascent steepens for a short sprint. After a few switchbacks, you will arrive at 2 more trail options. For now, let's call this Two Fork Pass. The trail to your right continues to Lake Wanoksink and Pine Meadow Lake along the old Pine Meadow Road West. You will eventually return along this road to get back to the parking area. For now, fork left and continue on the hard-packed double-track, which will link the Conklin, Pine Meadow, and Woodtown roads, passing some interesting swamps with a history.

The Minsi, Big Green, and Squirrel swamps now fill the basins of Ice Age–old lakes that have long since been dried up and filled with rocks, soil, and vegetation. Imagine an ice wall thousands of feet thick gouging out the landscape and leaving depressions in the land as if a meteor had fallen. This land was severely changed during the Ice Ages. Take this trail on your left and after about .3 mile, a small, single-track trail leads to your left in an easterly direction.

Turn onto this smooth, well-conditioned single-track and travel over solid bedrock that has been rounded and smoothed over by the dense, heavy glaciers.

If you look closely enough, you might see the north-south striations found on top of most exposed rocks in the northeastern United States. These striations are giant scratches that were created when the glaciers dragged rocks and other debris over the surface. An abundance of mountain laurel borders the trail and is quite common along most of the route. You will intersect with Woodtown Road in about .8 mile. Turn left to get to Second Reservoir in about 1.5 miles. Turn right and pass Big Green Swamp on your right. You will come to a three-fork intersection; take the rightmost road. This is Conklin Road.

As you travel along Conklin Road, you will ride along a ridge overlooking a large, swampy meadow on your right. This is known as Minsi Swamp, another ancient dried-up lake. Views of Lake Wanoksink will start opening up on your right about a quarter-mile after the swamp. Conklin Road travels beside the lake and then descends near the rocky shoreline. As you reach the shore of the lake, look for a place to rest and have lunch, as there are many fine spots here.

The trail turns sharply to your left, and you will soon see a small path to your right going over a dam. Turn down here. There is a 10-minute bike portage along an unmarked path that soon intersects with a larger dirt road. Turn right on the wide dirt road, travel along the southern shore of Lake Wanoksink, and descend a short path to Pine Meadow Road. Turning left will take you to Pine Meadow Lake. The route descends from the 1,082' elevation of Lake Wanoksink to Pine Meadow Lake's 972' level. You will pass by large broken boulders. Near the lake a solid granite promontory juts into the water. This granite stone has been chipped from very large mountains that once existed here. After millions of years of weathering and erosion, these rock fragments have fractured from their cliff faces and tumbled into the lake. This granite was formed deep in the earth and was pushed up to form the ancient mountain system over hundreds of millions of years. The trail continues past Pine Meadow Lake along 2 miles of rough roads and terminates at private property. You must turn around at that point.

On your return along Pine Meadow Road, you will ascend in a north-easterly direction along a wide, double-track, hard-packed road through an attractive hardwood forest. After 1.5 miles you will reach Two Fork Pass. Turning left takes you down the road you originally arrived on from Seven Lakes Drive.

RIDE 20 *BLACK ASH SWAMP*

Want to do some easy, yet stimulating, riding on ten miles of wide, rolling, double-track trails? Sure you do. Beginner riders will be moderately challenged throughout the winding up-and-down paths, while dirt disciples will

RIDE 20 *BLACK ASH SWAMP*

appreciate the route's variety of terrain. This rolling, ten-mile (five miles one way), out-and-back, old forest road varies from smooth to rocky. It's fast and tough at times with lots of short climbs, descents, and great scenery. The route winds past wetlands, deep woods, and the picturesque Lake Skenonto, once a glacial swamp and now filled with water. There are plenty of places to stop and picnic on the hilly western shore of the lake.

Lake Skenonto owes its existence to the glaciers. The last ice age peaked 18,000 years ago when the landscape was hidden beneath huge masses of ice and snow, reaching depths of thousands of feet. Look up in the sky, but make sure to stop your bike, and imagine how high 2,000 feet reaches. Pick that spot, then imagine a sheet of ice as thick as that point in the sky. The climate in those days was a lot different from today, and when it snowed it really snowed, with accumulations of a few thousand feet. "Blizzard" would be an understatement. As the snow accumulated and piled onto the glaciers, the glaciers slowly moved across the terrain. These massive monuments of ice steadily ravaged the land. When the ice melted, what remained was a landscape pockmarked by huge boulders, lakes, ponds, swamps, and valleys. Along the Black Ash Swamp route is an opportunity to explore the recent geologic and glacial history of the region.

General location: The trailhead is approximately 1.75 miles from Kanawauke Circle on Old Route 210, in the center of Harriman State Park.

Elevation change: The trail hovers around an elevation of 900', except for some minor hills and a steady descent at the end of the trail, to 600'.

Season: The best season is the period from Labor Day to Memorial Day. The summer months are very busy in Harriman State Park. If there is no snow cover on the trails, do not let winter's cold stop you; just put on more clothing and enjoy the solitude of having popular trails all to yourself.

Services: Nearby Sebago Beach offers food, beverage, and telephones from Memorial Day to Labor Day weekends. Sebago Beach can be reached by continuing south for about 2 miles on Seven Lakes Drive from Kanawauke Circle.

Hazards: The ride occasionally traverses rough sections of trail, but even with these sections of exposed rocks and roots, the ride does not require any special technical skills and is fairly easy to maneuver.

Rescue index: The park road, Old Route 210, is well traveled and help can be flagged down from passing vehicles. Park police usually patrol all the roads in Harriman State Park.

Land status: The trail is within the Harriman Bear Mountain State Park and is managed by the Palisades Interstate Park Commission.

Maps: The New York–New Jersey Trail Conference "Harriman Bear Mountain Trails," Trail Map 3, "Harriman Park South Half," is a waterproof and tearproof map that provides the best detail. It can be found at most outdoor-type stores for $6.95 or can be purchased at the Park Visitor Center on the Palisades Interstate Parkway. The USGS, 7.5 minute series, Sloatsburg and Thiells quadrangles also provide good detail.

Finding the trail: Take the Palisades Interstate Parkway north to Exit 14A/ Lake Welch Drive. During the winter when this road is closed use Seven Lakes Drive from Long Mountain Circle, which can be reached by continuing farther on Palisades Interstate Parkway. You can then take Seven Lakes Drive directly into Kanawauke Circle.

At Kanawauke Circle take Old Route 210 west. Kanawauke Lake is on both sides of the road. Immediately after passing the lake, turn into a large parking area on your left. You can also try to park farther along on Old Route 210, since the trailhead begins 1 mile down the road after passing Little Long Pond. There are spaces for 2 cars on your right, opposite Little Long Pond, but these are usually occupied on the weekends. Whatever parking location you have chosen, continue past Little Long Pond and turn left through 2 concrete pillars and onto a small paved road. The trail leads through a small development of summer camps and begins beyond a green pole barrier after passing a tennis court on your right.

Sources of additional information:

Palisades Interstate Park Commission (PIPC)
Bear Mountain State Park
Bear Mountain, New York 10911-0427
(914) 786-2701

New York–New Jersey Trail Conference (NY–NJTC)
GPO Box 2250
New York, New York 10016
(212) 685-9699

Notes on the trail: The trail begins as a paved road proceeding past a few summer camps. Continue on the paved road and go beyond a green metal barrier. The road is still paved, but it becomes slightly overgrown with weeds and grass. After .9 mile, a small grass road leads off to your left down to Lake Sebago. Continue on the paved road and bear right. At the fork, bear left through a mature grove of pine trees and up a short hill. Turn down the four-wheel-drive road leading off to your right. The wide, double-track trail traverses gentle hills along the western shore of Lake Skenonto. At about 3 miles, you will come across Black Ash Swamp. This large, overgrown depression in the land once was a lake, but it dried up and filled in with vegetation to become the swamp it is today. After the swamp, you begin a descent into a small hollow with a stream, known as Deep Hollow. You should see red blazes on the trees at this point. Black Ash Mountain, at 1,044', is located to the north, and Smith Rock, at 1,047', is in the south. The trail descends from 800' to 600' in a little over a mile. You must pedal back up in order to get to the trailhead.

RIDE 21 *THE HOGENCAMP MINE TRAIL*

Five miles out and five miles back of double-track offers the gamut of riding possibilities, as well as a chance to explore a densely forested and rock-strewn landscape steeped in eighteenth- and nineteenth-century history. These mountains were rich in iron ore and became an important resource. Pass by the

To Palisades
Interstate Pkwy.

Arden Valley Rd.

Lake
Cohasset

To 17

SUREBRIDGE MOUNTAIN

Greenwood
Mine

Surebridge Swamp

Surebridge
Mine

Lost Rd.

Times Square

Seven Lakes Dr.

Swamp
Mine

Pine
Swamp

HOGENCAMP MTN.

Hogencamp
Mine

Lake
Kanawauke

N

0   1/4   1/2

MILES

To 17

Old Route 210

Little Long
Pond

To 17

NY

Note: *All trails are double-track.*

Greenwood mine, which furnished ore for the cannonballs used by the American forces for the War of 1812 and Civil War artillery. The densely wooded hills provided the fuel to keep the furnaces working. Along the trail, imagine the mining industry that thrived here, hauling tons of iron ore from depths of up to 6,000 feet across the same paths you are riding on. Mines were dug and villages built around the huge furnaces needed for extracting the ore. The nearby streams and rivers powered the bellows for the furnaces.

The route meanders along a wide, occasionally rocky and rugged path. It explores a land of romance—a dark, dense forest of mixed hardwoods and mature hemlocks. The double-track requires a minimum amount of technical skills and is great for advanced beginners who feel ready to try something more demanding than a flat trail, ready to develop the basic skills for traversing a rocky terrain. True hammerheads will thrive on this demanding double-track, testing their stamina and enjoying this magical land of a thousand souls, which surrounds the trail from beginning to end.

Huge glacier-polished rock outcrops with scattered erratics can be found on Hogencamp Mountain, another remnant of the Ice Ages. Glaciers thousands of feet thick transported rock fragments from just a few feet to tens of miles. Most rock that was carried far was reduced to gravel, sand, or mud, but some boulders survived. These transported "erratics" could not have been weathered off the bedrock beneath them or off the bedrock from a nearby cliff. Huge amounts of loose rock in Harriman Park are in this category. The white conglomerate was certainly carried from the Shawangunk Mountains. Again, imagine a very different world than what appears today. The route proceeds through a landscape that had been hidden beneath huge masses of ice and snow, reaching depths of thousands of feet. As the snow accumulated and fed the thickness of the glaciers, the glaciers traversed the terrain, tearing it up as it moved and creating lakes, swamps, ponds, and valleys and depositing huge boulders.

What once provided nineteenth-century workers with a utility road for carrying tools and ore, and villagers with a roadway into their tiny towns, now enchants the mountain biker with stretches of demanding hill climbs, fast descending double-track, and beautiful scenery. This tour makes for a full day of memorable riding.

General location: The trailhead is approximately .75 mile from Kanawauke Circle, on Old Route 210, in the center portion of Harriman State Park.
Elevation change: The double-track rides along the hilly terrain with some steep, short pitches. Elevations begin at 827' and top out at about 1,200'.
Season: The best season is the period from Labor Day to Memorial Day. The summer months are very busy in Harriman State Park. If there is no snow cover on the trails, do not let winter's cold stop you; just put on more clothing and enjoy the solitude.

The Hogencamp Mine Trail.

Services: Nearby Sebago Beach offers food, beverages, and telephones from Memorial Day to Labor Day weekends. Sebago Beach can be reached by continuing south for about 2 miles on Seven Lakes Drive from Kanawauke Circle.

Hazards: This ride occasionally covers some rough terrain. Although not technically demanding, it may be strenuous. Anyone attempting this ride should be prepared to push or carry a bike up a small, steep, rock-studded hill. During the fall, it may be hard to see rocks underneath fallen leaves, so take care when descending if you are not sure what lies underneath the leaves.

Rescue index: The park road, Old Route 210, is well traveled, and help can be flagged down from passing vehicles. Park police usually patrol all the roads within Harriman State Park.

Land status: The trail is within the Harriman Bear Mountain State Park and is managed by the Palisades Interstate Park Commission.

Maps: The New York–New Jersey Trail Conference "Harriman Bear Mountain Trails," Trail Map 4, "Harriman Park North Half," is a waterproof and tearproof map that provides the best detail. It can be found at most outdoor-type stores for $6.95 or purchased at the Park Visitor Center on the Palisades Interstate Parkway. The USGS, 7.5 minute series, Sloatsburg and Monroe quadrangles also provide good detail.

Finding the trail: Take the Palisades Interstate Parkway north to Exit 14A/ Lake Welch Drive. During the winter this road is closed, so use Seven Lakes Drive from Long Mountain Circle, which can be reached by continuing farther on Palisades Interstate Parkway. You can then take Seven Lakes Drive directly into Kanawauke Circle.

At Kanawauke Circle take Old Route 210 west. Kanawauke Lake appears on both sides of the road. Immediately after passing the lake, turn into a large parking area on your left. Park and unload. Take your bike back onto Old Route 210, turning left. You will pass a beautiful lake on your left called Little Long Pond. There is a small promontory jutting into the lake that makes an excellent picnic spot. The trail begins on your right as a small paved road across and past the turnout for the promontory. Remember that as you leave the parking area, there are 2 trails on your right. Take the second one. There will be 5 large spruces on the left side of the entrance to the trail. Do not take the first trail, which traverses up the northwest shore of Lake Kanawauke and ends soon after.

Sources of additional information:

Palisades Interstate Park Commission (PIPC)
Bear Mountain State Park
Bear Mountain, New York 10911-0427
(914) 786-2701

New York–New Jersey Trail Conference (NY–NJTC)
GPO Box 2250
New York, New York 10016
(212) 685-9699

Notes on the trail: A narrow paved road departs from Old Route 210, ascending for about .1 mile. The road makes a switchback to the right. It gradually ascends, in a northeasterly direction, along an eroded, rock-studded, wide road. In Harriman State Park, many of the roads that ascend any type of hill are eroded. Their poorer condition is a result of the erosive power of water that runs off and down the roadbed, washing away the sediments. As you get to the top of the hill, you will see a small cinderblock foundation on your left. Bear right at the fork. You pass by another cinderblock foundation on your right and continue straight ahead along the trail as its condition improves to a grass-covered road. Begin a short climb up a small hill, and when you get to the top bear right following the trail. In about 500', you will come into the vicinity of the Hogencamp Mine.

It's mostly level riding as you pass a swamp on your right and ride through a mature stand of hemlocks. These trees are a rare sight because most were cut down. Their bark was used in the leather tanning industry, and recently many have fallen prey to a disease. As you ride along, you will start to see how the hillside on your left has been tunneled out for mining purposes. The landscape you are now traveling through is very interesting, with large boulders and erratics strewn along the hillside. The hillside on your left (east) actually belongs to the slopes of the 1,200' Hogencamp Mountain.

As the trail climbs out of this small valley, you will pass a series of rocks in the process of flaking or exfoliating. The appearance of this flaking bedrock has an interesting background. The bedrock you see and are traveling over was formed miles under the earth, under enormous pressure. After millions of years of uplift, tremendous pressure was released due to the unloading and expansion. This caused sheets of rock, from a few inches to a foot or more thick, to split off as giant plates. You will pass by many of these flat plates that appear to be flaking off the rock beneath them.

You will soon pass Pine Swamp. This is a large, attractive swamp surrounded by conifers. About midway along the swamp will be a huge boulder on your left, about 15' high and 25' long. Soon there will be a small splash of orange paint on a tree on your left. This points to a hill where Swamp Mine is located. When you get to a large brook, the trail will ascend .4 mile to your left along a wide, rocky road. Continue in this direction. Check out the road that leads off to your right. Many interesting mining cuts were made in the hillside a long time ago. In just a 300' descent this trail, a large wide cut in the mountain, is surrounded by 30'-high walls of stone and leads into a dark passageway. In this area a small settlement of houses and stores prospered from the working mines. You can also bail out at this point by continuing along this stony road to connect to Seven Lakes Drive across from Lake Tiorati in about a mile. If you do bail out at this point, let me remind you there is one long, rocky road you must climb. It's not the steepness that will get to you, but all those rocks that seem to go on forever as you are trying to ride up the hill. You may have to portage your bike. With all this huffing and puffing, your overall escape from the trail at this point may take about 20 minutes.

Let's not quit yet. At the time of this writing there were three yellow rectangles on a tree marking the ascent. Continue west for .4 mile up a rocky road toward an area known as Times Square. The short, steep, rocky climb rises from the current elevation of 1,100' to 1,200'. You will come to a large erratic sitting at a trail junction known as Times Square. When you arrive at this junction point, you will see many trails intersecting—hence, the name. Look for a 15'-wide, hard-packed road known as Lost Road. It continues in a northwesterly direction through a dense evergreen stand. (It's hard to miss because the other trails that intersect at Times Square are narrow hiking trails.) Follow this road, which soon turns north and passes through a rhododendron-filled swamp. This section of the road may be muddy after wet weather, but it is passable. The road passes Surebridge and Greenwood mines. Surebridge mine is half a mile past Times Square. A large, water-filled hole is visible from the road. This mine produced over 400 tons of iron ore during the Civil War. A little farther on is the Greenwood mine with loose rock piles strewn about. This mine was last active in 1880.

The trail opens out along the east shore of Upper Lake Cohasset and ends at Arden Valley Road. You return the way you came or turn right onto Arden

Valley Road, which intersects with Tiorati Circle. From Arden Valley Road it's 1.5 miles to Tiorati Circle. From Tiorati Circle go south on Seven Lakes Drive for another 3.5 miles to Kanawauke Circle and then turn west on Old Route 210 and back to your parking area. I prefer this option. The scenery, as you pass 4 picturesque lakes along Arden Valley Road and Seven Lakes Drive, is spectacular and makes a nice reward after some hard trail riding.

RIDE 22 *TREASURE OF LETTERROCK MOUNTAIN*

This seven-mile loop is a mixture of double-track, single-track, and paved road. The tour is strenuous, technically difficult, and not for the faint of heart. The climb up to Letterrock Mountain and the long descent through a rugged forest require good bike-handling skills and endurance. The hills can be gruesome. The fallen trees and rocky trails are the stuff technophiles dream about, but if you can put up with more than a little physical pain, you are definitely in for the ride of your life. On the descent from Letterrock, you will practice isometrics, tensing all your muscles for the plunge down a trail that is rutted and covered with boulders and fallen trees. Put some heavy cream in the water bottle before starting off the summit and in little over an hour you should have fine butter.

An arduous one-mile climb to the 1,100-foot summit of Letterrock Mountain is rewarded by an open forest with a high canopy and plenty of spots to catch a snooze. After lounging around at the summit, begin the long descent through a primitive-looking forest alongside a magnificent gully. The trail is crisscrossed by many brooks and streams. The final reward comes in the form of an easy ride, which descends along the banked turns of paved Tiorati Brook Road. That roller-coaster experience is then followed by a fireball express return down Seven Lakes Drive to your parking area. The route is a good illustration of what can happen to a trail when it's left to the forces of nature. The constant drainage of water down a sloped hillside follows the path of least resistance, in this case a narrow road, washing away the soils from the road bed and exposing the rocks underneath.

The trail passes by Letter Rock, a huge boulder near the summit of the mountain that was the subject of a hidden treasure in the seventeenth century. The "letter," caused by weathering on the huge boulder, had marked the spot on a worn and wrinkled seventeenth-century map. Legend has it that some Spanish explorers hid a treasure of silver near the boulder on the summit. This tale eventually led four treasure hunters in the 1930s to seek their fortune and blast away on Letterrock Mountain. Silvermine Lake was romantically named after the unfound silver.

RIDE 22 *TREASURE OF LETTERROCK MOUNTAIN*

To Long Mountain
Circle and Palisades
Interstate Pkwy.

Silvermine
Lake

N

0   1/4   1/2

MILES

Double-track

Seven Lakes Dr.

Letter
Rock

Tiorati
Circle

Letterrock
Mtn.
1195

Lake
Tiorati

NY

Tiorati Brook Rd.

To
17

To Palisades
Interstate Parkway

General location: The trail is approximately 2.7 miles from Long Mountain Circle on Seven Lakes Drive in the Harriman State Park.

Elevation change: Begin your ride at 800' and then climb for about a mile to the 1,100' summit of Letterrock Mountain. This breathless ascent to the summit area and the descent down the back slope will make you sweat and breathe hard and will increase your heart rate. The remaining trails traverse a moderately rolling terrain.

Season: There is beautiful foliage through the autumn and plenty of shade in the summer. The best season is the period from Labor Day to Memorial Day,

My wife Barbara searching for the treasure of Letterrock Mountain.

because the summer months are very busy in Harriman State Park. If there is no snow cover on the trails, do not let winter's cold stop you; just put on more clothing and enjoy the solitude.

Services: There is a soda machine, some telephones, and a swimming beach at Lake Tiorati Beach near Tiorati Circle. Food services can be found all year at the Bear Mountain Inn on NY 9. A Park Visitor Center, located on the Palisades Interstate Parkway about a mile before the Long Mountain Circle, sells trail maps, books, guides, snacks, and coffee.

Hazards: This tour is not for sissies. Many sections of the trail are loaded with obstacles like rocks, deadfalls (fallen trees), roots, and just about any other conspiracy nature could think of. Approximately .7 mile from the summit's descent, a small section of the trail is incredibly gnarled with huge, derailleur-eating rocks and fallen logs laid out in nearly impossible-to-ride combinations.

Rescue index: After the 1-mile climb to Letterrock Mountain, you naturally have the option to bail out and return down the road you just climbed. Once over the summit and down the back of the mountain, you are faced with equal hardship whichever way you decide to go. Continue onward and finish the ride if you have any doubts.

Land status: The trail is within the Harriman Bear Mountain State Park and is managed by the Palisades Interstate Park Commission.

Maps: The New York–New Jersey Trail Conference "Harriman Bear Mountain Trails," Trail Map 4, "Harriman Park North Half," is a waterproof and tearproof map that provides the best detail. It can be found at most outdoor-type stores for $6.95 or can be purchased at the Park Visitor Center on the Palisades Interstate Parkway. The USGS, 7.5 minute series, Popolopen and Monroe quadrangles also provide good detail.

Finding the trail: Take the Palisades Interstate Parkway north to Long Mountain Circle. At Long Mountain Circle take the Seven Lakes Drive in the direction of Lake Tiorati. Two miles after leaving the rotary, you will find a small parking area on your left. It follows the Silvermine picnic and parking area on your left. The trail begins about .7 mile on your left beyond a green metal barrier on an overgrown, four-wheel-drive road.

Sources of additional information:

Palisades Interstate Park Commission (PIPC)
Bear Mountain State Park
Bear Mountain, New York 10911-0427
(914) 786-2701

New York–New Jersey Trail Conference (NY–NJTC)
GPO Box 2250
New York, New York 10016
(212) 685-9699

Notes on the trail: After leaving Seven Lakes Drive, the trail heartily ascends into the woods to an elevation of about 1,100', following white trail blazers for a short distance. These blazes soon follow another trail that forks to your right. Continue straight ahead and begin a gentle climb through a mixed hardwood forest, passing the infamous Highland boulder fields. Many rocks and large boulders tumbled down the hillside after melting glacial waters and heavy rains washed the debris downslope toward the valleys. In about .4 mile, a short, half-mile trail leads off to your left in the direction of the abandoned Silvermine Ski Area summit.

Continue on the main road, and begin a descent down a small valley, where a little brook passes through and eventually drains into Silvermine Lake 4 miles away. After crossing the brook, begin a demanding ascent out of the valley for .3 mile to Letterrock Mountain and the Letterrock shelter. Keep to the right and notice that the trail is marked with yellow rectangle paint splashes on trees. Once the shelter is in site, sit a spell, catch some breath, and take a break, because the next section is challenging.

Continue through the campsite area in a southeasterly direction with the shelter on your left, and look for an unmarked, grassy, single-track trail. It is referred to as the Dunning Trail on some maps. Continue past a campsite ring on your right. This trail descends alongside Stillwater Brook and down its handsome, rocky valley. Even though this segment of the tour is mostly downhill, what will make this section memorable is the numerous stream crossings and blowdowns that you will encounter. In the evening you will be counting logs, not sheep. This section may require you to shoulder and portage your bike. At about 1.6 miles a small trail leads off to your right. Ignore it and continue straight ahead, bearing a little to your left. You will soon see old white splashes of paint on the trees. Take a moment to look back on the huge gully you have just descended.

At this point the trail intersects with a trail blazed with a red cross on white paint. After what you have just descended, it is no coincidence this is aptly named the Red Cross Trail. The rocky double-track levels out and descends alongside the headwaters of Stillwater Brook for about .75 mile. This area is not as dry as prior portions of this tour, and a thicker vegetation is more prevalent. The trail crosses over numerous small streams and through a dense forest filled with mountain laurel and leads to the paved Tiorati Brook Road in less than a mile. You will soon climb to a dam with excellent views of Tiorati Lake. Continue to Tiorati Circle along the rolling and scenic road and then descend quickly on Seven Lakes Drive back to your car.

RIDE 23 *NAWAHUNTA FIRE ROAD*

This hearty eight-mile loop links two separate trail systems. The ride traverses along old wood roads and through boulder-strewn valleys and attractive hardwood forests. There is a little something for everyone. A combination of scenery, varied terrain, good riding, a scenic lake that provides solitude and a good lunch spot, and miles of nontechnical single- and double-track makes for a pleasant and complete day of riding. This loop trail can be broken up into separate rides by studying the map and choosing a section to explore. Listed below is a tour that encompasses the trail systems and requires the better part of a day to complete.

The trip begins on the Nawahunta Fire Road and meanders along a wide, occasionally rocky, washed-out, old forest road. The surface of this road has become rock-studded from the continual runoff draining down the hills. The route explores a dark, dense forest of mixed hardwoods and conifers and provides a first-class double-track that requires a minimum amount of technical skills. This rugged path is great for advanced beginners who feel equipped to try something more demanding than a flat trail and are ready to challenge themselves with the basic handling skills necessary for traversing a rocky terrain. The true hammerheads will thrive on this demanding double-track, testing their stamina and enjoying the pristine, secluded wilderness that surrounds the trail from beginning to end.

RIDE 23 *NAWAHUNTA FIRE ROAD*

Note: *All trails are double-track.*

The road is not in very good condition due to insufficient maintenance. The tremendous erosional forces of the mountains, one of the chief factors in trail erosion, comes from poor drainage along the route. Rains wash down a trail and eventually expose some of the rocks and roots underneath the road bed. The object of some trail maintenance programs is to divert some of this runoff and preserve the surface of the trail. This is important because people often take trail maintenance for granted. In reality, some of the best riding and hiking is along trails that have been meticulously maintained, often with hours of volunteer effort. It helps to appreciate and understand what's visible on the trail and the efforts that made it rideable.

This trail leads through an erratic-filled valley almost two miles in length before it intersects with Long Mountain Parkway. After crossing the parkway, the second leg of the tour begins, linking with a three-mile double-track path that leads to the scenic Turkey Hill Lake. Previously a swamp, this body of water was re-created into a beautiful lake by the Civilian Conservation Corps in 1933 for use as a reservoir. Summer Hill Road, which borders the northeast side of the lake, was built for access to the dam site. Turkey Hill Lake is located in a valley surrounded by Long Mountain on the west, Summer Hill on the south, and Turkey Hill to the east. It's an ideal spot for a mountain bike–style picnic. From the lake, return to the parking area via a short stretch of Seven Lakes Drive.

General location: Approximately 2.7 miles from Long Mountain Circle on Seven Lakes Drive in Harriman State Park.
Elevation change: The elevation begins at 780' and gradually ascends to about 900' at the end of the fire road. The elevation of the second trail system begins on Long Mountain Parkway (US 6) at an elevation of 900'. From the parking area, a double-track path descends gently to the 600' elevation of Turkey Hill Lake. The return route from Turkey Hill Lake along Seven Lakes Drive leads you gently up from the Long Mountain Circle at about 500' to your parking area at 780'.
Season: The best season is the period from Labor Day to Memorial Day. The summer months are very busy in Harriman State Park. If there is no snow cover on the trails, do not let winter's cold stop you; put on more clothing and enjoy yourself.
Services: Food services can be found all year at the Bear Mountain Inn on NY 9. A Park Visitor Center, located on the Palisades Interstate Parkway about a mile before the Long Mountain Circle, sells trail maps, books, guides, snacks, and coffee.
Hazards: If you're traveling in fall, be careful of the hidden rocks beneath the leaves on the ground. Pay attention to the rocky road beds that become wet and slippery after some rainy weather.
Rescue index: You can bail out of the loop at the end of the Nawahunta Fire Road and coast down U.S. 6 to Long Mountain Circle instead of taking the Turkey Hill Lake link. The only problem is you have to ascend 2 miles back up Seven Lakes Drive to your parking area. The ride along this section of Seven Lakes Drive, from Long Mountain Circle to your parking area, is idyllic. You will pass by beautiful Queensboro Brook and a rocky landscape of dense forest. You might wish it were longer than 2 miles.
Land status: The trail is within the Harriman Bear Mountain State Park and is managed by the Palisades Interstate Park Commission.

Maps: The New York–New Jersey Trail Conference "Harriman Bear Mountain Trails," Trail Map 4, "Harriman Park North Half," is a waterproof and tearproof map that provides the best detail. It can be found at most outdoor-type stores for $6.95 or can be purchased at the Park Visitor Center on the Palisades Interstate Parkway. The USGS, 7.5 minute series, Popolopen and Monroe quadrangles, also provide good detail.

Finding the trail: Take the Palisades Interstate Parkway north to Long Mountain Circle. At Long Mountain Circle take the Seven Lakes Drive in the direction of Lake Tiorati. Two miles after the rotary, you will find a small parking area on your left. It follows the Silvermine picnic and parking area on your left. Get back on Seven Lakes Drive and turn left. The trail begins about 50' to your right down an old, wide, hard-packed, four-wheel-drive road.

Sources of additional information:

Palisades Interstate Park Commission (PIPC)
Bear Mountain State Park
Bear Mountain, New York 10911-0427
(914) 786-2701

New York–New Jersey Trail Conference (NY–NJTC)
GPO Box 2250
New York, New York 10016
(212) 685-9699

Notes on the trail: This tour starts on Nawahunta Fire Road, which begins on Seven Lakes Drive. Take the wide, flat Nawahunta Fire road for 2 miles over a moderately rolling terrain until it terminates at US 6, Long Mountain Parkway. If you have decided to link the Nawahunta Fire Road and the Turkey Hill Lake trails, cross Long Mountain Parkway and ride into the parking area directly across from the end of the fire road. Ride through the parking area from south to north and look for a splash of blue paint on a rock on your right side. Beyond this rock is a hard-packed gravel path leading through trees with blue markers. Dismount and walk this shared section of hiking trail. The trail descends into a small narrow valley to an intersection. Look for a tree with 3 white markers and red dots in the middle and make a sharp right in a southerly direction. You will travel through a small, short valley with steep sides. Notice the many trees on the slope that have been blown down. This valley acts as a wind tunnel during storms, and the trees cannot hold onto the steep-sided slopes. Take the middle fork after .2 mile and continue on the main double-track.

After 1 mile from the beginning of this valley road, a white-blazed double-track leads in a northerly direction from the main road you are on. That path descends to the southern shore of Turkey Hill Lake and at the time of this writing was marked with white paint blazes. The tour I have detailed here proceeds straight ahead in a southwesterly direction on the main road and

Summer Hill Road leading to Turkey Hill Lake.

ends at Long Mountain Circle. From Long Mountain Circle another old wood road takes you along the northern shore of Turkey Hill Lake. Continue on the main southerly double-track, as it will soon ascend a quiet forest in a southwesterly direction. The trail will come out near a salt storage facility. Continue on the paved road, keep bearing left, and ascend to another storage facility area. Go around the mounds of sand and look for two big cement blocks with a rusted iron gate. A wide, moderately rocky jeep road known as Summer Hill Road begins beyond this gate and ascends for 1 mile to the northern shore of Turkey Hill Lake. Long Mountain, elevation 1,157', can be seen to the northwest across from Turkey Hill Lake.

Return down Summer Hill Road to Long Mountain Circle and take Seven Lakes Drive in the direction of Lake Tiorati. There is a wide shoulder to ride on, and although it's mostly uphill, the scenery is splendid and should take your mind off the pain in your thighs. You should reach your parking area about 1.7 miles from the rotary.

If you have time, try the old fire road just before you get to the Silvermine Lake parking area. The trail begins a little over 1.2 miles from the rotary off Seven Lakes Drive. It is a mile in length and takes you out and back on a fairly level gravel road, with views of the lake and Black Mountain.

RIDE 24 *BEECHY BOTTOM ROAD*

This hard-packed dirt road is wide, level, and four miles long (one way). It provides an enjoyable passage for family and a complete day of mountain biking, picnicking, swimming in a large outdoor pool, and spoonfuls of Italian ices. The well-maintained roads and trails make it an ideal place for a beginner biker to venture off the road and get accustomed to the riding equipment and to gain a little confidence before graduating to more demanding double-track and single-track. The wide gravel roads provide a good surface for someone new to off-road riding to get the feel of the bike off the pavement. It's a great ride for those wanting to try out mountain bike riding without its technical demands. An afternoon pedaling this well-maintained path provides an opportunity to access a pristine and attractive wooded environment. The easy riding puts the focus on the surrounding woodlands and valley, rather than on the twists, turns, and maneuvering that would normally be required on a more technical trail.

The former road was built in 1933 at the base of Beechy Bottom Valley after the creation of Harriman Park. A mica mine dating back to 1893 can be found 50 feet below the intersection of Beechy Bottom Road and the short trail leading from the parking lot. Mica can be found near the opening of the mine at the bottom of the steep slope.

The demands for this ride are simple. A drive to the park, some sandwiches and snacks, a couple of bikes and some friends or family. Mix for a few hours and *voila,* a recipe for some great fun.

General location: Near the Anthony Wayne Recreation Area, off the Palisades Interstate Parkway within Harriman State Park.
Elevation change: Negligible.
Season: All seasons are ideal for riding. The summer months are very busy in Harriman State Park. This is a great place to spend a hot summer afternoon. Take a ride in the woods, cool off in the large outdoor swimming pool, and follow it up with some cool Italian ices. However, if it's winter and there is no snow on the trails, this ride is an ideal event to coax you off the couch. Get some fresh air and enjoy some popular trails all to yourself.
Services: The ride is located near the Anthony Wayne Recreation area, which offers parking, food concessions, a large outdoor pool to swim in, telephones, and bathrooms.
Hazards: This tour follows an old abandoned road. The riding is easy and you may feel encouraged to put the pedal to metal. But take precautions, as other people use the trails and may be around a blind corner. If you are approaching a turn, signal with a whistle or just yell out, "Rider approaching."

RIDE 24 *BEECHY BOTTOM ROAD*

Note: *All trails are double-track.*

Rescue index: The trail parallels Palisades Interstate Parkway and is within close proximity to the Anthony Wayne Recreation Area. This area is stocked with telephones and people.

Land status: The trail is within the Harriman Bear Mountain State Park and is managed by the Palisades Interstate Park Commission.

Maps: The New York–New Jersey Trail Conference "Harriman Bear Mountain Trails," Trail Map 4, "Harriman Park North Half," is a waterproof and tearproof map that provides the best detail. It can be found at most outdoor-type stores for $6.95 or can be purchased at the Park Visitor Center on the Palisades Interstate Parkway. The USGS, 7.5 minute series, Popolopen and Monroe quadrangles also provide good detail.

Finding the trail: Take the Palisades Interstate Parkway north, exiting at the Anthony Wayne Recreation Area. A $4 fee may be collected from Memorial Day to Labor Day weekends. Park at the northern end of the large parking lot. Pedal down to the tollgate, and about 200' past the tollgate you will see 2 stone pillars with wooden gates. The trail begins just beyond these gates.

Sources of additional information:

Palisades Interstate Park Commission (PIPC)
Bear Mountain State Park
Bear Mountain, New York 10911-0427
(914) 786-2701

New York–New Jersey Trail Conference (NY–NJTC)
GPO Box 2250
New York, New York 10016
(212) 685-9699

Notes on the trail: The road leading beyond the wooden gates ascends a short distance. A trail intersects midway and leads in a southerly direction through the lower picnic area, but you should continue straight ahead up to the next **T** intersection. The dirt road to your left (north) is about 1 mile in length. If you do turn left, upon reaching the end you must return on the same road. After this short 1-mile-out and 1-mile-back path, continue in a southerly direction. The trail extends for another 2.3 miles. Toward the end of the path, the last .7 mile descends from an elevation of 800' to 600'. To return to the parking area, head back on this same trail.

Northern New Jersey Tours

Those who are not familiar with the state have an image of New Jersey as an industrial wasteland. Far from the oil refineries and heavily industrialized sections are rich, low-lying, forested mountains and an abundance of fine mountain biking trails. Old lumber and carriage roads and single-tracked forest paths lace the northern New Jersey region. These hilly mountains offer a gamut of riding possibilities and a chance to explore the beautiful, historic, rugged woodlands. Some of these old roads and footpaths existed prior to the acquisition of the land for public use. Some trails date back to the Depression, when a federal program to help unemployment fostered the Civilian Conservation Corps. Public works projects spawned park and recreation facilities as viable today as when they were first constructed in the 1930s.

The beauty of mountain biking in the Garden State lies in its variety of terrain, from the flat, nineteenth-century mining and logging roads to the hilly and rocky highlands in the north. In between are swamps, woods, and grasslands.

Geologists divide the state into four primary regions. In the northwest, the Appalachian Ridge and Valley Province contains the highest elevations in the state and cuts a diagonal running southwest to northeast. Here, in what was once a major mountain range (since leveled by erosion), are a series of parallel valleys and ridges composed of sandstones and conglomerates approximately 400 million years old. The Ridge and Valley Province extends for over 1,200 miles from Alabama to Canada and, because of its regularity, is used as a navigational landmark by migrating birds. Hawk sightings along the main ridges are common during the fall migration. Stokes State Forest and High Point State Park together preserve nearly all the mountainous portions of this province.

Southeast and parallel to the Ridge and Valley Province lies the New Jersey Highlands Province. This area is composed of rocks that are 800 million years old—more ancient than those of the Ridge and Valley Province. The flat-topped summits of this province lie a few hundred feet lower than those in the Kittatinny Mountains. This mountain range extends north into New York as the Hudson Highlands and south into Pennsylvania as the Reading Prong. Numerous lakes and reservoirs grace state and county parks, including the large Wawayanda State Park, as well as the vast holdings of the Newark Watershed Conservation and Development Corporation, which supplies drinking water. Both parks have miles and miles of trails.

Sources of additional information:

Ramapo Valley Cycling Club, Inc.
18 Boulevard
Haskell, New Jersey 07420-1136
(201) 331-6199
(201) 839-4304

Wheelsport Cycle Club
15 Hillside Avenue
Mahwah, New Jersey 07430
(201) 529-1467

New Jersey Division of Travel and Tourism
20 West State Street, CN826
Dept. T1A
Trenton, New Jersey 08625
(609) 292-2470
(800) JERSEY 7

RIDE 25 *ALLAMUCHY MOUNTAIN STATE PARK*

Allamuchy State Park, with its 12 miles of forest roads and single-track, is a place worth seeking out. Riding is a mixed bag, including everything from easy cruising on well-graded forest roads to challenging opportunities on an equal amount of single-track.

A convenient network of old farm and lumber roads winds through this secluded and relatively unknown New Jersey State Park only 50 miles from Manhattan, providing a pleasant mountain biking experience for riders of all levels. Plenty of hills and lively single-track challenge the average hammerhead, with as much cruising material to go around for the less technically inclined. A wide, hard-packed forest road penetrates the Allamuchy forest and ends at Deer Park Pond just four miles later. Several other trails head off into the woods and pass through more densely forested habitat.

The rugged areas of northern New Jersey have a reputation for history, picturesque landscapes, and outdoor recreation opportunities. Allamuchy Mountain State Park is a prime example of this combination of culture, scenery, and activities. The trails pass through more than 4,000 acres of oak hardwood and hemlock-spruce forests and northern marshlands. Replanting projects from 30 years ago have helped certain acreage to regrow and flourish. These areas are known as succession fields and help to retain the natural habitat of the forest. The diversification of wildlife flourishes throughout this rich forest and supports an active population of animals. Deer Park Pond boasts a large group of

To Andover

To Pennsylvania

80

Viewing Area

ALLAMUCHY MOUNTAIN STATE PARK

Yellow Tr.

Blue Tr.

White Tr.

Red Tr.

Red Tr.

Yellow Tr.

80

To 206

To New York City

517

Deer Park Pond

CLEAR SPRINGS WILDERNESS AREA

White Tr.

Yellow Tr.

604

To Hackettstown

N

0   3000   6000
FEET

NJ

beavers, and several of their lodges can be seen from the shoreline. Ducks, Canada geese, and osprey nest at the lake, as well. A large white-tailed deer population makes this an ideal spot for hunting. Bow hunting is the only sanctioned hunting sport during the regular hunting season.

The first inhabitants of this rugged area were the Delaware Indians. The region was named after their leader, Chief Allamuchahokkingen, whose name translates as "place within the hills." Of course, that was a mouthful, and the name of the first settlement in 1715 was changed to Mamuchahoken and then finally to Allamuchy. The majority of the land that composes Allamuchy Mountain State Park was part of the Rutherford and Stuyvesant estates. These families are distinguished as the direct descendants of Peter Stuyvesant, the last governor of New Amsterdam.

A good amount of riding can be done in this park, so gear yourself up and come prepared for a full day of sizzling road and track.

General location: The park is approximately 50 miles west on Interstate 80 from the George Washington Bridge and 10 miles south of the town of Andover.
Elevation change: The forest trails traverse up and down with a maximum elevation change of 200'. The general elevation of the area is between 800' and 1,000'.
Season: The trails in the winter provide excellent cross-country skiing, providing there is snow. Under these conditions, the trails are unrideable. However, once the snow melts, get out there and explore this wonderful park.
Services: Ten miles north of Allamuchy State Park on NJ County Road 517 in the town of Andover is Andover Cycles and some food and gas services. Allamuchy Mountain and Stephens State Parks provide fishing opportunities year-round and make a great spot to cast a line.
Hazards: Parts of Allamuchy Mountain State Park are available for hunting. Call the park office for information on the current hunting season.
Rescue index: Some trails receive a fair amount of traffic, and encounters with other trail-users may be frequent, especially during the weekend, as this park has become increasingly popular with mountain bikers. A pair of bow hunters helped me get to know the forest trails during one of my visits.
Land status: New Jersey State Park Service.
Maps: You may call the park office to see if they can send you a park map in the mail. This park map provides some good coverage of the area. Allamuchy State Park is also covered by the USGS, 7.5 minute series, Tranquillity quadrangle.
Finding the trail: Take US Interstate 80 west from the George Washington Bridge and then take Exit 19; turn south on CR 517 toward Hackettstown. After about 2 miles on CR 517, look for Deer Park Road, an unimproved dirt access road. It comes up on the left immediately past an Italian restaurant called Mattars. Drive .7 mile over some small hills and many potholes to the

Foliage paints the forest of Allamuchy State Park with a
bold hand.

park entrance, which leads to a parking area. You will see a brown wooden
park sign indicating Allamuchy Natural Area, Allamuchy Mountain State
Park. There will be a large grass-covered parking area in another 50'. After
you have parked and you are ready to roll, put your back to the parking area
and turn to face a small, brown, wooden shed. The yellow-blazed single-track
begins to your right beyond some short trees, and the wider, easier dirt road
that leads to Deer Park Pond leads to your left.

Source of additional information:

Allamuchy Mountain State Park
Hackettstown, New Jersey 07840
(908) 852-3790
(201) 398-7010

Notes on the trail: Alternate rides can be assembled as you cruise on the easy 3.5-mile main dirt road, which leads down to Deer Park Pond, making this a total of 7 miles out-and-back. The principal trail that will be described is the main dirt road, but I will mention the other, more challenging rides throughout the description.

Two trails lead from the parking area: an easy, wide dirt road and a more difficult yellow-blazed, single-track trail, which leads from the northwest section of the parking area. The yellow trail leads into the forest and then reconnects with the dirt road in a little over 1.5 miles, making a loop.

As you begin your ride at the parking area for the easy ride, face the brown wooden shed and turn left down the wide dirt road past a wooden sign indicating Green Acres. There is a gradual ascent for about 1 mile up this road through an open forest of oak. In another .4 mile, you will approach parking area 1. Immediately before that, the yellow trail that began from the parking area intersects here. Continue on the wide dirt road and pass by several field regrowth programs, known as succession fields and planted 75 years ago. In another .7 mile you arrive at the last parking area, 2. Continue straight on the wide road beyond a yellow metal road bar gate. Immediately past the gate, notice a white-painted, blazed trail leading to the north and away from the dirt road. You may take this white trail as it heads north for a little over 1 mile. When you arrive at a wildlife-viewing area, continue on the white trail in an easterly direction. In a little under 1 mile, bear right at the next fork. Remain on the white blazed trail, which then leads south. The white trail terminates at Deer Park Pond in over half a mile.

As you continue on the dirt road past this gate, the trail will swing to the east almost immediately. Begin a long, gradual descent through an attractive deciduous forest of oak and maple to Deer Park Pond. The road is marked with white markers on trees. One of the most striking feelings as you proceed through this section of the forest is the openness and the expansiveness of the terrain. The forest floor is nearly all ferns, particularly on the right, and above that is nothing but open space until the lowest branches of some very large trees are reached. As you walk on, a portion of the lake appears through the trees on the left. This is Deer Park Pond. Beavers have built lodges in the area and the northern shore of the pond was completely denuded several years ago by these tree-felling, bark-chewing little mammals. You will notice some of their lodges around the pond. The road continues down to the pond over a dam and spillway and along the eastern shore. Notice the tall stands of hemlocks and pines right on the water. Thousands of acres of large hemlocks were decimated in the forests of northern New Jersey as well as in New York. Their bark was used for tanning leather products during the nineteenth century. It is rare to come across a stand of mature hemlocks.

The road ends at the lake, but there are several other trails that reach into the hills. Near the spillway, the blue trail leads in a northeasterly direction and creates a loop that returns you to the lake. Take the blue trail up a small hill passing the yellow trail and follow the blue trail for a little over 1 mile. Take a left at the next **T** intersection and go past the next left, turning left at the next white blazed trail, which leads you to the pond in a southerly direction. There is your loop. Return along the main wide dirt road.

RIDE 26 *ECHO LAKE*

This moderate, six-mile, out-and-back ride (three miles one way), is an easy tour through a pleasant woodscape. The trail is located in the southern portion of the largely unknown and secluded Pequannock Watershed in the New Jersey Highlands. This fast, double-track trail through a picturesque, young hardwood forest with numerous rock outcroppings, borders the large scenic Echo Lake, and gets into some fast-paced country cruising that is also beginner-friendly. The fairly level, wide, four-wheel-drive road is connected by two interesting spur trails. These trails do not require any special technical skills, and for the beginner it's an opportunity to get out into some secluded woods and test nascent skills without being too technical.

This ride takes your mind off the rocks under your tires and pulls it into the scenery. There are various spur trails to explore and lots of scenery. One short spur leads to Echo Lake, where you can walk or ride on the rocky shore trail circling the lake. The other spur, known as Conklin Road, traverses a thick understory of mountain laurel and a forest of young beech and oak. It is crossed by several streams.

The trail traverses the Pequannock Watershed, located in the forested and water-rich Highland region of northern New Jersey, known for its scenic and historic resources. The region provides habitat for a wide variety of birds, mammals, fish, and reptiles, and supports a wide range of recreational uses for the public. It is managed through a controlled access program by the non-profit Newark Watershed Conservation and Development Corporation (NWCDC), which was established to preserve the area's scenic and recreational qualities. The Pequannock Watershed covers almost 35,000 acres of land. This natural area is made up of many smaller watersheds that collect precipitation and channel their waters into the Newark water supply system. Numerous trail opportunities, including single-track, double-track, and old roads, fill the region. A special permit must be purchased before using these lands, which are popular with hunters, anglers, and hikers, but the extra effort is well worth the payback from exploring these lands.

General location: The trail is located in the western section of New Jersey's scenic Passaic County. It is north of NJ 23 and off County Road 513 (Union Valley Road), near the town of Newfoundland.

Elevation change: The ride starts out at 1,000' and descends to 800' near the turnaround point. The elevation change is spread fairly uniformly and there are no steep hills to climb. An ascent back to 1,000' from the turnaround point will be required, and you'll stay at this elevation for the remainder of the ride.

Season: January to the end of September provides the best riding. The trails may be soggy in the spring, and summer is usually hot and buggy. Hunting season usually begins about September 30. It is a good idea to check with the NWCDC for more up-to-date details.

Services: There are service stations, outdoor supply stores, and food along NJ 23 before the turnoff onto CR 513, Union Valley Road.

Hazards: If you insist on riding during hunting season, make sure you do not wear white. You might be mistaken for a white-tailed deer, which is the prime hunting target, so be safe and wear the bright orange hunting colors. It's always recommended to stop in at the NWCDC Office at Echo Lake and get the latest word on the watershed.

Rescue index: The route is not complex and is very easy to follow. You are never more than 1 mile from Union Valley Road. Nearby towns include Newfoundland and Postville.

Land status: Pequannock Watershed, owned by the city of Newark, is managed by the nonprofit Newark Watershed Conservation and Development Corporation (NWCDC). The land was purchased by the city of Newark in the 1900s to provide clean water for Newark and its neighbors.

In order to provide and conserve these natural resources, continued conservation maintenance of the region is required. Newark's stewardship of the area has provided a means to control access and monitor impact in order to preserve land that is unique and ecologically sensitive and that provides habitats for a diverse wildlife population. The requirement of permits is one of the ways in which controlled access can help moderate the human impact and at the same time sustain the wide range of recreational uses by the general public.

Maps: The NWCDC provides you with a general map of the area after you purchase your permit, either by mail or in person at their office at 223 Echo Lake Road. The New York–New Jersey Trail Conference "North Jersey Trails Western Portion," Trail Map 21, is waterproof and tearproof, provides the best detail, and can be found at most outdoor-type stores.

Finding the trail: Take Interstate 80 west from the George Washington Bridge to Exit 53/NJ 23. Take Route 23 north for about 16 miles and turn right (north) onto Union Valley Road. Follow this road north approximately 3.5 miles and turn right (east) onto Gould Road. Take this winding road until the intersection with Wooley Road. The trail begins opposite this intersection of Wooley Road with Gould Road as a wide, noticeable jeep road.

Sources of additional information: Biking in this area is by permit only. To obtain further information call or write:

Pequannock Watershed
Newark Watershed Conservation and Development Corporation
(NWCDC)
P.O. Box 319
223 Echo Lake Road
Newfoundland, New Jersey 07435
(201) 697-2850

Newark Watershed Conservation and Development Corporation
(NWCDC)
40 Clinton Street
Newark, New Jersey 07102
(201) 697-2850

Notes on the trail: The wide, four-wheel-drive road, also known as Kanouse Road, begins at Gould Road at the intersection of Wooley and Gould roads. The trail leads you in a southerly direction at the fairly level elevation of 1,000'. In just under 2 miles, notice a spur merging from the left. This will lead to the shore of Echo Lake, elevation 892', in about a quarter-mile. The trail is very rocky and you can only ride it halfway, at which point you must shoulder your bike or leave it locked to a tree. The lake is quite attractive and a great place to hang your helmet or just spend a few moments taking in the scenery. Another semirideable trail encircles the lake close to the shore, which is quite rocky at places and will require you to dismount and carry your bike.

Continuing on the main trail, Kanouse Road, you will arrive at another spur in half a mile that will lead in a northerly direction. This old wood road, known as Conklin Road, travels for a little over a mile. It's worth the time to investigate and explore the scenic woodscape, with its large understory of mountain laurel. You can continue on Conklin Road to Union Valley Road. If you have an urge to return to your parked vehicle, I suggest turning back the way you came and taking Kanouse Road to avoid the large hills on Union Valley and Gould roads.

After the intersection with the Conklin Road spur, the main trail, Kanouse Road, descends gently for approximately another mile, crossing the Kanouse Brook and reaching the town of Newfoundland. To return, you may turn right onto Union Valley Road, CR 513, and turn right onto Gould Road, which is hopefully where you parked your car. To return through the woods, just turn your bike around and head back in the same direction you came.

RIDE 27 *HANKS POND LOOP*

This tour may be technically and physically demanding along its many sections of rocky trail and is not for the weak of heart, but the primitive wilderness is charming. Nature is your companion, and the accompanying serenity is well worth the effort of this rigorous trail. It's not the hills that will get you, but rather the maneuvering over and around the rocky trail. This ride is for dedicated hammerheads who enjoy a good bone-jarring, teeth-grinding double-track. There are many sections of smooth trail, but a generous portion of rocky trail will keep you busy. The trail is so seldom used that thick green moss blankets many sections.

The trail traverses the Pequannock Watershed, located in the forested and water-rich Highland region of northern New Jersey known for its scenic and historic resources. The region provides habitat for a vast array of birds, mammals, fish, and reptiles, and offers many recreational facilities. It is managed through a controlled access program by the nonprofit Newark Watershed Conservation and Development Corporation (NWCDC), which was established to preserve the area's natural splendor and potential. The Pequannock Watershed is a very large region, covering almost 35,000 acres of land. This natural area is made up of many smaller watersheds that collect precipitation and channel their waters into the Newark water supply system. Numerous trail opportunities, including single-track, double-track, and old roads, traverse the region. A permit must be purchased before using these lands, which are popular with hunters, anglers, and hikers, but the small expense is more than worth the payback of exploring these lands.

This seven-mile loop trail consists of the Hanks East Trail, which goes north to its terminus at Stephens Road. To extend the ride another two miles, there is an alternate trip along a lovely old forest road. It begins at Stephens Road and runs north until it reaches an old pipeline. After reaching its terminus, turn around and return along the same route. It's along the mostly level Hanks West Trail, which follows an old wood road.

About 20 years ago, Pennsylvania outlawed bear hunting. Not only did the bear population increase, but it migrated into these mountains. After I shared a coffee with a local police officer, he smiled wryly and said, "Don't be surprised if you run across a few in the woods. Just make some noise, they are not that big." Last year, he had to remove a 700-pounder from an unfortunate accident with a car. "And you should have seen that car," he continued, until I bid a speedy farewell and began my ride. Nevertheless, I began with some trepidation. For the first portion of my ride, I would stop and listen for bear noise and wonder if I was going to ride into one. As it turned out, the only animals I saw were deer and turkey. I was told later that the bears hang

RIDE 27 *HANKS POND LOOP*
RIDE 28 *PARADISE ROAD*

To
Clinton Rd.

Stephens Rd.

Red Blazed

White Blazed

To Upper
Greenwood
Lake

Ride #28

Buckabear
Pond

To
West
Milford

Blue
Blazed

Dunker
Pond

Clinton Reservoir

Hanks Pond   Ride #27

N

28

Schoolhouse
Cove Rd.

Paradise Rd.

27

Clinton Furnace

0   1/2   1
MILES

To
Port Jervis

Clinton Rd.

23

NJ

To 80
and New
York City

around the residential areas where they pillage the garbage cans for food scraps. So do not worry and enjoy the ride.

General location: The trail is found in the western section of New Jersey's scenic Passaic County, south of Wawayanda State Park and north on NJ 23, near the town of Stockholm.

Elevation change: Hanks Pond is at 1,033', which is considered high for a body of water in the Northeast. A 1,100' ridge extends the full length of the Hanks East Trail, and the trail is somewhere in between the ridge and Hanks Pond. The Hanks East Trail travels along at a slightly higher elevation than the pond, but is fairly level along the east side of Hanks Pond.

The return along the Hanks West Trail is at a lower elevation, close to that of Hanks Pond, where access to the pond's shoreline is easier. This trail might also be wetter as a result of its close proximity to the pond.

Season: January to the end of September provides the best riding. The trails may be soggy in the spring, and summer is usually hot and buggy. Hunting season usually begins about September 30. Check with the NWCDC for more up-to-date details.

Services: There are service stations, outdoor supply stores, and food along NJ 23 before the turnoff onto Clinton Road.

Hazards: If you insist on riding during hunting season, make sure you do not wear white. You might be mistaken for a white-tailed deer, which is the prime hunting target, so be safe and wear the bright orange hunting colors. It's always recommended to stop in at the NWCDC Office at Echo Lake and get the latest word on the watershed. During the summer months, do not forget to bring bug repellent.

Rescue index: The route is well marked and simple to follow. At most points you will be about 4 miles from help and from the paved Clinton Road.

Land status: Pequannock Watershed is owned by the city of Newark. It is managed by the nonprofit Newark Watershed Conservation and Development Corporation (NWCDC). The land was purchased by the city of Newark in the 1900s to provide clean water to Newark and its neighbors.

In order to provide and conserve these natural resources, continued conservation maintenance of the region is required. Newark's stewardship of the area has provided a means to control access and monitor impact in order to preserve land that is unique and ecologically sensitive and that provides habitat for a diverse wildlife. The requirement of permits is one of the ways in which controlled access can help moderate the human impact and at the same time sustain the wide range of recreational uses by the general public.

Maps: The NWCDC provides you with a general map of the area after you purchase your permit, either by mail or in person at their office at 223 Echo Lake Road. The New York–New Jersey Trail Conference's "North Jersey Trails Western Portion," Trail Map 21, provides very good detail of the Pequannock Watershed and is waterproof and tearproof. It sells for $6.95

and can be found at most outdoor-type stores. USGS, 7.5 minute series, New-foundland quadrangle also provides coverage.

Finding the trail: Take Interstate 80 west from the George Washington Bridge to Exit 53/NJ 23. Take Route 23 (north) for about 17 miles and turn right onto Clinton Road. Follow this road north. After a little over 1 mile, fork right. The road left is Schoolhouse Cove Road and connects to the Paradise Road tour.

After bearing right you will ride along the eastern shore of Clinton Reservoir and then come to another intersection with a road leading off to your right. This is Van Orden Road. Turn right and about 50' on your right is parking area P1. You will see the lettering on a nearby telephone pole. Directly across from this parking area the trailhead begins on a wide, hard-packed dirt road.

Sources of additional information: Biking in this area is by permit only. To obtain further information call or write:

Pequannock Watershed
Newark Watershed Conservation and Development Corporation
 (NWCDC)
P.O. Box 319
223 Echo Lake Road
Newfoundland, New Jersey 07435
(201) 697-2850

Newark Watershed Conservation and Development Corporation
 (NWCDC)
40 Clinton Street
Newark, New Jersey 07102
(201) 697-2850

Notes on the trail: The loop consists of 2 designated named trails. The tour begins on the Hanks East white-painted marked trail and returns on the Hanks West white-and-light-blue marked trail. From the parking area, continue past the metal barrier onto a wide, gravelly road. There are white trail blazes on the trees. At .2 mile, go right onto a smaller forest road that will bear the same painted white trail blazes. This trail is known as the Hanks East Trail and travels on high ground above Hanks Pond for over 3 miles. For the first .7 mile it continues along the eastern shore of Hanks Pond as a single-track on semirocky terrain.

After 2 miles, you will approach an intersection with a blue-blazed hiking trail. If you must bail out, you can portage your bike for a short distance and connect with Hanks West Trail, which is the return route, back to the parking area.

Hanks East Trail continues for another 1.5 miles to intersect with the wide dirt Stephens Road. Shortly after turning left onto Stephens Road, turn left into the woods on the white-and-blue-blazed Hanks West Trail. Take this all the way back toward Hanks Pond and then back to the parking area. The latter section of Hanks West Trail is a wider, flatter wood road. There are numerous places along the shore to stop and rest and take in the scenery.

As an alternate ride, you may consider trying the blue-marked trail off Stephens Road, which heads north for 2 miles. Before you turn left onto the white-and-blue-blazed Hanks West Trail, turn right onto this old wood road.

RIDE 28 *PARADISE ROAD*

This ride features two trail systems carving the middle section of the Pequannock Watershed region. The route is bordered to the east by Clinton Reservoir and Bearfort Mountain, and to the west by Canister Reservoir and the Hamburg Mountains. Paradise Road, as the name suggests, is an invigorating and easy seven-mile cruise (3½ miles one way) along a wide, flat, dirt country road. An alternate hilly route requiring endurance continues for approximately 3½ miles from the parking area, but it hits a dead end. This road feels remote as it traverses a low mountain and mixed hardwood forest and then a hemlock forest with many streams, brooks, and marshes.

As an added attraction, another road through the woods spins through a fast 2½-mile double-track and heads deep into the heart of the region's surrounding forests. This route can be explored as a loop and is a bit more demanding than the Paradise Road route. It's well worth the effort. Both trails traverse the Pequannock Watershed, located in the forested and water-rich Highland region of northern New Jersey, known for its scenic and historic resources. The region provides habitat for a broad variety of birds, mammals, fish, and reptiles, and supports recreational uses for the general public. It is managed through a controlled access program by the nonprofit Newark Watershed Conservation and Development Corporation (NWCDC), which was established to preserve the area's scenic and recreational qualities. The Pequannock Watershed is very large, covering almost 35,000 acres of land. This natural area is made up of many smaller watersheds which collect precipitation and channel water to the Newark water supply system. Numerous trail opportunities, including single-track, double-track, and old roads, traverse the region. A special permit must be purchased before using these lands, which are popular with hunters, anglers, and hikers. There are many surprises for the curious. These rides pack it all in for a full day of fun and wilderness exploration.

General location: Located in northern New Jersey, south of Wawayanda State Park and north on NJ 23, near the town of Stockholm.

Elevation change: Paradise Road begins at 1,000' and gently rolls up and down, dead-ending at 1,200'. The alternate forest road loop trail begins at 1,100' and climbs to 1,200', where the trail levels out and then descends back to 1,100'. The maze consists of some small hills that vary between 1,100' and 1,300'.

Season: January to the end of September provides the best riding. This region usually sees plenty of snow and cold weather. The hard-pack dirt road doesn't get too soft after rains and can be ridden in wet weather, but the alternate forest road loop may get muddy in places and grow big puddles. Hunting season usually begins about September 30, but check with the NWCDC for more up-to-date details.

Services: There are many services along NJ 23 on your way up to the Pequannock region. Outdoor outfitters and food stores can be found along this popular scenic thoroughfare. There are no stores once you head up Clinton Road to the trailhead.

Hazards: If you insist on riding during hunting season, make sure you don't wear white. You might be mistaken for a white-tailed deer, which is the prime hunting target, so be safe and wear the bright orange hunting colors. It's always recommended to stop in at the NWCDC Office at Echo Lake to get the latest word on the watershed. During the summer months, don't forget to bring bug repellent.

Rescue index: Paradise Road has a simple layout. You go in one direction and return the same way. The alternate forest road loop tour could be a little more tricky, so pay attention to the trail description below. You'll encounter other trails on the way that are not mapped, so if you go exploring, just make a note of your starting point and return to it after your little discovery journey is finished. You are never more than 3 miles from Clinton Road. It is well traveled, and there is usually some traffic passing by.

Land status: Pequannock Watershed, owned by the city of Newark, is managed by the nonprofit Newark Watershed Conservation and Development Corporation (NWCDC). The land was purchased by the city of Newark in the 1900s to provide clean water to Newark and its neighbors.

In order to provide and conserve these natural resources, continued conservation maintenance of the region is required. Newark's stewardship of the area has provided a means to control access and monitor impact in order to preserve land that is unique and ecologically sensitive and that provides habitat for a diverse wildlife. The requirement of permits is one of the ways in which controlled access can help moderate the human impact and at the same time sustain the wide range of recreational uses by the general public.

Maps: The NWCDC provides you with a general map of the area after you purchase your permit, either by mail or in person at their office at 223 Echo Lake Road. The New York–New Jersey Trail Conference's "North Jersey Trails Western Portion," Trail Map 21, provides very good detail of the

Pequannock Watershed and is waterproof and tearproof. It sells for $6.95 and can be found at most outdoor-type stores. USGS, 7.5 minute series, Newfoundland quadrangle also provides coverage.

Finding the trail: Take Interstate 80 west from the George Washington Bridge to Exit 53/NJ 23. Take Route 23 (north) for about 17 miles and turn right onto Clinton Road. Follow this road north for 1.2 miles. Turn left on Schoolhouse Cove Road, a gravel road with good views of Clinton Reservoir. After 1 mile, make a right turn onto Paradise Road. Proceed .1 mile, and you'll see a small parking area on your right with a small wooden stake with "P9" labeled on it. This is parking area P9. Leave your car here.

Sources of additional information: Biking in this area is by permit only. To obtain further information call or write:

> Pequannock Watershed
> Newark Watershed Conservation and Development Corporation
>   (NWCDC)
> P.O. Box 319
> 223 Echo Lake Road
> Newfoundland, New Jersey 07435
> (201) 697-2850

> Newark Watershed Conservation and Development Corporation
>   (NWCDC)
> 40 Clinton Street
> Newark, New Jersey 07102
> (201) 697-2850

Notes on the trail: Just before you turn off onto Schoolhouse Cove Road from Clinton Road, notice an old stone structure to your right located alongside Clinton Brook. This is the remains of the Clinton Furnace, one of the very few surviving furnaces used during the region's iron-making period and built near the running water of Clinton Brook, which was necessary to power the waterwheel-driven bellows. Notice also the series of waterfalls immediately to the side of Clinton Furnace. This provided substantial energy to keep the furnace fired up and burning for months at a time. The iron ore was loaded from the top, and so the furnace's location is at a lower level than the road.

You can ride along the out-and-back Paradise Road and turn back at about the 3.5-mile point, which will tally 7 miles. The road is wide and fairly easy to follow. Return to the parking area and try your wheels on the alternate forest road loop, which leads from the parking area.

If you have chosen to ride on the alternate old forest road, many combinations can be put together. I will describe one loop which will begin from the parking area, head into the forest on the old wood road, and then loop around, emptying out onto Paradise Road only .2 mile from the parking area.

I was quite surprised when I discovered that one. I had been riding for a good hour and came out onto this dirt road, which I thought looked familiar. So I turned left and in 2 turns of my crank, there was my car.

The basic scheme of this ride is to head in from the parking area. The trail is obvious as a wide, double-track road. You soon come to a fork. The trail bearing to your right is a short trail that hugs the western shore of Clinton Reservoir and provides nice views of this large body of water but is only rideable for about half a mile. It was originally used by the Civilian Conservation Corps during the Depression in the 1930s as a horse trail.

Bear left at the fork up a small hill along a rocky trail. The trail levels and smooths out soon and continues on past an old stone house. At the T intersection about 1.5 miles into the ride, turn left and take this wide dirt road for about 2 miles until it ends at a larger, smoother dirt road. This is Paradise Road. Turn left and in a blink of an eye, there's your car.

RIDE 29 *HIGH POINT STATE PARK*

This dated north-south forest road trail rests along the crest of the Kittatinny Mountains located in Sussex County in the northwest corner of New Jersey. It passes through a very scenic forest packed with oaks, hickory, red maple, white ash, and young chestnut. The 14,056-acre state park is tantalizing, with its breathtaking scenery and breath-stealing double-track. High Point State Park within the Kittatinny Mountains boasts New Jersey's highest peak, High Point, at 1,803 feet, and a challenging double-track trail system. The dominating part of this tour is the five-mile (one-way) Iris Trail (described below), but two other short trails are worth mentioning and exploring. The black-marked Ayers Trail is only 1.5 miles in length, passing an old farm built after the Civil War. The one-mile, yellow-marked Mashipacong Trail traverses an old farm road lined with the foundations and stone fences of long-gone houses and farms and overgrown apple orchards. The not-too-difficult Iris Trail runs through deep woods on abandoned logging and farm roads that have resulted in rugged trails. The route serves as a popular snowmobile and cross-country ski trail in the winter. This tour is not for the weak of heart. Keep a light touch on the brakes; the trail requires some technical handling as you traverse the rocky surface of the eroded road beds.

The trail descends through a varied hardwood forest, crosses springs, and supplies a scenic overlook of picturesque Lake Rutherford. The return trip is demanding. An alternative could be the paved Deckertown Turnpike, County Road 650, and Sawmill Road, which, although just as steep, would avoid the ascent up the rocky Iris Trail.

Cool off during the summer in the spring-fed 20-acre natural Lake Marcia, almost 1,600 feet above sea level. Lake Marcia also has changing areas, showers, and a food concession.

General location: High Point State Park is located in the extreme northwest corner of New Jersey along the ridge of the Kittatinny Mountains in Sussex County and extends from the New York state line southwesterly 8 miles, where it joins Stokes State Forest. It is approximately 70 miles from Manhattan.

Elevation change: The trail begins at approximately 1,500' and descends to Lake Rutherford at an elevation of 1,400' over 1.5 miles. The trail continues to descend over the next 3.5 miles to an elevation of 1,200', whereupon you must turn around and head back up the trail.

Season: Winter in this section of New Jersey and at these elevations, usually guarantees snow, but cold weather has never kept me away from riding in the woods, so if there's no snow, I'd say year-round riding is possible. During early spring, the trails tend to get wet from snow-melt runoff and rains, but a quick call to the park office will inform you of the trail conditions.

Services: A concession stand near Lake Marcia and the town of Sussex is located on NJ 23, 8 miles before the park, and provides most services. There are some excellent accommodations if you would like to camp overnight in the park. There are over 50 tent campsites set along Sawmill Lake, with sanitary facilities and drinking water nearby. Reservations may also be made for 2 remotely located wilderness cabins on the shore of Steenykill Lake which are open from May 15 to October 15. They have 3 bedrooms, full kitchens, and a bathroom with hot water.

Hazards: Even though this is an old forest road, erosion has exposed an abundance of rocks and tree roots, so check your speed when encountering such areas. Ticks can be a problem if you go off the trail, so it is generally recommended that you stay on the trails. These are moderately strenuous trails, so before you set out, make sure you saddle up with some water and energy food.

Rescue index: An increase of activity on these trails occurs between May and September, and help from another trail user is usually available. A first-aid station is open during the summer near Lake Marcia, but it is a good idea to bring a small first-aid kit with you any time you ride.

Land status: The park is managed by New Jersey State Park Service.

Maps: Call the park to receive a park map in the mail or wait till you get there and pick up one in the park headquarters building.

Finding the trail: Although far from New York City, the riding possibilities are well worth the trip. The park can be reached by beginning your 70-mile journey on Interstate Route 80 in New Jersey west from the George Washington Bridge. Take scenic NJ 23 north all the way to the park entrance and turn left into High Point State Park. Lake Marcia can be reached by turning right

RIDE 29 HIGH POINT STATE PARK

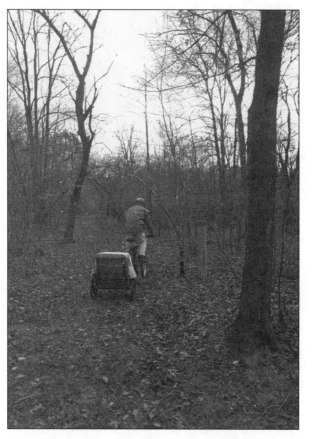

Uh, let's see, the sign says Chicago to the left and Boston to the right.

into High Point State Park, but turn left into the park and leave your car near the park office headquarters on your left.

Source of additional information:

High Point State Park
1480 State Route 23
Sussex, New Jersey 07461-3605
(201) 875-4800

Notes on the trail: At the southerly end of the parking area near the park office headquarters will be a small, brown, wooden shed used for the storage of firewood. Immediately beyond this shed, a yellow-marked trail can be seen leading off into the woods. Follow this trail for a short distance until it merges with a trail marked with painted white blazes. Bear right as the trails merge and after approximately .2 mile you will arrive at a 3-way intersection with yellow, red, and white marked trails. Take the leftmost wider trail marked with red disks. As a secondary reference, there will also be a 3'-high cement marker with the name "Iris Trail" painted on it. Secondary insurance always helps. The trail follows the rock-studded, eroded roadbed over rolling terrain and passes by Lake Rutherford. As you pass by Lake Rutherford, notice the stumps and rotten logs in and around the lake. These are all that remain from the American chestnut blight of the 1920s, which destroyed the great fruit-bearing chestnut forests of the northeast. The current chestnut tree has been stunted to a height of only 20'.

In the next 2.5 miles you will begin a more noticeable gradual descent to Deckertown Turnpike, CR 650. You may turn back the way you came or turn right on Deckertown Turnpike, and in 2 miles, turn right again on Sawmill Road. Sawmill will take you back to NJ 23 and the park office headquarters. You may also want to try the two alternative rides which can be accessed from Sawmill Road.

The black-marked Ayers and yellow-marked Mashipacong trails are old farm roads that lead off to your left about 4 miles up Sawmill Road, past the second road leading from the Sawmill Lake camping area. Pass the Sawmill Lake camping area and take a left onto Ayers Trail. The 1.5-mile Ayers Trail cuts through a large hardwood forest filled with oaks, hickory, red maple, and some young chestnut. You will pass through the fields and the site of Ayers farm built after the Civil War. The stone walls and fallen foundations are all that remain today. Take Ayers Trail until it **T** intersects with paved Park Ridge Road. Turn right on Park Ridge Road, and then after a mile turn right onto the yellow-marked Mashipacong Trail, which then travels in an easterly direction. Mashipacong Trail is an old, well-used farm road that takes you through a large overgrown field, fence rows, and apple trees. Follow this trail all the way to NJ 23. It leaves you a short distance south of the park office headquarters.

RIDE 30 *THE LABYRINTH*

There's a whole day's worth of cruising in the labyrinth of interconnecting trails in the 4,000-acre Ringwood State Park. With any spare time, consider a tour of the historic Tudor mansions of Ringwood and Skylands and the botanical gardens.

This trail system, like a maze, consists of hard-packed nineteenth-century carriage roads leading through a beautiful wooded landscape with five attractive ponds. An eight-mile loop trail leads along an interesting yet challenging route that is also beginner-friendly. It meanders through a moderately hilly landscape and doesn't require any special technical skills, but it gives the

Shepherd
Lake

Glasmere
Ponds

Weyble
Pond

Gatum
Pond

Brushwood
Pond

RINGWOOD
STATE PARK

N

0   1/4   1/2
MILES

NJ

experienced mountain biker a good workout. The ride is also suited for novices ready to try something more demanding than a flat trail but seeking an endurance test on more hilly terrain. What once provided turn-of-the-century visitors with a horse-drawn carriage tour through a beautiful woodland forest now enchants the mountain biker with stretches of demanding hill climbs, fast, descending double-track, and beautiful scenery.

Ringwood State Park is situated within the Hudson Highlands, a large, ancient mountain range that extends from Pennsylvania to Connecticut in a northeasterly direction. The range was formed over 1 billion years ago when continents collided and caused a huge mountain system to rise along the North American coast. These mountains once looked similar to the Himalayas in Asia, but 500 million years of erosion have leveled them to their roots, which extend miles deep within the earth. The remaining hills and small mountains are the result of these roots getting pushed up and creating the Highlands.

The Hudson Highlands were mined from the eighteenth to twentieth centuries, bringing great wealth to the industrialists in this region. Forges and furnaces were constructed during the middle of the eighteenth century to supply the metal products crucial to the colonies. George Washington made Ringwood his headquarters on several occasions. Ownership of the land and mansions was passed on for generations. Ringwood Manor, located in the park and on the surrounding land, is a fine example of the splendor and wealth of the ironmasters of the nineteenth century. The botanical gardens were inspired by the classical designs on the grounds of the famous Palace of Versailles in France. Iron for munitions for every major armed conflict from the French and Indian War to World War I was forged here. The Ringwood iron mines operated intermittently from the 1920s until they ceased operations in 1957. Spend a day exploring the myriad of trails and, if time allows, visit the Ringwood or Skylands mansions.

General location: Northeast Passaic County near the town of Ringwood.
Elevation change: These are mountains. You should expect some hills and valleys with elevations ranging from 600' to 1,000'.
Season: The trails are available from late spring until the first snows. After heavy rains or melting snowpacks, the roads tend to get very muddy. Ringwood State Park doesn't prohibit use of the muddy trails. However, use your own discretion as to whether or not the trails should be ridden during these periods.
Services: Concession services near the Ringwood Manor House are available from Memorial Day to Labor Day weekends. Boating and bathing is available from Memorial Day weekend through Labor Day weekend at the 74-acre Shephard Lake.
Hazards: Ringwood State Park does permit hunting in designated areas, but to avoid being in the wrong place at the wrong time, call the park office to get the dates when you should stay away.

Old stone ruins at Ringwood State Park.

Rescue index: In terms of getting lost, many trails are marked improperly or not marked at all. You may feel that it's very easy to lose your way with so many trails, intersections, and choices. Many times I stopped another rider and asked where they had come from and was told that they weren't quite sure, that they had been riding for a few hours but were confident they would end up back at the parking area. On most weekends there will be plenty of trail users to stop and ask questions of and hopefully they will give you more information than the riders I met. All the trails eventually do lead back to Honeysuckle Lane and the parking areas that are located along it. Stay on the wide dirt roads and keep descending. There are ranger services at the Ringwood Manor House for an emergency. During the hunting season, certain areas are off limits, so check with the park ranger for exact details. During hunting season, Sunday is always a day of quietude for the hunters, which means it's a day you should get on the trails.

Land status: The park is managed by the New Jersey Division of Parks and Forestry. There is a $3 fee for parking from Memorial Day to Labor Day.

Maps: You may call the park office to inquire if they can send you a free park map in the mail. The New York–New Jersey Trail Conference "North Jersey Trails Western Portion," Trail Map 22, provides good detail as well. The Trail Conference maps sell for $6.95 and are available from most outdoor-type retail stores, such as Eastern Mountain Sports.

Finding the trail: The park can be reached by taking the New York State Thruway, Interstate 87, to Exit 15-A. This exit leads you onto NY 17. Take

NY 17 north and turn left (west) onto Sloatsburg Road. Go past Ringwood Manor and turn left on Morris Road, going past Hewitt School and Carletondale Road. Skylands Manor House of Ringwood State Park is 1.5 miles up Morris Road at the top of the hill. Go through the tollgate and try to park at parking area A. If by chance that is full, use parking field B.

Source of additional information:

Ringwood State Park
RD Box 1304
Ringwood, New Jersey 07456
(201) 962-7031 or (201) 962-7047

Notes on the trail: Regardless of the parking area, pedal down the park road and return to the tollgate you passed when you came into the park. After the tollgate, turn right going toward Shepard Lake. Turn right again at the stop sign; a wide dirt road leads off beyond the area of the boat rental building. Proceed along this route, which is marked with faint red paint blazes. All of these trails are on wide, four-wheel-drive, jeep paths used as equestrian bridle paths, mountain bike paths, and hunting vehicle routes. The trail hugs the southern shore of Shepard Lake and you will soon come to a 3-way fork. The right fork and middle fork eventually merge into one trail. The right fork takes you up a steep hill with a screaming descent, and the left fork leads you on a more gently rolling ride along the shoreline.

From the point at which these two trails merge, continue straight until you come to a clearing. There will be a high-pressure gas pipe indicator made out of white plastic. Here again are another 3 forks. Take the right fork. You will soon come across 2 ancient stone buildings with a stone archway where the trail passes beneath. Go through the archway and continue straight for a short while and make a left at an intersection with a trail blazed with green paint on the trees. The mileage up to this intersection is about 4 miles.

Proceed on a gradual climb on this green-blazed trail until you come to a large intersection. Notice a trail to your left leading in a northeast direction up an incline. This is the continuation of the green-blazed trail and switches back in the direction you just came, continuing in a steady climb up the mountain. Bear right around the next bend in the trail as the trail continues to climb. At about 6.1 miles, you come to another intersection with a trail leading off to your left. Continue straight and start a descent. Weyble Pond will appear on your left. Bear left at the next fork. Proceed past a small pond on your right and take a right on the next dirt road immediately past this pond. This trail descends past an old stone wall on your right. Keep descending and soon you will approach Gatum Pond, where you bear right at a fork that switches you onto a trail marked with white paint blazes. This white trail descends for a short while and intersects with another trail. Turn right and then make a quick left to remain on the white trail. This intersection is about

7 miles from the start. Fork right at the next intersection following the white trail markers and continue straight at the next intersection, always remaining on the white trail. At the next 4-way intersection, continue straight up a small steep hill, remain straight, and bear left at the next 3 forks. You should end up at parking area B, near Swan Pond. This is Honeysuckle Lane. Turn right and continue past the botanical gardens to parking area A.

RIDE 31   *WAWAYANDA YAHOO*

Wawayanda is a beautiful 10,000-acre state park in the New Jersey Highlands. Laced with centuries-old logging roads and natural beauty, this park provides a wild and magnificent setting for mountain biking. A moderately challenging eight-mile loop trail along a road through the woods leads to a pristine forest of large rock outcrops, evergreens, hardwoods, and wetlands.

Beginners will be put to the test by trails that loop around small hills, dip into creek valleys, climb rolling ridge crests, and skirt major hilltops. Gonzo gearheads, when not blasting along on some smooth double-track, may have time to appreciate the interesting natural arena. While riding, notice how the forest changes from the dark, shady evergreens to zones of tall hardwoods. It's a varied and unique woodscape dotted with trees, ponds, boulders, and streams. Up and down the small ravines, the woodscape switches from the conifer-dominant wetland forest of lower valleys to the hardwood sections of the higher plateau.

Since Wawayanda is nestled in the Ramapo Mountains, one expects larger hills and mountains throughout the park, but the 10,000 acres appear to reside on a plateau. It is not a plateau in the geological sense. Rather, it's a level mountain top with elevations around 1,200 and 1,300 feet. The riding is challenging and there are many trails available. Most are fairly level and serve as cross-country skiing routes when there is snow. Another great feature is that Wawayanda Lake provides some great boating and swimming. Mountain bikers should bring their nonbiker friends.

The name Wa-wa-yanda, from the Lenape Indians, means "water on the mountain." It's a reference to the 255-acre lake with almost six miles of wooded shoreline and the other lakes and ponds found on top of the mountain. The park contains a maze of old logging roads that are testament to the heavy logging during the 1940s.

In the beginning of the ride, you'll see an old charcoal furnace—all that remains of New Jersey's iron ore industry in Wawayanda. Built in 1846, it was used to smelt the iron ore from local mines. It operated continuously for ten years until cheap coal became available in Pennsylvania, making it more

RIDE 31 *WAWAYANDA YAHOO*

economic to transport the ore for smelting to the hotter and more efficient furnaces. On an average day, seven tons of iron would be produced from this type of furnace and would be poured off at noon and midnight. Wawayanda iron was of such superior quality that it was used to manufacture railroad wheels. During the Civil War, shovels and swords were forged. During the time of greatest activity, a small village developed in the vicinity to house the workers and provide services such as a post office, store, gristmill, and sawmill. The village has since disappeared, and the chatter of wildlife has brought back the natural solitude of the area. The miles of old logging roads left behind from another era provide an opportunity to access a historic and pristine forest environment. Spend a day at Wawayanda silently gliding through the woods.

General location: The park is located along the New York border in Sussex and Passaic counties. The main entrance to the park is located on Warwick Turnpike approximately 3 miles north of Upper Greenwood Lake.

Elevation change: The Wawayanda "plateau" is not a geological plateau but rather a flat-topped mountain ridge with elevations ranging from 1,200' to 1,300'. The majority of trails described in this ride explore old wooded roads that reside at those elevations.

Season: From mid-April to the first snows. Due to the higher elevation of the Wawayanda "plateau," snows can arrive early. If there is no snow, do not let winter's cold stop you; just put on more clothing and enjoy the solitude. During the summer months, try not to arrive too long after 9 A.M. to be sure of a parking space.

Services: Greenwood Lake provides most food and gas services along Warwick Turnpike. During the summer, you can cool off in Wawayanda Lake at the lifeguard-protected bathing beach. This picturesque location provides a great rest spot to cool off your tires and grab some concession food.

Hazards: Some equestrians and hikers use these trails as well, so the usual courtesy should be extended to these other trail users. At this point there are no conflicts. Remember that your actions as a rider have a great deal to do with any policy of sharing multiuse trails. On weekends the trails are popular, so exercise some caution when zipping down the hills because other trail users may be zipping down the trail too.

Rescue index: You are within a well-used park. The well-marked trails are within 3 miles of the park office. Help is never too far away.

Land status: New Jersey State Park.

Maps: The New York–New Jersey Trail Conference's "North Jersey Trails Western Portion," Trail Map 21, provides good detail of Wawayanda Park and is waterproof and tearproof. It sells for $6.95 and can be found at most outdoor-type stores. USGS, 7.5 minute series, Wawayanda quadrangle also provides coverage.

Finding the trail: Take Interstate 80 west from the George Washington Bridge to Exit 53, which will lead to Route 23. Take Route 23 north for about 16 miles and turn right onto Echo Road, NJ 513. Follow NJ 513 north to its end and turn left (west) onto Macopin. Continue for about 4 miles and bear left at a fork onto Union Valley Road. The fork is obvious, but extra landmarks are the gas station on the right and the small shopping center on the opposite side. At the next fork bear left onto White Road. You will see a sign for Wawayanda State Park. This road will end at a stop sign and intersection with Warwick Turnpike. Turn left onto Warwick Turnpike and continue to the Wawayanda Park entrance on your left. Enter the park. Between Memorial Day and Labor Day weekends, a parking fee of $5 for weekdays and $7 for weekends and holidays is charged. Continue past the toll booth and take the park road until you see the large parking area near the beach. Turn left into this parking area. There is a park office at the entrance if you need additional maps or other information.

Source of additional information:

Wawayanda State Park
PO Box 198
Highland Lakes, New Jersey 07422
(201) 853-4462

Notes on the trail: If you have parked near Wawayanda Lake beach area, the trail begins beyond the wooden barrier between the beach and the parking area. There are usually people walking, riding, or running on this portion of the trail. Turn left onto this trail and follow it as it passes through another parking area for boat rentals. Keep hugging the lake's shoreline and continue straight and a bit to the left as you pass a stone dam at the end of the lake. You will soon come to the remnants of the old charcoal furnace at a 4-way intersection. It had been used at Wawayanda for the manufacture of shovels and railroad car wheels. Continue across the road. You will be returning from the trail that leads off to your right.

Cross a wooden bridge and fork right as you enter a small campground. Turn right at the next turn and then make another quick right; you'll notice a green metal barrier with a beautiful forest road leading beyond it. Go past the green barrier and pick up a trail that is marked by yellow paint blazes on the trees. This trail is known as Double Pond Road. Proceed up a small incline where the wide road soon levels out through an attractive hemlock forest, and after about 1.5 miles cross a small wooden bridge spanning a small stream. This is one of the many streams that carve and drain south from the New Jersey Highlands. Soon after the bridge, turn right at the next intersection onto a red-marked trail. Take this trail south through an attractive hemlock forest. If you would like to add another 4 miles onto this loop, do not turn right onto the red trail but continue along the yellow-marked Double Pond for about another 1.5 miles. You will arrive at a parking area. Turn south onto another yellow-marked trail known as Banker Trail. Take

Somewhere in the middle of Wawayanda's glorious nowhere.

this south for another 2 miles where it ends at the wider four-wheel-drive Cherry Ridge Road. Turn right onto Cherry Ridge Road and follow it in a general northwesterly direction. You will soon come to the exit point to which the red trail leads you.

So now let's continue down the red-marked trail. After a while, you will come to a fork where the red trail seems to go left and right. Bear right at this fork. Ride for a bit more and then you come out of the hemlocks into a clearing, where again the red trail goes left and right. Turn right, continuing in a southerly direction. At about 3 miles from the beginning of the ride, you will come to a fork. The red trail leads to your left and returns to Double Pond Road. Bear right onto the unmarked trail in a southwesterly direction. In about .3 mile, a stream will appear on your right with a small rock bridge across it. Carry your bike over this rock bridge and continue on the unmarked trail as it picks up on the other side of the stream. A single-track leads up and away from the stream and eventually opens up into a four-wheel-drive trail. In a little less than a mile, you come to a **T** intersection with the wider Cherry Ridge Road.

Turn right onto Cherry Ridge Road. At about .2 mile turn right at the **T** intersection, heading in a northerly direction. Ride for another .4 mile and arrive at a larger intersection. The yellow-blazed Laurel Pond Trail leads north through a beautiful forest of beech, elm, and hemlock. The trail descends for a small distance, levels off, and then begins a steady climb to an elevation of about 1,370'. You will pass a large ravine on your right lined with huge boulders. They have been split and fractured many times and now have trees growing in their cracks. Notice the 1,375' rocky ridge of an unnamed peak farther ahead to your left. It's all downhill from this point on. You pass a small blue-marked trail leading to your left. Continue straight on the yellow trail, which eventually leads into the 4-way intersection where the old furnace is located. At the furnace turn left and head up the hill between 2 wooden fence posts. This will return you to the Wawayanda Lake beach parking area.

Westchester Area Tours

As you cycle along the many paths throughout the parks and wilderness regions of Westchester County, it's hard to believe that the Native American Algonkian tribes or European Dutch settlers encamped along the same routes you will explore on these tours. Native Americans cut trails through the primitive forests for the purpose of establishing seasonal hunting routes. The European pioneers built dirt roads for transporting supplies and linking their tiny settlements to the larger populated city of New York.

Imagine yourself as an adventurer, a modern-day Henry Hudson, who in 1609 sailed up the river that now bears his name. There were no million-dollar homes, no highways, no corporate headquarters in Westchester back then. Just beautiful hills and valleys, fertile lands, and the promise of a bountiful future.

By 1664, others had sensed the area's great opportunities. The imperialist English took over the region from the Dutch and settlements grew as the Royal Governor granted large tracts of land, known as lordships or manors, to ambitious pioneers and settlers. Westchester County became a magnet for settlers forming small villages, manors, and subsistence farms, the precursors of today's towns and localities. It became the most prosperous county in the colony of New York, and ultimately, as centuries passed, one of the wealthiest counties in the United States.

The setting, however idyllic through most of its history, became war-torn on October 18th, 1776, when the British army and the American Revolutionaries fought at the Battle of Pelham. The earlier Native American and pioneer encampments became those of the British and American troops. General George Washington camped for six weeks in Westchester as part of his strategy to defeat the British.

With the war ending, the small farms of Westchester returned to productivity, taverns and inns opened their doors to weary and hungry travelers, and the county's charm was restored. One unusual industry which developed in northeastern Westchester in the 1820s was the traveling animal menagerie. The area was the birthplace of the American circus of Barnum and Bailey. The county began to change from an agricultural to an industrial economy after 1850 as factories were built along the Hudson and Bronx rivers and along the Long Island Sound. The iron industry developed in Croton and Peekskill, employing large numbers of immigrant laborers from central and eastern Europe. The need for water by New York City led to the county's huge dam and aqueduct projects built primarily by Irish and Italian laborers.

Southeastern New York is dominated by the Hudson River, which flows past the wonders of its cities and industries. At the same time, the river touches some of the state's wilder lands, where the mountain biker can quickly escape the centers of civilization that dot the Hudson's banks. This area includes a variety of rides that will introduce you to the best of southeastern New York's wild lands not far from the Hudson.

Trains to the trails: Transportation service by rail to some of the towns where the trails reside can be found on the commuter trains of the Metro North Railroad. Traveling on the trains with a bicycle requires a $5 bike pass and the obligatory passenger fare. The bike pass, by the way, is good for life. To acquire a pass, go to Window 27 at the Grand Central Terminal or call (212) 340-2176 to request an application. Train service schedules can be found at most train stations.

Various restrictions apply for individuals portaging bikes on the trains.

Bikes cannot be carried on the trains during New Year's Eve, New Year's Day, St. Patrick's Day, Mother's Day, Rosh Hashanah Eve, Thanksgiving Eve, Thanksgiving Day, Yom Kippur Eve, Christmas Eve, and Christmas Day, or between the hours of 12 P.M. and 8 P.M. on the Fridays or day before Memorial Day, July Fourth, and Labor Day weekends.

Weekday restrictions apply during the rush-hour commuting periods. No bikes are allowed on departing trains from Grand Central between 7 A.M. and 9 A.M., and 3 P.M. and 8 P.M. No bikes are allowed on arriving trains into Grand Central between 6 A.M. and 10 A.M., and 4 P.M. and 7 P.M. For all other questions call Metro North, (212) 340-2176.

RIDE 32 *BEDFORD COUNTRY ROAD RAMBLE*

This ride tours the hilly, hard-packed country backroads that weave through the village of Bedford in Westchester County. It's of medium difficulty. Perhaps it's a blessing that it's not a technical ride because of the wonderful scenery— the working horse farms, magnificent country estates, nineteenth-century homesteads, and historic landmarks along more than 25 miles of wide roads. The beauty of this New England–type village and surrounding countryside is better appreciated with an easy cruising ride like this. It's classic New England countryside down country lanes that intersect and tempt further exploration. This tour consists of a variety of roads which form an 11-mile loop.

Many of these roads double as bridle paths and are labeled with yellow markers on trees. These markers have a black arrow pointing in the direction that the bridle path follows and are marked with the letters "BRLA" for Bedford Riding Lanes Association. Since cars travel on these roads, keep your eyes and ears open when rounding a blind curve. When approaching horses, be careful not to spook them by riding too close to them or by coming up fast on them from either direction on the road.

These country roads were once part of a parcel of land that had been purchased from Chief Katonah in 1680. Old Post Road passes by the town

RIDE 32   *BEDFORD COUNTRY ROAD RAMBLE*

common, a small triangular park in front of the post office which was the original center of the village. Several village streets date back to this period. Bedford was one of the most important towns in northern Westchester during the American Revolution. American Revolutionary forces marched through Bedford to defeat the British at Yorktown.

Many old wood paths penetrate pristine wilderness areas and make great mountain biking routes. Moreover, these routes are unique. They have a rare, heavy historical flavor extending 300 years into the past.

General location: Approximately 30 miles north of Manhattan; Exit 4 off Interstate 684.

Elevation change: Although the roads are hard and compact, the riding is made more challenging by the short, steep climbs up the many hills throughout the area. However, the scenic rewards and sense of history are well worth the effort.

Season: This is an all-season territory, and with a little snow blanketing the ground the serenity of these old houses is splendid.

Services: Most services can be found in the town of Bedford. If you're in the mood for some snacks and home-baked cakes and brownies, stop by the deli facing the town common on Old Post Road.

Hazards: These roads are shared by people out for a stroll, groups of equestrian riders, bicycles, and cars. If you intend to tuck and burn down a hill with all that wind rushing past your ears, pay close attention around the turns, for you may not be able to hear the cars.

Rescue index: The roads are well traveled and you might be able to flag someone down. Bedford Village is never more than 2 miles away.

Land status: Town roads in the village of Bedford.

Maps: Hagstrom's "Upper Westchester County," which costs $2.75, provides sufficient detail for this ride and is available in most book stores.

Finding the trail: Take the Hutchinson River Parkway north to I-684 and take Exit 4. Turn right (east) onto NY 172 and left (north) onto NY 22, proceeding into Bedford Village. Park anywhere that allows parking. Take your bike and get back onto NY 22 going north. Shortly after the town you will come to the intersection of NY 22 and NY 121. Begin your tour with a left onto Guard Hill Road directly across from NY 121.

Source of additional information:

> Westchester County Department of Parks
> Recreation and Conservation
> 19 Bradhurst Avenue
> Hawthorne, New York 10532
> (914) 593-PARK

Notes on the trail: Head down Guard Hill Road, passing beautiful old farms and estates and bearing right at the first intersection. Continue up a small hill and turn right onto Narrows Road. Take that fine country road for about 1 mile to its end at Bedford Center Road. For a small 3-mile detour, turn right and then left at Davids Hill Road, bearing right until it ends at Harris Road. Turn right onto paved Harris Road, heading downhill. At it's end, turn right on Bedford Center Road. You have just made a small detoured loop.

Continuing on Bedford Center Road, pass Davids Hill Road (which you just took for this loop) and in under a mile, bear left onto Broad Brook Road as you come to a bend in the road that bears right. Continuing on Broad Brook

Road you may make a left onto Succabone Road to shorten the 11-mile loop by 3 miles or continue straight ahead and turn left at West Patent Road. Both these roads lead back to Guard Hill Road, which you can then take all the way back to where you started.

Take some extra time and explore Succabone Road, Clark Road, Clinton Road, and Fox Lane. They all pass through magnificent countryside.

RIDE 33 *CLARENCE FAHNESTOCK MEMORIAL STATE PARK*

There are a variety of trails in this 6,500-acre state park, located in the northern half of the Highlands, only 50 miles north of Manhattan. The rolling terrain is crisscrossed by forest roads, bridle paths, and nineteenth-century railroad beds and is sprinkled with several picturesque lakes. If you wish to get off the trails and into the water, Canopus Lake offers a beautiful sandy beach and boating facilities. This state park offers something for everyone. The four trail systems described in this chapter provide a wide range of riding opportunities. You can cruise on wide, hard-packed dirt roads and blast down some awesome single-track descents.

This wild and heavily wooded countryside consists of deep forests of tall hemlocks and maple stands among numerous lakes and marshes. Deer are numerous and beaver can be spotted in the swamps. The trail runs along the railroad beds built in 1862 to carry ore from the Sunk Mine to the Greenwood mine in Harriman Park. This ore was used for the Union Army artillery during the Civil War. The entire area was once the site of considerable activity and evidence of early settlements, and overgrown wood roads, cellar holes, and stone walls can be seen along the routes. Iron ore attracted miners in the early part of the nineteenth century. Mining survived until 1873. The surrounding land was purchased by Dr. Clarence Fahnestock in 1915 and then given to the state as a gift in 1929 by his son, Dr. Alfred Fahnestock, in memory of his father.

General location: Approximately 50 miles north of Manhattan, about 8 miles east of the historic town of Cold Spring.

Elevation change: The terrain is rolling with some short, steep hills.

Season: Due to the higher elevation of this park, there is greater exposure to snowstorms and cooler weather than the surrounding areas. Some fine riding can be found from late March to the first snows. If there is no snow on the ground in the winter months and you come prepared with warm clothes, the solitude on these trails is unparalleled. The extra effort it might take to get here on a cold morning will be worth the exhilarating experience you will come away with.

RIDE 33 CLARENCE FAHNESTOCK MEMORIAL STATE PARK

To N.Y.C.

NY

0   1/2   1
MILES

To Oscawana
Lake Road

Canopus Creek

Dirt Road

Dennytown Rd.

Services: Canopus Lake offers a concession stand, locker room, shower, and toilet facilities. Tent and trailer camping are available for those wishing to camp overnight. Boat rentals are also available. Main Street in the town of Cold Spring has some restaurants and delis.

Hazards: There is an unstated courtesy expected on multiuse trails such as the bridle paths. Hikers, equestrians, and mountain bikers at this point coexist in relative harmony. Let's keep it that way. When approaching horses, be careful not to spook them by riding close or fast from either direction on the road. Raccoon rabies are present in this area of New York, so do not approach or feed these animals in the park. If you do see an animal behaving strangely, please contact a member of the park staff.

Rescue index: The park receives a lot of visitors and is very popular with equestrians, hikers, and other bike riders. You are bound to run into someone on a trail. Besides, you will be about 2 miles from the well-traveled paved roads that surround the park.

Land status: New York State Park.

Maps: A vague park map is available free from the park services. The New York–New Jersey Trail Conference's "East Hudson Trails, #3" provides good detail of Clarence Fahnestock State Park and is waterproof and tearproof. It sells for $6.95 and can be found at most outdoor-type stores. The USGS, 7.5 minute series, Oscawana quadrangle also provides coverage.

The horse trails designated by a yellow disk with a horseshoe and horse's head in the center are easily followed.

Finding the trail: Take the Taconic State Parkway north and exit at NY 301 going west. There are 2 different parking locales in the park. The first parking locale can be reached just after you get onto NY 301. Turn left into the park and park at the end of the campsite road. This gives you access to the trails in the northern half of the park. The second locale offers two parking areas on Dennytown Road, which divides the lower southern half of the park. This gives you access to Sunk Mine Road and the horse trails that penetrate the southern half. I have listed 4 trails below, but there are numerous other possibilities for assembling your rides.

Sources of additional information:

Clarence Fahnestock State Park
RFD 2
Carmel, New York 10512-9802
(914) 225-7207

Taconic State Park and Recreation Commission
Old Post Road
Staatsburg, New York 12580
(914) 889-4100

Notes on the trail: The trails available throughout the park for biking are independent of each other and do not necessarily interconnect. I have listed 4 unique and distinctive trails worth exploring. They each offer a little different terrain and scenery. However, you can spend days just riding and discovering more.

Northern Locale: Turn left into the park entrance just after you exit the Taconic Parkway onto NY 301.

Trail 1: The trail begins at the south end of the parking area. The out-and-back mountain bike designated trail is roughly 2 miles in length, making it 4 miles total. It passes along the west shore of Stillwater Pond. This ride can be extended by turning left at its termination at the T intersection. Continue on the same horse trail for another 4 miles as it meanders in a southerly direction along the eastern spur of the park property. Fortunately, horses and mountain bikers understand each other in this state park, and a mutual respect of each other's rights on the trails is evident from encounters on the trails.

Trail 2: Get back onto NY 301 and turn right (east). Go about .9 mile past the Taconic Parkway intersection with Route 301 and start looking for a bridle/snowmobile path on your right leading in a southerly direction. If you pass the power lines, you have gone too far. This bridle and snowmobile trail is a little over 2 miles in length. It goes over moderately hilly terrain and ends on Dicktown Road. You may link with Trail 1 near Stillwater Pond by turning right onto Dicktown Road and gingerly crossing the Taconic Parkway. A path leads down to Stillwater Pond. Just beyond the west shore of the pond, you can pick up the horse trail from Trail 1. Head north and *voila,* you have completed the loop.

Southern Locale: Take NY 301 south and turn left onto Dennytown Road. There is a parking area just past Sunk Mine Road on your left.

Trail 3: This 8-mile loop tour follows along a 16'-wide, hard-packed, dirt, town road called Sunk Mine Road, descending and winding through the midsection of the park. There is an interesting spur trail about .9 mile from the start. It appears as a double-track trail on your left just after the small pond and follows a meandering brook. This abandoned mining road ascends to Sunk Mine. About 1.7 miles from the start, turn right onto the dirt Bell Hollow Road. Take this for about 2.5 miles as it follows along the Canopus Creek through a beautiful rugged ravine. Dennytown Road will come in from the north at an angle, so turn north and follow it for 2.7 miles to your parking area.

Trail 4: This trail begins across Dennytown Road from which Sunk Mine Road leads. Look for the circular, yellow, horse trail markers. This 5-mile loop includes 3 miles of single-track on a yellow-marked horse trail, with a 2-mile return along a scenic backcountry road. The trail takes you through quiet stands of pine, young tree growth, and mountain laurel. There are some small climbs along the horse trail, but the scenery is well worth the effort.

RIDE 34 INDIAN BROOK ROAD LOOP

Hard-packed country roads supply ample mileage to explore some of Putnam County's rolling terrain. Three country roads can be connected to form a nine-mile loop with a detour at an eighteenth-century tavern for a full-course meal. The Bird and Bottle Inn was established in 1761 before the Revolutionary War. It was an important stagecoach stop along Old Albany Post Road. The inn still retains the ambiance of the colonial era, with woodburning fireplaces, beamed ceilings, wide plank floors, and authentic antiques. Call ahead to reserve a table for brunch. Work off your eats by finishing the last leg of the trip. Pass by scenic ponds and stop by the Taconic Outdoor Education Center. Call to find out what programs are being sponsored. On one occasion, there were lectures on drawing sap from trees to make syrup.

General location: Approximately 50 miles north of Manhattan, about 8 miles east of the historical town of Cold Spring.

Elevation change: The terrain is rolling with some short, steep hills to climb, but mixed in are a fair share of reciprocal, well-earned descents.

Season: These roads are great in all seasons, and if the cold doesn't bother you, saddle up and get on the trail. These are wide, hard-packed dirt roads that provide access to many homesteads. Plowing during winter is almost always performed, and the compacted roads barely show a dent or any rutting during wet periods. If you can brave the cold, I wouldn't hesitate to get out there and enjoy a brisk morning ride, followed, of course, by some warm cider at the local tavern.

Services: Overnight lodging is available at the Bird and Bottle Inn. Each room is furnished with a working fireplace and is decorated with furnishings of the eighteenth century. The neighboring town of Cold Spring provides some restaurants and delis on Main Street as well as attractive antique and craft shops.

Hazards: These roads are not well traveled. However, there is the occasional vehicle here and there, so take care on blind turns and listen for oncoming cars.

Rescue index: You will always be able to flag down a car if needed or you can ask for help at one of the residential homes along the way.

Land status: County roads.

Maps: The New York–New Jersey Trail Conference's "East Hudson Trails, #3" provides good detail of Clarence Fahnestock State Park and is waterproof and tearproof. It sells for $6.95 and can be found at most outdoor-type stores. The USGS, 7.5 minute series, Oscawana quadrangle also provides coverage.

Finding the trail: Take the Taconic State Parkway north and exit at NY 301 going west. Look for Dennytown Road on your left in just under 4 miles and turn left. Parking can be found on your left in three quarters of a mile.

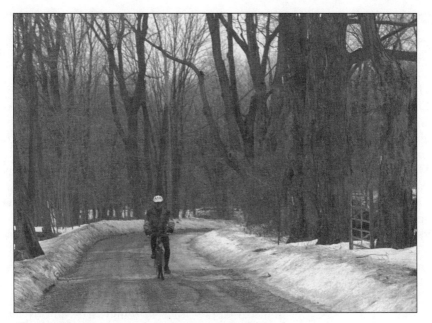

Ah, solitude. January on the Indian Brook Road Tour.

Source of additional information:

> New York–New Jersey Trail Conference (NY–NJTC)
> GPO Box 2250
> New York, New York 10116
> (212) 685-9699

Notes on the trail: After you park your car, return to Dennytown Road the way you came and turn left on Indian Brook Road. You will pass the Taconic Outdoor Education Center and Duck Pond. After about 3 mostly downhill miles, turn left at the stop sign and the Bird and Bottle Inn is directly on your right. A quick left onto Old Albany Post Road begins your return. The .6-mile ascent up Old Albany Post Road is a little demanding after having stopped at the inn, but the lovely homes will help distract you and keep your pedaling in good form as you climb the long, steady hill. When you reach the top after 1.5 miles, turn left onto Phillipse Brook Road, which at the time of this writing was marked with a road sign, and pass by an old farm with sheep. Take it to its end, where it meets up with Dennytown Road. Turn left and proceed uphill for about .2 mile. You should recognize the parking area coming up on your right.

RIDE 35 *THE MIANUS MAZE*

This unique trail system, located in the Mianus River Park near Greenwich, Connecticut, is a maze of single-track and hard-packed old carriage roads, a tantalizing network of mountain bike trails suitable for beginners and intermediates. It's all wrapped up in a primeval, densely forested park of only 220 acres, although the wealth of trails adds up to over 14 miles in linear distance. The five-mile loop trail described here is just one of the many configurations that can be created from this vast network of trails. There is just enough trail variety here to initiate the novice and invigorate the archetypal, total-bent dirt-head. The moderately hilly single-track has become a popular destination for local mountain bikers. Novices can cruise on the easy carriage roads through the park and the more technically inclined will find enough stream beds, rocks, and logs to cross and maneuver around. It makes for a full afternoon of riding. The scenery is packed with dense hardwood and conifer forests, and the trout-filled Mianus River runs through the park for over one mile.

Once in the park, the suburban sprawl that surrounds it is quickly left behind and this urban oasis takes on the dimensions of a full-scale wilderness with a large variety of flora and fauna. Large rock ridges and outcrops are found throughout the park and the forests consist of white pine, hemlock, willow, hickory, ash, birch, maples, and oak. Over 22 varieties of birds, including owls, hawks, and herons, live in these woods. Red fox, chipmunks, squirrels, and the white-tailed deer call this dense habitat home.

As you glide silently along the trails, think about the rich and colorful events that took place in the area that encompasses Mianus River Park. The river hosted the primitive cultures that settled and thrived in this region. Native Americans lived on the lands that surround the Mianus River long before the arrival of English and Dutch settlers in the seventeenth century. Fertile meadows stretched for miles along the river north and south of the Mianus Gorge, inviting settlements and leading to the creation of towns and villages.

Spend an afternoon riding the trails in Mianus River Park and share in this primeval wilderness.

General location: Greenwich, Connecticut.
Elevation change: There are some minor hills to climb and descend as you go over the ridges and into the stream valleys, but none exceed 100 feet.
Season: This is 4-season territory except during a snow cover.
Services: Most services can be found in the town of Greenwich.
Hazards: The park is beautiful and quite popular and is shared by other users, including hikers and equestrians. The current policy of trail usage is

managed by the individual, and for now the people involved in these activities coexist and respect each other's rights to use this special park. This implies that we, as mountain bikers, need to be sensitive while riding here. So let's keep the image of the eco-respectful mountain biker and use commonsense etiquette, and hopefully we will ensure our place on these trails.

Many ongoing projects are conducted throughout the park and are designed for preserving and developing the park's trail system. The Mianus Coalition is always looking for volunteers for their work crews to get out there and lend a helping hand. Write to them if you have the time and share in the work to protect this beautiful park.

Rescue index: This small park is surrounded by residential areas, and civilization is never more than 2 miles away.

Land status: The park is on municipal land shared by the town of Greenwich and the city of Stamford.

Maps: The map that accompanies this tour is one of the best for this park.

Finding the trail: The park is located approximately 40 miles from Manhattan. Take the New England Thruway north for about 24 miles and get off at Exit 5/ Riverside and Old Greenwich, in Connecticut. The exit ramp winds around and over the thruway. Turn left onto East Putnam Road, Route 1, going south. Continue on Route 1 just under a mile and turn right at the third traffic light onto River Road. At the stop sign turn right onto Valley Road. After about a mile, turn left onto Cognewaugh Road. Take Cognewaugh Road for 2 miles to a circular gravel parking area on the right side, just after Shannon Lane.

Sources of additional information:

The Mianus Coalition
116 Dean Street, Apt. B
Stamford, Connecticut 06902-6251
(203) 969-1183

Town of Greenwich Chamber of Commerce
21 West Putnam Avenue
Greenwich, Connecticut 06830
(203) 868-3500

Town of Greenwich Division of Parks and Trees
101 Field Point Road
Greenwich, Connecticut 06836-2540
(203) 622-7824

Greenwich Bicycle
40 West Putnam Avenue
Greenwich, Connecticut 06830
(203) 869-4141

RIDE 35 THE MIANUS MAZE

Note: ----------- = Stone Wall

NY

Private

Mianus River

Highest
Point
270

Mianus River

Merriebrook Lane

Swamp

Dam

Dry Lake

Cognewaugh Rd.

N

0   500   1000

FEET

A menagerie of landscape features shapes the primeval forest of Mianus River Park.

Notes on the trail: At the time of this writing the trails were not marked; there is quite an array of interconnecting trails, so try to follow the route description below.

From the parking area, a wide carriage road leads beyond a metal barrier in the northeast section of the parking area. It's hard to miss.

The carriage road soon passes by a swamp on your right, and at .4 mile you should bear left onto a wide, hard-packed single-track. The fork to your right is the trail you will be returning on. In about .2 mile, cross a small stream bed and bear left in a westerly direction up a steep hill. Ignore the trail to your right that parallels the stream bed. As the trail levels out, you begin a small descent, fork left, pass a small pond on your left and continue straight, ignoring a small trail to your right. Bear right at the next fork up a small switchback. There are many trails in this portion of the park, so pay attention to all the forking going on.

Bear right at the next fork and then left at the fork immediately after. The trail descends to a swampy area, crossing a small stream and generally heading in a northeasterly direction. Bear left at the next fork and ride parallel with the stream bed. You will notice some houses up on a hill to your left. The trail begins to turn away from the stream; at the **T** intersection, turn right, and head up a small incline. Bear right at the next fork and turn left at the next **T** intersection, which brings you to the wider carriage road at 2.1 miles.

Turn right on the carriage road. In another .2 mile, take the leftmost fork and soon after, fork right. You will ride along the Mianus River to your left. Notice a small path leading to your right; this can connect to the Service Road carriage trail. Continue straight and pass a large eastern hemlock grove on the river's edge to your left.

At 2.8 miles you reach an intersection with another carriage road. Bearing right will send you back, but bear left to continue cruising on this picturesque path. The park is home to about a mile of the Mianus River and is known for the brook, rainbow, and brown trout fishing. You pass several fishing spots. After .4 mile you reach a gate. Turn around, head back, and bear left at the intersection that brought you this way.

Pass 2 smaller single-tracks on your left and then turn left at the 4-way intersection with a wooden post in the ground, proceeding in a southwesterly direction. This carriage road leads you over some minor hills, and at the top you'll pass a large stone barrier and bear right. Continue straight until you reach another fork in about 1,000'. Bear left to return to the parking area, or bear right to do the loop again, but as a different configuration.

RIDE 36 *BABCOCK PRESERVE*

This park has rugged sections along its network of hiking and bridle paths set upon abandoned roads, but the trails are not overly difficult. An intermediate six-mile loop is described in this ride, but many other configurations can be created by analyzing the map and connecting the trails.

This tour is technically tricky along some portions of the rocky trail, but there is enough smoother double-track to whisk you through and quicken the pace. The trails are fairly level and gently roll over an interesting terrain of primitive wilderness habitat hosting a wide variety of birds and small mammals. Nature is your companion and serenity prevails in these woods as you travel over old, eroded, and overgrown forested roads that now serve as hiking and equestrian trails. There are many sections of smooth trail as well as a fair portion of rocky trail that will jar your teeth and keep you busy. The trail is seldom used by mountain bikers, and perhaps it's been decades since it served as a road.

General location: Just north of the town of Greenwich on North Street.
Elevation change: There are minor hills to climb, but the trail follows a gently rolling terrain.
Season: This is 4-season territory except when the trails are covered with snow. Then you might consider taking out your cross-country skis.

BABCOCK PRESERVE

Note: *Most trails are single-track.*

Services: Most services can be found throughout the town of Greenwich.

Hazards: The trails are shared with equestrians, so yield to the larger of the beasts and give them the right of way. The park is beautiful and may be popular on weekends. The current policy of trail usage is managed by the individual, and for now the people involved in these activities coexist and respect each other's rights to use this special park. We, as mountain bikers, need to be sensitive while riding here. So let's keep a positive image and use common-sense etiquette, and hopefully we will ensure our place on these trails.

Rescue index: The park is very small in terms of acreage, but it is always possible to get disoriented. The trails are well marked, with posted wooden signs indicating the direction you should take to return to one of the two parking lots. The ride described here will park you at the North Street parking area. Numerous private homes also border the park, so in the worst-case scenario, knock on a door.

Land status: The preserve is maintained and owned by the town of Greenwich.

Maps: An Eagle Scout project by Boy Scout Troop 37 completed a comprehensive map of the preserve; it hangs on a board beside the beginning of the trail on North Street.

Finding the trail: Take the Hutchinson River Parkway north and then follow signs for Merritt Parkway. Take Merritt Parkway and the North Street exit. At the end of the exit ramp, turn left and go about half a mile. The entrance to the parking area for the Babcock Preserve is on your left. Turn in and take the bumpy dirt road to its terminus. Park your car here and notice the wooden bulletin board erected to hold the preserve's map. Directly to the left of that, beyond a metal barrier and over a stone bridge, the trail will begin.

Sources of additional information:

Town of Greenwich Chamber of Commerce
21 West Putnam Avenue
Greenwich, Connecticut 06830
(203) 868-3500

Town of Greenwich Division of Parks and Trees
101 Field Point Road
Greenwich, Connecticut 06836-2540
(203) 622-7824

Greenwich Bicycle
40 West Putnam Avenue
Greenwich, Connecticut 06830
(203) 869-4141

Notes on the trail: The ride begins on a wide, hard-packed, dirt utility road crossing a stone bridge over a small stream and ascending a moderate hill in a westerly direction. This is Yellow Birch Trail, marked by yellow disks and square yellow tree markers. At the top of the hill, bear right at the fork. The

Self-portrait at Babcock Preserve.

trail follows a gently rolling terrain, first through an open oak forest and then through a dense undergrowth of huge mountain laurel. Turn right at a **T** intersection, descend into a small, shallow gully, and then climb out of it. Fork right at the next intersection and remain on Yellow Birch Trail. At 1.3 miles you come to a metal, barbed-wire fence. Notice several signposts indicating these trail crossings. To the right the White Ash trail follows the length of the metal fence. Bear left, continuing on the Yellow Birch Trail, which becomes more single-track. Soon you come to another intersection with the Flowering Dogwood Trail. Remain straight on the Yellow Birch Trail. After another 1,000', you come to a fork. The left path leads to a sign indicating the trail is closed, so bear right, and then at the next forked intersection bear left onto the blue-marked Blueberry Trail, which will lead you through the remains of an old stone boundary wall. You have now gone 1.8 miles. The Blueberry Trail is marked with round, wooden, blue disks that are very easy to follow. In .1 mile, cross a stream and continue straight, ignoring the small path leading off to your left. Descend a hill to a paved road. Turn right onto a single-track called the West Ridge Loop Trail. In about 100', a trail leads to your right, but continue straight through a stone fence and down a small incline, bearing right and then continuing straight on the trail that parallels a small brook to your right. Pass a small single-track leading to your left. This is the continuation of the West Ridge Road, which leads later into Red Maple Trail. Ascend a small hill and you will arrive at a clearing bordered by a stone wall. Bear right and then make a quick left to pick up the blue Blueberry Trail. Bear left at the next fork. The trail to your right is the Black Gum Trail, which leads back to the Yellow Birch Trail and the parking area.

At 2.8 miles you come to a 4-way intersection with Flowering Dogwood Trail. Continue straight on the Red Maple Trail. Bear left at the next T intersection after traversing some large rocks in the trail. Bearing right at the next fork will place you on the White Ash Trail, which will proceed along the metal fence. At the intersection with Yellow Birch Trail, near the opening of the fence, turn left. That will lead you back to the parking area. This loop is estimated to be about 6 miles.

RIDE 37 *TACONIC–HEREFORD M.U.A.*

The Taconic–Hereford Multiple Use Area, one of the largest M.U.A.s in Dutchess County, has been set aside for its great upland game hunting and other outdoor activities. It's a 909-acre oasis for mountain bikers and generally is not known as a mainstream mountain bike area. It's a gem and will fulfill anybody's wanderlust, with its easy yet stimulating 11 miles of four-wheel-drive roads and single-track.

Over eight miles of well-maintained, hard-packed, four-wheel-drive roads loop through a low, hilly terrain. The trail is fast-paced, exhilarating, and a joy to ride. Some spur trails take off and wind through an attractive, dense hardwood forest as single-track. The terrain consists of rolling hills with somewhat steep slopes, but none of the routes for riding require technical handling skills. Don't think. Just ride. These trails are perfect for easy or fast cruising, depending on your mood or how much caffeine you've imbibed.

The Taconic–Hereford M.U.A. is comprised almost entirely of deciduous hardwood forest and offers a compact and robust habitat for a variety of upland game animals like grouse, squirrel, woodcock, and rabbit. Throughout the ride are innumerable opportunities to view the cherished wildlife that flourishes here.

An M.U.A. provides recreational options for a variety of sportsmen and outdoor enthusiasts. Area use regulations allow individuals to hunt, fish, and even trap game. Access throughout these M.U.A.s is usually via networks of four-wheel-drive roads that, during winter, provide suitable snowmobile routes. The great concept here is that these roads provide some fine mountain biking paths as well, and during seasons when hunting is banned, the place is wide open to exploration by bike.

General location: Dutchess County in the town of Pleasant Valley. The Taconic–Hereford M.U.A. is located along the eastern side of the Taconic State Parkway and south of Tyrell Road.

RIDE 37 *TACONIC–HEREFORD M.U.A.*

Elevation change: The 8-mile loop traverses a low, hilly terrain and provides for some easy riding, while the more challenging riding takes place on the single-track spur trails.

Season: From April to September you're safe. I have been told by the New York State Department of Environmental Conservation (DEC) to wear orange during the hunting season to avoid being mistaken for a large squirrel or deer with a helmet on.

Services: The towns of Pleasant Valley along US 44 and Millbrook on NY 44A provide most services. In nearby Millbrook is a 250-acre Chinese-style garden called Innisfree Garden, with streams, waterfalls, and terraces. It is located on Tyrell Road. If you have time, it's worth checking out.

Hazards: This is a popular destination for hunters, and hunting seasons start at the end of September and end sometime in March. The area is available for riding around those dates. Call the DEC for exact dates and details.

Rescue index: You will not find the crowds you might encounter in southern Westchester County, so be smart and travel safe, tell friends or family where you are going, and carry a compass and a whistle (for scaring the bears). Even though the area is 909 acres, you might get disoriented. But not to worry; if you head long enough in one direction on the four-wheel-drive roads, you will eventually reach a paved road in under 4 miles, at which point you may flag down a passing motor vehicle and explain your predicament.

Land status: New York State Department of Environmental Conservation (DEC) manages the forest as a multiple-use area.

Maps: The DEC will supply you with a general map for this M.U.A., along with several other M.U.A.s in Dutchess County, in a small brochure.

Finding the trail: Drive north on the Taconic State Parkway. There are two access points, one of which is directly off the Taconic State Parkway. I have found, however, that as one travels at 55 mph, the entrance comes up a bit too fast, and I am always missing it. I usually take the second exit, Tyrell Road. Turn right onto Tyrell Road, which turns into a dirt road. You will soon come to the DEC sign for the Taconic–Hereford M.U.A. There is parking immediately to your left.

Source of additional information:

> New York State Department of Environmental Conservation
> Region 3
> 21 South Putt Corners Road
> New Paltz, New York 12561-1696
> (914) 256-3000

Notes on the trail: The four-wheel-drive road heads in a southerly direction into the woods. Notice two single-track spurs, one on your left and one on your right, that lead off into the woods about 200' into the ride. These paths are worth investigating and follow a perimeter path around the area. For now just remain on the four-wheel-drive path. You will pass by a few double-track paths leading off to your right in a westerly direction, but continue straight. At a **T** intersection with another four-wheel road, turn left in an easterly direction. At the next intersection you may do one of two things. You can turn left and head in a northerly direction to end up on Tyrell Road, where you will just have to turn left again, and you will have returned via a loop to your parking area.

Or bear right and head in a southerly direction. After crossing a small bridge, the road turns into Pond Gut Road. Turn right at the next road, Sidley Road. Turn right again at the next road, which is parallel to a stream. At the next intersection, Rossway Road, turn right and head north to the Taconic Parkway. Travel for a short distance north on the side of the Taconic and you will soon reach the first entrance into the Taconic–Hereford area, which I have always missed by car. Turn into the woods on the wide four-wheel-drive road and at the next intersection with a four-wheel-drive road, turn left in a northerly direction toward your parking area near Tyrell Road.

RIDE 38 *YE OLDE CROTON AQUEDUCT*

The Old Croton Aqueduct, while no longer supplying water to New York City, provides an enjoyable passage for the mountain bike family seeking an easy ride along a wide, hard-packed dirt road. It's great for those new to mountain bike riding without the technical skills necessary for different terrain. The generally flat path is three miles (one way) and provides easy, pleasant cruising. Often, the twists, turns, and maneuvering that more technical trails demand serve to distract from gazing upon the scenery. The riding in this tour, however, allows attention to be focused on the woodland and distant scenery of the Hudson River and surrounding valley.

What makes this ride so interesting is the history that rounds out the package. This path was part of a project to bring life-saving fresh water into a desperate New York City in 1830. Diseases from filth and contaminated drinking water were claiming lives across all social and economic classes. During these times, fires raged throughout the city and there was not enough water to fight them. The decision to import water into Manhattan led to the design and construction of the Old Croton Aqueduct. It drew water from the Croton River through a masonry-enclosed structure that ran 41 miles into New York City. Gravity pulled the water along. The scope of this engineering project was massive yet not innovative, since the Assyrians and Romans had long ago built similar aqueducts using much of the same basic technology. Construction began in 1837 and was completed by 1842 with the help of 4,000 immigrant Irish laborers earning a mere 75 cents a day and working 10-hour days. The water filled the Yorkville Reservoir, now the Great Lawn in Central Park, and the Murray Hill Reservoir, now the site of the New York Public Library at 42nd Street and Fifth Avenue. Although designed to last for centuries, the aqueduct was discontinued in 1890. By 1925, the Great Lawn of Central Park had filled in to become the vast playground and outdoor concert setting of today. Spend a morning or afternoon riding along this path. It's another opportunity to enjoy a setting with a unique place in history.

General location: Town of Cortlandt in northern Westchester County and only 4 miles from Croton.

To Points
North

To Taconic
State Parkway

Taconic State Pkwy.

Croton Dam Rd.

Dam

To
N.Y.C.

N

0   1/2   1
MILES

Maple St.

To
Peekskill

129

Croton River

Quaker Bridge Rd.

General Electric
Mgt. Institute

9

NY

9A

To
Crotonville

CROTON
POINT
ST. PARK

To
Ossining

Hudson
River

Elevation change: Generally flat and wide with some gradual grades.

Season: The trails are available year-round, but when snow arrives and covers the trail, cross-country skiing becomes the sport. It's a good idea to stay away from the trails during wet weather, as they have a tendency to become muddy.

Services: The town of Croton provides most services. There is a small deli on Quaker Bridge Road as the trail nears its turnaround point at the General Electric Management Institute.

Hazards: Keep an eye out for walkers and watch for motor vehicles when the trail crosses a paved road.

Rescue index: The park is situated in a residential area. The route sees a fair amount of traffic from walkers and other bike riders, so help is usually close at hand.

Land status: New York State Park. There will be a sign labeling this area as the Old Croton Trail Way State Park.

Maps: The path is fairly straightforward and the map I have drawn should provide enough detail.

Finding the trail: Take the Taconic State Parkway north to the Underhill Road exit, just past the bridge that crosses the New Croton Reservoir. Proceed west on Underhill Road to where it ends at Route 129, Croton Lake Road. Turn right on Route 129 and after approximately 3.5 miles you can turn left into Croton Gorge Park in the town of Cortlandt. There is a $6 parking fee. You can also turn left onto Croton Dam Road before the park, cross the dam, and find parking for your vehicle in a small parking area on your right directly after the dam.

Sources of additional information:

Taconic State Park and Recreation Commission
Mills–Norrie State Parks
Old Post Road
Staatsburg, New York 12580
(914) 889-4100

Franklin D. Roosevelt State Park
2957 Crompond Road
Yorktown Heights, New York 10598
(914) 245-4434

Notes on the trail: If you have left your car in the small parking area on Croton Dam Road, the white stone gravelly path begins just beyond the metal fence. An alternative would be to leave your car in the parking area of Croton Gorge Park. Take the maintenance road past and behind the rest rooms. It is visible from anywhere in the parking lot. This road makes a few switchbacks as it reaches the level of the aqueduct path. Keep bearing left until you reach the top, where the white gravel road you are on swings left. Take a sharp right in a southeasterly direction onto the aqueduct path. The path to the left leads you to a metal, fenced gate that leaves you on Croton Dam Road. If you are geared up for another tour, look up the Croton Dam Road tour, another ride in this book.

The 10'-wide, hard-packed dirt road leads you through an attractive and covered hardwood forest with rock outcroppings along the way. You will soon encounter a large, cylindrical stone structure. There are several along the way. These ventilator shafts were built to aerate the flowing water within the underground aqueduct and to maintain the water's fresh flavor and prevent if from being pressurized. The water traveled through the conduit at about 1.5 miles an hour, and the ventilators were originally placed every mile.

The path crosses the paved Quaker Bridge Road several times and skirts the north edge of Gerlach Park in Crotonville, following a grassy trail until you near the Indian Creek Culvert. You may turn around when you reach the General Electric Management Institute that looms in front where the path ought to be.

After you have turned back and returned the way you came, if you have some extra time, continue on the aqueduct trail until it reaches Croton Dam Road. Turn right on Croton Dam Road and follow it around for about 4 more miles of riding. This wide country road provides for some pleasant riding accompanied by great views of the surrounding countryside and Croton Reservoir.

RIDE 39 *BLUE MOUNTAIN NIRVANA*

A magnificent network of designated mountain bike trails winds through some spectacular scenery in the Hudson Highlands. Blue Mountain Reservation in Peekskill, New York, is one of the rare Westchester County parks that still allow mountain biking. One can travel over seven miles of reasonably challenging carriage roads and single-track that comb through 1,600 acres of hilly park. There is something here for every level of rider. Novices can enjoy the scenery along the gently rolling carriage roads. The more advanced rider can take on the tough hills that climb through a densely wooded landscape. The trails are strictly cardiovascular, not technical, and the rewards are in the fast-paced and well-controlled descents. The park has rules about riding at speeds that are out of control or threatening to hikers, plants, or wildlife. Remember to ride courteously and responsibly. It's the best way to ensure that these mountain bike nirvanas will long be available to us. Spend a complete day wandering past spectacular rock outcroppings and scenic ponds, exploring the eclectic terrain of this primeval forested park.

The region went through extensive geological faulting, in which sections of bedrock thrust hundreds and even thousands of feet up causing extreme

RIDE 39   *BLUE MOUNTAIN NIRVANA*

placement of the mountains and valleys. This type of faulting caused the steep-sided, narrow-topped ridge rising to Blue Mountain and Spitzenberg Mountain to grow to a height of more than 700 feet from the sea-level Hudson River. As you ride throughout the park, notice the other parallel gullies that run north-south as well. After these ridges were pushed up to these heights, they were intensely eroded by the gigantic continental ice sheets of the last ice age, which at times were over one mile high. Many of the rock outcroppings on the trails include trees growing on the top or clinging to the sides with the roots set in the cracks. These distinctive characteristics of the terrain are the result of faulting and friction from the gigantic continental ice sheets of the last glacial period.

General location: A little over 40 miles north of Manhattan, located in the town of Peekskill in Westchester County.

Elevation change: This part of Westchester County is known for its hilly and rocky terrain. A robust mixture of ascents and descents awaits the rider. None are too long or steep, and elevation changes rarely exceed 400', but they may be rigorous.

Season: Year-round riding is available 7 days a week from dawn to dusk. A parking fee of $6 will be collected at the park's gate. If there is no snow, get onto the trails. Do not let winter's cold stop you; just put on more clothing and enjoy the solitude.

Services: The town of Peekskill provides most services.

Hazards: Hikers and horses can be found on the trails, and there is a Cyclist Responsibility Code that requires you to yield the right-of-way to them. If they find you riding at out-of-control speeds, stomping on plants, menacing hikers, or running over wildlife, you will be removed from the park. Courteous and responsible conduct will assure the mountain biker's presence in this park. When approaching hikers or horses, be careful not to spook them by riding close or fast from either direction on the trail.

Rescue index: The compact trail system never takes you too far from your parking area, and usage from other recreational users puts you in close contact, in case you need it. The park is surrounded by the residential community of Peekskill.

Land status: Westchester County Department of Parks Recreation and Conservation.

Maps: The park provides a well-detailed trail map with the rider-level designated mountain bike paths. You may call and ask the Weschester County Department of Parks (phone: (914) 593-PARK) to send you a map.

Finding the trail: Take the Taconic Parkway north to the Briarcliff Manor exit. Route 9A will merge with Route 9. Turn right onto Welcher Avenue and proceed east to the park entrance.

This park can be reached by the Metro North Railroad, Hudson Division Line. Disembark at the Montrose Station. Cross the tracks and take Montrose Station Road for 1 mile and then make a left on Washington Street. Remain on Washington Street for 1 mile and then turn right onto Welcher Avenue into the park.

Sources of additional information:

Blue Mountain Reservation
Welcher Avenue
Peekskill, New York 10566
(914) 737-2194 or (914) 593-PARK

Peekskill Chamber of Commerce
One South Division Street
Peekskill, New York 10566
(914) 737-3600

American Cycle Corporation
1770 Crompond Road
Peekskill, New York 10566
(914) 739-7533

Toddville Bike Center
2141 Crompond Road
Cortlandt Manor, New York 10566
(914) 737-7255

Notes on the trail: Continue past the park gate and bear left to the last parking area. You will notice a wide carriage road leading past a yellow triangular sign adjacent to a sign listing the rider responsibility codes. Begin your ride here.

Ride a short, steep pitch and you will soon encounter a yellow-marked trail on your left; continue straight. One very pleasant item about riding at the Blue Mountain Reservation is that the trails are color-coded and easy to follow. The coding system indicates three levels of riding skills. Yellow is for beginners, orange and green are for intermediate, and red is for advanced. The colors are painted on the trees. Don't be scared off by the red trail. If you are a beginning or intermediate rider, it will not be long before you master the required gnarliness.

Continue straight on the orange and green trail and bear left at the next intersection with a trail on your right. Keep bearing left at the next intersection with a small trail leading off to your right. Bear left again at the next intersection. Remain on the green trail and ignore the red trail leading off to your right. You will soon come to a **T** intersection. Bear right onto the orange and green trail. Turning left onto the red trail will take you back to the parking area. Continue on the orange and green trail, and climb a short, steep, rock hill that levels out soon. As you come to a large blowdown, take the small blowdown-influenced single-track on your left that soon rejoins the trail. After passing through some magnificent rock outcroppings you will exit the forest into a small field with a swamp to your right. Take a sharp left up a small hill. If you were to continue straight ahead, the orange and green trail would take you up toward Mount Spitzenberg. The path soon re-enters the forest where the blazes become blue. Proceed over some rocky terrain. Notice a yellow arrow on a brown sign at the next intersection, and bear left at the fork.

Descend along a moderately rocky trail through a beautiful hemlock forest. Several major rock outcroppings line both sides of the trail. You are in a general descent-mode and will be for about half a mile. It's a nice reward for all

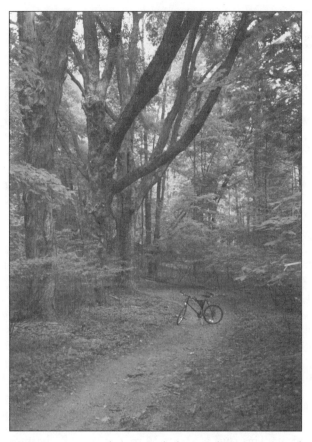

Mature sugar maples sentinel along a divine section of
Blue Mountain double-track.

the climbing you did before. Descend two long switchbacks and pass by
5 100-year-old maple trees on your left. The forest you are traveling through
at this point is all maple trees. Fork left at the red trail and you will soon
come to another fork; bear right. From this point on it's mostly single-track
marked with blue and orange **V** blazes on the trees. You will soon emerge
onto a paved road. Turn left and in about 50' turn left again back into the
woods. Descend a steep hill and continue straight, ignoring the trail on your
right. Continuing on this rolling section of trail, you will emerge in a parking
area. Turn left at the clearing and continue along the trail that runs along the
left side of the lake. At the end of the lake will be a red wooden building.
Make a left onto a small trail and bear right at the next fork, which leads you
down to a carriage road. Turn left onto the carriage road. Make another left
at the next intersection and continue down a hill over a small bridge. The single-
track changes into a carriage road and ends at a road. Return to your parking
area from here or head back in for another loop.

RIDE 40 *ALBERTO'S FAVORITE*

The North County Trailway is great for the beginner mountain biker and the entire family. I learned about it from Alberto, an attendant at a gas station near the town of Ossining. I inquired about directions, and Alberto observed my mountain bikes on top of my car. He asked me where I was biking. I told him I was looking for routes, and he shared one of his favorites, which was just off Route 9 not too far from where we were.

This trailway comprises ten miles (five miles one way) of out-and-back fun. It provides a great opportunity to bring the young ones who want to ride through the woods with a minimum of exertion or technical prowess. Since the trail is paved, it's a confidence builder for those new to the sport and looking to break in and get accustomed to their new machine before graduating to the mightier challenges of double-track and single-track. The trailway passes through an oasis of woodlands amid the urban sprawl. Fall is splendid in this setting, and the foliage at peak periods is intense.

This path runs mostly over the right-of-way of the former Putnam Railroad that was in service from 1881 to 1958. It was also the old stagecoach route that ran north from White Plains and into the many northern hamlets of Westchester. At full operation, the Putnam Railroad served 22 stations, some of which still exist today. Thanks to the National Trails System Act of 1983, the rails-to-trails program converts abandoned railroad tracks into public, recreational trailways throughout the United States.

General location: This tour is about 34 miles from Manhattan in northwest Westchester near Eastview and Tarrytown.
Elevation change: The trail travels over a railroad grade but is nevertheless quite smooth and slightly inclined.
Season: This is 4-season territory except when the trail is covered with snow.
Services: Most services can be found in Tarrytown along NY 9.
Hazards: In the beginning of the ride the path crosses Saw Mill River Road, and one should take care to look for cars coming in both directions since they will be coming around turns. Another hazard I would like to mention is that this path tends to be busy on weekends. Runners, roller bladers, and bikes going faster than they should are often seen darting around on the path. Pay attention and stay alert to these obstacles. You do not often have the solitude on this trail as you might have in the woods on some quiet double-track.
Rescue index: The trailway receives a fair amount of use, and there is usually someone who can provide assistance. The trailway is also surrounded by residential areas and is in close proximity to help if needed.
Land status: The trailway is managed by the Westchester County Department of Parks, Recreation and Conservation.

RIDE 40   *ALBERTO'S FAVORITE*

To Yorktown

100

133

N

0   4500

FEET

Taconic State Parkway

To New Castle

117

To Scarborough

NY

Saw Mill River Pkwy.

To N.Y.C.

Tarrytown Reservoir

Saw Mill River Rd.

To Mt. Pleasant

To N.Y.C.

Easy cruising along the North County Trailway.

Maps: The Westchester County Department of Parks will send you a general map of the trailway system, but the paved trail is straightforward, goes in one direction, and is easy to follow. Unless you ride with your eyes closed it's almost impossible to become lost.

Finding the trail: Take the Saw Mill River Parkway north to Exit 23. The sign says Saw Mill River Road, Eastview. Turn left and go about 1.5 miles around the Tarrytown Reservoir. Look for the parking area on your right. Turn up Sunnyside Road perpendicular to the parking area and turn left onto the North County Trailway.

Source of additional information:

> Westchester County Department of Parks
> Recreation and Conservation
> 19 Bradhurst Avenue
> Hawthorne, New York 10532
> (914) 593-PARK

Notes on the trail: The path is very straight, with few turns. It starts by skirting the Tarrytown Reservoir through a dense wooded corridor with sufficient canopy to block summer's midday sun. After 1 mile the path reaches the reservoir's pump station and ends on Saw Mill River Road. Cross the road and continue up a short, steep hill and then down another short, steep hill, bearing left at the bottom of the hill. From this point on, you will be on a gradual incline. This is characteristic of the old rail bed, which was designed to rise no more than 2 degrees from level. This portion of the ride continues for another 4 miles to the turnaround point. Return along the trailway toward where you began.

RIDE 41 *THE OLD "PUT" PATH*

This is an exciting and easy trail wrapped in the beautiful pastoral landscape of Westchester County and its history. Although not technically challenging, this partially paved and wide, hard-packed cinder trail is ideal for beginners testing out new equipment but also a lot of fun for novices. It's a great opportunity to bring the young ones in tow on a child seat or on small bikes. Spin some tales about what might have taken place in history along this very same route. This route is along the North County Trailway, which passes through an attractive and protected woodland corridor. In the fall, the foliage is breathtaking. From the parking area described below, you may pedal south for 8 miles or north for about 13 miles. The path is fairly straight and easy to follow. It is mostly paved except for a four-mile segment in the northern section, which is encountered approximately two miles north of the parking area.

The path travels over the former Putnam Division Railway right-of-way. The old "Put" line of the New York Central Railroad ran from 1881 to 1958, connecting over 56 miles of track and serving 22 stations. Some still exist. Through a nationwide rails-to-trails program, created in 1983 by the National Trails System Act, many abandoned railroad tracks have been converted to recreational paths. It has been said that the route was used for carrying George Washington's wounded to nearby Chappaqua following the battle of White Plains in October 1776. The French general, Rochambeau, also marched his forces along the route on his way from Newport, Rhode Island, to Yorktown, Virginia, in 1781. Begin your ride in the hamlet of Millwood, named after a local grain mill.

The old "Put" trail not only provided a means of transportation, it combined a pleasant day in the country. The railroads spurred the development of Chappaqua and Millwood, creating opportunities for commerce in the region. Although the line was primarily used for passengers, local farmers also used the old Put to ship milk, cider, apples, and other produce to the New York markets. The Millwood station was constructed in 1880. More development ensued, and there was extensive acquisition of watershed lands and the construction of the network of reservoirs and aqueducts for the New York Water Supply System. Within Westchester, the development of this system involved the construction of three aqueducts, six reservoirs, and seven major dams starting in the 1830s and continuing to the early 1950s. In a

RIDE 41 *THE OLD "PUT" PATH*

number of locations, the railroad lines were built along or near the reservoir's watershed or the aqueduct's right-of-way lands, thereby taking advantage of the spectacular views. Your ride covers one of these paths.

General location: Northwest Westchester. This tour is about 40 miles from Manhattan near the towns of Millwood and Chappaqua.
Elevation change: The trail travels over a railroad grade and is quite smooth and slightly inclined.
Season: This is 4-season territory except when the trail is covered with snow.

Services: Most services can be found in Tarrytown along NY 9.

Hazards: This path tends to be busy on weekends. Runners, roller bladers, and bikes going faster than they should are often seen darting around on the path. Pay attention and stay alert to these obstacles. You do not often have the solitude on this trail that you'd find in the woods on some quiet double-track.

Rescue index: The trailway receives a fair amount of use, and there is usually someone who can provide assistance. The trailway is also surrounded by residential areas and is in close proximity to help if needed.

Land status: The trailway is managed by the Westchester County Department of Parks, Recreation, and Conservation.

Maps: The Westchester County Parks Department will send you a general map of the North County Trailway system, but the trail is very straightforward and easy to follow. The trailway is paved and travels in one direction. Many other trail users can be seen on the trail, and unless you ride with your eyes closed it's almost impossible to get lost.

Finding the trail: Take the Taconic State Parkway north to the Millwood exit, NY 100/NY 133. At the end of the exit ramp, turn left and then turn right at the stop sign onto NY 100/NY 133. Go to the traffic light (Mobile Service Station) and take a right turn onto NY 133. Look for a parking area in about .25 mile on your right. Park there and the path begins directly in front of the parking area.

Source of additional information:

> Westchester County Department of Parks
> Recreation and Conservation
> 19 Bradhurst Avenue
> Hawthorne, New York 10532
> (914) 593-PARK

Notes on the trail: The path is straightforward, with few turns. This chapter describes the section of the pathway that leads 13 miles in a northerly direction. An optional 8-mile section lies south of the parking area, too. Begin your journey by turning left onto the special paved North County Trailway path that will take you in an easterly and then northerly direction and will soon cross Millwood Road. The paved portion of the trail extends for about 2 miles and terminates alongside a small pond. Look for a small dirt single-track leading to your right. Continue down a small dip that will cross a wet section of trail and then climb above the small rock retaining wall where you will find the continuation of the trail. The trail becomes more single-track at this point, but it is wide and smooth and takes on the level of the original railroad grade. One small section of the path where the trail surface undulates reminded me of a roller coaster. The path soon enters a densely wooded forest with such a thick canopy that it feels like riding through a tunnel of trees. You will emerge from the woods in front of the railway trestle bridge that carried the trains over the Croton Reservoir. It is quite a sight and a great place to stay a while and take in the scenery. You can cross the bridge and continue on a single-track for another 5 miles, passing through the old stations of Yorktown Heights, Amawalk, and Baldwin Place. To return, face the direction you came from and start to pedal. It is that simple.

RIDE 42 *NINHAM MOUNTAIN M.U.A.*

A multiple use area (M.U.A.) is a parcel of land that provides recreational options. Area use regulations allow individuals to hunt, fish, and even trap game. Networks of four-wheel-drive roads often provide the transportation pathways necessary for accessing M.U.A. resources. Hunters use these roads during the fall. During the winter, these routes are often used as snowmobile trails. For mountain bikers, these dirt roads mean an opportunity to gear up and get out. During seasons when hunting is banned, these unique wilderness areas are wide open to explore on bike.

This particular M.U.A. is located in the town of Kent, just north of the West Branch Reservoir and about three miles east of the village of Carmel. There are approximately eight miles of four-wheel-drive roads through 1,023 acres. Two major dirt road systems begin from the parking area and wind through a mixed hardwood forest. There's a four-mile, out-and-back route with one road ascending for one mile with a two-mile single-track (one mile, one way) linked at its end. The other dirt road descends for two miles and terminates at Boyds Road on the West Branch Reservoir. From that point it is a five-mile return to the parking area, forming a seven-mile loop.

The rolling plateau and steep, densely wooded slopes of the Ninham M.U.A. make for challenging terrain that is not terribly technical but requires good stamina. The one-mile climb along the dirt road ascending Ninham Mountain is a real lung stretcher and worth attempting. A 1½-mile single-track traverses a ridge near the summit, and then the return descent deals the payback. The second road winds through another section of the M.U.A. You are east of Clarence Fahnestock Park and close to some of the rides detailed in that park. NY 301 connects both areas.

The mountain is named after Daniel Ninham, a member of the Wappinger Indians tribe and a devoted friend of the people who settled the area.

General location: Putnam County, near the town of Carmel.
Elevation change: There is only one serious hill climb and that is the 1-mile, four-wheel-drive road on the right side of the last parking area. While there may not be enough oxygen in the air to fill your lungs going up, the return descent will put a smile on your face as you blast your way down.

RIDE 42 *NINHAM MOUNTAIN M.U.A.*

Season: April to September provides the best riding opportunities. Call the Department of Environmental Conservation (DEC) to find out details of the hunting season. Wet weather does not affect or rut the hard-packed dirt roads, so a day after a rain shower should be no problem for riding.

Services: Services can be found in Lake Carmel and Kent Corners.

Hazards: Hunting seasons start in the beginning of October and end in March. The area is available for riding around those dates. Call the New York State Department of Environmental Conservation (DEC) for exact dates and details.

Rescue index: This is not one of your mainstream mountain biking areas so you will probably not see too many other bikers; carry an extra tube, water, and snacks. If you become disoriented just head downhill, which will eventually lead you to NY 301, which has a substantial amount of vehicular traffic on it.

Land status: New York State land. The New York State Department of Environmental Conservation (DEC) manages the forest as a multiple-use area. These state-owned parcels of land have been set aside to provide a place for hunters and other recreationalists who may not be affiliated with a hunting club or own suitable acreage for such activities. Hunting is often not permitted in many of the counties that are within easy driving distance of New York City. These lands are therefore inaccessible to the urban hunter. The DEC manages this state land as an M.U.A. for public outdoor recreational usage, including hunting.

Maps: The USGS, 7.5 minute series, Lake Carmel quadrangle provides sufficient detail of this area.

Finding the trail: Take the Taconic State Parkway north and exit at NY 301. Turn right and head east on NY 301 as it follows along the West Branch Reservoir. Just before you reach the road that passes over the dam of the West Branch Reservoir, turn left onto the unmarked Gipsy Trail Road. You will see signs for Putnam County Park at this intersection. Follow this road to the DEC sign for the Ninham Multiple Use Area, turn left and continue to the end of the dirt road, which terminates at a circular parking area. There will be two barriers, one to the left and the other, with a stop sign posted on it, to the right. The ascent up Ninham Mountain begins beyond the barrier on your right and the second, lower road begins beyond the left barrier.

Sources of additional information:

New York State Department of Environmental Conservation
Region 3
21 South Putt Corners Road
New Paltz, New York 12561-1696
(914) 256-3000

Taconic State Park and Recreation Commission
Old Post Road
Staatsburg, New York 12580
(914) 889-4100

Wheel and Heel
65 Gleniega Avenue
Carmel, New York 10512
(914) 228-1206

Notes on the trail: Start by passing the barrier on the right side and begin the gradual but steady climb. After 1 mile of a steady climb, the abandoned lookout tower will be within your sights. Just before you reach the top of your climb, look to your left and notice the large, 3-pole utility platform. Just to the right of that is a small, overgrown, grass-covered, two-wheel-drive road. The trail gradually descends through a primitive forest for about .8 mile and degrades into an unnegotiable single-track. Turn around and head back the way you came. As you get back to the lookout tower, catch your breath and then get ready for that lip-stretched descent on the mile-long hill you came up earlier.

The second dirt road leading from the parking area descends 2 miles to the West Branch Reservoir. After reaching the reservoir, turn left and proceed 5 miles to the parking area. Just before you reach the road that passes over the dam of the West Branch Reservoir, turn left onto the unmarked Gipsy Trail Road. You will see signs for Putnam County Park at this intersection. Follow this road to the DEC sign for the Ninham Multiple Use Area and turn left and continue to the end of the dirt road, which terminates at the circular parking area.

RIDE 43 *MOUNT TAURUS ASCENT TRAIL*

It takes five miles of an old forest road to reach the summit of Mount Taurus. This tour is not for the faint-hearted and delivers a thorough workout for the advanced rider. This is not a high-tech ride, but sections of the rough, washed-out road require good endurance and basic technical skills. The steep sections of the trail demand a good deal of strength too. Maneuvering through the eroded, exposed rock bed of the trail and learning to work the rocks on the hilly, rolling terrain is difficult but rewarding. You will gain confidence as you conquer the obstacles. Reaching the summit of Mount Taurus gives a sense of accomplishment. Mount Taurus, with its unsurpassed panoramic views of the Hudson River and the mountains to the west, is one of the premium summits in the Hudson Highlands, but it takes work getting there. Two steep pitches a tenth of a mile long and three tenths of a mile long lie ahead, requiring portaging your bike.

The poor condition of this road is an excellent example of what can happen to a trail when it is exposed to the tremendous erosional forces of nature and receives little or no maintenance. One of the chief factors of trail erosion is poor drainage along the route. Rains wash down a trail, eventually exposing some of the rocks and roots beneath the road bed. The road beds themselves become conduits for water runoff. The object of some trail maintenance

RIDE 43 *MOUNT TAURUS ASCENT TRAIL*

programs is to divert some of this runoff and preserve the surface of the trail. Much effort goes into trail maintenance. Unfortunately, it is taken for granted. Without it, we would not be able to enjoy many trails.

As you ride along the route, notice a large stone building. This was part of the Catskill Aqueduct system constructed in the nineteenth century. The conduit originated at the Ashokan Dam in the Catskills and passed beneath the Hudson River. The tunnel was bored 1,100 feet below the surface of the river and carried water down to the reservoir that used to exist where the Mid-Manhattan Library now stands. Engineers faced a major dilemma getting the water across the Hudson River and down to New York City to feed the reservoir that existed where the library on 42nd Street now stands. During the Roman Empire, multiarched bridges with the proper gradient carried water to faraway places. Dynamite and mechanical power in the nineteenth century made it possible to conduct the aqueduct's stream far below the river. Shafts were built on either side of the river where the tunnels were excavated and constructed. From the Hudson River, the tunnel continued beneath Mount Taurus and turned south toward New York City. The large stone building is one of the vents used along the aqueduct. It's hard to imagine that such a tunnel exists underground and through this mountain.

As you climb Mount Taurus, notice a large scar on the southern face of the mountain. It's from the 1930s when a quarrying operation removed huge chunks of rock.

General location: In northwest Putnam County, near the town of Cold Spring.

Elevation change: The ride climbs from the town of Nelsonville at elevation 200' to the summit of Mount Taurus, elevation 1,400'. There are several short climbs with an overall elevation gain of 1,200' over 5 miles. This is a ride for dedicated and strong hammerheads.

Season: These are 4-season trails as long as there is no snow on them.

Services: Restaurants and most other services can be found on Main Street in the town of Cold Spring.

Hazards: Prevention of deer ticks by spraying bug repellent on your clothing is a good idea. Be aware that portions of this trail go through private land, and there could be hunting during November and December. The trail is gnarled with rocks in sections and can be an endless conveyor of pain if you are not an advanced rider. When the trail is wet, the rocks conspire to throw you off your bike, so swing wide in these sections when there is room to move. The steep sections may require a dismount and a portage.

Rescue index: You are never too far out in the wilderness, and these trails are moderately popular.

Land status: Portions of this trail travel on private property. There is no conflict with landowners, according to local riders who ride the trail. Most of the trail travels through a remote section of wilderness with no houses around. The only precaution to take is to stay off the trail during the hunting season, which runs between September and April. Certain sections of the land are private, and the landowners have the option to hunt on their land during the hunting season. The last section of the trail passes through Highlands State Park, which is state land. This land is managed by the Taconic State Park and Recreation Commission.

Maps: New Jersey Trail Conference's "East Hudson Trails," Trail Map 2, provides complete coverage of this trail and the surrounding area and is waterproof and tearproof. It sells for $6.95 and can be found at most outdoor-type stores. USGS, 7.5 minute series, West Point quadrangle also provides detail.

Finding the trail: Take the Taconic State Parkway north and exit at NY 301. Go west on NY 301 until you get to the town of Nelsonville, where the trailhead begins. Cold Spring is the next town. Turn right on Cedar Street about 8.5 miles from the Taconic State Parkway. Parking is just a short way up near the intersection of Mountain and Cedar streets. The trail begins directly opposite from Mountain Street. You will see a small wood road leading into the forest in a northeasterly direction. Begin your ride here.

Sources of additional information:

Taconic State Park and Recreation Commission
Old Post Road
Staatsburg, New York 12580
(914) 889-4100

Clarence Fahnestock State Park
RFD 2
Carmel, New York 10512-9802
(914) 225-7207

Cold Spring-on-Hudson Chamber of Commerce
Cold Spring, New York 10156
(914) 265-9060

Putnam County Tourism
76 Main Street
Cold Spring, New York 10156
(914) 255-3066

Notes on the trail: Ride in about 200' and turn left onto the trail just before the stream. Continue until you reach an intersection. There will be a blue arrow painted on a large tree.

The trail is eroded in sections, with exposed rocks studding the road bed. After about .3 mile, you will cross a stream. After this the trail climbs steadily for about 2.5 miles. The trail is well defined, easy to follow, and marked with blue paint splashes on trees.

At 1.2 miles a small, steep pitch is encountered, and then at 1.7 miles a longer steep pitch is approached.

RIDE 44 *HUBBARD–PERKINS CONSERVATION AREA*

Over nine miles of abandoned, well-maintained wooded country roads traverse a serene and un-populated wooded landscape in the middle of Putnam County. The main course consists of a seven-mile (total) out-and-back, hard-pack road, while two short spur trails serve as the dessert on this full-course mountain bike meal. These roads flow through beautiful meadows and open forests and along a meandering stream. The trail passes by an undisturbed valley some four miles long and two miles wide and crisscrosses several streams. It is bordered by stone walls and full-grown, mature trees. Land parcels are delineated by these walls. The walls of the valley are steep, wooded slopes that rise 1,100 feet. Extensive stands of hemlock and mountain laurel are noticeable at the higher elevations.

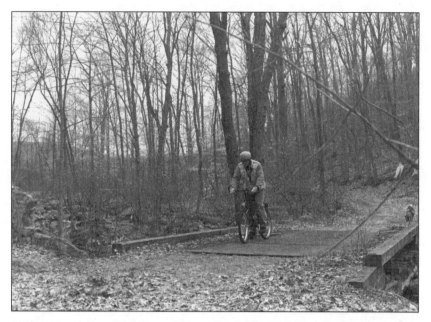

Bridge crossing a stream through the valley of the Hubbard–Perkins Conservation Area.

Bike-handling skill requirements are minimal. The easy grades and good cruising, except for one long climb at the end of the main route, make this an ideal ride for beginners who are ready to start advancing their skills. For the more experienced dirt disciple, this tour is remote and secluded, with lots of wildlife and an opportunity to get in some fast double-track.

Thanks to the Open Space Institute, a non-profit land preservation organization, the estates of Helen Fahnestock Campbell Hubbard and the adjacent Perkins estate (comprising approximately 4,000 acres of undeveloped mountains and woods) were combined. The lands were acquired for the preservation of open space in the Hudson Highlands.

The house at the entrance to the area belongs to Willie Conklin, who serves as caretaker on the lands. He removes blowdowns, maintains the trails, and is knowledgeable about the area. He said that around April, the coyotes go into mating and do a lot of hooting. The area is plentiful with deer, and Willie says there are bears in the hills as well.

General location: The tour is located in Putnam County just west of Clarence Fahnestock Memorial State Park, near the intersection of NY 9 and NY 301.

Elevation change: The first 2 miles are fairly level at 500', but the last 2 miles climb to an elevation of 1,100'.

Season: The trails should dry out by mid-April and provide good riding through December. If there is no snow on the trails, and if you do not mind the cold, get out there and enjoy the solitude and quiet of a winter day.

Services: Cold Spring offers most services along its popular Main Street.

Hazards: Raccoon rabies are present in this area of New York State, so do not approach or feed these animals in the park. The eastern deer tick spreads Lyme disease, so use insect repellent on your clothing and around your ankles and shoes.

Rescue index: At most you will be about 4 miles from the well-traveled NY 301.

Land status: New York State Office of Parks and Recreation, the Taconic State Park and Recreation Commission.

Maps: New Jersey Trail Conference's "East Hudson Trails," Trail Map 2, provides complete coverage of this trail and the surrounding area and is waterproof and tearproof. It sells for $6.95 and can be found at most outdoor-type stores. USGS, 7.5 minute series, West Point quadrangle also provides detail.

Finding the trail: Take the Taconic Parkway north and exit at Route 301 going west. Continue on Route 301 and turn north on Route 9. About a quarter of a mile on your right the trail begins. Park along the stone wall, but do not block the driveway.

Sources of additional information:

Taconic State Park and Recreation Commission
Old Post Road
Staatsburg, New York 12580
(914) 889-4100

Clarence Fahnestock State Park
RFD 2
Carmel, New York 10512-9802
(914) 225-7207

Cold Spring-on-Hudson Chamber of Commerce
Cold Spring, New York 10156
(914) 265-9060

Putnam County Tourism
76 Main Street
Cold Spring, New York 10156
(914) 255-3066

Notes on the trail: You will begin on an old, wide, paved road bordered by stone walls and old-growth trees. Families built their homes along this road, and the remains of the foundations of their homes can be seen along the sides of the trail. You will come to a fork in the road with a lesser road leading off to your right, blocked by a metal fence. Bear right onto this road, traveling over some metal bridges and crossing several brooks and streams. In about half a mile, you will pass by the remnants of an old stone entrance. That spur-trail road to your left leads uphill to the site of an old granite house that was buried for unknown reasons. Continue straight on the wide, four-wheel-drive, jeep road. At about 1.5 miles, an open clearing provides you with good views on your right of the 1,100' Round Hill and the smaller unnamed hill just north of it. The road climbs along the west bank of the stream for about .1 mile and levels out. After about 2 miles, a fork to the right begins a steep ascent to the end of the trail.

RIDE 45 *FRANKLIN D. ROOSEVELT STATE PARK*

Franklin D. Roosevelt State Park is evidence that good things, even places to mountain bike, come in small packages. This New York State Park is not deep in the heart of wilderness. It's not hammerhead heaven or the holy training grounds for technique. What this compact urban park does offer is some relaxing family riding, picnicking, boating on a picturesque lake, swimming in a large outdoor pool, and Italian ices. The well-maintained roads and trails make it an ideal place for a beginner mountain biker to venture off-road. The wide gravel roads provide a good surface for someone new to off-road riding and first getting the feel of a bike on surfaces other than pavement.

A five-mile loop of hard-packed dirt roads winds its way past two pleasant, scenic lakes (Crom Pond and Mohansic Lake) and through attractive hard-wood and conifer forests. There is a "family-style" single-track that children can attempt, but if you need to bail out switch to the wider dirt road that runs parallel to it.

Boat rentals are available at Mohansic Lake and a large swimming pool is open during the summer; you can cool off here and enjoy some nearby refreshments. Franklin D. Roosevelt State Park has something for everyone and provides a full day of diverse family fare.

General location: The park is approximately 30 miles north of Manhattan off the Taconic Parkway.

Elevation change: The trail follows fairly level grades with no strenuous hill climbs.

Season: These trails are great in any season, and if you do not mind the cold, dress warmly and enjoy the solitude of a popular park.

Services: Yorktown is next to the park and offers some services. Two concession stands are located in the park; one is near parking area 1 and the other is located near the swimming pool.

To Potnam Valley
and Points North

N

0   150   300
METERS

To
Yorktown

Crom Pond Rd.

To
Peekskill

P

P

FRANKLIN D.
ROOSEVELT
STATE PARK

NY

P

Mohansic
Lake

Pool

Taconic State Parkway

To New
York City

Hazards: During the weekends the paths might be crowded with walkers and other bikers, so drive cautiously and courteously. Raccoon rabies are present in this area of New York State, so do not feed, touch, or approach them. If you see one acting a bit strange, contact park personnel and inform them of its whereabouts.

Rescue index: Since this is an urban park, people are always around, and park personnel can be found at the park office near the entrance.

Land status: New York State Park.

Maps: A park map is available by paying the $3 entrance fee into the park, and it provides very good coverage of the trails.

Finding the trail: Take the Taconic Parkway north until you see signs for Franklin D. Roosevelt State Park. Exit the Taconic, pay at the park entrance, turn into the park, and bear left for parking area 1.

Source of additional information:

Franklin D. Roosevelt State Park
2957 Compound Road
Yorktown Heights, New York 10598
(914) 245-4434

Notes on the trail: Park at area 1, return to the park road, and turn left. A small, narrow, paved path to the right of the park's roadway runs parallel to it. Get onto that path, and soon views of Mohansic Lake open up. This path ends at the park road, which leads to the boat launching site. Do not turn right here, but rather continue straight ahead toward the swimming pool parking area up a short hill. Bear left at the fork near the parking area's entrance, and ahead on your right look for a brown sign labeled "Nature Trail."

Turn right and take the hard-packed, wide dirt road. The trail descends and T intersects with another wide, well-surfaced trail. Turning right will take you into the pool zone. Turn left onto the fairly level path, which soon ascends a small hill. As the path turns a corner, keep bearing left as you pass through a conifer forest of hemlock and spruce. You will see some other paths leading into the main trail you are on; however, continue straight ahead in the southerly direction you have been maintaining since rounding the bend.

The trail ends where you began in about 1.4 miles. Cross the paved park road directly across from this "nature trail" and look for a small single-track leading into the woods. Turn onto this trail and bear right. This is a great single-track to try the kids on, and it will take you through an attractive, dense forest for about 1.5 miles. It ends at a well-built wooden bridge that spans a small brook. Cross the bridge and turn right onto a gravelly paved road. This road will continue around a bend and proceed south. Continue straight up a small hill and past a low wooden barrier fence that runs along-side a picnic area and playing field. Turn right at the next intersection. If this path looks familiar, it should, as you have been down it once before. For the sake of a good full ride, let's do it again. Take it to its termination at the paved park road and turn right onto the wide, gravelly park road. Take this to its end and then return to parking area 1 or ride to one of the other attractions in the park.

RIDE 46 *TRAIL OF THE PATRIARCHS*

This is one of the big daddies of Westchester single-track. It is six miles (one way) of moderately challenging, enchanting, technical nirvana. There is only one catch. It is not a county-designated mountain bike trail. It is listed in a Westchester County recreation guide under bicycling and fitness. I telephoned the Department of Parks in Westchester and was told they preferred that mountain bikers not ride the trail. They did not authorize its use as a designated mountain bike trail as they had done with Blue Mountain Reservation. They also said that they would like to keep the trail for hikers and equestrians, but currently there are no strict regulations. The official word seemed confusing, but I did the ride anyway. I found many mountain bike tracks, but not one horse track. My guess is that the trail seems very narrow and would probably be difficult for a horse to maneuver on. The ride is listed here in the hopes that one day, Westchester County will share this beautiful recreational resource with our trail-conscious mountain biker community. I suggest you telephone the Department of Parks for a trail-status update before you go.

These six miles of single-track extend from Ryder Road in the town of Ossining up to the New Croton Reservoir, through a wilderness corridor of land. This park-land corridor was set aside along a popular pathway to preserve the habitat and share it with recreationalists. Until this trailway becomes more accessible and sanctioned for mountain bikers, we must abide by the rules.

General location: The trail begins about 38 miles from Manhattan in northwestern Westchester County.
Elevation change: The trail travels over fairly level ground with minor ups and downs. There is one major climb about 4 miles into the ride that ascends a substantial hill. The sweat equity earned from the climb puts a smile on your face and keeps you trucking.
Season: This trail could be very muddy during wet weather, and any type of heavy traffic would quickly aid in eroding the beautiful condition of the path.
Services: There is a service station, coffee shop, and small convenience store located about a quarter-mile west on Ryder Road, past the trailhead.
Hazards: This trail is primarily for hikers and equestrians. This is not an authorized, designated mountain bike trail, and as a courtesy it is expected that mountain bike riders will remain off the trail. The heart-wrenching

To Taconic State Pkwy.

To Taconic State Pkwy.

133

Pines Bridge Rd.

134

Grace Ln.

Spring Valley Rd.

To 9A

9A

To 133

To Crotonville

Ryder Rd.

To Ossining

To Ossining

N

FEET

0   1000   2000

dilemma is that this trail is nirvana and has the potential to be a technical holy land, but nobody else understands except those who ride it. The trail has become popular and there appears to be a trail-conscious understanding of use of it, from the mountain bikers I have spoken to. They respect the small leniency thrown to them from officials and tread softly and carefully, yielding to the occasional equestrian with humbleness and courtesy. Westchester County Park Police have jurisdiction on this land and will ask you to get off if they find you on these unsanctioned trails. They currently do not patrol the trails. Let's hope in the future that awareness of the low impact of mountain bikes opens these beautiful trailways.

Rescue index: The trail leads through a narrow wilderness corridor with private property and roads on both sides.

Land status: The trailway is built on land that was purchased in 1929 by the Westchester County Parkway Commission. Fortunately they never built the parkway, and a primitive wilderness corridor has survived to remain the home to beautiful forests and an abundance of animal wildlife.

Maps: Westchester County Department of Parks provides a general map of the trail. The trail is straightforward, and the map I have supplied will guide you sufficiently.

Finding the trail: Take the Taconic State Parkway north to the Pines Bridge Road exit. Turn left after the ramp and go west on Pines Bridge Road, which turns into Ryder Road. A brown sign labeled "Briarcliff Peekskill Trailway" indicates the beginning of the trail on the right (north) side of Ryder Road, approximately 2.6 miles from the exit ramp. It is immediately before a small bridge that crosses over NY 9A. Parking can be found a little farther up near a convenience store or in the small shopping center parking area in town along the same street. The Brookside Public School, on the left side of Ryder Road before you get to the trailhead, also provides parking.

Source of additional information:

Westchester County Department of Parks
Recreation and Conservation
19 Bradhurst Avenue
Hawthorne, New York 10532
(914) 593-PARK

Notes on the trail: The trail begins as single-track off Ryder Road and traverses a densely wooded corridor situated along and running parallel to the east side of NY 9A. The trail soon turns away from the sounds of the busy roadway and proceeds in a northeasterly direction along the banks of a small brook. Fork left over the brook and continue up a small rise. The trail is marked with green-painted trail blazes on trees. In 1.5 miles, the paved Grace Lane is crossed. Continue across the road and into the woods, where you may hear the sound of many dogs barking. At first I thought I was in the middle of

Wooden bridge bordering Teatown Lake.

a fox hunt, but it turned out to be some kind of dog kennel. The sounds diminish about .3 mile after you climb a short hill. At 2.3 miles, cross the paved NY 134 and continue straight into the woods. At 3.2 miles a small trail leads off to the right between two sawed-off logs. Do not turn right, but continue straight through a rich forest of maple and beech. It is interesting how the forest changes from hardwoods to conifers as you descend near stream beds and then rise above them where the trail dries out.

At 3.8 miles you cross Spring Valley Road. Turn left and look for the trail between 2 old fence posts, leading back into the woods about 50' on your right. Head into the woods again and there will be a small lake on your right. Keep bearing left and pass another small trail forking to your right and leading down to the lake. At this point the trail blazes become blue. At the next fork with a trail bearing yellow blazes, bear right onto the blue trail. Cross a small wooden bridge, fork left, and head up a small hill. As you crest that hill, there will be a small clearing with power lines traversing an open slope. Turn left and begin a long climb up this grassy hill. After you cross beneath one of the utility towers, continue straight and ignore the small trail leading off into the woods on your right. You will come into another clearing as you crest the top of the hill. Bear right around the bend and descend a very steep, rock-studded, wide, four-wheel-drive road. At the base of this descent is a 4-way intersection with a post with 2 green diamonds on a yellow arrow. Turn right into a young, dense, conifer and beech forest and descend moderately. Bear left at the next intersection and proceed through a swampy area. Traverse some wooden planking across a swamp and make a sharp right following the yellow and green markers. Bear right past another, larger overgrown road to your left. You will pass by numerous large rock outcroppings of fractured and tumbled rock. They are very impressive and quite enormous.

At 5.5 miles bear left, following the green trail. The yellow trail splits off to the right. Cross paved Blinn Road at 6 miles and continue straight. Turn around at the next road, which is Quaker Ridge Road. Return the way you came.

RIDE 47 *THE ORIENT EXPRESS*

Warning! At present there is a section of the trail that is not open to mountain bikers. There is a chance that it could be open in the future. According to park officials, there are early tremors of negotiations to open up this area to mountain biking. For now you must walk your bike along the interconnecting hiking trails.

This undeveloped park preserve consists of 3,900 acres of mysterious, primeval forest, with spectacular views of the Hudson River and Hudson Highland mountain range. This tour takes place in the enigmatic Hudson Highland State Park. The park is located on a ridge that once flanked a steep gorge through which the Hudson River flows. This abrupt rise, from sea level at the Hudson to 1,600 feet, is a part of the great fault that borders the Highlands on both sides of the river. The Hudson Highlands were once the roots of a great mountain system and have been leveled by half a billion years of erosion. The Hudson gorge was two or three times greater in depth. Today the Highlands, miles deep in the earth, are all that remain of the original mountain range.

This nine-mile loop runs behind Sugarloaf Mountain. In 1776, a fort was built on the north slope with the strategy of defending the Highlands from Connecticut to New Jersey. Only 60 miles north of Manhattan, this ride runs deep into the wilds of the Hudson Highlands and brings a real sense of solitude. The single-track crosses several brooks and streams and traverses a thick wilderness of beautiful hemlock evergreen woods and a rock-strewn landscape. The Ice Age glaciers left their mark when they melted and retreated over 10,000 years ago, sculpting the landscape with huge boulders and broken rock. Along the way, you will be challenged by the hills, charmed by the scenery and invigorated by the great riding. The ride is long. Start early so there is plenty of time to rest and enjoy the forest. At the end of the ride, follow an old wood road that leads along a creek and past a scenic lake.

To Garrison

To Cold Spring

NY

N

0 — 1/4 — 1/2

MILES

9D

403

Farm
Buildings

Hudson River

To South
Highland

Sugarloaf
Mtn.

9

Double-track

TO
N.Y.C.

9D

South Mtn. Pass Rd.

To
9

To Bear
Mtn. Bridge

The trails are a mixed bag and include grass-covered, flat double-track and rolling, well-padded, pine needle–covered single-track. The wide single-track is not technically challenging. Its smoothness, good condition, and gentle, rolling grade make this tour ideal for strong advanced beginners and a blast for the more experienced dirt disciples.

Although I have not had the pleasure of riding this trail, it comes as a strong recommendation from my friend and riding companion, Eddie Ortiz. He tried this trail and felt it had a place in my book.

The park is beautiful and popular and is shared by other recreational users. Walkers and hikers occasionally use these routes for connections with their hiking trails, which means that we, as mountain bikers, need to be especially sensitive when riding. When you approach a person or group of people from behind, let them know you are there before you get too near, and do not forget to smile and say hello, too. Courteous and responsible conduct along these old forest trails will help assure the mountain biker's presence in this rare and pristine park.

General location: In Putnam County north of the town of Peekskill.
Elevation change: The terrain has its share of hills, but they are gently sloped and can be managed with an extra energy bar or two. The ride begins in the parking area, climbs to a level, flat, single-track trail, and then ascends a gentle grade along a brook. The path then traverses a rolling terrain with no major hill climbs.
Season: These trails are good any time of the year. This area can be potentially ridden in all 4 seasons, with the exception that in winter, the higher elevations might collect substantial amounts of snow.
Services: Most services can be found in the town of Peekskill.
Hazards: Raccoon rabies are present in this area of New York State so do not approach or feed these animals in the park. The eastern deer tick spreads Lyme disease, so use insect repellent on your clothing. I usually spray some around my ankles and socks in case I go through overgrown trails. There is a bow-and-arrow season in some sections. Call the park superintendent for more detailed information. There are about 2.5 miles of riding on the semibusy NY 9D, which is at the end of the loop and returns you to the parking area. Pay attention to the passing cars.
Rescue index: At most you will be about 2 miles from the well-traveled road, NY 9D.
Land status: This state land is managed by the New York Department of Environmental Conservation.
Maps: The New York–New Jersey Trail Conference's "East Hudson Trails," Trail Map 1, provides very complete coverage of Hudson Highlands State Park and is waterproof and tearproof. It sells for $6.95 and can be found at most outdoor-type stores. The USGS, 7.5 minute series, Peekskill quadrangle also provides coverage.

Woodscape along the Orient Express.

Finding the trail: Take the Taconic State Parkway north and exit at NY 301. Go west on NY 301 until you get to the town of Cold Spring. Turn south on NY 9D. You will reach NY 403 in about 4.5 miles. About 1 mile past NY 403 on NY 9D look for 2 square stone markers on your left. The words "Castle Rock 1881" and "Wing & Wing 1857" are engraved on them. Turn in here and bear left at the fork. On your right is an old red barn. Park your car next to the barn or in the rock-enclosed parking area on a small hill behind the barn.

Sources of additional information:

Clarence Fahnestock State Park
RFD 2
Carmel, New York 10512-9802
(914) 225-7207

Taconic State Park and Recreation Commission
Old Post Road
Staatsburg, New York 12580
(914) 889-4100

Peekskill Chamber of Commerce
One South Division Street
Peekskill, New York 10566
(914) 737-3600

American Cycle Corporation
1770 Crompond Road
Peekskill, New York 10566
(914) 739-7533

Toddville Bike Center
2141 Crompond Road
Cortlandt Manor, New York 10566
(914) 737-7255

Notes on the trail: Pedal down to the fork and bear right. You will see a white sign indicating the start of the trail in 100 yards. Make a left at the next trail sign and cross a large, grassy field. You will probably have to push your bike up the last 50' to get on top of the small ridge running in both directions. Turn right to pick up a red-marked, single-track trail. There are beautiful views of the Hudson River and nearby farms. At about .2 mile you will come to an intersection. Bear right; the trail is unmarked and descends parallel to NY 9D. The trail takes a turn to the left, going back in a northeasterly direction. Begin a gradual uphill climb alongside a brook going through a large forest of mature hemlocks. You are now on the eastern side of Sugarloaf Mountain.

Due to current park regulations, this is where you must dismount and walk your bike. After about 1.5 miles, you will find a blue trail coming in from the south. Continue north on this trail for .2 mile and turn right at the next trail intersection, which will take you south for about 500' and then east. Take the white trail for about .3 mile. Immediately past an intersection with a blue-blazed trail leading off in a southerly direction, turn right at the second trail that is blazed with yellow markers. This will continue for another .3 mile, where the trail makes a sharp right turn in a southerly direction. Bear right at the next trail intersection, continuing south into an old wood road in just under a mile. Once on the old wood road you may mount and continue riding.

Take this forest road past Lake Alice and where it comes out onto a hard-packed dirt road. South Mountain Pass Road is reached in about half a mile. Turn right onto South Mountain Pass Road, which descends steeply to Route 9D. The last 3 miles of the tour require you to pedal along the shoulder of NY 9D. Notice the familiar 2 stone pillars. Turn in and ride up to where your vehicle is parked.

RIDE 48 SAXON WOODS PARK

Saxon Woods Park is more evidence that good things, even places to mountain bike, come in small packages. There are a variety of off-road opportunities for novice to intermediate mountain bikers in this woodland oasis. This

To Scarsdale

Woods Rd.

To White Plains

Pool Entrance

P

SAXON WOODS

Golf Course

Loop #2

Hutchinson River Pkwy.

To New Haven

To New York City

Loop #1

Park Entrance

N

0   1000

FEET

Loop #1

Mamaroneck Ave.

NY

To (87)

compact park provides a variety of riding in a variety of terrain along five miles of wide single-track and rolling fire roads. The trails are separated into two distinct loops, each approximately 2½ miles in length. They twist, turn, and wind through an attractive, hilly woodland. The trails running throughout the park do not offer any epic adventures, but their close proximity to New York City and challenging terrain provide several hours of exciting intermediate riding. Much of the single-track runs over small hills and into small drops in the landscape, prominent in the dense, mixed hardwood and conifer forest.

So what's the catch? It is not a county-designated mountain bike trail. I telephoned the Department of Parks in Westchester and was told they preferred that mountain bikers not ride the trail. They did not authorize its use as a designated mountain bike trail as they had done with Blue Mountain Reservation. They also said they would like to keep the trail for hikers and equestrians, but currently there are no strict regulations. The ride is listed here in hopes that one day Westchester County will share this beautiful recreational resource with our trail-conscious mountain biker community. Until these trails become more accessible and sanctioned for mountain bikers we must abide by the rules.

This trail comes as a strong recommendation from a friend and riding companion, Eddie Ortiz.

General location: The park is only 17 miles from Manhattan, near Mamaroneck in Westchester County.
Elevation change: The 2 loops traverse moderately hilly terrain, with no major hills to climb. There is an abundance of flat sections too.
Season: These trails can be swell in any season. Try not to ride on them when they are covered with slushy snow or during extremely wet conditions. This will minimize trail erosion and help preserve their excellent condition.
Services: White Plains offers most services.
Hazards: This trail is primarily for hikers. This is not an authorized, designated mountain bike trail, and, as a courtesy, it is expected that mountain bike riders remain off the trail. The heart-wrenching dilemma is that this trail is nirvana and has the potential to be a technical holy land, but the only people who understand that are those who ride it. The trail has become popular, and there appears to be a trail-conscious understanding and use of it from mountain bikers I have spoken with. They respect the small leniency thrown to them from officials and tread softly and carefully, yielding to the occasional equestrian with humbleness and courtesy. Westchester County Park Police have jurisdiction on this land and will ask you to get off if they find you on these unsanctioned trails. They currently do not patrol the trails. Let's hope in the future that awareness of the low impact of mountain bikes opens these beautiful trailways.

Saxon snowbirds show true grit pedaling some frozen turf.

Rescue index: You are never far from help in Saxon Woods Park. You are surrounded by residential areas on all sides of the park and can find park personnel, at most times of the day, near the park entrance.

Land status: Westchester County Park.

Maps: Westchester County Parks will send you a Saxon Woods Park map that can also be picked up at the park entrance.

Finding the trail: Take the Hutchinson River Parkway north to Exit 23 South/ Mamaroneck Avenue. After the exit ramp, turn right onto Mamaroneck Avenue. In less than a mile, turn right at the next traffic light at the Saxon Woods Park.

Source of additional information:

> Westchester County Department of Parks
> Recreation and Conservation
> 19 Bradhurst Avenue
> Hawthorne, New York 10532
> (914) 593-PARK

Notes on the trail: Of the 2 loops, Loop 2 is the better trail. It is smoother and less gnarled by rocks and roots. Both trails are marked with rectangular white and yellow disks nailed to trees. Let's begin with Loop 1 and then pedal into Loop 2. Enter the park on Mamaroneck Avenue just south of the Hutchinson River Parkway. Drive up the steep hill and proceed into the parking area.

After parking, pedal back out of the parking area and turn right onto the single-track as it leads into the woods in a southerly direction. This is the beginning of Loop 1. After about .75 mile, you begin a rocky descent to a stream crossing. In another 1,000', bear left at the fork and continue on the single-track. Follow the trail up a small hill and down into several dips along the trail as it courses south, west, and then north in the direction of the parking area. After approximately 2 miles from the last fork, turn right at the next fork. There will be rest rooms that appear as tiny bungalows at the intersection. Use these as your landmark for the fork. After another 1,000', you will come to a **T** intersection. Turn left to begin the Loop 2 portion of this route. Turn right to return to the parking area.

If you are heading toward Loop 2, continue on the single-track for about half a mile past the Hutchinson River Parkway. You will approach a fork, where you must bear right to begin the one-way Loop 2. Bear right at the next fork and in about 400' make a sharp left. Follow the trail as it winds through a dense forest, and in a little over 1 mile, turn left at the next fork. Several other trails intersect with the main trail of Loop 2, which I have designated on the map and which are well worth seeking out. The next .75 mile traverses close to the golf course. Watch out for golf carts on the trail. After .75 mile, the trail ends, and you'll turn left in an easterly direction. After over half a mile, turn right at the fork to return to the parking area. You will cross the Hutchinson River Parkway again and soon reach the parking lot.

Shawangunk Mountain Tours

Ninety miles north of Manhattan lies one of the finest mountain bike trail systems in New York. This trail system, comprised of mostly nineteenth-century carriage roads, is spread throughout 24,000 magnificent acres in the Shawangunk Mountains. The area includes a state park, private preserves, and the Mohonk resort property. The area is quite popular with hikers, equestrians, cross-country skiers, and mountain bikers. The charming college town of New Paltz caters to the needs of the outdoor set, while the grandeur and beauty of mountains and cliffs have attracted people primarily from the metropolitan New York and New England regions for over a century. There are many attractions. New Paltz has some of the oldest streets in America. Take a stroll down Huguenot Street, where several stone houses evoke a rural European village. They were built by homesick French Huguenot families 300 years ago. Several wineries, apple farms, and pumpkin patches in the area are worth visiting too.

The Shawangunk creation bears some very important geologic history. Hundreds of millions of years ago, a great landmass called Appalachia stretched from what is now Maine to Alabama. Erosion wiped out its identity and the region was submerged under a sea. Massive quantities of eroded material accumulated and gradually cemented together. After a great upheaval, the landmass was lifted out of the sea to great heights and folded into fantastic shapes. This mountain-building era is known to geologists as the Appalachian Revolution and is currently represented in the Appalachian Mountains. There are many different names to portions of this range. The 30-mile section in New York, where Lake Minnewaska and Lake Mohonk lie, was called Shawangunk by the Native Americans. Sedimentary rocks, made up of fragments of other rocks and eroded materials deposited under water, form the Shawangunks. Three general types of rocks are found in this area and are readily identified. The first is quartz conglomerate, which is very hard and resistant and contains many different materials from silt particles to pebbles. The second is sandstone, and the third is shale, which is much older than the other two. The last period in this creation story is the Ice Age, beginning perhaps 125,000 years ago and ending possibly 10,000 years ago. The glaciers of this period acted as nature's gigantic bulldozer. They moved from northeast to southeast gouging out deep ravines in the mountains and scattering thousands of boulders of immense proportions. The glaciers left a chain of lakes: Mohonk, Minnewaska, and Awosting, among others.

A maze of several mountain bike paths winds through the impressive terrain of Minnewask State Park. This beautiful park is characterized by unique and sensitive environments, valuable for their many rare geologic and ecological features. The park is situated on the dramatic Shawangunk Mountain ridge, which rises more than 2,000 feet above sea level. The ridge dominates the park and its immediate environs as well as the rolling agricultural landscape of the surrounding towns and hamlets below.

The Mohonk Mountain House, a sprawling 125-year-old Victorian castle, sits on 2,200 acres and offers a few spectacular bike trails, and others that are equally impressive and designated for hiking. The Mohonk Mountain House is a national historic landmark. The building complex and surrounding land are included in the landmark designation. The Mohonk Preserve, which adjoins the resort, provides an additional 5,500 acres of woodlands and trails.

The mountain bike possibilities in the Shawangunk Mountains are nearly endless. Day rides from New York City usually entail an early start and a late return. Consider staying overnight at one of New Paltz's many bed-and-breakfasts or motels, and make it a long, memorable weekend.

RIDE 49 BONTICOU ROAD TOUR

Roughly ten miles of hard-packed carriage roads traverse the unique mountain ridges of the scenic and spectacular Shawangunk Mountains. Over 5,600 acres of precipitous, craggy cliffs, glens, mountain lakes, and mixed forests cover the land, which is part of the Mohonk Preserve.

Some of the most spectacular and scenic double-track can be found in these mountains on this ten-mile loop tour. It's easy to spend hours and hours cruising along nineteenth-century carriage roads that were built for vacationers of past eras who visited these mountains often. These trails are considered among the finest in the East. Beginning in the early nineteenth century, America entered the Romantic period, during which renewed emphasis was placed on the arts and nature. A good view was held in high regard. The aristocracy and intelligentsia of New York, who often took the long trip up the Hudson River by boat, found this an area of abundant natural beauty and prime meeting grounds.

Along these pleasant trails are great panoramic views of the distant pastoral farmland of the Wallkill, and the expansive Roundout River Valleys lie below. These carriage roads generally follow the contours of the land and do not require any great stamina or special technical skills. The exception is the steep Link Trail, which connects the Mohonk Preserve Visitor Center parking area to the beginning of the Bonticou carriage road.

What once provided turn-of-the-century visitors with a horse-drawn carriage tour through a beautiful woodland forest now benefits mountain bikers with stretches of gentle hill climbs and beautiful scenery. A tour at Bonticou makes for a day of memorable riding.

MILES

0   1/4   1/2

N

NY

MOHONK PRESERVE

Bonticou Crag 1194

Spring Farm 690

Spring Farm Rd.

Cedar Dr.

Spring Farm Rd.

Bonticou Rd.

Knolls Rd.
Upper 27

6

Bonticou Rd.

Mohonk Rd.

Spring Farm Rd.

Guyot Hill 1260

P

To 209, High Falls, and Stone Ridge

MOHONK PRESERVE

To Mohonk Lake Trails

To Mohonk Lake

Bonticou Rd.

Big Hill

Mountain Rest Rd.

To 87 and New Paltz

Visitor Center

General location: Travel about 90 miles north of Manhattan on the New York State Thruway, Interstate 87, to Exit 18/New Paltz.

Elevation change: The trail begins at a little over 900' and gradually climbs to 1,100'. The route then levels out and follows the contour of the mountain. There are some ascents to Guyot Hill and some descents as you go down Cedar Drive, but nothing too taxing.

Season: Fall is absolutely breathtaking, with colors filling the surrounding valleys. Winter usually brings snow, but if there is no snow on the trails, put some extra layers of clothing on and enjoy the popular trails for yourself. Late spring and summer are excellent, with warm breezes convecting up from the valleys.

Services: Most services can be found at New Paltz. Bicycles can be rented at Catskill Mountain Bicycle Shop in New Paltz.

Hazards: Many of the trails traverse the tops of flat ledges. Since you might feel more inclined to go faster on the level paths, pay attention to hidden turns along open ledges. This respect for speed and for the unknown beyond may be worth your while, to avoid becoming airborne over the Wallkill Valley below. If you are riding in the winter, watch out for ice and other slippery conditions that may be prevalent on the carriage roads. You are required to wear a helmet.

Rescue index: The Mohonk Preserve Visitor Center has telephones and first aid. On weekends, a volunteer mountain bike patrol known as GORP (Gunks Off-Road Patrol) rides a beat. They provide help and answer questions for other riders they encounter on the trail. They promote safety consciousness, from helmets to passing zone etiquette and first aid. This organization has also helped with fire prevention by riding the trails and scanning for flare-ups throughout the forests, and it encourages other mountain bike riders to join them.

Land status: The Bonticou Road and its network of trails pass through the Mohonk Preserve. Mohonk Preserve is a nonprofit organization working to protect the natural lands in the Shawangunk Mountains. There are special programs in environmental education and tours throughout the area. These 5,500 acres are open to the public from dawn to dusk for a small fee. A $10 yearly seasonal-use pass is charged for each bicycle. In addition, a day-use fee of $5 is charged each time you ride. You can become a Mohonk Preserve Member, which will cut down the day-use charges if you're planning to visit frequently. Whatever the cost, a wonderful day's outing awaits you in this unique setting of mountains, forests, and lakes.

Maps: After paying the day fee at the visitor center, ask for the mountain bike map. Take along hiking maps too, as they supply more detailed information on the trails. The New York–New Jersey Trail Conference's "Shawangunk Trails" waterproof and tearproof map provides the best detail and can be found at most outdoor-type stores for only $6.95. Map 10 and 10A, Mohonk Preserve, Lake Mohonk Resort and Virginia Smiley Preserve, provide the most

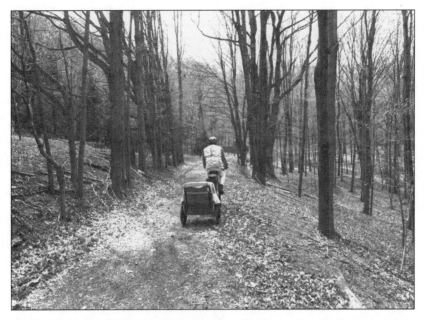

The family chariot gliding along Spring Farm Road.

detail for these rides. These roads are well marked. Bicycle trail blazes are posted on trees along the route. At important intersections, the name of the road you are traveling is posted on wooden signs.

Finding the trail: Take the New York Thruway (Interstate 87) north and exit at 18. Proceed past the toll booths and turn left onto NY 299 (west), which becomes Main Street. Proceed through the town, cross the bridge over the Wallkill River, and bear right at the next fork heading toward the Mohonk Mountain House. After the town of New Paltz, continue on County Road 6. Cross a bridge and bear right at the Mohonk Mountain House sign, continuing onto Mountain Rest Road. Head up this road for about 1.75 miles until you see the Mohonk Preserve Visitor Center on your right. Directly across from the center is the parking area. You can park here and ascend the .2 mile Link Trail that climbs from the parking area and intersects with Bonticou Road. The other option is to continue on CR 6 and park in the parking area just after the entrance to Mohonk Mountain House. There is a $6 fee for this parking area. Both alternatives lead to Bonticou Road.

Sources of additional information:

Ulster County Public Information Office
244 Fair Street
PO Box 1800
Kingston, New York 12401
(914) 331-9300

New Paltz Chamber of Commerce
257 ½ Main Street
New Paltz, New York 12561
(914) 255-0243

Mohonk Preserve
Mountain Rest Road
New Paltz, New York 12561
(914) 255-0919

Mohonk Mountain House
Mountain Rest Road
New Paltz, New York 12561
(914) 255-1000 or (800) 772-6646

Catskill Mountain Bicycle Shop
5 ½ North Front Street
New Paltz, New York 12561
(914) 255-3859

Notes on the trail: From the visitor center, take the Link Trail (yellow-marked) a short distance up a steep hill to the Bonticou carriage road. You will ascend from an elevation of about 950' to 1,100' in .4 mile. The Link Trail comes to an end at Bonticou Road. Turn right at the intersection. Bonticou Road is a wide, exquisite, level, hard-packed road that passes through forests of maple, oak, and hemlock and provides great views of the pastoral farmland of the Wallkill River valley to the east. After 1.3 miles a 4-way intersection offers 2 options.

Turning to the left will take you uphill along the Guyot Hill loop trail to an elevation of 1,260'. This small loop passes a small, picturesque pond and returns you to the same intersection with Bonticou Road. You can also take this loop to return to the visitor center, since there is a connection at the western end of the loop linking back down into Bonticou Road. Guyot Hill is unique. The Shawangunks are mostly made up of a hard conglomerate rock that covers the other rocks. This small hill is the highest mound of soft shale in the mountains not covered by the conglomerate. Guyot Hill and Bonticou Crag served as hiding grounds for militia during the Revolutionary War.

Continue on Bonticou Road by following the posted wooden sign reading, "Bonticou Road." Farther along the road, you will come across the tremendous block-like boulders that make up the "talus" of the Bonticou Crag. These huge rock fragments, sometimes the size of a house, have fallen from the face of the cliff as a result of faulting, fracturing, and erosion. The interesting item about this site is that you are looking at rock that should be horizontally laid out. The tremendous pressures from beneath the earth's surface have caused these landmasses to be pushed up vertically through a process called faulting.

As you ride along, views of the fallen rocks of Bonticou Crag come into view. Consider taking a short, vigorous rock scramble up the Crag to the summit where beautiful mountain-top views of the surrounding valleys and Catskill Mountains can be had.

A quarter-mile later, you will come to another intersection. Let's become oriented and stand at the intersection with our noses facing north. Continue to your right down Cedar Drive as it leads off in a northerly direction through a mature hemlock forest. Cedar Drive takes you downhill to an intersection with Spring Farm Road. Continue on the main carriage road bearing left. Turn left uphill at the intersection with Spring Farm Road.

Continue up Spring Farm Road, bearing left at the intersection with Bonticou Road. The right fork will take you away from your parking at the visitor center, but it will link you from Bonticou Road into the Mohonk Lake trail systems. Spring Farm Road, the left fork, will take you back to CR 6, the Mohonk tollgate, and the Mohonk Preserve Visitor Center parking area.

RIDE 50 *LAND OF OZ*

Imagine riding along smooth, wide, hard-packed, dirt carriage roads and traversing precipitous, craggy ledges that rise up hundreds of feet with magnificent views of distant farmland and river valleys. Does it sound like a mountain biker's dream? Perhaps, but it is within your reach. Just click your heels and get an early morning start for a full day of riding. Then take in 14 miles of carriage roads that weave along this unique mountain plateau in the scenic and spectacular Shawangunk Mountains.

The trails on this 14-mile loop encircle the Lake Mohonk area, whose landscape was sculpted by the last ice age. Mohonk, a Native American name meaning "top of the sky," towers above the nearby valleys and can be seen as a long ridge of high cliffs running in a north-south direction. Ironically, they were once a landmass submerged deep within a large sea. Forces deep in the earth pushed this landmass out of the sea to great heights and creased it into bizarre shapes. Freezing water fractured the vertical cliffs, causing large boulders to plummet down the escarpment. The mile-high continental ice sheets from the last ice age became nature's bulldozers and gouged out deep clefts in the mountains, scattering thousands of tons of boulders of immense sizes and shapes across the landscape. The glaciers carved out a ravine on the top of this ridge along a faultline and created a chain of lakes, among them Mohonk and Minnewaska. About this time, one of the glaciers pushed tremendous quantities of rock and debris into the south end of Lake Mohonk. When the ice melted, the materials settled into a solid mass, preventing any water from

RIDE 50 *LAND OF OZ*

Note: *All trails are carriage roads except where marked.*

passing through. Rains that fell on these mountains seeped through the landscape and fed underground streams that built up the lake through hidden channels and replenished its waters.

Visit the nineteenth-century Mohonk Mountain House overlooking the lake. It was purchased as a rundown tavern in 1869 by the Smiley brothers and has evolved into a 305-room hotel. It's still owned by the Smiley family. Surrounded by the Mohonk Preserve, the environs of the area reflect the lifestyle of leisure and elegance of bygone eras. Cruise along the faultless carriage roads and meander through the exquisite Shawangunk Mountains, with their exposed, craggy rock ledges and thick hemlock forests. A century ago, horse-drawn carriages rode along the same trails. Park your bikes near the Mohonk Mountain House and stroll through the nearby gardens and around the spring-fed half-mile-long mountain lake in front of this huge Victorian castle.

General location: About 90 miles north of Manhattan on the New York State Thruway to Exit 18, near the town of New Paltz.

Elevation change: The ride begins at the Mohonk House parking area, elevation 1,100', near the gatehouse. The trail basically follows the contour of the land, with some moderate hills punctuating the route. The long, traversing ascent along Kleine Kill Road at the end of the tour will be the most rigorous climbing you have to do. Once at the top, it's all level riding with one last long downhill ride to the parking area.

Season: In the winter, cross-country skiers can be found on the groomed tracks. If there is no snow, get your bike out, dress warmly, and take in the views. Don't forget to grab a hot chocolate at the Mohonk Mountain House. Fall fills the surrounding valleys with breathtaking colors. Winter usually brings snow. Late spring and summer are excellent, with warm breezes moving up from the valleys.

Services: Most services can be found at New Paltz, and bicycles can be rented at Catskill Mountain Bicycle Shop in town. Within the Mohonk area, Picnic Lodge, a visitor center located 1.5 miles from the gatehouse, has a snack bar, gift shop, and picnic area.

Hazards: Weather conditions can make routes icy, wet, and slippery along the edge of the cliffs. Tread carefully and control your speed when conditions are less than secure. Many of the trails travel the tops of flat ledges. If you feel more inclined to go faster on the level paths, pay attention to what may lie beyond a hidden turn. During the winter watch out for ice and other slippery conditions. In spring and summer, the open ledges and rocks can be sunning spots for snakes. During one ride we crossed the path of a 5' slithering friend, making his way across the trail to one of those spots.

Rescue index: Telephones can be found at the Mohonk Mountain House. It's fairly difficult to become lost since most trails end at or near the main grounds. Trail names and road signs are abundant throughout the tour and are worthwhile when you are in doubt about which direction to take.

Land status: This network of trails passes through the Mohonk Resort. Mohonk Preserve is a nonprofit organization working to protect the natural lands in the Shawangunk Mountains. There are special programs in environmental education and tours throughout the area. These 5,500 acres are open to the public from dawn to dusk for a small fee. A $10 yearly seasonal-use pass is charged for each bicycle. Each time you ride, a $5 day-use fee is charged. If you are planning to come frequently, you can become a Mohonk Preserve Member. It will reduce the day-use charges considerably. Whatever

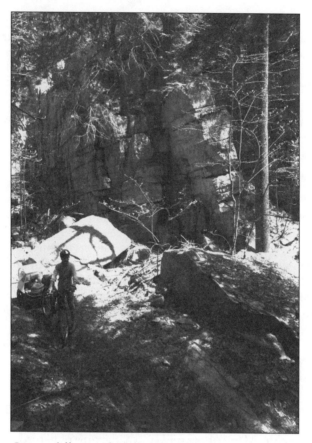

Craggy cliffs, once buried under a large sea, tower above the trails in the Mohonk Preserve.

the cost, a wonderful day's outing awaits you in this unique setting of mountains, forests, and lakes.

Maps: A bicycle map is supplied when you stop by the visitor center to pay the day fees. Take along their hiking maps too, as they supply a little more detailed information on the trails. The New York–New Jersey Trail Conference's "Shawangunk Trails" waterproof and tearproof map provides the best detail and can be found at most outdoor-type stores for $6.95. Map 10 and 10A, Mohonk Preserve, Lake Mohonk Resort and Virginia Smiley Preserve, provide the most detail for these rides. These roads are well marked, with bicycle trail signs and the name of the road you're traveling on posted on trees. Things could not get much better than this.

Finding the trail: Take the New York Thruway (Interstate 87) north and exit at 18. Proceed past the tollbooths and turn left onto NY 299 (west), which becomes Main Street. Proceed through town, cross the bridge over the Wallkill River, and bear right at the next fork heading toward the Mohonk Mountain

House. After the town of New Paltz continue on County Road 6, cross a bridge, and bear right at the Mohonk Mountain House sign onto Mountain Rest Road. Head up this road for about 2 miles until you see the Lake Mohonk Gate House on your left. Turn in here. There is a $6 fee for parking. Return to CR 6 and turn left, pedaling down a steep hill for about 200'. Look for a carriage road on your left leading into the forest. This is Bonticou Road west. Begin your journey there.

Sources of additional information:

Ulster County Public Information Office
244 Fair Street
PO Box 1800
Kingston, New York 12401
(914) 331-9300

New Paltz Chamber of Commerce
257 ½ Main Street
New Paltz, New York 12561
(914) 255-0243

Mohonk Preserve
Mountain Rest Road
New Paltz, New York 12561
(914) 255-0919

Mohonk Mountain House
Mountain Rest Road
New Paltz, New York 12561
(914) 255-1000 or (800) 772-6646

Catskill Mountain Bicycle Shop
5 ½ North Front Street
New Paltz, New York 12561
(914) 255-3859

Notes on the trail: This portion of Bonticou Road continues on the west side of County Road 6 and is a continuation of the Bonticou Road tour found in this book. It connects several other carriage roads to form a 14-mile loop through the Lake Mohonk area.

This portion of the hard-packed carriage road takes you through mature stands of hemlocks and past a hillside dotted with fallen talus from the Shawangunk conglomerate ledges. The landscape is very interesting and unique and the carriage roads are easy to cruise on, leaving you time to focus on the scenery and not on the difficulties of a trail. At about .7 mile a trail comes in from the right; keep bearing left on the main carriage road. You will soon come to an intersection with North Lookout and Rockrift roads. Bear right onto Rockrift Road; there are signs indicating that bicycles are not allowed any farther on North Lookout Road, so you can only turn right at this point. Descend past more large rock crevices and bear left onto Cedar Drive. Bear left at the intersection onto Mossy Brook Road. Each of the roads has signs indicating which route it is.

There is a half-mile steady climb up the four-wheel-drive Mossy Brook Road. Turn right when you reach the intersection with single-track Maple Path indicated by blue markers on a tree. Ascend Maple Path a very short distance and turn left where the trail levels off along some utility lines. In about 50' you come to an intersection with Stokes Trail; bear right to continue on Maple Path. The trail ascends and travels through a forest with an understory of mountain laurel and past more open ledges. Some sections of Maple Path are uncharacteristically rockier than what is found along the other carriage roads, but the remaining trails are in excellent condition. The final descent from Maple Path takes you through a huge arena of broken rock known as Rock Pass and down to the Laurel Ledge carriage road. Turn right toward the Rhododendron Bridge. Laurel Ledge Road is a wide, fairly level carriage road. It passes along the base of a great broken-up talus slope. The placement of these huge boulders has created a unique landscape that has become a home for plant and animal communities to thrive in. After about 1.5 miles along Laurel Ledge Road, you will come to an area filled with huge rhododendrons. You will notice a road higher up on a ridge to your right. That is Overcliff Road. Keep bearing left to the bridge that spans a small stream. This is Rhododendron Bridge. Proceed over the bridge and make a right onto Oakwood Drive. Take this carriage road bearing left. At a large intersection with Duck Pond Road, Kleine Kill Road, and Oakwood Drive, take Kleine Kill Road, and climb heartily for .7 mile toward Rock Spring Bridge, past great views of Sky Top along this wide, hard-packed, dusty road. Continue straight toward Woodland Bridge and Huguenot Drive. When you reach the paved Huguenot Drive, a turn to the right will bring you back to the parking at the Mohonk Gatehouse. Turning left will take you up toward Mohonk Lake and the Mohonk Mountain House and picnic area.

RIDE 51 *THE TRAPPS*

This area of the Mohonk Preserve is popular with hikers, mountain climbers, and cross-country skiers. The five-mile loop consists of two wide, hard-packed dirt roads known as the Undercliff and Overcliff roads. The tour of the Trapps should not be left out of any mountain biker's itinerary of the Shawangunk Mountains. The scenery is awesome. These two roads encircle dizzying, craggy ledges that rise hundreds of feet, with panoramic views of

Note: *All trails are carriage roads.*

distant farmland and river valleys. This fairly level ride is not technically challenging, and its smoothness, good condition, and gentle rolling grades provide opportunities to shift your gaze from the ground and peer out across the landscape. This area has a universal appeal to bikers of all skill levels. Beginners will be exhilarated by the accessibility of such scenery. The more experienced rider will appreciate the opportunity to get in some fast double-track riding. They can also network into the Mohonk Lake area's trail system, readily accessed via the Rhododendron Bridge at the end of Undercliff Road.

Undercliff Road follows the 2,000-foot Shawangunk Mountain Ridge with wide open views of the Wallkill River valley and all its wineries and farms. Millions of years ago, sediments, eroding and washing down from the Shawangunk Mountains, filled the valley to the east. These soft sediments were then carved out by streams and rivers flowing from the higher, surrounding mountains. The glaciers from the last ice age finished the job. They bulldozed a tremendous trough running north-south along the eastern side of the Shawangunk Range, creating the present-day fertile lowlands of the Wallkill River valley.

Undercliff Road, built in 1903, is considered an engineering feat because it crossed a talus slope of rock fragments varying in size from pebbles to house-size boulders. These tremendous blocks of white conglomerate rock were wedged loose by ice and growing plants and tumbled down the face of the cliffs, settling as talus. Notice the talus blocks that are more angular. These are the newer blocks that have recently fallen as opposed to the older, more rounded blocks.

Undercliff Road traverses one of the most popular mountain climbing regions in the eastern United States, called "The Gunks." As you ride past these vertical cliffs and steep faces, notice all the climbers suspended from or attempting an ascent up the ledges. The rock is unusually solid and trustworthy and provides excellent handholds and footholds in tiny ledges and horizontal cracks.

General location: Travel about 90 miles north of Manhattan on the New York State Thruway to Exit 18, near the town of New Paltz.
Elevation change: This loop basically follows the contours of the land at an elevation of about 1,000'. There are a few short, graded hills to climb, but nothing too strenuous.
Season: In the winter cross-country skiers can be found on the groomed tracks; but if there is no snow take your bike out, dress warmly, and enjoy the solitude of a fresh winter day. Fall is absolutely breathtaking with colors filling the surrounding pastoral valleys. Winter usually brings snow. Late spring and summer are excellent, with warm breezes coming up from the valleys.
Services: Most services can be found at New Paltz. There is a sandwich and beverage truck in the parking area near the trailhead. Bicycles can be rented in New Paltz at the Catskill Mountain Bicycle Shop on Front Street.

Hazards: Most of the riding is along ledges, and weather conditions can make routes icy, wet, and slippery. The area is beautiful and quite popular. Expect considerable traffic from hikers and other riders in the beginning of the ride. Ride courteously and defensively, and be prepared to drastically reduce your speed on a busy weekend.

Rescue index: Telephones and a small deli can be found near the intersection of NY 55 and NY 299. Undercliff and Overcliff roads are popular trails, and there are usually Mohonk Preserve rangers patrolling the area.

Land status: The Trapps are part of the Mohonk Preserve and the roaming park rangers require a daily-use fee. Mohonk Preserve is a nonprofit organization working to protect the natural lands in the Shawangunk Mountains. There are special programs in environmental education and tours throughout the area. The area is open to the public from dawn to dusk for a small fee. A $10 yearly seasonal-use pass is charged for each bicycle. Each time you ride, a day-use fee of $5 is charged. You can become a Mohonk Preserve Member, which will cut down the day-use charges, if you're planning to visit frequently.

Maps: The New York–New Jersey Trail Conference's "Shawangunk Trails" waterproof and tearproof map provides the best detail and can be found at most outdoor-type stores for $6.95. Map 10 and 10A, Mohonk Preserve, Lake Mohonk Resort and Virginia Smiley Preserve, provide the most detail for these rides. The loop consists of only carriage roads. It is hard to become lost.

Finding the trail: Take the New York State Thruway (Interstate 87) north and exit at 18. Proceed past the toll booths and turn left onto NY 299 (west), which becomes Main Street. Proceed through town, cross the bridge over the Wallkill River, and bear left, staying on NY 299. The road provides a good perspective of the Shawangunk Ridge as the mountains fill up your front windshield. Turn right at the intersection with NY 55. After the hairpin turn, begin looking for available parking anywhere along the side of the road. Due to the area's popularity, you will probably see many other vehicles parked along the side too. People get there early to begin climbing. After you have parked along the road, proceed to the small pedestrian bridge that crosses NY 44. This is Trapps Bridge. The trail begins on the northeast side of NY 44 or the right side coming from New Paltz.

Sources of additional information:

Ulster County Public Information Office
244 Fair Street
PO Box 1800
Kingston, New York 12401
(914) 331-9300

New Paltz Chamber of Commerce
257 ½ Main Street
New Paltz, New York 12561
(914) 255-0243

Mohonk Preserve
Mountain Rest Road
New Paltz, New York 12561
(914) 255-0919

Mohonk Mountain House
Mountain Rest Road
New Paltz, New York 12561
(914) 255-1000 or (800) 772-6646

Catskill Mountain Bicycle Shop
5 ½ North Front Street
New Paltz, New York 12561
(914) 255-3859

Notes on the trail: Pedal up the steep embankment to the top of the bridge and take Undercliff Road leading off to the right. The road passes under the cliffs where you will see many climbers and their gear hanging from the crevasses and ledges.

Stay on Undercliff Road until you come to a 4-way intersection at about 2.5 miles. If you feel like extending your loop, you can network with the Mohonk-area bike trails. Take a right over the Rhododendron Bridge onto Oakwood Drive, which connects with Old Stage Road. Then return to the intersection. Refer to the map for better detail of this loop extension.

To continue on the Trapps loop, take the farthest left-hand road and ascend a short hill to Overcliff Road. Take this wide carriage road back to Trapps Bridge. If you are charged up and would like to continue riding, pedal across the bridge and continue along the hard-packed road known as Trapps Carriage Road. This wide dirt road continues on for another 3.5 miles.

RIDE 52 *SHANGRI LA*

Minnewaska State Park is to the East what Moab, Utah, is to the West: a mecca for mountain bike riders. This area may not be a dirt disciple's technical dream because the trails are primarily wide, hard-packed, dirt carriage roads. However, once your knobbies touch down on this 11-mile loop, it's a rider's taste of heaven. Hammerheads may not find many steep, narrow, and twisting trails that stretch the limits of their abilities. So what. They will find miles of old carriage roads that seem to have been divinely created just for cruising on a mountain bike. The network of trails is situated on the Shawangunk Mountain Ridge, which rises more than 2,000 feet above sea level. There are overlooks and panoramic vista points of incredible beauty along the trails, which roll through the evergreens and hardwoods garnering the

Note: All trails are carriage roads.

1,500-foot dazzling white craggy cliffs. Dense thickets of laurel and azalea, blooming in May, are abundant along the carriage roads. Ride through a unique habitat. The Shawangunk Mountain Range displays a transition in flora between the northern boreal forests of the Catskill high peaks and the southern forests that are distinguished by hardwoods, oak, hickory, and pitch pine. The Shawangunk ridge is used as a corridor for animal migrations. Hawks, falcons, and vultures use these migration pathways or flyways and can be seen soaring above the warm updrafts rising above the escarpment.

After a day of warm-weather riding, cool off or picnic around the two beaches set among the gem-like Lake Minnewaska or Lake Awosting. Nestled among the craggy cliffs of dazzling white conglomerate garnered with evergreens and hardwoods, is the clear, deep, blue-green Awosting Lake. This "Shangri-la" bares incredible beauty. The Shawangunks were once the bed of a large sea. Forces deep within the earth forced this landmass out of the sea to great heights and into bizarre shapes. Freezing water fractured the vertical cliffs, causing large boulders to plummet down the escarpment. The mile-high continental ice sheets from the last ice age scoured the land and carved deep clefts in the mountains, scattering thousands of tons of boulders. The glaciers carved out a ravine in the top of this ridge along a faultline, forming the Mohonk, Minnewaska, and Awosting lakes, and many more. Lake Awosting lies within one of these fault zones and is replenished from underground springs that channel the rains falling on these mountains and seeping into the landscape. This land has much to offer.

General location: Travel about 90 miles north of Manhattan on the New York State Thruway to Exit 18, near the town of New Paltz.
Elevation change: The carriage roads gradually climb from 1,200' to 2,000' and drop to about 1,800' during the course of the ride. There are short ups and downs, but nothing too strenuous, as well as a fair share of level riding.
Season: In the winter cross-country skiers can be found on the groomed tracks, but if there is no snow take your bike out, dress warmly, and enjoy the solitude of a winter day. Fall is absolutely breathtaking, with colors filling the surrounding pastoral valleys. Winter usually brings snow. Late spring and summer are excellent, with warm breezes rising from the valleys.
Services: Most services can be found at New Paltz. There is a sandwich and beverage truck in the parking area near the trailhead. Bicycles can be rented in New Paltz at the Catskill Mountain Bicycle Shop on Front Street. There is an energy-supply truck with sandwiches, coffee, and cool, refreshing beverages in the parking area near Lake Minnewaska. Portosans, those friendly mobile toilets, can be found below the parking area near the lake. During the summer there is also a swimming dock by the lake.
Hazards: Most of the riding is along ledges, and weather conditions can make routes icy, wet, and slippery. The area is beautiful and quite popular. Expect considerable traffic from hikers and other riders at the beginning of

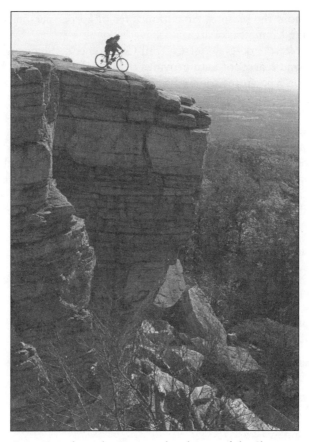

Centuries of weathering scar the plateau of the Shawangunks.

the ride. Ride courteously and defensively, and be prepared to drastically reduce your speed on a busy weekend. The hiking trails are off-limits to bikers, so if you are looking for single-track try somewhere else. Horseback riding is allowed on the carriage roads, so as a courtesy pull to the side and allow them to pass. There is currently no conflict between equestrians and mountain bikers, and all share and enjoy the same trails. Be careful not to spook horses by riding close or fast from either direction on the trail. Fall weekends during peak foliage make for difficult parking. Get there between 9 A.M. and 10 A.M.

Rescue index: There is a ranger station next to Lake Minnewaska. There is also considerable people traffic on the carriage roads during the busier seasons. Help is never too far away.

Land status: The Palisades Park Commission manages this New York park. The park is open daily at 9 A.M. and closing hours, which are posted, may vary throughout the seasons. An entrance fee of $5 per person is charged to enter the Lake Minnewaska area.

Maps: The New York–New Jersey Trail Conference's "Shawangunk Trails" waterproof and tearproof map provides the best detail and can be found at most outdoor-type stores for $6.95. Map 9, "Minnewaska State Park/Ice Caves Mountain," provides the most detail for these rides.

Finding the trail: Take the New York Thruway (Interstate 87) north and exit at 18. Proceed past the toll booths and turn left onto NY 299 (west), which becomes Main Street. Proceed through town, cross the bridge over the Wallkill River, and bear left, staying on NY 299. The road provides a good perspective of the Shawangunk Ridge as the mountains fill up your front windshield. Turn right at the intersection with NY 44/NY 55. Continue on this road for about 5 miles until you see a sign posting the park entrance. Turn left into the Minnewaska park entrance and pay the individual entrance fees.

Sources of additional information:

Ulster County Public Information Office
244 Fair Street
PO Box 1800
Kingston, New York 12401
(914) 331-9300

New Paltz Chamber of Commerce
257 ½ Main Street
New Paltz, New York 12561
(914) 255-0243

Lake Minnewaska
P.O. Box 893
New Paltz, New York 12561
(914) 255-0752

Catskill Mountain Bicycle Shop
5 ½ North Front Street
New Paltz, New York 12561
(914) 255-3859

Notes on the trail: Leave the parking area and head toward the north end of Lake Minnewaska. You will see some picnic tables overlooking the lake. Descend to the lake. There will be several signs with trailhead names and mileage posted. Several loop configurations can be created within this park. For the sake of choosing one, I am going to propose the following route, which offers the most diversity, fun, and scenery.

Our goal is to picnic or snack at Lake Awosting. Lake Awosting, Lake Minnewaska, and Mohonk Lake are surrounded by a very tough and durable, quartz-pebble conglomerate wall of rock. The lakes are thought to lie along a fault zone where the bedrock was broken up. The Ice Age glaciers scooped up and carried off the rocks, leaving a basin to be filled by the melting glaciers.

Look for the blue-blazed Castle Point carriage road trail. This wide, hard-packed road takes you along a very scenic escarpment with many panoramic viewpoints. The 3 miles of gradual ascent needed to reach the downhill trail to Lake Awosting will go unnoticed because you will become lost in the natural beauty that appears around every turn. There are some gazebos built along the ledges for resting and taking in the scenery. Take a moment to sit in one and look out over the landscape. A very unusual and interesting feature along the route is the huge blocks of rock that have split off the cliffs and tumbled down to lean against each other. The wide crevasses in the ledges you see along your ride are the beginnings of the jointing and fracturing of these rocks. At about 4.3 miles from Lake Minnewaska, you will come to an intersection with the yellow-blazed Hamilton Point carriage road trail. If you wish to return at this point or create a shorter ride, make a left onto this path and continue straight until you reach the parking area in about 3 miles.

To continue to Lake Awosting, make a right at Castle Point's trail junction with Hamilton Point and descend to the lake. Fork left and you will be on the black-marked Awosting Lake carriage road loop. Take the loop and stop at the stone swimming beach located along the middle of the lake. If it's summer, this is a great place to stop, rest, and swim. There are 2 more great places for stopping. A little farther on, 2 rock promontories jut into the water, which is more secluded and is situated in a beautiful setting.

Make your way around the lake. At the end of the lake a black-blazed road comes in from your left. Stay to your right and cross the small dam at the north end of the lake. Bear left onto the green-marked Awosting Lake carriage road and return to the parking area, which takes over 3 miles. If you are riding in the winter, you will see some very large frozen falls created by water seeping over the cliffs along this road.

RIDE 53 *WALLKILL VALLEY RAIL TRAIL*

This beautiful, 12-mile hiking and biking trail (6 miles one way) passes through two quaint seventeenth-century villages, skirts farms, passes through woods, and crosses over rivers and streams. The elevated rail bed provides a view of the surrounding area, including woodland ponds, the Wallkill River, and the Shawangunk Mountains in the distance. Wood turtles, woodcocks, songbirds, broadwing hawks, great horned owls, fox, white-tailed deer, and raccoons are frequently sighted.

RIDE 53 *WALLKILL VALLEY RAIL TRAIL*

To
Tillson

32

New Paltz

299

To Lake
Minnewaska

To New York
State Thruway

87

Wallkill River

208

NY

208

N

0   1/2   1

MILES

To
Wallkill

The well-maintained cinder trail is essentially flat. It can be ridden as an out-and-back or as a loop, by returning to the start via 1 of 21 paved roads that cross the trail. The trail passes through the New Paltz Historic District, which features seventeenth-century stone houses and the old railroad station that served the trains on this former Conrail route. There is also a Mexican restaurant, a bistro, a bakery, and several pizza parlors to top off a leisurely ride.

Although I have not covered this trail personally, I would be remiss not to include it. It's listed in another book in this series, by Joe Surkiewicz, entitled *The Mountain Biker's Guide to Central Appalachia*.

General location: The ride begins in the town of New Paltz, 15 miles south of Kingston and 1.5 miles from the New York State Thruway (I-87).

Elevation change: Negligible.

Season: The best riding is from late spring to mid-fall.

Services: All services, including 2 bike shops and rentals, are available in New Paltz. Gardiner has several bed-and-breakfast inns.

Hazards: Parts of the southern section of the trail are frequently covered with water after heavy rain. The bridge over the Wallkill has been slated for repair; if the work is not completed before your visit, take special care.

Rescue index: Help can be flagged down on the paved roads that cross the trail or from nearby residences.

Land status: The linear park is jointly owned by the village of New Paltz and the Land Trust of Wallkill Valley.

Maps: The New York–New Jersey Trail Conference's "Shawangunk Trails" waterproof and tearproof map provides the best detail and can be found at most outdoor-type stores. Map 10, Shawangunk Trails–North has the most detail. The USGS, 7.5 minute series quadrangles are Gardiner and Rosendale. Brochures of the trail include a map and are available at the Town Hall on North Chestnut Street in New Paltz. Phone (914) 255-0100.

Finding the trail: Take the New York State Thruway (Interstate 87) north and exit at 18. Proceed past the toll booths and turn left onto NY 299 (west), which becomes Main Street. At approximately 1.5 miles from the exit, the Wallkill Valley Rail Trail crosses the road. Park on a side street in the village or in the lot near the historic district.

Source of additional information:

Wallkill Valley Rail Trail Association
P.O. Box 1048
New Paltz, New York 12561

Notes on the trail: From the parking area the path leads in both a northerly and southerly direction. You have the option of traveling in either of those directions.

Catskill Region Tours

Within the sprawling, 700,000-acre Catskill Park region lies the state-protected Catskill Forest Preserve, which includes the Catskill Mountains. This range is west of the Hudson River, which carves the valley running north-south through eastern New York. Actually the Catskills are not true mountains. Rather, the Catskills are eroded portions of a plateau millions of years old. Four hundred million years ago this area was beneath a shallow ocean. The region was pushed up as the earth's continental plates collided and merged. The ice ages, whose glaciers covered the northern half of North America, weathered this plateau into the many valleys and mountains visible today.

These mountains offer virtually unlimited possibilities for rugged, scenic biking. I have included ten tours which sample some of the best terrain. Endless miles of dirt roads also crisscross this beautiful landscape. The forests are laced with dirt roads, jeep trails, and single-track hiking trails. The Catskill Forest Preserve is dotted with campsites and offers diverse recreational activities for all who visit.

Exploitation of the mountains began in the early nineteenth century. Decades upon decades of relentless, uncontrolled cutting and burning left the 250,000-acre preserve denuded and wasted in the latter half of the nineteenth century. It was a wilderness thought to be inexhaustible, but full-grown majestic hemlocks, maples, and oak trees were reduced to stumps. Green pastures became barren dirt fields. When one sees the verdant mountains today, it's hard to imagine that long ago they were just studded with stumps.

Unlike the White Mountains of New Hampshire and the Green Mountains of Vermont, the Catskills were protected from exploitation well into the nineteenth century and stayed unchanged until the forces of the Industrial Revolution ravaged the land. The forests of this great park were initially exploited for their bountiful supply of hemlock bark, used in the process of turning animal hides into leather. Massive numbers of trees across the valleys and mountainsides were leveled.

Hunter, now a popular ski resort town, was the site of the first tannery. It thrived, and soon after, more tanneries were built, and then more, and they all thrived on surrounding hemlock forests and ample water supplies. The industry continued to grow until shortly after the Civil War, when all reachable tracts of hemlocks were gone, and the demand for the Catskill-tanned leather, which played a large role in outfitting the Union troops, dried up.

Today, a virgin hemlock grove is a rarity. The few surviving trees are spotted only by those hikers or woodsmen who venture deep into the wilderness or have a sharp eye, or perhaps a mountain biker pausing at just the right spot. The forests of New York became the bastion of several industries that came and went over the decades. As tanneries sprung up, so did quarries for the excavation of bluestone. However, close to the end of the nineteenth century, the quarries became obsolete with the discovery of the less expensive Portland cement.

Logging, another mountain industry, continues today, as does the tourist industry with its growing legions of hikers, mountain bikers, and nature lovers. It's an industry with roots traceable to the early 1800s, when America acquired a renewed appreciation for the arts and nature.

As we approach the twenty-first century, despite the ravaging of the land and pockets of poverty, the Catskills remain rich in beauty and history. Generations of the well-to-do and famous came to the large hotels, which over the decades, changed ownerships, were renovated, or simply closed during hard times. The region's golden era stretched from the 1940s to the 1960s; it became the vacation paradise for families and the weekend retreat for singles looking for that perfect someone, long before the Hamptons were the in spot.

Europeans escaping the world wars immigrated to America for sanctuary and then made summer migrations from the cities to the Catskills for vacations. Small Catskill towns became havens for Irish, Italians, Germans, and Eastern European Jews. Railroad and steamship lines, originally laid down for industrial purposes, were now transporting populations of new Americans to the mountains.

It was the great escape from the industrial age, the strife of the city, and the problems of the past. Many owe it all to the 1885 creation of the Catskill Forest Preserve. It reshaped the land and charted the future as a major source of year-round recreational activities and miles and miles of excellent hiking, cross-country ski, and snowmobile trails. The rich history of this region is an attraction, especially for mountain bikers. Old lumber and carriage roads provide many miles of potentially awesome mountain bike experiences.

Sources of additional information:

Department of Environmental Conservation (DEC)
Region 3 Headquarters–
 Ulster and Sullivan Counties
21 South Putt Corners Road
New Paltz, New York 12561
(914) 255-5453

Department of Environmental Conservation (DEC)
Region 4 District Office–
 Schoharie and Delaware Counties
Route 10
Stamford, New York 12167
(607) 652-7365

Department of Environmental Conservation (DEC)
Region 4 Sub-Office–Green County
439 Main Street
Catskill, New York 12414
(518) 943-4030

IMBA-Affiliated Club
Fats in the Cats Bicycle Club
61 John Street
Kingston, New York 12401
(914) 331-9800
(914) 338-3552

RIDE 54 NORTH LAKE TRAILS

The setting for this moderately challenging five-mile-out, five-mile-back trail is the unique and natural habitat of the Catskill Forest Preserve's North Lake area. The tour includes spectacular views of the Hudson Valley and explores an area steeped in nineteenth-century Catskill history. The legendary Catskill Mountain House once stood here and played host to an assemblage of famous people. A combination of horse and wood roads, set on top of an elevated plateau, gently traverse the eastern face of the 2,000-foot escarpment. The trail passes through a forested habitat and features plants and trees from three geographic forest types. This is the only area in the Catskills where pitch pine, common to southern forests; maple and beech hardwoods of northern forests; and the spruce and firs of the mountain summits can be found in the same place. On a clear day, five states can be seen from the rocky, flat ledges that make up the eastern edge of the Catskill escarpment.

What once provided turn-of-the-century visitors with a horse-drawn carriage tour through a beautiful woodland forest now enchants mountain bikers with stretches of demanding hill climbs and fast, descending double-track. The great views and mysterious, craggy mountains make for a day of captivating riding. Camp overnight at the North-South Lake Campground and ride for a second day if you can't do it all in one.

For centuries, the Catskills were Native American hunting grounds. Native Americans lived and fished in the fertile river valleys and hunted in the dark, hemlock-filled valleys and wooded slopes of the mountains they called Onteora or "land in the sky."

Beginning in the early nineteenth century, America entered the Romantic period, when the arts and nature took on greater significance. A good view was held in high value. Despite the ravaging of the land from the lumbering and tanning industry during this time, the Catskills still held abundant natural

RIDE 54 *NORTH LAKE TRAILS*

NY

North-South Lake
State Campground

North
Lake

South
Lake

Laurel House Rd.

Schutt Rd.

To
Tannersville

Catskill Mtn.
House Site

Laurel
House
Site

Hotel
Kaaterskill Site

Palenville
Lookout

N

0   1/4   1/2

MILES

beauty. The aristocracy and intelligentsia of America sought out this area as
a prime meeting ground. Grand hotels with spectacular mountain views were
built for the rich and famous who flocked to the Catskills. From the mid-
nineteenth century to the turn of the century, two large hotels, the Catskill
Mountain House and Hotel Kaaterskill, built right on the escarpment, had
guest registers that included presidents, entertainers, industrialists, and other
celebrities. The views from the escarpment inspired famous painters, poets,
and writers. The North Lake Area's reputation made it the place to be for New
Yorkers downriver. Carriage roads were built into and on the escarpment to

bring guests to the most spectacular vantage points. Take your time at North Lake. There is a lot to see, and one of the best ways to get it all in is to camp out in the North-South Lake Campground.

Although I have not had the pleasure of riding this trail, it is strongly recommended by two friends. John Lowe and his son Mathew rode the trails and fell in love with them. As you silently glide through miles of bridle paths and wood roads, enjoy the history and the pristine forest environment.

General location: Exit 20 off the New York State Thruway (Interstate 87), near the town of Haines Falls and Tannersville and about 9 miles east of the town of Hunter. If you package it as a weekend, it will certainly be worth the time it takes to get there.

Elevation change: The elevations of horse trail and forest road along the escarpment vary between 2,400' and 1,800'. If you continue past the turn-around point on this ride, you will keep descending to about 700'. To return, you have one heck of a climb back.

Season: Spring, summer, and fall are excellent seasons to ride along these trails. This region usually sees plenty of snow and cold weather. If there is no snow on the trails and you feel like braving the cold weather, dress warmly and get out on the trails for one very brisk ride.

Services: Most services can be found along NY 23A in Haines Falls or the town of Hunter. The North-South Lake public campground provides the base for your travels and offers tent and trailer sites, 2 lakes, 2 beaches, and 2 picnic areas with tables and fireplaces. Rowboat and canoe rentals and fishing complete the gamut of recreational opportunities. The campground opens for spring camping in mid-May and remains open until late October.

Hazards: It tends to be busy on the weekends so keep an eye out for other trail users. A portion of the trail is shared by equestrians. You will encounter equestrians and hikers on the same trails, so display a mutual respect and courtesy for each other and these beautiful trails will remain a recreation item for all to enjoy. A passing hello has always been met with one in return from equestrians and hikers. They are glad to see you enjoying the park also. Most share the trails, knowing that these lands are to be respected and enjoyed. I would also like to caution that many of the trails contain sections that are located along high ledges and sometimes on open rock. In most places, there are no railings or fences. Do exercise caution when the views get too close and look too good to be true.

Rescue index: These are well-traveled trails and help could be available from one of the other trail users. Campground personnel are usually around most times of the day.

Land status: New York State Department of Environmental Conservation (DEC) manages the New York State Forest Preserve lands of the Catskills.

Maps: The New York–New Jersey Trail Conference's "Catskill Trails," Trail Map 40, provides complete coverage of this region and is waterproof and tearproof. It sells for $11.95 and can be found at most outdoor-type stores. Another trail map is usually available in the North-South Lake campground area near the registration booth.

Finding the trail: Take the New York State Thruway, Interstate 87, north to Exit 20, the Saugerties exit. Turn north onto County Road 32 for approximately 6 miles and then west on NY 23A. Stay on NY 23A to the village of Haines Falls. Make the first right turn in Haines Falls onto County Route 18 and continue north for 2 miles to the end of the road. Just before you reach the campground entrance, turn right onto Schutt Road. You will find a parking area to your immediate right.

Sources of additional information:

North Lake Campground Office
PO Box 347
Haines Falls, New York 12436
(518) 589-5058

Greene County Tourism
Box 527
Catskill, New York 12414
(800) 355-CATS

Notes on the trail: Facing east away from the parking area, look for and get on the blue-blazed Escarpment Trail. The trail turns south and intersects with the red-blazed Schutt Road Trail in about half a mile. Bear left (south) on the Schutt Road Trail. After .3 mile, bear right onto a yellow-blazed trail and in another quarter-mile, fork left onto the horse trail, marked with yellow horse-trail disks with a black horse head in the middle. Follow this trail for another .7 mile. Continue past a trail leading north and soon you will reach a **T** intersection. Turn left onto the forest road. Turning right will continue to lead you on the horse trail and down the face of the escarpment and eventually to Route 23A. You then will be faced with the agonizing climb back up 1,700'.

Continue left onto the forest road for a little over half a mile, where you arrive at another **T** intersection. Turn right on a short spur trail to the Palenville Lookout. Continue back up the trail and straight on the forest road for another 2 miles, passing over the old railroad grade that brought visitors up to the Catskill Mountain House. This tour only covers 2 more miles past the Palenville Lookout. Then you approach an intersection with another forest road. The forest road that lies beyond is not documented on this tour, so turn back at this point.

Travel for 2 miles and make a right onto the forest road that **T** intersects with the road you are on. Continuing straight will take you out to the Palenville Lookout. After another half-mile you will come to the intersection with the horse trail. Continue northwest on the horse trail back to the parking area.

RIDE 55 *OVERLOOK MOUNTAIN ASCENT*

This ride is not for the weak of heart. Just outside the town of Woodstock lies a graded, wide jeep road that ascends the 3,100-foot Overlook Mountain. Not many roads reach a summit in the Catskill Mountains. Although this nontechnical climb demands great stamina and lung capacity, the rewards of cresting this mountain with a bike are incomparable. The effort to climb the summit is more than compensated by the views from the top. Additional rewards are a remote wilderness lake and a gonzo, turbo-charged descent. At the summit are spur trails on open ledges facing the Hudson Valley. There is also a fire tower at the summit providing some spectacular views after a short climb up the stairs.

The nine-mile (total mileage), out-and-back, wide, smooth jeep road passes the ruins of the historic Catskill Hotel site. Beginning in the early part of the nineteenth century, America entered the Romantic period, when arts and nature became priorities. A good view was held in high regard. Despite the ravaging of the land at the time, the Catskills still held much natural beauty. The region became a magnet for the aristocracy and intelligentsia. Grand hotels with glorious mountain views were built for the rich and famous, who flocked to the Catskills. As the West was discovered, the Catskill crowd thinned and the great hotels closed, one by one. Built in 1870, the Overlook Mountain House, which housed about 300 guests, was situated at an elevation of over 2,900 feet, the highest of them all.

After reaching the summit, explore a rocky jeep trail that descends two more miles to the secluded and picturesque Echo Lake. It's a great place to rest, feast, snooze, and meditate.

General location: Just outside the village of Woodstock in the Catskill Mountains from Exit 20 on the New York State Thruway (Interstate 87).
Elevation change: The ride up Overlook Mountain climbs about 1,400' in a little under 3 miles and will whip you up into shape.
Season: Spring, summer, and fall are excellent seasons to climb the summit. This region usually sees plenty of snow and cold weather. The hard-pack dirt road doesn't get too soft after rains and can be ridden in wet weather, but traction on the rocky jeep trail descending to Echo Lake can be slippery.
Services: The village of Woodstock is basically an artist community of painters, writers, and musicians and is an interesting place to visit. The village has a great variety of restaurants and unusual shops.
Hazards: The descent from the summit may entice you to exceed the speed limit. While it is nice to bomb down the road, remember that hikers and other bikers may be coming up the road. Exercise control in case you have to stop

RIDE 55 *OVERLOOK MOUNTAIN ASCENT*

or move to the side for another trail user. Try not to ride any faster than you can handle. At the summit, use caution on the ledges where rattlesnake dens have been spotted.

Rescue index: Other bikers and hikers use this popular trail often and could be a source for help, should the occasion arise. Becoming lost is not an issue since it is one road in and one road out.

Land status: New York State Department of Environmental Conservation (DEC) manages the New York State Forest Preserve lands of the Catskills. The trail is on New York State land.

Maps: The New York–New Jersey Trail Conference's "Catskill Trails," Trail Map 41, provides complete coverage of this trail and is waterproof and tearproof. It sells for $11.95 and can be found at most outdoor-type stores.

Finding the trail: Proceed north on the New York State Thruway, Interstate 87 to Exit 20. Take NY 212 west toward Woodstock. Turn right (north) onto County Road 33 in the village of Woodstock, which then turns into Meads Mountain Road. Ignore the intersection with Glasco Turnpike, which is also labeled CR 33, and continue on Meads Mountain Road. After about 2 miles past the intersection with Glasco Turnpike, on Meads Mountain Road, look for a parking area on the right. Park here.

Sources of additional information:

Ulster County Tourism
P.O. Box 1800
Kingston, New York 12401
(914) 331-9300

New York State Department of Environmental Conservation
50 Wolf Road, Room 111
Albany, New York 12233
(518) 457-3521

Notes on the trail: The red-blazed jeep trail, referred to as the Overlook Spur Trail, leaves the trailhead at the parking area and begins to climb steadily for about 2.5 miles in a northeasterly direction. After reaching the site of the ruins of the Overlook Mountain House, follow in an easterly direction a short, half-mile spur trail that leads to the summit of Overlook Mountain and the State Fire Tower.

If you wish to ride to Echo Lake, return on the spur to the ruins and bear right down a blue-blazed trail known to hikers as Overlook Trail. Descend for about 1.5 miles and turn left onto the yellow-blazed Echo Lake Trail for another .8 mile. You can hang around the lake, relax, take in some lunch time, snooze a bit, and then commence your climb out of this serene setting. Retrace your steps, bearing right on the blue-blazed trail up to the summit of Overlook Mountain, and then descend the red-blazed jeep trail to the parking area.

RIDE 56 *HIGH POINT KANAPE BROOK TRAIL*

The rewards of this ride are twofold. This journey ascends gently through a secluded and attractive valley of the Kanape Brook. The ride terminates three miles later at the 2,000-foot, forested saddle between High Point and

Mombaccus mountains. Kanape Brook flows along a rock-and-boulder-studded streambed and passes through a typical Catskill forest of beech, birch, and maple. Once there, take an optional hike up to the 3,000-foot High Point Mountain, with its panoramic views. Stay for lunch and soak in the scenery.

The trail parallels the Kanape Brook for most of its length and is an old, hard-packed, dirt and gravel road. The road is in very good condition even though it receives no maintenance. It seems to survive the tremendous erosional forces of the mountains. Trail erosion results from poor drainage along the route. Rains wash down a trail, eventually exposing some of the rocks and roots beneath the road bed. The object of some trail maintenance programs is to divert some of this runoff and preserve the surface of the trail. An effort was made a long time ago to divert the water flowing down the mountain through several stone culverts that had been constructed to lead the water beneath the trail. An encroaching, growing forest can cause trails to disappear. Along the ride, notice the many old stone walls and ditches that were constructed. This helps to keep the forest from growing over the trail. The trails have a history and require upkeep. Do not take this fact for granted. Giant efforts are required to maintain trails for all of us who want to enjoy them.

Although I have not had the pleasure of riding this trail, it is strongly recommended by my friend and riding companion, Bruce Horowitz. We have logged many miles together on our bikes in our quest for the ultimate single-track.

General location: Southeastern Catskills, near Kingston, New York.
Elevation change: The ride gradually ascends from an elevation of 1,200' to 2,000', to the height of land. The optional hike to High Point covers another 1,000' over 1 mile and reaches the summit of High Point at 3,000'.
Season: Late spring, summer, and early fall. The Catskills usually get a blanket of snow after Thanksgiving, but it can snow earlier.
Services: Services can be found along NY 28, west of Kingston.
Hazards: This is not a mainstream mountain bike trail. It is secluded and seldom used. Hikers use these trails to gain access to the climb up High Point Mountain. If you are riding near hikers, slow down. If you are approaching from behind, let them know of your presence with a whistle or a friendly greeting.
Rescue index: These are not well-traveled roads, but to get out of this wilderness, all you have to do is pedal downhill toward Peekamoose Road, where several country homes are located.
Land status: The trail is on New York State land. New York State Department of Environmental Conservation (DEC) manages the New York State Forest Preserve lands of the Catskills.
Maps: The New York–New Jersey Trail Conference's "Catskill Trails," Trail Map 43, provides some detail of this trail and is waterproof and tearproof. It sells for $11.95 and can be found at most outdoor-type stores. USGS, 7.5 minute series, West Shokan quadrangle also provides decent coverage.

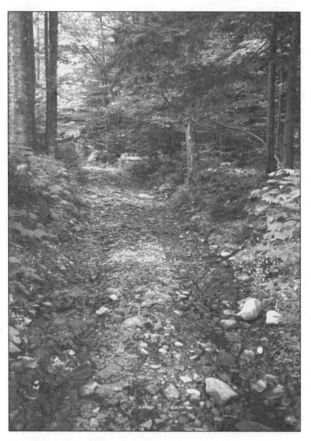

Catskill rocks require good shocks.

Finding the trail: Take the New York State Thruway, Interstate 87, north to the Kingston exit and get on NY 28 West. In a few miles fork left onto NY 28A. Take that road around the southern shores of Ashokan Reservoir. Follow 28A to County Road 42 (Peekamoose Road). Proceed through the town of West Shokan and look for a small parking lot in about 3 miles on your right. Notice the state land and forest preserve signs. Pedal across the road and go over the wooden bridge across Kanape Brook. The trail begins beyond a large, open, grassy area on the other side of a wooden bridge.

Sources of additional information:

Ulster County Tourism
P.O. Box 1800
Kingston, New York 12401
(914) 331-9300

New York State Department of Environmental Conservation
50 Wolf Road, Room 111
Albany, New York 12233
(518) 457-3521

Notes on the trail: Take the trail southeast along the brook. It travels uphill through the beech, birch, and maple forest and slowly climbs up and away from Kanape Brook on your right. Notice the stone culverts you cross over, which are used to divert water from the mountainside. Bear right at the next fork, staying on the more established trail. You will soon cross Kanape Brook into a clearing, where the brook forms a large pool. The area is surrounded by a conifer forest, and as you continue on the trail, balsam fir and hemlock begin to appear. Follow this wide trail and ascend about 500' in 1 mile. The height of land between Mombaccus Mountain and High Point, elevation 2,050', is reached with little effort. Here, an unmarked hiking trail starts up to High Point. The hike is only 45 minutes and 1 mile in length. The panoramic view from the small rock ledge summit is a place worth seeking out and is well worth the trip. Views from east to southwest open up. The Ashokan Reservoir, Shawangunk Mountains, and Hudson Highlands can be seen. From the saddle, turn back and return the 3 miles, all downhill.

RIDE 57 *VERNOOYKILL FALLS TRAIL*

One of the commodities mountain bikers can be thankful for is that snow-mobilers know a good trail when they see one. This eight-mile, out-and-back (four miles one way), old town road doubles as a snowmobile trail in the winter and remains one of the best-kept secrets in Ulster County for mountain bikers. It's secluded, quiet, and interesting to explore for a few hours. The trail passes through a tall, attractive forest of beech and hemlock. At the end of the ride, you might want to visit Vernooykill Falls, which can be reached by following the turquoise paint blazes on the trees. Lock up your bikes and take a hike. The series of cascades, called the Vernooykill Falls, are part of the Vernoy Kill, which flows south toward the Rondout Reservoir. The falls make a superb location to sit down and munch some of the food you should bring along. Walk and follow the falls for a short distance south, where a sturdy wooden footbridge crosses the creek and provides great views of this area.

This is not a strenuous ride, but sections of the rough, washed-out, old town road require some basic technical skills to maneuver through the eroded, exposed rock bed of the trail. A beginner-intermediate rider will feel their confidence building as they tackle these minor obstacles along the rolling terrain. Learning to work the rocks on a steep hill is more difficult because

RIDE 57 *VERNOOYKILL FALLS TRAIL*

you have other impediments, like fear, which cause you to stop prematurely and perform an end-over.

Along this four-wheel-drive road you will come across a spur leading to a remote swamp. This half-mile spur trail leads to a remote beaver pond in a primitive wilderness setting known as Balsam Swamp. There are even a few campsites on the road down to the pond. It's quite interesting to see how the beavers have colonized this pond.

If you get an early start, you can do this tour and one of the other nearby southeastern Catskill tours such as Willowemoc, Flugertown Road, or Denning Road.

Wide hardpack along the Vernooykill Falls Tour.

General location: Ulster County in the southeastern Catskills, near Kerhonkson, New York.

Elevation change: The old road travels over rolling terrain with some minor hills, but nothing too hard to handle. There is a half-mile descent to Balsam Swamp.

Season: Late spring, summer, and early fall are the best seasons. The fall foliage is superb and laid on with a heavy hand.

Services: B.Y.O.W.B.—bring your own water bottle. There is a bar on County Road 55 past the Rondout Reservoir. Ellenville is a large town with gas, stores, and even a bike shop known as Moto-Mark Cycles.

Hazards: During foliage season, leaves may cover up some rocks protruding on the trail. Be aware that these rocks become slippery during wet periods. Though this is not a well-traveled path, keep an eye out for other trail users. When I was there, a jeep came up the road.

Rescue index: This is not a well-traveled path, but you are only within a few miles of County Road 46, which has residences and traffic.

Land status: The trail is on New York State land. The New York State Department of Environmental Conservation (DEC) manages the New York State Forest Preserve lands of the Catskills.

Maps: The USGS, 7.5 minute series, Kerhonkson quadrangle provides coverage for this area.

Finding the trail: Take the New York State Thruway (Interstate 87) north and exit at NY 17/U.S. Route 6 West. Take NY 17 north and exit at the Ellenville,

NY 209 exit. Turn right onto NY 209, going north. Proceed past Ellenville and take County Road 55 north. Bear right at the fork with County Road 55A. This takes you on the northeast side of the Rondout Reservoir. You will ride along this attractive body of water at an elevation of 1,440'. Turn right at the intersection with Ulster County Road 46 and continue north. There are some amazing views along this road to your east. Look for Greenville Road, which intersects from the left at the end of CR 46. Turn left onto Greenville Road, and you will soon notice a wide town dirt road leading off to your right. This is Cross Road, the beginning of your ride. Look for a small turnout that will serve as parking a short distance past Cross Road on your right.

Sources of additional information:

> Moto-Mark Cycles
> Route 209
> Ellenville, New York 12428
> (914) 647-6068

> Ulster County Tourism
> P.O. Box 1800
> Kingston, New York 12401
> (914) 331-9300

Notes on the trail: Take Cross Road a short distance to its end at Dymond Road. At the intersection, continue straight ahead onto the designated snowmobile trail. Two brown New York State DEC trail signs indicate that the trail type is a snowmobile trail. Cross Dymond Road and head into the forest on the four-wheel-drive road. The trail follows a gently rolling terrain with some rocky and wet sections where water runoff has eroded the road bed and exposed the rocks. Many drainage streams tumble down these mountainous slopes and cross the trail at points.

A little after 1 mile, you will start picking up blue markers on the trees. Bear left at a fork. You reach the end of the trail in 3 miles. The right fork will lead you down to Balsam Swamp in about half a mile.

RIDE 58 *THE HOLY LAND*

The operative word on this huge parcel of land is diversity. Seven thousand acres on the Stewart Airport property, in Newburgh, have been packaged as a cooperative area, available for hunters and other outdoor enthusiasts. This domain is the "holy land" to the local mountain biking community because of its excellent and competitive single-track trail system over a variety of challenging terrain. The cooperative area is composed of a combination of active

Note: *This is a very rough outline of the single-track that is available here.*

and abandoned farmland, apple and pear orchards, and second-growth forest-land. Ponds and marshes dot the landscape, along with several small streams. Twelve miles of wide, gravelly, hard-pack dirt roads crisscross the hilly interior, providing long, sweeping descents from hills. These roads are perfect for the novice or experienced rider hungry for some genuine fat-tire fun.

For the more serious riders and technicians, there are wads of intermediate and advanced high-tech single-track. These trails traverse what seems to be an unlimited supply of hills and tight turns punctuated by a myriad of jumps. They can be attacked aggressively or handled slowly. The lunar, ten-mile, jackhammer, single-track loop described below is for dedicated hammerheads with a purpose. Good bike handlers will get an excellent workout. Sections of the ride are actually banked and pitched at an angle, keeping you off the brakes and moving fast. As you navigate through the many twists and turns of the trail, the riding begins to take on a Zen-like quality. You're not over-braking or oversteering, and the tires seem to carve like skis. You come out of corners with just enough momentum, as if the trail is controlling the bike and you're just along for the ride.

The Stewart Airport Cooperative area, a.k.a. "the holy land," is a great place to come with a group of people with different riding skills. There is plenty of track for those who would like some easy peddling through scenic countryside. For the dirt disciples who are not happy unless they have shred-ded some rock and come back bruised and battered and have conquered every hill, this is heaven.

General location: Located in northeastern Orange County between the city of Newburgh and the village of Maybrook. The area is bounded on the north by Interstate 84, on the east by the New York State Thruway (Interstate 87), and on the south by NY 207.

Elevation change: The topography is generally flat and gently rolling. The layout of the single-track loop takes full advantage of the hilly terrain and varied woodland, including as many short-haul ascents and descents as can fit into the trail's 10 miles. There are no major long hauls up any mountain, just lots of tiny hills. The double-track rolls gently along the interior dirt roads with no appreciable gain or loss in elevation.

Season: Due to its use as a hunting area, the "safe" season is from April 1 to September 30. It's a good idea to check with the New York State Department of Environmental Conservation (DEC) for exact dates and any other relevant information about the area.

Services: Many service stations and convenience stores are located on NY 207. Nearby Newburgh will make up for the rest, with other general services.

Hazards: Hunting seasons start in the beginning of October and end in March. The area is available for riding in this period. Call the New York State Department of Environmental Conservation (DEC) for exact dates and details. I would also like to mention that becoming lost while doing the single-track routes is a very real possibility. Unless you frequent this area quite often and are familiar with the myriad trails that interlace this terrain, stay on the route described here. I was warned by veterans. The general condition of the single-track is good, but sections are blemished occasionally with roots and rocks to keep it challenging. Some sections of trail are pitched at an angle to keep you off the brakes and moving fast.

Rescue index: If you do become lost and you do not have a compass, watch for airplanes overhead departing or arriving at nearby Stewart Airport. The landing and takeoff patterns are usually in an east-west line. Just keep heading in the direction the landing aircraft is heading toward, which is east. However, do not follow it after takeoff! As you head in the direction of the airport, you will eventually reach a paved road called Drury Lane. Depending upon where you are in the 7,000 acres, the distance to Drury Lane is no more than 3 miles. On Drury Lane turn right, going in a southerly direction to reach NY 207. Turn right on NY 207, west, back to the parking area.

Land status: The land is owned by the New York State Department of Transportation (NYSDOT), but the New York State Department of Environmental Conservation manages the forest as a cooperative multiple-use area.

In 1957, the New York State Legislature passed the Fish and Wildlife Management Act. It established a set of standards to provide for good fish and wildlife management practices on private lands and waters and to ensure the orderly use of them. The act establishes a cooperative effort between New York and the private land owners. It helps to protect and enhance fish and wildlife resources, to provide hunting and fishing opportunities for the public, to improve landowner and sportsmen relations, and to safeguard the interests and rights of landowners. The cooperative agreement provides public access on these lands through permit stations where fees and permits may be collected. The landowners, in return for sharing their land, receive services such as general maintenance and clean-up, free shrubs and trees, as well as some law enforcement provided for by the DEC. Cooperative agreements provide for orderly public recreational access while protecting the interests of the landowner.

Maps: There is no accurate map of this area. The DEC map supplied to you when you pick up your permit indicates the major dirt roads that are part of the double-track trail option described below. Unfortunately, it does not detail the incredible network of single-track. Bring a compass! There are also no USGS Topo Series maps to provide the fine detail you might need. There are zillions of small twists, turns, and loops that are difficult to map but incredible to ride. The map our cartographer and I have supplied will give you the general flow and direction of the route and an idea of where things are located. The trail is well marked, and if you follow the markers you can't get lost.

Finding the trail: You must first pick up a permit, good for one season of riding in the area, from the Stewart Airport administrative building. From there it's only a few minutes to the parking area. Take the New York State Thruway north to the Newburgh exit. After the exit ramp, follow the signs for Stewart Airport which will eventually land you on NY 207. Turn into Stewart International Airport off NY 207 and follow the signs for the terminals. Turn right at the terminal sign, go past the terminal, and turn right on First Street. You will find the Stewart Airport administrative building on your right in the second-to-last brick building. There will be a yellow sign outside reading, "Receptionist." Go inside and present your driver's license and then the "receptionist" will issue you a 2-part permit, 1 to keep in the car and 1 to keep on your person. You are now on your way.

Go back out to NY 207 and turn right. Approximately 3.7 miles down NY 207, you will turn right at the Stewart Airport Cooperative Hunting Area, State of New York DEC sign. Parking can be found right in front of the gate.

Source of additional information:

New York State Department of Environmental Conservation
Region 3
21 South Putt Corners Road
New Paltz, New York 12561-1696
(914) 256-3000

Notes on the trail: The easy, cruising double-track and the advanced single-track briefly described above are detailed below:

Advanced Single-Track: Continue past the parking gate down a wide, gravelly, paved road. Pass some cornfields on the left and a brown wooden shack on your right. Continue through a 4-way intersection with New Road (not a new road) and Ridge Road. Continue for about .2 mile and on your left will be the single-track. Usually orange streamers are tied around the trees where the path goes through. This route is occasionally used as a race route and is marked with spray paint or streamers, which helps in navigating your way. Continue through an apple grove and then into a dense hardwood forest. After about 2 miles, cross a paved road and head back into the forest on the single-track. There are several sections of exposed roots from trail use and natural erosion. Since this single-track is used as a race course, many banked turns are built up. This gives you the freedom to get into the rhythm of the course. Once your pace is set, you and your bike are swept into one turn after another. There are some rocky sections where it might be necessary to portage your bike, but you will soon turn into the hard-packed single-track that is prevalent throughout the course.

At about 3.2 miles you will come to another single-track intersecting from the right, but just remain straight. You start hitting some demanding small hills at the 4-mile mark, with one major ascent out of a gully that will shame us all and require a dismount. For the next half-mile the course runs along a ridge and skirts some magnificent corn and farm fields. At about 4.9 miles, you pass by a small pond on your left, and bear right as another road joins it from the left. Continue on the wide dirt road between some cornfields. Some trails will lead off it, but keep straight on the main wide road. At about 5.7 miles fork left on the main wide dirt road. At about 6 miles, make a left at the **T** intersection with another dirt road, and then make a quick right into the woods. The trail climbs through a hardwood forest for a short distance and then descends to a 4-way intersection. Continue straight. In another mile you will come into a clearing; continue to your right. Bear left at the next fork and proceed up a short hill. At the top, bear right into the forest. When you get to the top of another hill, bear right where the orange streamers could and should be, if they are still clinging to the trees. At 7.5 miles turn right at another intersection. After descending a short hill, you will see an orange arrow spray-painted on a tree. Bear right at this fork, riding along solid rock which runs for a short distance along a ridge. Shortly, you will descend sharply to your left down a steep hill. After 2 more sharp descents, bear left at another fork and up another hill to a long rock ledge. If you are not Arnold or super-bikeman, you will probably have to walk and push the bike up and over. Another orange arrow spray-painted on the rocks indicates the direction to take. At the next 4-way, single-track intersection, continue straight, and at 8.4 miles bear right at the next **T** intersection. At about 9 miles you will merge with another four-wheel-drive road; continue straight, bearing left through an overgrown pear orchard. Finish your ride at 10 miles on the same old paved New Road where you started. Turn left to return to the vehicle parking or try the loop again if you dare. The pros do it 3 times in 1 race.

Beginner Double-Track: Continue past the parking gate down a wide, gravelly, paved road. Pass by some cornfields on the left and a brown wooden shack on your right. Continue through a 4-way intersection with New Road and Ridge Road. Ridge Road will be the road you return on. Continue north on New Road. In less than a mile, you approach a clearing with another wide dirt road. The road leading off to your left is Giles Road, which continues onward to NY 207. Remain on New Road. Shortly after that turnoff you pass Drakes Lane and then another road on your left; continue on New Road. You will soon pass some cornfields and arrive at another intersection with Linsey Lane on your left. Linsey Lane could be a candidate as an additional country road to tour on, but for now just remain straight. Climb gently and notice several single-tracks crisscrossing New Road. It just gives you a hint of the extent and amount of single-track out there. Continuing straight ahead on New Road, the wide, gravelly road turns paved and starts making a turn toward the southeast and runs parallel to I-84. At 5.5 miles you approach a 4-way intersection after what seems like a long climb. To your left will be a gate and bridge that goes over I-84. Straight ahead is Maple Avenue. Turn right at this intersection onto the wide Ridge Road. The road turns gravelly as you descend a small hill. Climb gently up another hill over a paved section of road. It gets a little steeper before it levels out and earns its name as the "Ridge." The views are great and you can see for miles. Cruise for another mile and soon you will pick up the scent of apples from an abandoned apple orchard on your left. At a little over 9 miles you reach the intersection with New Road. Turn left to reach the vehicle parking area.

RIDE 59 BASHAKILL

This trail runs along an abandoned railroad corridor and is graded for comfortable riding. The tracks have long since been removed and the wide path is flat and level and travels through a fascinating wildlife area known as the Bashakill Wildlife Management Area. In total, over ten miles of riding are possible on the old railway bed, providing a perfect opportunity to experience this unique resource. Over five miles run along the eastern side of the 2,175 acres, and more mileage after the path leaves the northern edge of this multiple-use area.

The operative word is cruising. There will not be a lot of steep, winding single-track to test your skills, just a long straight path through the natural beauty of a lowland freshwater wetland, the largest in southeastern New York. The long wide valley is geologically known as the Port Jervis Trough. It is banked by views of the Allegheny Plateau to the west and the steep Shawangunk Ridge to the east. The ridge rises almost 700 feet. This ridge is part of the same mountainous ledges found around the Lake Minnewaska and Mohonk bike trails. The trough is a depression in the land that began when the Shawangunk Mountains were lifted and pushed up from the valley floor. Streams and rivers flowed through the valley guaranteeing the erosional pathway. The arrival and departure of the glaciers during the last continental glaciation, which reached as far south as Pennsylvania, caused the valley to be wide and flat. This freshwater wetland is home to a diverse biotic community resulting in a variety of fish and wildlife. White-tailed deer, grouse, rabbit, turkey, fox, raccoon, beaver, muskrat, and many species of waterfowl provide great opportunities for wildlife observation and photography. While traveling on the rail path, notice the many bird houses built in the marshy waters. These houses are used to study wood ducks and bluebirds. Wildlife management programs protect and maintain habitat diversity through construction of these structures. You will also see some nesting platforms, used to attract osprey.

General location: In southeastern New York approximately 65 miles northwest of New York City, south of NY 17.
Elevation change: The trail travels over a railroad grade that is slightly inclined.

RIDE 59 *BASHAKILL*

To Monticello

To Wurtsboro

N

0   1/2   1
MILES

209

17

To
87

Haven Rd.

South Rd.

Delaware and Hudson Towpath

63

To Port
Jervis

Indian
Orchard Rd.

Otisville Rd.

NY

Season: From April to September.

Services: Most of the exits off NY 17 have gas and convenience stores. The nearest large towns are Wurtsboro and Monticello.

Hazards: Hunting seasons start in the beginning of October and end in March. The area is available for riding around those dates. Call the New York State Department of Environmental Conservation (DEC) for exact dates and details.

Rescue index: US 209 is a heavily traveled road and help can usually be flagged down from passing motorists.

Land status: The New York State Department of Environmental Conservation manages the state-owned forest as a multiple-use area. The land was purchased in 1980 as part of the Environmental Quality Bond Act to preserve unique wilderness areas.

Maps: The DEC provides a Bashakill Wildlife Management Area brochure with a basic map of the area. It contains sufficient detail to follow the trail.

Finding the trail: Take the New York State Thruway (Interstate 87) north and exit at NY 17/US Route 6 West. Take NY 17 north and exit at the Ellenville, NY 209 exit. Turn left after the exit ramp, and after 2.2 miles turn left onto Haven Road. About .3 mile down this road is the first access parking area for the Bashakill. Continue down the road, crossing a small bridge that spans the wetland, and you will soon come to the second access parking area. Turn left down a wide dirt road and the parking will be on your right. The trail exists in both directions to the northeast and southwest of the parking area beyond some barriers.

Source of additional information:

New York State Department of Environmental Conservation
Region 3
21 South Putt Corners Road
New Paltz, New York 12561-1696
(914) 256-3000

Notes on the trail: From the parking area, you can proceed to the right in a northeasterly direction beyond the barrier or southeasterly by crossing Haven Road and continuing beyond the concrete barrier. Both paths run parallel along the open wetland. The eastern side of the trail faces an upland mixture of forests, old fields, and abandoned orchards.

The trail that leads south can be made into a loop. Follow it for about 3.4 miles. Exit onto Otisville Road and then turn right on paved County Road 63. Take that a short distance to US 209. Turn right on US 209 and then take another right onto an unmarked road. You will enter an open field. Look on your left for another unmarked double-track trail. If you reach the stream you have gone too far. Turn north (left) onto this wide trail. After about .4 mile, look for a hard-packed, double-track trail on a ridge beyond a line of trees.

This is the old Delaware and Hudson towpath. Horses would pull floating barges and work their way down the path. The trail is slightly elevated above the landscape and provides good views. Continue on the tow path to Haven Road. Turn right on Haven Road to return to your parking area.

RIDE 60 *FLUGERTOWN ROAD*

Combine eight miles of easy cruising along a beautiful, forested country road. Add another eight miles of single-track through the dense hemlock forests in the New York State Catskill Forest Preserve. Throw in a campground, many small ponds, and some marshmallows, and it's a recipe for a great weekend. The rolling Flugertown Road is wide and semipaved and turns into an old wood road that runs through a tall, dense, hardwood and conifer forest along the Willowemoc Creek. Beginner riders will be pressed by the winding, four-mile (one way), up-and-down dirt road. The more experienced will want to tackle a rolling, four-mile (one way), narrow single-track leading to the Mongaup Pond State Campground. Adventurers will be charmed by this secluded single-track as they are immersed in a dense Catskill forest of mature conifers and hardwoods. The entire area teems with plant and animal life. Silently glide through this pristine wilderness setting. Take a moment to assimilate the surroundings. The large Mongaup Pond awaits at the end of the ride.

Take your time. There is a lot to see. One of the best ways to get it all in is to camp overnight at a campsite by a brook or stream. There is a lean-to on the edge of Long Pond stationed about .9 mile from Flugertown Road in a secluded, primitive wilderness setting. It is an ideal campsite. Look for beaver lodges and dams near the outlet at the southern end of the pond. If you are camping, drive your car up Flugertown Road and park by one of the campsites near the DEC signs. You can then ride along Flugertown Road and tackle some of the single-track described below.

General location: North of Monticello off NY 17, on the border of Ulster and Sullivan counties in the southeastern Catskills, about 100 miles from New York City. If you package it as a weekend, it will certainly be worth the time it takes to get there.
Elevation change: Flugertown Road is fairly level with some minor hill climbs. The 4-mile single-track along the snowmobile trail leading to the Mongaup Pond campground climbs to about 400', levels off, and then drops 300'. The single-track to Long Pond begins steeply but levels out as it reaches the pond. The unnamed road that leads to Sand Pond is fairly level, with some minor climbs.

RIDE 60 *FLUGERTOWN ROAD*

Season: Late spring, summer, and early fall provide the best riding opportunities.
Services: Liberty is about 15 miles south of this area, but overall there is not much in the neighborhood, so come prepared and carry what you will be using during your stay.
Hazards: Mongaup Pond State Campground is a popular area during the summer months. It sees its fair share of crowds, but as you head out on the trails, the din of tents and trailers will diminish. Slow down if you are approaching hikers so you won't surprise them.

Rescue index: While this area seems remote, the popular trails are well used and you will usually encounter other individuals camping or hiking. Becoming lost should not be a problem because the routes described in this ride are not part of any network or loop and are one-direction, out-and-back paths.

Land status: The trail is on New York State land. New York State Department of Environmental Conservation (DEC) manages the New York State Forest Preserve lands of the Catskills.

Maps: The New York–New Jersey Trail Conference's "Catskill Trails," Trail Map 43, provides complete coverage of this area and is waterproof and tearproof. It sells for $11.95 and can be found at most outdoor-type stores.

Finding the trail: Take the New York State Thruway (Interstate 87) north and exit at NY 17/US Route 6 West. Take NY 17 north and exit at Parksville/ Cooley, Exit 98. The exit is actually a stoplight. Make a right onto County Road 85. If you need to fuel the car or yourself, do it at the convenience store at the corner of this stoplight, because there is not much up ahead. The road turns into CR 84 after the intersection with Cooley Mountain Road. After about 8 miles, you will reach an intersection with a stop sign; continue straight. You will soon come to a small bridge, where you will pick up the intersection of Flugertown Road and CR 84. Make a left onto Flugertown Road and take the left fork. You can park on the left side in a small turnout and take your bike up Flugertown Road. There is also the option of driving farther up Flugertown Road to the New York State DEC signs. If you choose the latter, you will miss out on the fun and beauty of Flugertown Road. If you are camping, you will need to haul in your equipment. In this case, drive up Flugertown Road to the DEC signs and park closer to one of the campsites in the area.

Source of additional information:

Department of Environmental Conservation (DEC)
Region 3 Headquarters–Ulster and Sullivan Counties
21 South Putt Corners Road
New Paltz, New York 12561
(914) 255-5453

Notes on the trail: There are 4 riding opportunities in this tour. Continuing on Flugertown Road, the paved section ends and the wide dirt country road begins after about 1 mile. You will soon come to an open field on your left. There will be a four-wheel-drive, unmarked path leading off to your left before the field. It proceeds in a northeasterly direction to Sand Pond. Two miles in length, it makes an excellent spur trail to explore one of the unique ponds that exist on these lands. This double-track intersects with the yellow-blazed, Mongaup-Willowemoc Trail in about 1 mile. Turning left in a westerly direction will lead you to Mongaup Pond and its campgrounds. Turning right in a northwesterly direction leads out to an intersection farther up on

Flugertown Road. Continue straight on the unmarked Sand Pond Trail, cross a small brook, and reach the pond in about 1.5 miles.

If you have just returned from Sand Pond and are standing on Flugertown Road, pedal along the wide, hard-packed Flugertown Road past open land. You will soon pass an attractive country house on your left. Continue straight ahead into a dense portion of woods beneath a canopy of hardwoods. You will soon come to the New York State DEC sign for the Long Pond Trailhead. The red disks indicate the snowmobile trail that leads to your right and ascends to Long Pond in .9 mile. It requires a short, steep climb until you get to the level of land near the pond. After the second wooden bridge, fork right and ascend steeply to Long Pond. The Long Pond lean-to is off a spur from this path.

Turning back to Flugertown Road, continue down the road. Another DEC sign will be on your left. This is the 4-mile, one-way Mongaup-Willowemoc Trail. It begins along the snowmobile trail, which is marked with red disks nailed on trees, and then veers to the left along a trail marked with yellow disks.

You can continue on Flugertown Road; bear right in a northeasterly direction until you see the private road signs posted by the Peters Hunting Club. This trail description ends here, but Flugertown Road continues for another 4 miles and intersects with Willowemoc Road. According to the DEC, these roads are public and you can ride on them. If you are riding during the fall hunting season, pay attention at this point on the road, since this is a hunting club and they post signs. You might want to turn around here during hunting season.

RIDE 61 *WILLOWEMOC ROAD*

This strenuous, six-mile (total), out-and-back, wide, country dirt road is for tough bikers. Its climb demands great stamina and lung capacity. But the rewards are there, as you pass a wilderness of mature hemlock, old abandoned apple orchards, and clearings with some great mountain views. Need I mention the turbo-charged, fireball descent?

The road traverses the Beaver Kill Range, which consists of two 3,300-foot summits. They rise to the north and offer open vistas of a large, densely forested valley with streams feeding the West Branch River that joins the Neversink River.

Willowemoc Road can be ridden in conjunction with the Flugertown Road tour by continuing on Flugertown Road to its termination at Willowemoc Road.

General location: North of Monticello off NY 17 on the border of Ulster and Sullivan counties in the southeastern Catskills, about 100 miles from New

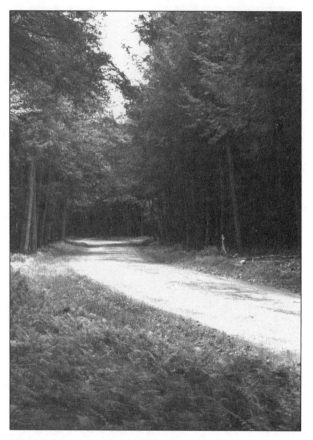

The Willowemoc Road leads through a dense primeval forest.

York City. It's a good idea to combine this ride with the Flugertown Road tour.

Elevation change: The general trend of this tour is up, but oh my, what a ride down. There is about a 500' elevation gain over 3.5 miles.

Season: Late spring, summer, and early fall are the prime seasons. The hard-pack dirt road does not get too soft after rain and can be ridden in wet weather.

Services: Liberty is about 15 miles south of this area, but overall there is not much in the neighborhood, so come prepared and carry what you will be using during your stay.

Hazards: Watch for vehicles coming and going on the road. There are a few hunting lodges as you get closer to the top of your ride. Club members and visitors contribute to the small amount of vehicular traffic on the road. Pay close attention around the turns as you descend, as there are often vehicles coming up the road.

Rescue index: There are several residences along the road, and in case of emergency a knock on a door may be an option.

Land status: Ulster County secondary road.

Maps: The New York–New Jersey Trail Conference's "Catskill Trails," Trail Map 43, provides complete coverage of this area and is waterproof and tearproof. It sells for $11.95 and can be found at most outdoor-type stores.

Finding the trail: Take the New York State Thruway (Interstate 87) north and exit at NY 17/US Route 6 West. Take NY 17 north and exit at Parksville/Cooley, Exit 98. The exit is actually a stoplight. Make a right onto County Road 85. If you need to fuel the car or yourself, do it at the convenience store at the corner of this stoplight, because there is not much up ahead. The road turns into CR 84 after the intersection with Cooley Mountain Road. After about 8 miles, you will reach an intersection with a stop sign; continue straight. You will soon come to a small bridge where you will pick up the intersection of Flugertown Road and CR 84. Ignore the intersection with Flugertown Road and keep bearing right. You will be continuing on Pole Road. As you approach an intersection with another road on your left you will see the New York State DEC sign for Long Pond and Balsam Lake trails. This is across from a small body of water called Round Pond. Make a left and about 500' on your right is a parking area.

Source of additional information:

Department of Environmental Conservation (DEC)
Region 3 Headquarters–Ulster and Sullivan Counties
21 South Putt Corners Road
New Paltz, New York 12561
(914) 255-5453

Notes on the trail: If you are approaching Willowemoc Road from the Flugertown Road tour, continue to the end of Flugertown Road. The intersection with Willowemoc Road is approximately 4 miles past the Peters Hunting Club sign. Turn left, heading north on Willowemoc Road.

If you are beginning from the parking area, turn right onto Willowemoc Road and in less than a quarter-mile you will come to a fork. The fork to your left is actually the alternate end of the Flugertown Road tour and is blazed with red disks, indicating a snowmobile trail known as Basily Road. It will eventually connect with Flugertown Road.

Bearing right at the fork, continue up a long, gradual incline for about 2 miles. You first proceed through a mature hemlock forest and then into a forest of beech as you get to the higher elevations. In about .7 mile you pass an abandoned apple orchard, and views start opening up to the east of some 3,000' mountains. The valleys you look across are the drainage basins for the Fall Brook stream networks, which all flow into the West Branch River that joins the Neversink River farther south.

At about 3 miles, you will see a sign indicating that the road ahead is private. It passes through the Wild Meadows Game Preserve and belongs to the Shannon Hunting Club. You have to turn around at this point. The ride down should be a real screamer.

RIDE 62 *THE DENNING TRAIL*

This great Catskill tour follows the scenic Denning Road for five miles along a beautiful country road. The ten-mile (total), out-and-back road passes along old meadows bordered by 100-year-old sugar maples and dense woodland. The easy riding cuts through an area that is part of the primitive wilderness of the Catskills, partially settled long ago. The countryside resembles old but well-maintained country estates. The gently rolling, semipaved road parallels the wide East Branch of the Neversink River and passes through the Neversink River flood plain, which deposited rich soils long ago. The result: beautiful, fertile meadows for apple orchards and farms that existed for more than 200 years. For centuries, the Catskills were hunting grounds for Native Americans. They lived and fished in the fertile river valleys, and hunted in the dark, hemlock-filled valleys and wooded slopes of the mountains they called Onteora or "land in the sky." American farmers shared these woods with the Native Americans of the Northeast and began searching the mountainous region for rare, flat parcels of land to farm. This flood plain provided a fertile piece of land in the rocky, craggy Catskill Mountains and was a prime location to grow an orchard or cultivate a small farm.

Try to imagine the impressions this land made on those who discovered it. Beginner and advanced riders can share and embrace the rich history that embodies these mysterious woods and surrounding lands. One cannot help but feel the exhilaration when riding through this rich, forested land.

General location: North of Monticello off NY 17 on the border of Ulster and Sullivan counties in the southeastern Catskills, about 100 miles from New York City.

Elevation change: The ride is fairly level and the elevation change is minimal.

Season: Late spring, summer, and early fall are great seasons to ride. The winter brings snow. The hard-packed dirt road does not get too soft after rain and can be ridden in wet weather.

Services: Liberty is about 15 miles south of this area, but overall there is not much in the neighborhood, so come prepared and carry what you will be using during your stay.

Hazards: Watch for other vehicles on the road. Getting lost is not a problem since the road is straight.

RIDE 62   *THE DENNING TRAIL*

Rescue index: Denning Road passes some country homes, and a trailhead at the end of Denning Road is used by hikers. There are always some vehicles on their way to the trailhead or to one of the country homes.

Land status: This is a town road surrounded by private and state land.

Maps: The New York–New Jersey Trail Conference's "Catskill Trails," Trail Map 43, provides complete coverage of this area and is waterproof and tearproof. It sells for $11.95 and can be found at most outdoor-type stores.

Finding the trail: Take the New York State Thruway and exit at NY 17/US Route 6 West. Take NY 17 north and the Liberty exit. Take County Road 55 for about 12 miles and then turn left, going north on CR 19 toward Claryville. Look for parking near the intersection of Red Hill Road and Denning Road, or anywhere along Denning Road.

Source of additional information:

Department of Environmental Conservation (DEC)
Region 3 Headquarters–Ulster and Sullivan Counties
21 South Putt Corners Road
New Paltz, New York 12561
(914) 255-5453

Notes on the trail: The ride begins on the paved section of Denning Road. After a short distance, the road degrades to a wide, hard-packed country road and you will pass by some charming homesteads. Climb a short hill for about a quarter-mile and then descend to the level of the Neversink River. Continue past the dead-end signs for another 3 miles. Do not turn right onto New Road Hill. At a fork, bear right. You will pass by a Japanese-style house with peaked roofs and rock gardens that was built at the turn of the century. The estate was and is still owned by the Tison family. The parking area for the Denning hiking trailhead is reached soon after at about the 5-mile mark. This will be your turnaround point.

RIDE 63 *VERTIGO AT PLATTEKILL*

On a remote road in the Catskill Mountains, a rustic ski center provides lift service for you and your mountain bike up Plattekill Mountain. Forty miles of novice, intermediate, and advanced single- and double-track trails crisscross and descend the mountainous terrain. Cross-country ski trails run along the ridges that encircle the ski center and provide rolling single-track trails through dense conifer and deciduous forests. Wild raspberries grow freely along the trails.

Plattekill Mountain attracts a lot of serious riders. Don't stand in the middle of any path on a busy weekend. You might encounter one of these fully armored and padded road warrior–style bikers bulleting down on a full-suspension mountain bike. For a relatively short chairlift ride, you have access to a variety of trail options. Wide, steep switchbacks across the ski runs and hard-packed, sometimes rocky single-track lead down the mountain. A group of cross-country trails at the top of the mountain provide rolling, single-track terrain.

Laszlo Vajtay is the owner of Ski Plattekill, the small, 1000-vertical-foot slope outside of Roxbury. The recently opened mountain biking center on the premises is run solely by Vajtay. He has encouraged the building of stimulating routes. His staff and volunteers have creatively hacked out and constructed single-track trails and high-speed switchbacks through the dense hardwood forests.

The easy novice-rated trails are wide and gently sloping and utilize the beginner downhill ski trails. The intermediate trails are steeper and narrower and include the single-track. The advanced trails are for the aggressive rider seeking technical, race-quality, extreme, and vigorous downhill and single-track. All-day, long-distance rides are also available, as are instructions and guided tours for riders of all levels.

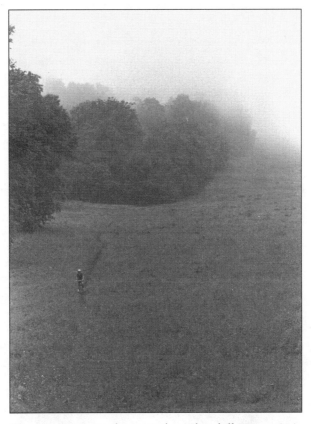

The way to master the vertical on Plattekill Mountain is to go along with it.

General location: Approximately 40 miles west of Kingston in the western Catskill Mountains.

Elevation change: The mountain provides 1,000' of vertical. An all-day lift ticket allows you to pile up many descents.

Season: The area is open to mountain biking from Memorial Day weekend through Thanksgiving Day weekend, weather permitting.

Services: Don't be fooled by the ski center's rustic appearance. Prices are on the high side for rentals and lift tickets. Good-quality, Gary Fischer front-suspension and full-suspension bikes are available; at the lodge you can kick back, chat, and drink some cold ones.

At the time of this writing an all-day lift ticket was $18. This does not include mountain bike rentals. Rigid bikes go for $20, front-suspension bikes go for $30, and full-suspension bikes are priced at $40. Add another $5 for a helmet, and it might be wiser to purchase a mountain bike before going. On weekends it is a good idea to call in advance and reserve a bike.

T Bar
Peak

Chair Lift
Peak
3250

Sunshine Triple Chair

Base
Lodge

Plattekill Mountain Rd.

To
Arkville
and

NY

N

| 0 | 1000 | 2000 |

FEET

Note: *More trails exist in this area than can be shown on this map. Maps are available at the mountain. All trails are numbered.*

Climbing Plattekill Mountain.

Hazards: Sections of the single- and double-track trails that descend through-out the terrain can be classically Catskill rocky. Caution is advised on all descents, as the rocks cause your tires to skip and lose traction. After a few runs you become acquainted with this kind of riding. There are some sharp turns throughout the forested trails and these, too, require some caution.

Rescue index: Help can be found on the premises. A first-aid station can be found at the lodge.

Land status: Ski Plattekill is owned by Laszlo Vajtay.

Maps: Upon purchasing a lift ticket, you are supplied with a comprehensive map of the ski bowl and trails.

Finding the trail: Take the New York State Thruway and Kingston Exit 19. Follow NY 28 west for approximately 35 miles to Arkville. Turn right just before the railroad crossing. Proceed about 1 mile and turn right (north) on NY 30. You will begin picking up the signs for Ski Plattekill. Turn left onto Cold Spring Road, follow the signs, and park in one of the ski center's park-ing areas.

Source of additional information:

Ski Plattekill Mountain Biking Center
Plattekill Mountain Road
P.O. Box 187
Roxbury, New York 12474
(607) 326-3500 or (800) GOTTA-BIKE

Notes on the trail: A large array of trails awaits the energetic mountain biker at Plattekill Mountain. A tremendous number of riding configurations can be created on the maze of trails that descend from the top of the chairlift. They will fill up an entire day of bike riding and exploration. After picking up your lift ticket at the lodge, grab a map, pick a trail, and just begin riding. Most of the routes are marked as they appear on the map. If you do get lost, just keep descending. All trails lead to the lodge and chairlift.

RIDE 64 *THE D & H HERITAGE CORRIDOR*

This is an exciting and easy trail wrapped in the beautiful pastoral landscape of historic Ulster County. The six-mile (one way) hiking/biking rail-trail connects two quaint seventeenth-century villages: Hurley and High Falls. The well-maintained, level path passes through a dense, deciduous woodland, paralleling tranquil farmland and crossing over rivers and streams. It's a splendid setting, particularly in the fall, and the foliage at peak periods is intense. Although not technically challenging, this wide, hard-packed cinder rail-trail is ideal for beginners and gently paced for riders seeking placid terrain and scenery. In total, there are 12 miles of out-and-back fun. Only a minimal amount of exertion and technical prowess is required. This route passes through the attractive and protected woodland area known as the Delaware and Hudson Canal Corridor.

What was the former Ontario & Western rail bed now provides a two-wheeled passage through history. The trains, which ran until 1957, hauled coal and local farm products.

It can be an out-and-back ride or a loop (by returning to the start via one of the paved roads that cross the trail). The trail begins near the historic village of Hurley, which features eighteenth-century stone houses. It terminates near High Falls, settled in 1669.

In Hurley, the past comes to life as you pass along the main street lined with stone houses. The Van Deusen house, built in 1723, served as the temporary capitol of the state after the burning of Kingston in 1777. The Esopus-Minisink Trail passes through town. This Native American trail connected the Delaware Valley with the Hudson River and was used before and during the American Revolution. While riding, you pass the Old Guard House, used to hold a British spy, Lieutenant David Taylor, who was hanged from an apple tree on October 18, 1777. In High Falls you can walk or ride down to the scenic Rondout Creek. Nearby and across from the historic Depuy Canal House Restaurant and tavern on NY 213 is the old stone aqueduct built in 1825 by the D & H Canal Company. The Depuy Canal House Restaurant is housed in a stone building built in 1797 by S & A Depuy, which also kept a

RIDE 64 *THE D & H HERITAGE CORRIDOR*

tavern there. To this day, the menu is still great. It was completed in 1828 and abandoned in 1889. The 108-mile canal was conceived in 1823 as a means of transporting coal from Honesdale, Pennsylvania, to Eddyville, New York, and became an important source of much-needed energy. The coal was then carried to New York City on barges floating down the Hudson River.

The construction of the rail path began with support from special interest groups and the Environmental Quality Bond Act Fund that provides monies for parks and recreation throughout several state counties. Thanks to the

Rondout Creek.

efforts of a group of local bicyclists and the Delaware and Hudson Canal Heritage Alliance, the path is maintained and kept in very good condition.

Ride with an effort to protect the trail and the environment. Be thoughtful about sharing the trails with others, including hikers and joggers, and maintain proper etiquette while enjoying the beauty of this path. Riding in muddy conditions hastens erosion. Now get out there and ride.

General location: Travel about 90 miles north of Manhattan on the New York State Thruway, Interstate 87, to Exit 19/Kingston.

Elevation change: The smooth trail travels over a flat and generally rolling grade.

Season: Fall is absolutely breathtaking, with colors filling the surrounding valleys. Winter usually brings snow, but if there is no snow on the trails, get some extra layers of clothing on and enjoy hearty cold-weather riding.

Services: Services are available at Hurley and can be reached off US 209 or at High Falls on NY 213. Stewart Shops in Hurley is a convenience store and gas station.

Hazards: You may at times share the path with hikers, joggers, and other bike riders. Extend the usual courtesy when approaching from behind and let other users know that your presence is near. Be thoughtful about sharing the trails with others so mountain bike riders can enjoy the use of beautiful trails like these.

Rescue index: The trail receives a fair amount of use and there is usually someone who can provide assistance. The path is also surrounded by residential areas and therefore in close proximity to help if needed. Further help could be found in High Falls or along US 209.

Land status: The path passes through the Hudson Valley Greenway Countryside Corridor/The D & H Canal Heritage Corridor. The Rail-Trail Park marks the beginning of the trail. The D & H Canal Corridor extends between the Catskill and Shawangunk mountains.

Maps: The trail is easy to follow and the map I have drawn up provides the best detail. USGS, 7.5 minute series, Kingston East quadrangle and St. Regis quadrangle, provides good detail for these unimproved dirt roads.

Finding the trail: Take the New York State Thruway (Interstate 87) north and exit at 19, Kingston. You must bear right (west) on NY 28 and then follow the signs for US 209. After traveling for about 3.2 miles on US 209, look for a blue trailhead sign on your left. The trailhead sign reads "1986 Environmental Quality Bond Act, the Hurley-Marbletown O & W Rail Trail through the D & H Canal Heritage Corridor." Turn off US 209 and find a small, gravel-covered parking area before the trailhead that is marked with a small, wooden, informational kiosk.

Sources of additional information:

Ulster County Public Information Office
244 Fair Street
PO Box 1800
Kingston, New York 12401
(914) 331-9300

Catskill Mountain Bicycle Shop
5 ½ N. Front Street
New Paltz, New York 12561
(914) 255-3859

Kingston Cyclery
478 Broadway
Kingston, New York 12401
(914) 331-2814

D & H Canal Museum
P.O. Box 23
High Falls, New York 12440
(914) 687-9311

Notes on the trail: The path is straightforward with few turns. Begin your journey by pedaling beyond the metal gate and the wooden informational kiosk. The wide, hard-packed dirt path proceeds in a southwesterly direction through a dense woodland for about 2 miles, followed by a long, narrow wetland area. Cross Marcot Road at 3.5 miles and begin pedaling on a wide, hard-packed single-track. The next road you cross is Cottekill Road. You have now covered about 4.5 miles. Continue across the road and pass some farm fields and attractive pine plantations. At 6.4 miles the path terminates on Leggett Road.

You may turn back at this point to the parking area, making this about a 13-mile round-trip. You can also continue your ride into High Falls. To do so, head east (left) on Leggett Road and then make a quick (.2-mile) right (south) on Lucas Turnpike. Turn left (east) at the next intersection with NY 213. Cross the bridge spanning Rondout Creek and proceed into High Falls. Be sure to check out High Falls Historic Park on NY 213 and the D & H Canal Museum in town on Mohonk Road.

Adirondack Region Tours

Adirondack Park is simply enormous. With over 6 million acres of public and private lands in the northern third of New York, the park could practically cover the entire state of Vermont. Established in 1892, it remains the largest state park in the nation.

Despite its vast, original, natural beauty, the Adirondacks for decades were largely taken for granted and abused by industrial interests. During the mid-nineteenth century, legions of lumberers and loggers pounced on the landscape, denuding it of virgin timberland as the nation's demand for wood grew. New York became the nation's leading lumber-producing state. Majestic white pines—strong and straight as telephone poles—were logged while hemlock was left to rot on the forest floor after having been stripped of bark used for leather tanning. The spruce trees made the finest pulp for paper and were relentlessly cut down. Erosion from rains and snow meltwater washed over the barren hillsides, and these remote, primitive forests became a memory.

Fortunately, the massive abuse did not go unnoticed forever. Conservationists forced the government to establish in 1885 the New York State Forest Preserve. As a result, ten years later 900,000 acres of land were protected. The area within the preserve was declared "forever wild."

Forty-two percent of this land is public; 58 percent is private. Most of the state land is designated as "wilderness" or "primitive" and is off-limits to bicycles and motorized vehicles. That's one giant step for protecting the environment, but not good news for off-road bike riders. However, in 1985, the State Land Master Plan allowed access throughout the preserve on land that was designated as "wild forest." Any foot trails, dirt roads, and horse and snowmobile trails on these particular lands labeled as "wild forest" became open for bicycling. This wild forest amounts to about 1.2 million acres of backcountry wilderness mountain bike yahoo potential, with the exception of routes posted closed. In effect, Adirondack Park provides the most extensive mountain biking opportunities in the eastern United States.

All-terrain biking began in the Adirondacks at the end of the nineteenth century and soon became popular. A local biking club was formed in Keene Valley in 1897. Many of its members had to ride over rough roads with sections filled with tree stumps and logs and without the benefit of today's modern suspension systems.

Many of the routes throughout the Adirondacks were once in a primitive state. The early roads, literally hacked out of the dense woodland, were later paved with logs, making for a very bumpy ride. The waterways, ancient paths of least resistance, were the first travel corridors and became the preferred method of travel. Native Americans and early explorers, hunters, and trappers paddled the lakes and rivers by canoe. Prior to the sixteenth century, not many year-round residents chose the Adirondacks for settling and raising a family. The Native Americans avoided the densely forested mountains and preferred to settle in the gently rolling Champlain Valley where they engaged in agriculture. The Adirondack region proved to be excellent hunting territory, which attracted Native Americans, hunters, and trappers. Bear, moose, deer, mountain lion, and wolf were plentiful, and the 2,800 lakes and ponds and 6,000 miles of rivers and streams were well-stocked for fishing. The region was also a popular tribal warground. There were numerous skirmishes among the Iroquois from the south and the Algonquins and Hurons from the north.

Heavy settlement of the region didn't begin until the latter part of the eighteenth century, after the Adirondacks were discovered to be a tremendous source for lumber. Recreation began after the Civil War, and from 1870 to 1910 the Adirondacks were the preferred location for many vacationers. The burgeoning tourist industry spawned hotels, rustic guides, and roads. At the beginning of this period, steamships and other boats were used to transport people in and out. The railroad came next. The tracks and trains that were built to haul lumber became a convenient way to bring tourists. It wasn't until the twentieth century, with the advent of the automobile, that roads were built and improved. I have included some rides that follow along these ancient corridors of travel.

The Adirondacks are a wilderness that beckons explorers and adventurers of any age or era. And that includes mountain bikers. Snowmobile routes, forest roads, and single-tracks are abundant in the Adirondacks and make for prime two-wheel travel rides for all levels of riders.

The Adirondacks evoke the deep meaning of wilderness. To quote Edward Abbey, in his book, *Desert Solitaire,*

> Wilderness invokes nostalgia, a justified not merely sentimental nostalgia for the lost America our forefathers knew. The word suggests the past and the unknown, the womb of earth from which we all emerged. It means something lost and something still present, something remote and at the same time intimate, something buried in our blood and nerves, something beyond us and without limit. Romance—but not to be dismissed on that account. The romantic view, while not the whole of truth, is a necessary part of the whole truth.
>
> But the love of wilderness is more than a hunger for what is always beyond reach; it is also an expression of loyalty to the earth, the earth which bore us and sustains us, the only home we shall ever know, the only paradise we ever need—if only we had the eyes to see.

Happy trails.

RIDE 65 *JOHNSON POND–PARADOX TOUR*

Tucked above the small hamlet of North Hudson lies a 22-mile loop through a mixed hardwood and evergreen forest. This hearty feast of a ride requires about a good half-day. If you take your time, you could fill up a full day. Get an early start and explore these mostly hard-packed dirt roads. After finishing this tour exit north on Interstate 87 to the Lake Placid and Keene Valley area and sample some of the great tours available in that area. North Hudson resides in a quiet corner of the Champlain Valley and offers a mixture of paved and dirt roads. The historic settlement is just north of the popular and attractive Schroon Lake and Lake George. Views of ponds, forests, and hillsides add to your ride's delight.

General location: Thirty-eight miles north of Lake George near the village of North Hudson in Essex County, in northeastern New York.

Elevation change: The terrain is rolling and there are some gradual climbs, but nothing very steep. This tour is primarily a challenge based on distance versus a mountain bike technical dream.

Season: These routes are rideable providing they are not covered with deep snows and have dried out after the spring thaws. The approximate dates are early May through November. However, it always depends on the severity of the winter and the amounts of snow that fall.

Services: There are better options for food and shops 6 miles south in Schroon Lake. Gear up and fill up there before you tour.

Hazards: During mud season, which begins from the first thaws and lasts until late April, the roads are deceptively moist and soft. The roads are frozen with water during the winter, and when they begin to thaw out riding on them is like riding on quicksand.

Rescue index: You are riding along seldom-traveled roads. Some summer residences are scattered along the roads, though. During my first jaunt along these routes, I had to ride back down to NY 9 before I could find some assistance.

Land status: The route travels through the pristine Hammond Pond Wild Forest on public roads.

Maps: *The New York State Atlas and Gazetteer*, published by DeLorme Mapping Company, provides some topographical detail as well as route layout. The topographic details shown on the maps include 160' contour intervals. The popular atlas is available at most bookstores in the Northeast.

Finding the trail: Take the New York State Thruway (Interstate 87) north to Exit 24 (Albany). Take I-87 north to Newcomb/North Hudson, Exit 29. After the exit ramp, turn right at the stop sign to pick up NY 9 north. Follow it for .3 mile and turn right onto Johnson Pond Road (Essex County Road 2).

RIDE 65 *JOHNSON POND–PARADOX TOUR*

Park your car anywhere along the road. To avoid a major steep section, drive your car .6 mile and park anywhere along the road soon after it levels out.

Source of additional information:

Lake Placid/Essex County Visitors Bureau
Olympic Center
Lake Placid, New York 12946
(800) 2PLACID

Notes on the trail: I know the beginning is painful, but once out of the way, the remaining passage is a piece of cake. The first .6 mile climbs steadily up the semipaved, rough road. It does level out and pass through an evergreen forest. Catch your breath and take a moment to admire the raging stream that tumbles alongside the road. Johnson Pond Road (CR 2) changes into a dirt road soon after passing Johnson Pond on your right. After pedaling 5 miles from NY 9 along Johnson Pond Road, turn left (northeast) at the intersection with Old Furnace Road. Paradox Creek and the 600' Bald Pate and Moose Mountain will accompany you on your left to the north. This 5-mile leg leads you to Ironville, the location of the Penfield Museum.

From Ironville pedal south, winding along the western shore of Penfield Pond. In just under 2 miles, turn right on Stoney Lonesome Road. Continue another 5 miles, passing Flemings Pond on your left. You can turn left on Letsonville Road to reach Paradox Lake and NY 74. Turn right on Letsonville Road and connect with Johnson Pond Road in just under 2 miles. If you are riding in the summer, make sure you stop to swim at Paradox Lake near the state campsite.

RIDE 66 *THE WILD ONE*

In the High Peaks region of the Adirondacks is a rugged valley surrounded by spectacular scenery and the site of a unique and challenging mountain bike trail. Old Mountain Road traverses the valley, located northwest of Pitchoff Mountain. This six-mile (one way) route passes through meadows and mixed woodlands with spectacular views of the rocky northern cliffs and crags of nearby Pitchoff Mountain. The ride provides an excellent intermediate-level, double-track trail. Except for trail erosion exposing a few rocks along the route and some small hills, this trail is ideal for those who would like to challenge themselves and experience true mountain-pass scenery. As you pedal along, you will pass numerous beaver ponds. They often flood the trail and may require a small detour with a carry.

The ride follows one of the original routes across the Adirondacks before the eighteenth century. The route connected Lake Champlain to the St. Lawrence Valley and was known as the Northwest Bay Road. This section, which ran from Keene to Lake Placid, was long considered to be the most difficult and treacherous. Stagecoach passengers often had to get out and help push their coach through the 2,350-foot pass. By the mid-nineteenth century stagecoaches traveled along the present NY 73 route through Cascade Pass. Ironically, the severe winter weather in Cascade Pass often made people prefer

RIDE 66 *THE WILD ONE*

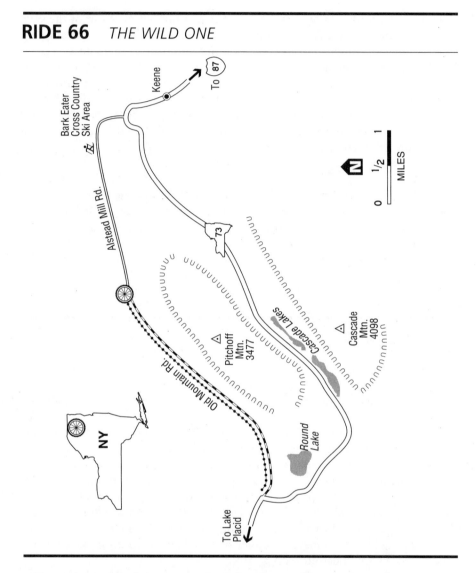

Old Mountain Road. From 1810 to 1860 this route was the only direct road-way from Keene and the east to North Elba and the west. Cars passed along the same route until 1930. After 1930 the eroded route was only passable by four-wheel-drive vehicles. And then came the mountain bike, opening up this exciting route for two-wheel travel and discovery.

General location: Near the village of Keene, about 14 miles south of Lake Placid in the High Peaks area of Adirondack Park in northeastern New York.

Elevation change: Heading east from Alstead Mill Road, the elevation begins at 1,800', rises to 2,350' at the pass, and descends to 2,100' as the trail leads into NY 73.

Season: The trails are available almost year-round, and if there is no snow cover, winter is an ideal time in these primitive woods, providing the ground is frozen (sans ice) and there is no snow. The route follows a deep valley within a high mountain notch and can be muddy and flooded in sections during wet weather. The black flies can be fierce in late spring, so bring some repellent. Try to avoid mud season, which begins after the first thaws in March and can last until early May.

Services: We stayed at the Bark Eater, a true country inn, located on Alstead Mill Road. The inn provides the mountain bike rider with a base camp to launch several bike excursions along the miles of trails just beyond the Bark Eater's perimeters. Originally a stagecoach stopover, the Bark Eater Inn has been in operation since the early nineteenth century. The farmhouse atmosphere still reflects these early times with wide board floors, stone fireplaces, and antiques everywhere. It is located on a spacious, 350-acre farm in the heart of the Adirondack High Peaks. Joe Pete Wilson, a former Olympic and world competitor in Nordic skiing, biathlon, and bobsledding welcomes mountain bikers year-round. His experienced staff is eager to help you enjoy your time there. Placid Planet Bicycles and High Peaks Cyclery rents and sells mountain bikes in Lake Placid.

Hazards: An 800' vertical descent awaits the rider after reaching the height of land at the pass.

Rescue index: NY 73 is a well-traveled route and is never more than 5 miles away.

Land status: New York State Department of Environmental Conservation manages the Forest Preserve land through which the route passes.

Maps: The Adirondack High Peaks Region Area Map published by Plinth, Quoin & Cornice Associates provides excellent topographical detail of the route and surrounding terrain and can be found at most outdoor-type stores in New York for approximately $4.95. It is based on the USGS, 15 minute series, at a scale of 1:62,500 and a contour level of 20' where 1 inch = .98 mile.

Finding the trail: Take the New York State Thruway (Interstate 87) north to Exit 24 (Albany). Take I-87 north to Exit 30. Pick up NY 9 north and follow it for 2 miles to NY 73. Continue on NY 73 toward the Lake Placid area. The start of the tour is located on NY 73, 9 miles from Keene and 5.8 miles from the traffic light in Lake Placid. The end point is the termination of Alstead Mill Road in Keene. From Keene's center, proceed west on NY 73 and turn right on Alstead Mill Road. Turn left after 1.4 miles at the Bark Eater Touring Center and continue straight to the top of the road at 3.9 miles. You will notice a small parking area in a pretty meadow beside 3 buildings that are used for an Adirondack guide service organization. The trail begins at the end of the parking area. The end of the tour is located on NY 73, 9 miles from Keene and 5.8 miles from the traffic light in Lake Placid. If you are shuttling, park your car in the small lot near the intersection of Old Military Road (on the maps as Old Mountain Road) and NY 73 (half a mile east of Cascade Ski Touring Center). You can also just ride up to the pass and back down again.

Sources of additional information:

The Bark Eater
Alstead Mill Road
Keene, New York 12942
(518) 576-2221

Placid Planet Bicycles
200 Saranac Avenue
Lake Placid, New York 12946
(518) 523-4128

High Peaks Cyclery
331 Main Street
Lake Placid, New York 12946
(518) 523-3764

Adirondack Park Agency
PO Box 99, Route 86
Raybrook, New York 12977
(518) 891-4050

New York State Department of Environmental Conservation
P.O. Box 296
Raybrook, New York 12977
(518) 897-1200

Lake Placid/Essex County Visitors Bureau
Olympic Center
Lake Placid, New York 12946
(800) 2PLACID

Notes on the trail: This tour can be as short as a 6-mile jaunt over a mountain pass if someone is willing to park a second car at the end of the route, or an 18-mile loop if you have to make it back to your starting point by yourself.

Proceed past the parking area onto forested, grassy double-track. The trail follows the Nichols Brook. You will soon cross a wide plank bridge just above the convergence of 2 streams. Begin a gradual climb of 1 mile and come out of the woods near a large, stump-filled beaver pond. Look to your south to take in Pitchoff Mountain. After half a mile the route narrows to single-track. Pass by another 3 small beaver ponds. Try to catch a glimpse of some of their lodges amid the stumps and fallen dead trees. Just before the

Panoramic views surround you along Alstead Mill Road.

last pond, look for the deep valley to your south. You are ascending along its side and just a few feet to the left the ground seems to fall away into this valley. You will soon begin a short descent to the last pond.

The last pond is about 2.8 miles from the parking area and is a great spot to take in the tree-enshrined cliffs of Pitchoff Mountain. Proceed west on the trail. It may be wet in spots, but just take the higher route, which lies north of the trail. It is a well-defined herd path. A gentle descent through a birch, beech, and hemlock forest delivers you to the western trailhead. Continue straight (west) to NY 73. You are now .8 mile northwest of the Mt. Van Hoevenberg Ski Center, which hosts another 25 miles of trail.

RIDE 67 *THE BARK EATER BACKROADS*

A menagerie of old country roads winds through farm and forest and provides a good half-day of pleasurable riding. The hard-packed dirt Bartlett Road is six miles in one direction. Connect it with two other dirt roads and it forms a 16-mile loop around the Bark Eater Inn. The steep descents and hearty climbs along Limekiln and Lacy Roads provide some challenging but not impossible riding. The rewards unfold as you pass through beautiful beech and hemlock forests and pass in and out of mountain farms and

meadows. Gushing, babbling brooks crisscross your path under bridges and alongside roads. Forests, horse farms, and meadows combined with the mountain backdrop of the Hurricane Mountain Primitive Area to the east make for some spectacular scenic mountain bike riding.

General location: Near the village of Keene, about 14 miles south of Lake Placid in the High Peaks area of Adirondack Park, in northeastern New York.

Elevation change: There are some great descents, but the price is some steep climbs. Elevations range from 800' where NY 73 is, to 1,500', the height of land on Bartlett Road. The greatest climb is along Limekiln Road heading south and up toward its intersection with Alstead Mill Road.

Season: The trails are available year-round, and if there is no snow cover winter is a time of solitude on these roads. If the roads are firm, free of snow, and not spongy from spring thaws, winter to spring is a great time to explore these backroads.

Services: We stayed at the Bark Eater, a true country inn, located on Alstead Mill Road. The inn provides the mountain bike rider with a base camp to launch several bike excursions along the miles of trails just beyond the Bark Eater's perimeters. Originally a stagecoach stopover, the Bark Eater Inn has been in operation since the early nineteenth century. The farmhouse atmosphere still reflects these early times with wide board floors, stone fireplaces, and antiques everywhere. It is located on a spacious, 350-acre farm in the heart of the Adirondack High Peaks. Joe Pete Wilson, a former Olympic and world competitor in Nordic skiing, biathlon, and bobsledding welcomes mountain bikers year-round. His experienced staff is eager to help you enjoy your time there. Placid Planet Bicycles and High Peaks Cyclery rents and sells mountain bikes in Lake Placid.

Hazards: An 800' vertical descent awaits the rider after reaching the height of land at the pass.

Rescue index: These roads are not too remote—only about 1 to 2 miles from well-traveled NY 73. There is usually someone around the Bark Eater Inn who can provide a phone or some aid.

Land status: These are public roads.

Maps: The Adirondack High Peaks Region Area Map published by Plinth, Quoin & Cornice Associates provides excellent topographical detail of the route and surrounding terrain and can be found at most outdoor-type stores in New York for approximately $4.95. It is based on the USGS, 15 minute series, at a scale of 1:62,500 and a contour level of 20' where 1 inch = .98 mile.

Finding the trail: Take the New York State Thruway (Interstate 87) north to Exit 24 (Albany). Take I-87 north to Exit 30. Pick up NY 9 north and follow it for 2 miles to NY 73. Continue on NY 73 toward the Lake Placid area. After the village of Keene turn right onto Alstead Mill Road. Look for signs

The scenic Bark Eater back roads.

for the Bark Eater Inn. You may park along Alstead Mill Road, or if you are staying at the Bark Eater Inn, just go out your door and start pedaling.

Sources of additional information:

The Bark Eater
Alstead Mill Road
Keene, New York 12942
(518) 576-2221

Placid Planet Bicycles
200 Saranac Avenue
Lake Placid, New York 12946
(518) 523-4128

High Peaks Cyclery
331 Main Street
Lake Placid, New York 12946
(518) 523-3764

Adirondack Park Agency
PO Box 99, Route 86
Raybrook, New York 12977
(518) 891-4050

New York State Department of Environmental Conservation
P.O. Box 296
Raybrook, New York 12977
(518) 897-1200

Lake Placid/Essex County Visitors Bureau
Olympic Center
Lake Placid, New York 12946
(800) 2PLACID

Notes on the trail: Begin your ride on Alstead Mill Road and turn right (north) on Bartlett Road. After about half a mile, notice a dirt road to your right. This is Lacy Road, which you will turn down after returning from the one-way Bartlett Road. Turning left leads you to the Clifford Falls waterfalls. You can take Bartlett Road for about 6 miles and then turn around. Turn left (east) onto Lacy Road, which descends toward the East Branch of the Ausable River and NY 73. At a yield sign, you may continue straight to the river or turn right and ascend Limekiln Road. Take Limekiln Road over 1 mile to its **T** intersection with Alstead Mill Road. Turn right on Alstead Mill Road to wherever your car is parked.

RIDE 68 *THE MYSTERY OF PINE POND*

The 12-mile, round-trip (6 miles one way), hard-pack, double-track route leading toward scenic Pine Pond, on the northern edge of the High Peaks Wilderness Area, is one of Lake Placid's most popular trails. Due to the restrictions on riding in designated Wilderness areas, this trail travels through the state's "Wild Forest" zone and is permissible and ideal to ride.

Pine Pond, a tiny, isolated gem rimmed by stands of old-growth white pine on its wide, sandy shores, is beautiful in all seasons. The pond was formed when a large chunk of ice from the Ice Age fell off one of the glaciers. The ice surrounding this large piece melted faster than the chunk. The result is that sand filled in around the sides of this chunk of ice, and when it finally did melt a large hole in the ground remained. Naturally over time this hole filled with water. Pine Pond is known as a kettle hole. The Adirondack landscape has been extensively sculpted by the glaciers that dominated North America during the ice ages. The glaciers that were sometimes 1,000 feet thick completely covered the mountains.

Your trip into Pine Pond will be exciting, easy, and scenic. This well-worn trail is easy to follow and a must-do for all ability levels.

RIDE 68   *THE MYSTERY OF PINE POND*

General location: Northeastern New York, Adirondack Park. The trailhead is located within minutes of the village of Lake Placid.

Elevation change: The grade of the trail going to the pond is a gradual descent with the exception of the initial climb. A few rolling hills are thrown in for fun and the trip back from the pond will nevertheless be generally uphill. The most technical part of the ride is at the beginning, an uphill with rocks to maneuver around followed by a rocky downhill. After this, the trail is rolling and has several areas with mudholes that may be deceptive in depth. Don't forget to allow for adequate time and energy for the longer return uphill. Once dark falls, what was first an easy trail can quickly become an evening's nightmare.

Season: The black flies can be fierce in late spring, but the trail can be ridden in most seasons except when there is snow on the ground.

Services: Most services can be found in Lake Placid, which is full of lodging, restaurants, and shops. Placid Planet Bicycles rents and sells mountain bikes.

Hazards: This is a popular trail among cyclists, hikers, horses, four-wheelers, hunters, and a variety of wildlife. Follow and respect the rules of the trail; treat these other users the way you want them to treat you, and continued use of special trails like these will continue.

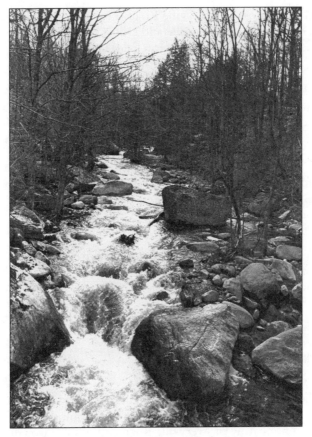

Rocky stream in the Adirondack High Peaks region.

Rescue index: The trail is fairly worn, straightforward, and hard to get lost on. You are never more than 6 miles from Lake Placid and there are usually other trail users in the vicinity.

Land status: New York State Department of Environmental Conservation manages the Forest Preserve land.

Maps: The Adirondack High Peaks Region Area Map published by Plinth, Quoin & Cornice Associates provides excellent topographical detail of the route and surrounding terrain and can be found at most outdoor-type stores in New York for approximately $4.95. It is based on the USGS, 15 minute series, at a scale of 1:62,500 and a contour level of 20' where 1 inch = .98 mile.

Finding the trail: Take the New York State Thruway (Interstate 87) north to Exit 24 (Albany). Take I-87 north to Exit 30. Pick up NY 9 north and follow it for 2 miles to NY 73. Continue on NY 73 for 28 miles to the Lake Placid area. In Lake Placid, take Old Military Road, also known as Old Mountain

Road, (near ski jumps) to Averyville Road (note the Northville–Placid Trail sign). Turn left (south) on Averyville and follow this until the pavement ends; continue past a barn and through a farm field. Upon entering the woods, continue until you find parking at the side of the road.

Sources of additional information:

Placid Planet Bicycles
200 Saranac Avenue
Lake Placid, New York 12946
(518) 523-4128

Adirondack Park Agency
PO Box 99, Route 86
Raybrook, New York 12977
(518) 891-4050

New York State Department of Environmental Conservation
P.O. Box 296
Raybrook, New York 12977
(518) 897-1200

Lake Placid/Essex County Visitors Bureau
Olympic Center
Lake Placid, New York 12946
(800) 2PLACID

Notes on the trail: The trail is fairly straightforward and easy to follow. Stay on the most worn path and don't stray onto any errant deer paths. The route is actually a continuation of Averyville Road and passes through potato fields and then enters the woods. Once in the woods you will begin to pick up the state's red snowmobile markers which blaze the trail. Proceed through the hardwood forest for about 1 mile. The next mile, along a sometimes washed-out logging road, is a steep, rocky descent; the exposed rock can be slippery when wet or when covered with fallen leaves. The track then narrows to about 4', and the forest changes to pine and hemlock. The final portion of the trail is mostly pine needle–covered trail with tree roots to maneuver over. Cold River enters from the left, and the trail follows its banks for a few hundred yards before intersecting a T junction. A left turn takes you to Pine Pond's north shore and a right takes you to Oseetah Lake. Return to your car by the same route.

RIDE 69 *MCKENZIE MOUNTAIN LOOP*

This challenging 13-mile loop traverses a beautiful mountain pass on an old tote road. The double-track passes between McKenzie Mountain, elevation 3,861 feet, to the north and Haystack Mountain to the south, and goes through a pristine forest. Sections of the trail may be difficult to ride due to exposed rocks from the weathered trail bed, but the riding is exciting and the scenery rewarding. The forest has been left in its natural state and saved from the infamous logging of the nineteenth and early twentieth centuries. New York was the leading lumber-producing state in the nation by 1850. The nation's demand for wood escalated in the early part of the nineteenth century, and lumber barons established logging operations throughout the Adirondacks. They stripped the forests of the majestic white pines that were valued for their strength and straight grain. Rivers were used to transport the logs, and roads were cut throughout the woodlands. Fortunately for the donations of the Shore Owners Association of Lake Placid, the land was bought up by the state before the former land owners, the International Paper Company, could log it. The Shore Owners Association that began in 1893 maintained trails in and around this small wilderness area. The association was formed to fight the massive fluctuations of the levels of water that resided in Lake Placid. These fluctuations were caused from logging near the lake. Eventually the associations won control.

During the winter this trail is part of the extensive Jackrabbit Cross Country Ski Trail System that extends from Keene Valley west to Lake Placid and Saranac Lake. The Jackrabbit Ski Trail was constructed in 1986 to improve the cross-country skiing in the Lake Placid–Saranac Lake area. It is named in memory of Herman "Jack Rabbit" Johannsen, who laid out many of the trails himself. He was a pioneer of Lake Placid skiing from 1916 to 1928 and died in 1987 at age 111.

There is only one catch. It is listed in several local mountain bike brochures, but when I telephoned the Department of Environmental Conservation, I was told they preferred that mountain bikers not ride the trail. They did not authorize its use as a designated mountain bike trail. The ride is listed here, in hopes that one day this beautiful recreational resource can be shared with our trail-conscious mountain biker community.

Until this trailway becomes more accessible and sanctioned for mountain bikers, we must abide by the rules.

General location: Just west of the village of Lake Placid in the High Peaks area of Adirondack Park, in northeastern New York.

RIDE 69   *McKENZIE MOUNTAIN LOOP*

Elevation change: The first .3 mile rises sharply along an eroded road from approximately 1,900' to 2,400'. The trail then levels out, climbs some more, and drops very steeply to McKenzie Pond at 1,660'.

Season: The trails are usually dried out after spring thaw around the middle of May and are good to ride on until the first snows appear. This abandoned tote road gets very wet and soggy for a high pass route.

Services: Placid Planet Bicycles is located on the corner of Whiteface Inn Road and rents and sells mountain bikes and supplies.

Hazards: There is one awesome descent after reaching the height of land at the pass. Care should be taken if the trail is wet and/or covered with leaves.

Rescue index: The route passes through a wilderness that is not far from condominiums near Whiteface Landing on Whiteface Inn Road, and the well-traveled NY 86 is only a mile away.

Land status: New York State Department of Environmental Conservation manages the Forest Preserve land.

Maps: The Adirondack High Peaks Region Area Map published by Plinth, Quoin & Cornice Associates provides excellent topographical detail of the route and surrounding terrain and can be found at most outdoor-type stores in New York for approximately $4.95. It is based on the USGS, 15 minute series, at a scale of 1:62,500 and a contour level of 20' where 1 inch = .98 mile.

Finding the trail: Take the New York State Thruway (Interstate 87) north to Exit 24 (Albany). Take I-87 north to Exit 30. Pick up NY 9 north and follow it for 2 miles to NY 73. Continue on NY 73 for 28 miles to the Lake Placid area. Proceed west from Lake Placid on NY 86. Turn right (north) onto Whiteface Inn Road (Essex County Road 31) toward the Whiteface Inn Resort. After approximately 1.2 miles there will be parking on your left. Across the road from the golf course entrance on the left are signs for the Jackrabbit Trail. Take the second trailhead about 200' farther down the road to access the beginning of this old logging road. There will be 2 large stones about 75' in on the trail. A New York State Department of Environmental Conservation sign specifies the routes' destinations. The McKenzie Pond Road is 5.5 miles and Saranac Lake is 7 miles.

Sources of additional information:

Placid Planet Bicycles
200 Saranac Avenue
Lake Placid, New York 12946
(518) 523-4128

Adirondack Park Agency
PO Box 99, Route 86
Raybrook, New York 12977
(518) 891-4050

New York State Department of Environmental Conservation
P.O. Box 296
Raybrook, New York 12977
(518) 897-1200

Lake Placid/Essex County Visitors Bureau
Olympic Center
Lake Placid, New York 12946
(800) 2PLACID

Notes on the trail: The route proceeds steeply along the old, eroded logging road and levels off after .3 mile. The trail is washed out with cobblestones but is rideable. The forest changes from old-growth beech and birch to a mixed second-growth forest with evergreens. At 1.6 miles, you will reach the Placid Lean-to in a flat section of trail. It sits by a small stream and is in bad shape, waiting for the next storm to level it. Continue toward McKenzie Pass, and at 1.9 miles you arrive at an intersection. The trail left (south) leads to NY 86 in 3.6 miles. The trail to the right (north) climbs 1.6 miles to the summit of McKenzie Mountain. Continue straight (west), climbing to the top of the pass toward McKenzie Pond, which will be reached in another 2.5 miles. Descend with caution, as about 1,000' of elevation is lost in slightly more than a mile. The trail is rocky, with several washed-out culverts. After reaching the bottom, continue straight past a side trail on the right to emerge on McKenzie Pond Road. Turn left onto the road and left again at the stop sign. Follow NY 86 back toward your parking area on Whiteface Inn Road.

RIDE 70 *SCARFACE*

The following description was adapted from the Placid Planet Bike Shop's trail brochure:

Only four miles from Placid Planet in the metropolis of beautiful Raybrook are the access trails to Scarface Mountain. At 3,088 feet, Scarface Mountain stands out; its sheer rock face can be seen while driving on NY 86. The trails up the actual mountain itself are not suitable for riding, and you are requested to abstain from riding up Scarface. You are encouraged to stash your bike in the woods and hike up. An awesome eight-mile network of trails winds through a dense spruce and white pine–forested wilderness. The route traverses a combination of single- and double-track trails. The undulating terrain is pure heaven for mountain biking. There is a touch of the surreal as you ride over pine needle–covered single-track through dense plantations of conifer woodland.

Rumor has it that these trails were reconditioned for a European cross-country ski team to train for the 1980 Olympic Games in Lake Placid. Whatever the reason for their existence, they are a great ride—not too technical but fun for riders of most abilities. In late summer, the wild blueberries are wonderful. Keep in mind that this area is very popular with hunters; dress appropriately in season. This tour was high on the Placid Planet Bicycle staff's favorite mountain bike ride list and is a must-do if you're visiting the area.

RIDE 70 *SCARFACE*

General location: Just west of Lake Placid in the village of Raybrook, located in the High Peaks area of Adirondack Park, in northeastern New York.

Elevation change: The terrain is mostly rolling with 1 major ascent from the bridge crossing the pond into which Ray Brook flows. The ascent is from 1,600' to 1,700' in half a mile.

Season: The trails are available year-round, and if there is no snow cover winter is an ideal time in these primitive woods. The black flies can be fierce in late spring. While many trails throughout Adirondack Park are wet and

How about a child seat for my birthday?

unrideable until mid-May, these trails are very dry. The peaty composition of the ground is very absorbent and there are rarely any muddy spots.

Services: The village of Raybrook located farther west on NY 86 has a great barbecue takeout restaurant. An ice cream store and some wood craft stores and cottage lodging round out this rural town's occupancy in the wilderness.

Hazards: The trails are fun to ride, and the tight turns demand some extra attention so that you don't knock over one of the trees with your head. Call the New York State Department of Environmental Conservation (NYSDEC) for specific hunting season dates.

Rescue index: You are only a few miles from well-traveled NY 86. The ascent trail to Scarface Mountain is a favorite among hikers, and if you didn't whiz past them on the trail, I'm sure they would be willing to lend you a hand if such an occasion should arise.

Land status: New York State Department of Environmental Conservation manages the forest.

Maps: The Adirondack High Peaks Region Area Map and the Adirondack Canoe Map published by Plinth, Quoin & Cornice Associates provide excellent topographical detail of the route and surrounding terrain and can be found at most outdoor-type stores in New York for approximately $4.95.

Finding the trail: Take the New York State Thruway (Interstate 87) north to Exit 24 (Albany). Take I-87 north to Exit 30. Pick up NY 9 north and follow it for 2 miles to NY 73. Continue on NY 73 for 28 miles to the Lake Placid area. Head toward Saranac Lake on NY 86 and turn left (south) onto Ray Brook Road. It is across from the state police barracks just past the Mobile gas station. One hundred or so yards down Ray Brook Road is a parking area on the left. This is the trailhead.

Sources of additional information:

Placid Planet Bicycles
200 Saranac Avenue
Lake Placid, New York 12946
(518) 523-4128

Adirondack Park Agency
PO Box 99, Route 86
Raybrook, New York 12977
(518) 891-4050

New York State Department of Environmental Conservation
P.O. Box 296
Raybrook, New York 12977
(518) 897-1200

Lake Placid/Essex County Visitors Bureau
Olympic Center
Lake Placid, New York 12946
(800) 2PLACID

Notes on the trail: The first 1.5 miles take you through a dense, spruce-filled forest over undulating terrain. This portion of the trail is new and was rerouted in 1981 after a federal correctional facility was built nearby. The route is marked with red disks and is a lot of fun to ride. You will soon cross an abandoned railroad right-of-way. These were the Fairytale Railroad tracks, which ran between Remsen and Lake Placid. Left will take you on what could be a great ride to Lake Placid but is so overgrown it is considered a real disaster by some. Going right on the tracks will take you near the Adirondack Correctional Facilities. The chances are better than average that you will be questioned by people with guns about why you are there, even though it seems obvious by your Lycra shorts, jersey, and helmet that you are just cruising on your mountain bike. Like anyone with more than 2 brain cells would intentionally go to a prison wearing Lycra. Anyway, go straight and you cross an interesting walking bridge that crosses over an attractive pond which the Ray Brook flows into. It is an impressive-looking bridge and a wooden plaque proclaims its construction history. At the far end of the bridge a staircase takes you back into the woods. You will soon traverse an open meadow filled with blueberry bushes. The route proceeds southwest over fairly level ground. You will soon enter a majestic white pine forest and intersect a wood road at 1.3 miles.

Backcountry utopia along the Scarface Trails.

Continue straight at 1.5 miles onto an old tote road whose width will narrow somewhat. The trail to the summit of Scarface leads to the left (south) at 1.7 miles. Continue straight through the mixed deciduous and conifer forest. Bear left at the next fork and descend for about half a mile. At the **T** intersection, turn left. You may take this for another 1.5 miles to Roger Brook, but then you must return along the same route. After returning from this short spur, pedal past the first trail and take a right (east) onto the second trail, a few hundred yards later. This trail will reconnect with the original trail you came in on. At the time of this writing there were no posted signs indicating private property. If there are, don't trespass. It is a privilege to ride on these lands. Just turn back and head down another trail.

RIDE 71 *THE PENINSULA TRAILS*

This small network of interconnecting double-track and single-track trails provides an excellent mountain bike warm-up if you are staying in the village of Lake Placid and plan on riding the many trails in the area described by this guide. The distance only adds up to about three miles. The trails are conveniently located at the northern end of the village of Lake Placid, so while some of your party may want to shop the town, you can head on out to the trail at the edge of town. I rode them after a big pasta dinner one evening just before sunset, and it was a great way to end the day. This small maze consists of four named trails.

The easy-cruising, wide, hard-packed dirt Access Road Trail is .7 mile long. The hard surface makes this a delight for families with small children and those new to the sport. The trail is also important for reaching the other more technical trails. There is an intermediate dirt road called the Ridge Trail. This .8-mile-long, hard-packed single-track travels through a beech forest. The intermediate Boundary Trail is of the same character and provides another .6 mile. The Lake Shore Trail is the only advanced single-track and is .4 mile long. Its condition is very rooty, as it meanders along the shore of Lake Placid. The views of Lake Placid (the lake) from the technical Lake Shore Trail single-track are a sight to behold and worth the trail effort. Beautiful homes line the shores of the lake and benches are located at key viewing locations. In the western horizon are also views of the 2,800-foot Mount Colburn and the smaller Mount Tamarac behind it to the right. The 3,861-foot McKenzie Mountain lies behind them. This network of trails is proof that good things can also come in small packages.

General location: Northeastern New York on the north side of the village of Lake Placid.

Elevation change: The riding is fairly level with no major elevation changes or tough climbs.

Season: Mountain biking is allowed on these trails during all seasons, providing the trails are not too wet or covered by snow.

Services: All services can be found in Lake Placid. Bike rentals can be found at Placid Planet Bicycles and High Peaks Cyclery.

Hazards: The trail system is popular with hikers and joggers. Use caution on the fast, flat trails and enjoy the serenity and beauty of the woods. This will minimize conflicts and provide mountain bikers with a good reputation.

Rescue index: The trails are all within 1 mile of Lake Placid.

Land status: New York State land.

RIDE 71 *THE PENINSULA TRAILS*

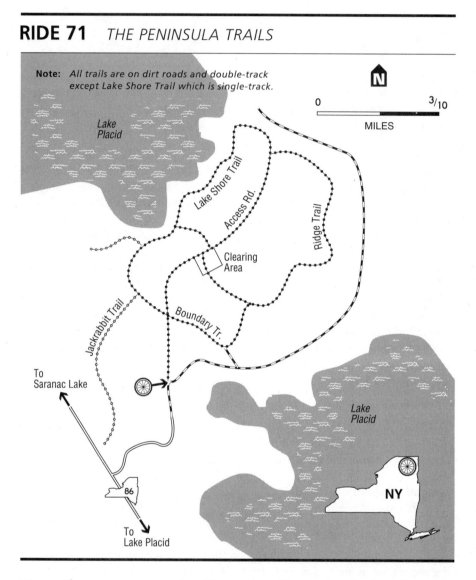

Note: *All trails are on dirt roads and double-track except Lake Shore Trail which is single-track.*

0   3/10

MILES

Lake Placid

Lake Shore Trail

Access Rd.

Ridge Trail

Clearing Area

Jackrabbit Trail

Boundary Tr.

To Saranac Lake

Lake Placid

To Lake Placid

86

NY

Maps: The map accompanying this tour provides the best basic trail outline and is easy to follow. Trail signs along the route also give adequate indication of which way to go.

Finding the trail: Take the New York State Thruway (Interstate 87) north to Exit 24 (Albany). Take I-87 north to Exit 30. Pick up NY 9 north and follow it for 2 miles to NY 73. Continue on NY 73 for 28 miles to the Lake Placid area. Pass through the village of Lake Placid on NY 86 and turn right (east) onto the paved road just after the Howard Johnson Restaurant. You will see a sign for

Brewster Peninsula Trails. Turn in and continue up the road for .3 mile. The road will swing to the right and the parking will be on the left, just before a yellow metal gate with a stop sign. The trail begins beyond this gate.

Sources of additional information:

High Peaks Cyclery
331 Main Street
Lake Placid, New York 12946
(518) 523-3764

Placid Planet Bicycles
200 Saranac Avenue
Lake Placid, New York 12946
(518) 523-4128

Adirondack Park Agency
PO Box 99, Route 86
Raybrook, New York 12977
(518) 891-4050

New York State Department of Environmental Conservation
P.O. Box 296
Raybrook, New York 12977
(518) 897-1200

Lake Placid/Essex County Visitors Bureau
Olympic Center
Lake Placid, New York 12946
(800) 2PLACID

Notes on the trail: The Access Road Trail begins north of the gate. As you pass through a clearing with a picnic bench, notice the single-track that leads east into the woods. This trail connects with the Ridge Trail. Continue straight through the clearing. Pass another trail to your left. This trail leads down to the Lake Shore Trail. Don't turn here yet. The end of the Access Road Trail turns into Lake Shore Trail and you may return along this trail to your left. Continue northeasterly along the Access Road Trail. It ends at a **T** intersection with the Lake Shore Trail and Ridge Trail. Turning left will take you along the blue-marked, advanced single-track that twists and turns through a dark conifer forest over many exposed roots and rocks, and meanders along the shore of Lake Placid. The trail is about .4 mile in length and leads back in a southwest direction. Near its end it leads into the Boundary Trail. You can take the red-marked Boundary Trail, crossing over the Access Road Trail into the Ridge Trail in about .6 mile. Turn left onto the yellow-marked Ridge Trail. This trail winds through a beautiful hardwood forest mixed with hemlock and balsam and traverses rolling terrain. The higher ground the trail passes over is ideal for the hardwoods growing on it versus the conifers near the lake's shore-line. The trail ends at the Access Road Trail. Turn left (south) onto the Access Road Trail back to the parking area.

RIDE 72 *A DAY AT THE RACES*

Mount Van Hoevenberg was the Olympic Cross Country Ski center during the 13th Winter Olympic Games in 1980. Over 30 miles of wide, well-graded trails are open to the public on this state-owned and -operated ski area. The ride-challenge index ranges from easy cruising to hard hill climbs. It is not a technical single-track dream, although you can put together some good mileage on the wide, double-track paths. The beauty of Mount Van Hoevenberg is the multitude of trails to choose from and the terrain the routes traverse.

The area is named after Henry Van Hoevenberg, who in 1910 began constructing the system of trails and shelters for hikers in the High Peaks area. These trails and shelters are now maintained by the New York State Department of Environmental Conservation. Van Hoevenberg was also the original builder of the Adirondack Lodge during the late nineteenth century. A trail leading up to Mount Marcy is named after him too.

The ski trails at Mount Van Hoevenberg were created in the early 1960s and first used for competition in 1969. Additional loops were put in for the biathlon events, and another expansion created more trails suitable for Olympic competition. The successive expansions of this large cross-country trail's complex have led to a crazy-quilt nature in the trail layout. Fortunately, signs along the trail and detailed maps available at the Mount Van Hoevenberg ski center help you navigate the maze. For cross-country skiers these courses are considered equal to any in the world, and they offer a supreme test of a skier's ability. The labyrinth-like trail layout furnishes mountain bikers with endless excitement and a full day of riding.

General location: Northeastern New York, about 5 miles south of the village of Lake Placid on NY 73.

Elevation change: The trail system resides on a low mountain, compared to the high peaks that surround it. The multitude of trails traverses a whole range of minor elevation changes. It is a hilly area, and there are many trails. You could accumulate a bunch of vertical after a full day of riding.

Season: Mount Van Hoevenberg officially opens sometime in late June. It all depends on the conditions of the trail and their moisture content. I would call the Lake Placid Chamber of Commerce before heading out. You can ride around the trails prior to the area's opening, but the routes tend to be soft and soggy.

RIDE 72 *A DAY AT THE RACES*

To
Lake Placid

73

Mt. Van Hoevenberg
Ski Area Entrance

To
Keene

Stadium

N

0   750   1500

FEET

NY

Note: *More trails exist in this area
than can be shown on this map.*

Crossing a field at Mount Van Hoevenberg.

Services: Open daily from Sunday to Thursday, 10 A.M. to 5 P.M.; Friday, 10 A.M. to 8 P.M.; and Saturday, 9 A.M. to 8 P.M. Trail fees are $4 per day and $6 for 2 days. High Peaks Cyclery operates a mountain bike center in the Mount Van Hoevenberg sports complex. They offer rentals and repairs and advice on where the hot trails are. Bike rentals are $20 per day. For further information call the bike shop at (518) 523-3764.

Hazards: The terrain is varied at the Mount Van Hoevenberg Ski Area and can be hilly and challenging. Be prepared with water and nourishment if you intend to spend many hours riding the myriad of trails.

Rescue index: The Mount Van Hoevenberg area is a popular place and offers other recreational activities to draw people in. Everybody is friendly, and a helping hand is never far away.

Land status: New York State Department of Environmental Conservation manages the forest as a multiple-use area.

Maps: Maps of the mountain bike trail system can be picked up after paying the day-use fee.

Finding the trail: Take the New York State Thruway (Interstate 87) north to Exit 24 (Albany). Take I-87 north to Exit 30. Pick up NY 9 north and follow it for 2 miles to NY 73. Continue on NY 73 for 23 miles to the Lake Placid area. There will be a sign for the Mount Van Hoevenberg Ski Area on NY 73. Turn left (west) into the complex. You'll see several parking areas as you ride along the access road. Proceed straight to the stadium and park there.

Sources of additional information:

Olympic Regional Development Authority
Lake Placid, New York 12946
(518) 523-1655

High Peaks Cyclery
331 Main Street
Lake Placid, New York 12946
(518) 523-3764

Placid Planet Bicycles
200 Saranac Avenue
Lake Placid, New York 12946
(518) 523-4128

Adirondack Park Agency
PO Box 99, Route 86
Raybrook, New York 12977
(518) 891-4050

New York State Department of Environmental Conservation
P.O. Box 296
Raybrook, New York 12977
(518) 897-1200

Lake Placid/Essex County Visitors Bureau
Olympic Center
Lake Placid, New York 12946
(800) 2PLACID

Notes on the trail: A large array of trails awaits the energetic mountain biker at Mount Van Hoevenberg. A tremendous number of riding configurations can be created on the maze of trails and will fill up an entire day of bike riding and exploration. Check in at the office, grab a map, pick a trail, and just begin riding. The routes are well marked and a large map of the trail system at the stadium will help you determine and plan which trail to take.

RIDE 73 *WHITEFACE—A PLACE IN THE SUN*

Mountain biking has come to Whiteface Mountain's alpine ski area. The year 1996 marked the first time mountain bikes could be hauled up by chairlift and riders could disembark and descend onto a variety of intermediate and advanced utility road bike trails. Two chairlifts are used to open up 2,100 feet of vertical descent. Wide, hard-packed, dirt maintenance roads, ranging from one to three miles in length, crisscross the 4,867-foot mountain and make for some very fast riding. Make sure your brakes are in good condition.

Whiteface Mountain stands sentinel above Lake Placid. Its massif is isolated from the other mountains that belong to the High Peaks and lie further south. Its face is carved by challenging alpine ski trails and ancient landslides that have left vertical, treeless strips of exposed bedrock. Excessive moisture and rains peel off the thin layer of soil, plants, and trees from the steep, smooth bedrock. This phenomenon occurs on many Adirondack mountains.

It is a busy mountain. The summit is used by the Atmospheric Sciences Research Center. An auto-toll road ascends to the summit where a restaurant, tunnel, and elevator have become popular tourist attractions. The mountain also hosted the 1980 Olympic alpine events.

During its turbulent past, settlers cleared the lower slopes for agricultural purposes. The mountain's upper hillsides were logged for its abundance of hardwoods. Logging was rampant throughout the Adirondacks and the forests were decimated. Whiteface Mountain has gone through its reforestation and recovered with a diversity of tree species not found on any other mountain in the Adirondacks. Over 19 types of trees have repopulated the areas the old-growth virgin woodland once occupied. In summary, Whiteface inspires awe in all who visit it. Whether you hike it, climb it, or ski or bike down it, this mountain will guarantee you full-blown fun.

General location: Northeastern New York, about 10 miles northeast of the village of Lake Placid on NY 86.

Elevation change: The second Little Whiteface chairlift leaves you at a point where you can descend 2,100'. That's vertical.

Season: Whiteface Mountain Ski Center officially opens sometime in late June. Call the Lake Placid Chamber of Commerce before heading out. You can ride around the trails at the base of the mountain that wind through the valley along the river prior to the area's opening, but the routes may be soft and soggy.

Services: Open from June 15 to October 14, 9 A.M. to 4 P.M. Fees for trail access only are $5 per day for adults and $3 per day for children. Chairlift and trail access fees are $15 per day or $8 per trip for adults and $10 per day

RIDE 73 *WHITEFACE—A PLACE IN THE SUN*

West branch of the Ausable River near Whiteface Mountain.

or $6 per trip for children. Bike and helmet rentals are available in Base Lodge, as are food and beverages.

Hazards: This is an intermediate-to-advanced mountain. Make sure your bike is tight and your brakes are in good working order. You will need them on your descent.

Rescue index: The Whiteface Mountain Ski Center is a popular place and offers other recreational activities that draw people to it. Everybody is friendly, and a helping hand is never far away.

Land status: The area is managed by the Olympic Regional Development Authority.

Maps: Maps of the mountain bike trail system can be picked up after paying the day-use fee.

Finding the trail: Take the New York State Thruway (Interstate 87) north to Exit 24 (Albany). Take I-87 north to Exit 30. Pick up NY 9 north and follow it for 2 miles to NY 73. Continue on NY 73 for 28 miles to the Lake Placid area. From Lake Placid it's approximately another 10 miles. Follow the signs for Whiteface Mountain Ski Center.

Sources of additional information:

> Whiteface Mountain Ski Center
> P.O. Box 1980
> Route 86
> Wilmington, New York 12997
> (518) 946-2223

> Olympic Regional Development Authority
> Lake Placid, New York 12946
> (518) 523-1655

> Adirondack Park Agency
> PO Box 99, Route 86
> Raybrook, New York 12977
> (518) 891-4050

> New York State Department of Environmental Conservation
> P.O. Box 296
> Raybrook, New York 12977
> (518) 897-1200

> Lake Placid/Essex County Visitors Bureau
> Olympic Center
> Lake Placid, New York 12946
> (800) 2PLACID

Notes on the trail: Whiteface offers some great trails along the ski mountain's maintenance roads. To get the most out of this area, begin by taking the Mid-Station Shuttle chairlift. An array of intermediate bike trails can be accessed from this point. If you're brave and want something more challenging, take the Little Whiteface chairlift and descend the advanced terrain for a full 2,100'. A large network of trails awaits the energetic mountain biker. Check in at the office, grab a map, pick a trail, and begin your riding.

RIDE 74 *THE FLUME FALL*

A combination of old roads and cross-country ski trails provides up to five miles of well-maintained, double-track and single-track mountain bike riding. Portions of the trails have been used for competition mountain bike races. This maze of trails can be found just over one mile north of the entrance to the Whiteface Mountain Ski Area. The trails are adjacent to Whiteface

RIDE 74 *THE FLUME FALL*

Mountain and parallel the clear, bouldered West Branch of the Ausable River. The trailhead begins just beyond a bridge that spans a gorge known as the Flume Fall.

For thousands of years the Ausable River has tumbled and carved a wide path through the solid rock, and the area makes an impressive spot to sit, think, relax, and have a bite to eat. This mountain stream flows through a zone of geologic phenomenon known as the Wilmington Notch. Over 500 million years ago, the bedrock buckled and faulted, causing a series of northeast-trending fracture zones. This notch, which lies within one of those zones, extends from Lake Placid to Wilmington. This fracture zone had become the preferred drainage route for rivers and glaciers and causes rapids, waterfalls, and small pools to occur as the Ausable River flows through it. In other parts of the Adirondacks, these fracture zones have become deep, lake-filled valleys. The grandeur of the Adirondacks deserves special attention. They are filled with geologic and ecological wonders that have inspired study and awe.

General location: The trailhead lies just north of Lake Placid in the High Peaks area of Adirondack Park in northeastern New York, and about 1 mile past the entrance to Whiteface Mountain Ski Area.

Elevation change: The tour traverses gently rolling terrain. There are some minor climbs, but nothing too challenging. The trails near the Ausable River are the most level and can be found by bearing left after the parking area. They are part of the Riverview Loop.

Season: During the winter these trails are used as cross-country ski trails, but as the spring season opens up and the trails dry out, the riding can begin and continue until the first snowfalls. Remember, the black flies can be fierce in late spring.

Services: The area offers convenient camping near the beautiful West Branch of the Ausable River. Two miles south is a public campground on the banks of the Ausable, which makes a great spot to park your car and pitch a tent.

Hazards: Some sections of the trail are prone to flooding after periods of wet weather. They may be muddy and crossed by small streams. When I rode during one Memorial Day weekend, a 100' section of trail had been flooded. So be prepared for nature's surprises.

Rescue index: You are within earshot of NY 86, and help is never far away.

Land status: The trails are within the Saranac Lakes Wild Forest on New York State land.

Maps: There are currently no maps available for these trails.

Finding the trail: Take the New York State Thruway (Interstate 87) north to Exit 24 (Albany). Take I-87 north to Exit 30. Pick up NY 9 north and follow it for 2 miles to NY 73. Continue on NY 73 for 28 miles to the Lake Placid area. Take NY 86 past the Whiteface Ski Area, and after about 1 mile you will see the Hungry Trout Motor Lodge and Restaurant. Proceed over the bridge that spans the West Branch of the Ausable River and pull into the parking area on the left.

Sources of additional information:

High Peaks Cyclery
331 Main Street
Lake Placid, New York 12946
(518) 523-3764

Adirondack Park Agency
PO Box 99, Route 86
Raybrook, New York 12977
(518) 891-4050

New York State Department of Environmental Conservation
P.O. Box 296
Raybrook, New York 12977
(518) 897-1200

Expert rider Dave Moin negotiates a beaver dam along the Flume Fall Trail.

Lake Placid/Essex County Visitors Bureau
Olympic Center
Lake Placid, New York 12946
(800) 2PLACID

Notes on the trail: Route-finding is fairly straightforward. The trail network consists of 2 basic loops. Two hard-pack dirt roads lead from the parking area. The first loop, known as the Riverview Loop, is the beginner-level loop. The second, more advanced Race Loop follows the Riverside Loop.

The Riverview Loop should be ridden in a clockwise direction. Begin at the parking area and bear left (west) onto the leftmost hard-packed dirt road that parallels the river. You will soon pass a beaver pond on your right. The trail leads in a southwest direction. After about half a mile, turn right onto a single-track leading north. You will begin a .2-mile gradual ascent, passing over a few stream crossings, and then you'll connect with a wider, hard-packed woods road. To complete this 1.3-mile loop and return to the parking area, turn right (northeast) onto the smooth, needle-covered dirt road. Some trails lead to your left. Continue straight and descend to the parking area.

The second loop, known as the Race Loop, is mostly single-track and can be accessed by continuing straight on the first half-mile of the Riverside Loop. Go past 2 large boulders and climb gently in a westerly direction. Some sections may be rocky. You approach a small parking area. Turn right (north) onto a dirt road at the parking lot and go past the maintenance building. Climb steeply onto a single-track for about half a mile and connect to an upper trail. Turn right (east) and descend on a somewhat rocky trail, crossing several streams. You will join the Riverview Loop in approximately 1 mile.

RIDE 75 *THE BLOOMINGDALE BOG TRAIL*

This tour along an abandoned railroad bed is a great ride for novice mountain bikers and provides access into a remote, scenic wilderness. The 20-mile, out-and-back (ten miles one way) route is wide, flat, and smooth. The double-track trail passes over level, grassy sand flats and through an interesting bog and wetland environment. Two meandering brooks, the Twobridge and Negro, provide the open water areas filled with wildlife, trees, and plants in the relatively dry area. The straight route was used in 1887 by the Chateaugay Division of the Delaware and Hudson Railroad to connect Plattsburgh to Saranac Lake. The sandy flats and level terrain were ideal for a rail bed. The trail is straight. You can see where the path leads on the horizon, which gives you a feeling of space and distance. Contrary to many of the winding trail systems in the heavily wooded Adirondack forests, this trail has a slightly western flavor. The railroad grade makes an easy cruising bike path walk and introduces you to an

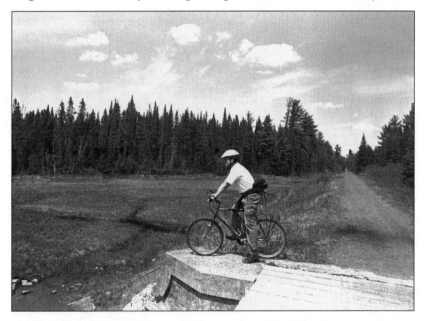

Wandering brooks meander through the evergreen-lined Bloomingdale Bog.

NY

To
Plattsburgh

Onchiota

30

Negro Brook

Oregon Plains Rd.

Vermontville

Blue
Hill

Merrill
Rd.

Bigelow
Rd.

To Paul
Smiths

Gabriels

Negro
Hill

192

86

Bloomingdale

Twobridge Brook

3

N

0   1   2

MILES

Saranac
Lake

3

86

To Lake
Placid
and 87

To Tupper
Lake

abundance of fauna and flora. I spotted otters and osprey along one section of the route. In winter, the route is an excellent ski trail. Several roads cross the railroad and provide more territory in this unusual corridor to explore.

As you pedal along the trail, look for the clumps and mounds rising out of the bogs; these are known as leatherleaf. Several other trees and plants distinctive to bogs can be seen along the way. Rhododendron, cranberries, black spruce, and tamarack grow in the wetter areas, whereas the pines and balsams grow on the dryer borders. Early settlers drained portions of these bogs to grow vegetables.

This tour is long, flat, and usually smooth. Riders of all levels will enjoy experiencing the solitude of the forests and fast-cruising double-track.

General location: North of the village of Saranac Lake, Franklin County, in the Adirondacks of northeastern New York.

Elevation change: The trail travels along an old, abandoned railroad bed and is relatively flat with little elevation gain.

Season: The route travels through wetlands and is best ridden during early summer after the black flies have found better things to do with themselves. You can ride well into the winter providing there is no snow on the ground.

Services: Most services can be found in the village of Saranac Lake, approximately 7 miles from the trailhead on NY 86.

Hazards: Bugs.

Rescue index: Several roads cross the route, and you are never more than 5 miles from one of these roads. Help is never too far away.

Land status: New York State Forest Preserve.

Maps: USGS, 7.5 minute series Saranac Lake quadrangle and St. Regis quadrangle provides good detail for these unimproved dirt roads. The Adirondack Canoe Map published by Plinth, Quoin & Cornice Associates provides excellent detail of the route and can be found at most outdoor-type stores in the Adirondacks for approximately $4.95.

Finding the trail: Take the New York State Thruway (Interstate 87) north to Exit 24 (Albany). Take I-87 north to Exit 30. Pick up NY 9 north and follow it for 2 miles to NY 73. Continue on NY 73 for 28 miles to the Lake Placid area. Pass through Lake Placid and continue on NY 86 toward Saranac Lake. Look for a dirt road 1.3 miles north of the hospital in Saranac Lake on NY 86. NY 86 makes a big bend to the west, and there is a dirt road heading north at the beginning of the bend. Turn right onto the dirt road, bear left, and park your vehicle at the gate.

Sources of additional information:

Saranac Lake Area Chamber of Commerce
30 Main Street
Saranac Lake, New York 12983
(800) 347-1992, (518) 891-1990

Placid Planet Bicycles
200 Saranac Avenue
Lake Placid, New York 12946
(518) 523-4128

Notes on the trail: In this easy ride on the level railroad bed, the bog and wet-lands are interesting to peruse. These wetlands arise from Twobridge and Negro brooks. At 3.7 miles you'll intersect with NY 192. There is a short stretch of exposed roots, but generally it's smooth riding. At 4.2 miles, inter-sect with the gravel Bigelow Road. After Bigelow Road you will see Negro Hill at 1,800' to the west. You will encounter some deep sandy spots north to Merrill Road. At 6.1 miles intersect Merrill Road (dirt). Looking west, notice Blue Hill at 2,300'. At 7.8 miles intersect Oregon Plains Road (paved). At 9.8 miles arrive at CR 30 (near Buck Pond State Campground).

Note: Several shorter loops are possible by parking at other access roads and returning on Oregon Plains Road.

RIDE 76 *THE DEER POND ODYSSEY*

An eight-mile loop through pristine wilderness leads the rider past three attrac-tive ponds. The first part of the loop is composed of an old semipaved road. The path changes into an up-and-down single-track as it passes Deer Pond and the little-frequented Mosquito Pond. You ascend a number of ridges on the way, but the overall relief change is minimal. An optional one-mile spur trail leads to Lead Pond. The riding is moderately challenging and not too techni-cal. The undulating terrain provides a pleasant roller-coaster ride for mountain bikers. The trails are well marked and Deer Pond makes an idyllic spot for a picnic. This tour comes highly recommended from the folks at Placid Planet Bicycles.

General location: Sixteen miles west of the village of Saranac Lake, in Franklin County in Adirondack Park, northeastern New York.
Elevation change: The trail skirts around 3 hills with elevations of 1,600', 1,700', and 1,800'. There is no climbing of these hills on this tour, and the rid-ing is moderately easy over undulating terrain.
Season: The black flies can be fierce in late spring. The trails are available from late spring, when they dry out, through September 14. Hunting season begins in mid-September, and although you may don an orange hunting vest, it is still risky to be moving through the forest at the speed of a young buck.
Services: The village of Saranac Lake is about 16 miles east of the trailhead on NY 3.

RIDE 76 *THE DEER POND ODYSSEY*

Hazards: Bugs can be fearsome foes in late spring as the area thaws and dries out. Bring plenty of bug repellent in May and June.

Rescue index: The tour is fairly close to well-traveled NY 3, and help is not far away.

Land status: The route follows roads and trails in the Saranac Lakes Wild Forest. The Wild Forest classification on this state public land of Adirondack Park is available for mountain biking. Mountain biking is presently prohibited in designated Wilderness areas of Adirondack Park and where signage is posted.

One of the 3,700 lakes and ponds found in the Adirondack Preserve.

Maps: USGS, 15 minute series Saint Regis quadrangle provides good detail for this route. The Adirondack Canoe Map published by Plinth, Quoin & Cornice Associates provides excellent topographical detail of the route and surrounding terrain and can be found at most outdoor-type stores in New York for approximately $4.95.

Finding the trail: Take the New York State Thruway (Interstate 87) north to Exit 24 (Albany). Take I-87 north to Exit 30. Pick up NY 9 north and follow it for 2 miles to NY 73. Continue on NY 73 for 28 miles to the Lake Placid area. Continue through Lake Placid west on NY 86. At Saranac Lake, take NY 3 west for about 16 miles. At .6 mile west of the junction of NY 3 and NY 30, turn right (north) onto Old Wawbeek Road. A New York State Department of Environmental Conservation trailhead sign marks the road entrance to the parking area.

Sources of additional information:

Saranac Lake Area Chamber of Commerce
30 Main Street
Saranac Lake, New York 12983
(800) 347-1992, (518) 891-1990

Placid Planet Bicycles
200 Saranac Avenue
Lake Placid, New York 12946
(518) 523-4128

Notes on the trail: Continue from the parking area west on Old Wawbeek Road for 2.3 miles, paralleling NY 30 for about 1 mile. The road is full of potholes, and sections are heaved up from freezing and thawing.

After 2.3 miles, turn right (north) onto a technical single-track. The trail passes through a thick plantation of European spruce, and you begin to descend to a small beaver pond. The vegetation around the beaver pond is in stark contrast to the barren understory of the heavily shaded conifer plantation. Traverse another ridge before the trail dips again to skirt the east shore of Mosquito Pond. Begin a small ascent out of Mosquito Pond to a ridge crowned with mature beech and sugar maples. The route then drops from this hill to the shores of Deer Pond. The trail leads you along the southern shore of Deer Pond and intersects with another trail at 4.4 miles. The trail to your left leads north and passes along the eastern shore of Deer Pond and some nice picnic spots. Continuing farther on this spur trail will lead you to the western shore of Lead Pond.

To continue on the loop, bear right at this intersection and head east. After about half a mile you must cross wetland. A stringer bridge several hundred feet long crosses the area and then connects to a truck trail. Turn right (south), following the truck trail for another 1.5 miles back to the trail head.

RIDE 77 *MOSS LAKE*

This moderate five-mile loop includes three miles of wide, flat, double-track trails and about two miles of challenging snowmobile trails. The area is popular among hikers and passes by two attractive ponds. The trail begins at the Moss Lake trailhead on Big Moose Road. A three-mile loop around the attractive lake with spurs down to the lake shore will warm you up, and then another out-and-back (one mile, one way) snowmobile trail leads to Bubb and Sis lakes.

Moss Lake was the site for the Moss Lake Camp for Girls between 1923 and 1972. Over 3,000 girls attended this tiny haven. In 1929, the 600-acre property consisted of three separate camps spread along the lake's northern and eastern shores. Each of these camps had its own sleeping bungalow, dining room and recreation hall, archery range, dance studio, and craftshop. Moss Lake provided a perfect waterfront for swimming, canoeing, and sailing. The property was sold to the Nature Conservancy in 1973. Later on that year, the tract was sold to New York and became a part of the Adirondack Park Forest Preserve. The buildings are long gone and the lake shore is now a public campground. The hard-packed surface of the three-mile trail around the lake, built in 1924, is the camp's former bridle path and makes an ideal track for beginning mountain bikers. The tour doesn't require any special

technical skills, allowing beginners an opportunity to get into some secluded woods and test their emerging skills without being too technically challenged. More experienced riders will appreciate the surrounding old-growth woodland, interesting spur trails, and lake scenery.

General location: Northeast of the village of Eagle Bay near Big Moose Lake, in Herkimer County in the west-central region of Adirondack Park, northeastern New York.

Elevation change: The loop around Moss Lake, elevation 1,758', traverses gently rolling terrain. The snowmobile trail climbs moderately to Bubb Lake, elevation 1,815', and Sis Lake, elevation 1,821'.

Season: You can ride after the wet season ends in April or May. It all depends on the amount of snow and rain in prior months. You can then ride until mid-September when hunting season commences. You may don an orange hunting vest, but it is still risky to move through the forest at the speed of a young buck. The fall is a beautiful time to ride through the mixed hardwood and conifer forests, though.

The black flies can be fierce in late spring and last until late June. Deerflies take over where the black flies leave off and can last into July. They look like miniature F-15 jets with their swept-back wings. Remember to bring bug repellent.

Services: Lodging, food, and other services can be found in nearby Eagle Bay or in Old Forge, approximately 5 miles west on NY 28.

Backcountry mountain bike tours are provided by Ted Christodaro from the bike store Pedals & Petals in Inlet. Daily and overnight tours are a great way to explore this abundant trail area. Ted is a good source for information on the condition of the trails. The shop provides repairs, supplies, and mountain bike sales. Call Pedals & Petals for any information on clinics, tours, festivals, and races. The Adirondacks have independent weather systems, and it's hard to determine the condition of trails from faraway cities. It's a good idea to telephone ahead before taking off on the trails.

Mountain bikes can be rented from the Mountainman Outdoor Supply Company on NY 28 in Inlet.

Just north of Eagle Bay, the Big Moose Inn along Big Moose Road is minutes from the trailhead and offers a hearty meal and lodging. The chef has been with the inn for 27 years and cooks a fine meal. The Bennet family welcomes mountain bikers and can offer some advice on current trail conditions.

Hazards: This trail is popular with hikers, and care should be taken when descending along sections of the route to keep control of your bike.

Rescue index: The trail's popularity among hikers and its proximity to the well-traveled Big Moose Road makes this tour close to civilization. Help is never far away.

Land status: Old Forge and the central region of Adirondack Park offer a variety of terrain with exceptional natural beauty. The route follows roads

My dog, Shogun, keeps pace on the snowy trails around Moss Lake.

and trails with the Wild Forests classification in Adirondack Park. They reside on state public land and are available for mountain biking. Mountain biking is presently prohibited in designated Wilderness areas of Adirondack Park and where signage is posted.

The town of Web has expanded the use of their well-maintained snow-mobile trails and opened the well-marked routes for mountain bikers. The potential use of the diverse Old Forge/Web trail system is limitless and is an exciting opportunity for mountain bikers to explore.

Maps: USGS, 7.5 minute series Eagle Bay quadrangle provides good detail for this route. The Adirondack West-Central Wilderness Area Map published by Plinth, Quoin & Cornice Associates provides excellent topographical detail of the route and surrounding terrain and can be found at most outdoor-type stores in New York for approximately $4.95. It is based on the USGS, 15 minute series, at a scale of 1:62,500 and a contour level of 20' where 1 inch = .98 mile.

Finding the trail: Take the New York State Thruway (Interstate 87) north to Exit 24 (Albany). Take I-87 north to Exit 25/Route 8, Chestertown and Hague. At the end of the exit ramp, turn left (west) onto NY 8 toward Loon Lake. After passing through Wevertown, turn right (west) at the stop sign onto NY 28. This scenic highway takes you through the towns of North Creek, Indian Lake, and Blue Mountain Lake. Whitewater rafting on the Hudson River is very popular, and there are many outdoor outfitters in the Indian Lake area. Continue on NY 28 west toward Inlet and Old Forge.

Northern access is from the west side of Big Moose Road, 2.2 miles north of Eagle Bay on the left. There is a New York State Department of Environmental Conservation sign and a large parking area.

Sources of additional information:

Pedals & Petals
Route 28, P.O. Box 390
Inlet, New York 13360
(315) 357-3281

Old Forge Tourist Information Center
P.O. Box 68
Old Forge, New York 13420
(315) 369-6983

New York State Department of Environmental Conservation (Region 6)
317 Washington Street
Watertown, New York 13601
(315) 785-2239

The Big Moose Inn
Big Moose Road
Eagle Bay, New York 13331
(315) 357-2042

Mountainman Outdoor Supply Company
Route 28, P.O. Box 659
Inlet, New York 13360
(315) 357-6672

Notes on the trail: From the parking area, continue straight to the loop and turn left onto it. You will pass through a hardwood forest that was logged years ago, resulting in the small trees you currently see. The trail is fairly level, and as you continue to circle around the lake the forest becomes more mature and richer with older deciduous trees and some conifer hemlocks. You soon encounter the intersection with the trail to Sis and Bubb lakes. They are approximately 1 mile away. Continue on this loop to complete it and then come back around and pedal the trail to Bubb Lake.

Continuing the loop, you will soon cross a bridge that spans the outlet in the southwest section of Moss Lake, about halfway around. This outlet eventually drains into the north branch of the Moose River. The stream leading away from Moss Lake is a typical Adirondack highcountry stream that winds its way through an extensive marsh area. Follow the clear, open trail as it curves around the pond. Just before reaching the parking area, notice the open area on the right. This is where the camp was located.

RIDE 78 *SAFFORD POND TRAIL*

The trip follows a snowmobile trail for a total distance of ten miles and puts you in contact with two beautiful, wild, and uninhabited ponds. Located in the Fulton Chain Wild Forest, the dense conifer trees make the primeval woods dark and mysterious. This out-and-back route is five miles in one direction and begins at the Safford Pond trailhead on Big Moose Road. The trail traverses fairly level terrain along a wide single-track. West Pond, a small pocket of fresh water with an attractive waterfall at the drainage point, is reached in just about one mile. Look for the old beaver dam and swamp. Safford Pond is a little farther along at four miles. The pond has a fine pebble beach and good swimming. The route ends at Lake Rondaxe five miles later.

General location: Northeast of the village of Eagle Bay near Big Moose Lake, in Herkimer County in the west-central region of Adirondack Park, northeastern New York.

Elevation change: The beginning of the trail climbs slightly to about 1,900'. After the spur trail to West Pond the trail descends moderately to 1,800' for about 2.5 miles until you reach Safford Pond. It is all level riding after Safford Pond to the trail's end at Lake Rondaxe.

Season: This is a low drainage area and an inviting home for insects. Black flies thrive under these conditions, and their season to swarm is usually in late spring (May). Try to avoid them if possible. The little buggers can be a fierce foe to fight in the woods. The trails are available from late spring, when they dry out, through September 14. Hunting season begins in mid-September, and although you may don an orange hunting vest, it is still risky to be moving through the forest at the speed of a young buck.

Services: Lodging, food, and other services can be found in nearby Eagle Bay and Old Forge, approximately 5 miles west on NY 28.

Backcountry mountain bike tours are provided by Ted Christodaro from the bike store Pedals & Petals in Inlet. Daily and overnight tours are a great way to explore this abundant trail area. Ted is a good source for information on the condition of the trails. The shop provides repairs, supplies, and mountain bike sales. Call Pedals & Petals for information on clinics, tours, festivals, and races. The Adirondacks have independent weather systems, and it's hard to determine the condition of trails from faraway cities. It's a good idea to telephone ahead before taking off on the trails.

Mountain bikes can be rented from the Mountainman Outdoor Supply Company on NY 28 in Inlet.

Just north of Eagle Bay, the Big Moose Inn along Big Moose Road is minutes from the trailhead and offers a hearty meal and lodging. The chef has

been with the inn for 27 years and cooks a fine meal. The Bennet family welcomes mountain bikers and can offer some advice on current trail conditions.
Hazards: In July 1995 a severe storm swept through this terrain and caused many large, old-growth trees to blow down. Many huge trees lie across the trail, making passage difficult. The trail is slowly being cleared of these trees at the time of this writing. It is a good idea to check with the New York State Department of Environmental Conservation on the condition of this trail before you attempt to ride it.

Before the storm, Safford Pond Trail was popular with hikers and snowmobile enthusiasts. Care should be taken when descending along sections of the route to keep control of your bike. The snowmobile trails are maintained on a regular basis, but the heavy forest can set down new wooden obstacles at any time.

Rescue index: The trail is close to the well-traveled Big Moose Road, and help can be found in Eagle Bay.

Land status: Old Forge and the central region of Adirondack Park offer a variety of terrain with exceptional natural beauty. The route follows roads and trails in the Wild Forests classification of Adirondack Park. They reside on state public land and are available for mountain biking. Mountain biking is presently prohibited in designated Wilderness areas of Adirondack Park and where signage is posted.

The town of Web has expanded the use of their well-maintained snowmobile trails and opened the well-marked routes for mountain bikers. The potential use of the diverse Old Forge/Web trail system is limitless and is an exciting opportunity for mountain bikers to explore.

Maps: USGS, 7.5 minute series Eagle Bay quadrangle provides good detail for this route. The Adirondack West-Central Wilderness Area Map published by Plinth, Quoin & Cornice Associates provides excellent topographical detail of the route and surrounding terrain and can be found at most outdoor-type stores in New York for approximately $4.95. It is based on the USGS, 15 minute series, at a scale of 1:62,500 and a contour level of 20' where 1 inch = .98 mile.

Finding the trail: Take the New York State Thruway (Interstate 87) north to Exit 24 (Albany). Take I-87 north to Exit 25/Route 8, Chestertown and Hague. At the end of the exit ramp, turn left (west) onto NY 8 toward Loon Lake. After passing through Wevertown, turn right (west) at the stop sign onto NY 28. This scenic highway takes you through the towns of North Creek, Indian Lake, and Blue Mountain Lake. Whitewater rafting on the Hudson River is very popular, and there are many outdoor outfitters in the Indian Lake area. Continue on NY 28 west toward Inlet and Old Forge.

In the town of Eagle Bay, turn right (north) onto Big Moose Road. Proceed about 5 miles. Access is from the Safford Pond trailhead at the Orvis parking area on Big Moose Road.

Sources of additional information:

Pedals & Petals
Route 28, P.O. Box 390
Inlet, New York 13360
(315) 357-3281

Old Forge Tourist Information Center
P.O. Box 68
Old Forge, New York 13420
(315) 369-6983

New York State Department of Environmental Conservation (Region 6)
317 Washington Street
Watertown, New York 13601
(315) 785-2239

The Big Moose Inn
Big Moose Road
Eagle Bay, New York 13331
(315) 357-2042

Mountainman Outdoor Supply Company
Route 28, P.O. Box 659
Inlet, New York 13360
(315) 357-6672

Notes on the trail: From the parking area, follow the blue-marked, wide, single-track south through a dark, mature conifer forest. Several small streams crisscross the trail but are easily forged. Safford Pond is approximately 3 miles from the trailhead and is the next pond you will encounter. A spur trail leads west to the pond. The main trail skirts the eastern edge of the wetland that lies east of Safford Pond. Another spur trail leads east to Goose Pond. The trail crosses a wide, wet area and then skirts the base of a hill. The trail is flat and continues to Lake Rondaxe. After reaching Lake Rondaxe (approximately 5 miles), you must return to the trailhead along the same route.

RIDE 79 *THE UNCAS TOUR*

This ride means many things to many people. The 18-mile loop can be ridden in total or broken up into segments you may wish to ride at different times. Along the way, you will be challenged by moderate, hilly terrain but charmed by the lake, pond, and river scenery you pass. The combination of

double- and single-track winds through dark, primeval forests. The tour is invigorating and provides a riding experience for just about every level of biker.

Uncas Road is an easy nine-mile, cruising, scenic dirt road and is perfect for family fun and novice mountain bike riders. A four-mile single-track winds through a majestic forest, past ponds and brooks. The remaining mileage traverses hard-packed dirt roads that were built sometime in the nineteenth century. They were the old roadways that connected the great camps and summer homes of J. P. Morgan and Alfred G. Vanderbilt.

A popular single-track leading from Eighth Lake Public Campground traverses hilly terrain for almost four miles, connecting scenic Eagle's Nest Lake and Bug Lake, and terminates at Uncas Road. From the village of Eagle Bay, Uncas Road parallels Eagle Creek, passing by the small Upper Pond and terminating at Raquette Lake. The wide, nine-mile, hard-packed dirt ride provides for some easy cruising, and its smoothness, good condition, and relatively flat grade gives you the freedom to enjoy nature's canvas, which surrounds you all the way. It was constructed during the late nineteenth century and provided passage for Adirondack camp owners and their guests, who were traveling between Eagle Bay on Fourth Lake and Raquette Lake.

Once at Raquette Lake, you have the option of taking it easy for the rest of the afternoon, going on a luncheon cruise on the WW *Durant,* and touring the lake shores. If you want to continue on the circuit and finish the loop, pedal from Raquette Lake to NY 28 and then take the hard-packed, fast-cruising Sagamore Road to Sagamore Lake. Tours at the historic Sagamore Lodge are available. From the Sagamore Lodge, ride five more miles on another part of Uncas Road back to NY 28. Pedal across NY 28 into the Eighth Lake Public Campground where you began your loop. The campground is an excellent spot to establish your base camp, so bring a tent and some sleeping bags and immerse yourself in these pristine woodlands.

General location: Near the town of Inlet, in Herkimer County, in the west-central region of Adirondack Park in northeastern New York.

Elevation change: The Uncas Road section is mostly level. Sagamore Road to the Sagamore Lodge traverses gently rolling terrain with no major climbs. The ride from the Sagamore area back to NY 28 on the "other" Uncas Road is more demanding, with elevation changes between 1,900' and 2,200', and might take your breath away, but it's just for 5 miles. A 3-mile single-track from the Eighth Lake Public Campground is a little more demanding but extremely exciting as it ascends from 1,800' to 2,200' and then descends back down to the first Uncas Road.

Season: You can ride after the wet season ends in April or May. It all depends on the amount of snow and rain from prior months. You can then ride until mid-September, which is when hunting season commences. You may don an orange hunting vest, but it is still risky to be moving through the forest at the speed of a young buck. Autumn is a beautiful time to ride through the mixed hardwood and conifer forests.

The black flies can be fierce from late spring until late June. Deerflies take over where the black flies leave off and can last into July. They look like minia-ture F-15 jets with their swept-back wings. Remember to bring bug repellent.

Services: Lodging, food, and other services can be found in Inlet, approxi-mately 6 miles west on NY 28.

Ted Christodaro from the bike store Pedals & Petals in Inlet provides daily and overnight backcountry mountain bike tours throughout this area and is a good source for information on the condition of the trails. The shop provides repairs, supplies, and mountain bike sales. Call Pedals & Petals for any infor-mation on clinics, tours, festivals, and races. The Adirondacks have indepen-dent weather systems, and it's hard to determine the condition of trails from faraway cities. It's a good idea to telephone ahead before taking off on the trails.

Mountain bikes can be rented from the Mountainman Outdoor Supply Company on NY 28 in Inlet. There is a state campground at Limekiln Lake if you are interested in camping out and sampling the Limekiln Trail and Moose River Plains Trails.

Hazards: The loop is long, and you must be in reasonable shape to attempt it. Of course, you can ride this tour in sections and thereby enjoy it at a differ-ent pace. Care should be taken when crossing the sometimes busy NY 28, and you should pay attention to the occasional vehicle that might be driving by on Uncas or Sagamore roads.

Rescue index: There are several bailouts and you are never actually commit-ted to the ride as in some other tours in this book. Help can be found by driv-ing back to well-traveled NY 28. Help can also be found in Raquette Lake and Inlet.

Land status: Old Forge and the central region of Adirondack Park offer a variety of terrain with exceptional natural beauty. The route follows roads and trails in the Wild Forests classification of Adirondack Park. They reside on state public land and are available for mountain biking. Mountain biking is presently prohibited in designated Wilderness areas of Adirondack Park and where signage is posted. This tour follows public roads, and the single-track passes through state land.

Maps: The Adirondack West-Central Wilderness Area Map published by Plinth, Quoin & Cornice Associates provides excellent topographical detail of the route and surrounding terrain and can be found at most outdoor-type stores in New York for approximately $4.95. It is based on the USGS, 15 minute series, at a scale of 1:62,500 and a contour level of 20' where 1 inch = .98 mile.

Finding the trail: Take the New York State Thruway (Interstate 87) north to Exit 24 (Albany). Take I-87 north to Exit 25/Route 8, Chestertown and

Taking a break at Bug Lake.

Hague. At the end of the exit ramp, turn left (west) onto NY 8 toward Loon Lake. After passing through Wevertown, turn right (west) at the stop sign onto NY 28. This scenic highway takes you through the towns of North Creek, Indian Lake, and Blue Mountain Lake. Whitewater rafting on the Hudson River is very popular, and there are many outdoor outfitters in the Indian Lake area. Continue on NY 28 west toward Inlet and Old Forge.

Approximately 6 miles east of Inlet on NY 28 is the entrance to the Eighth Lake Public Campground. Turn into the campground past the registration booth and park. Pedal straight ahead (west) in the campground on the paved road. The road turns into a double-track through a conifer forest. Follow the yellow DEC markers.

Sources of additional information:

Pedals & Petals
Route 28, P.O. Box 390
Inlet, New York 13360
(315) 357-3281

Old Forge Tourist Information Center
P.O. Box 68
Old Forge, New York 13420
(315) 369-6983

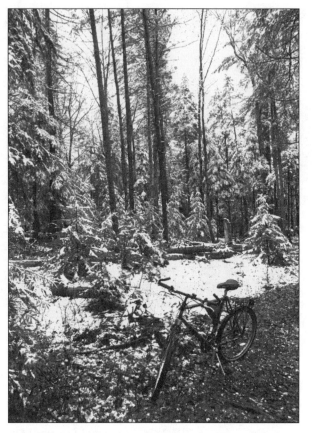

Snowfall adorns a grove of evergreens along the Uncas River.

New York State Department of Environmental Conservation (Region 6)
317 Washington Street
Watertown, New York 13601
(315) 785-2239

Mountainman Outdoor Supply Company
Route 28, P.O. Box 659
Inlet, New York 13360
(315) 357-6672

Notes on the trail: After leaving the campground, proceed on the double-track. It soon crosses a small bridge spanning the inlet of Seventh Lake and begins a small climb for .6 mile. Bear left at a fork in the trail. The right fork is the spur trail to Eagle's Nest Lake. Continue riding and cross the outlet stream of Bug and Eagle's Nest lakes. The trail continues along the west side of Bug Lake as a steady climb. Continue straight past a snowmobile trail that leads to the left in a southwest direction at 2.3 miles. You soon cross a long bridge over the inlet to the Brown's Tract Ponds, and at 2.7 miles you pass the Black Bear Mountain yellow-marked hiking trail. Continue straight in a northwest direction to reach the dirt Uncas Road at 3.5 miles.

Turn right onto the wide, flat Uncas Road and pedal for about 3 miles to approach Upper Pond. Soon after this body of water, bear right at a fork and proceed on the dirt road. This is an easier route to Raquette Lake. The left fork leads you to a steep climb around Fox Mountain. Raquette Lake is reached in 2.5 miles.

Once in Raquette Lake, turn right (south) to NY 28. Cross NY 28 and begin riding on Sagamore Road, which is directly across the road. Sagamore Road is a wide, hard-packed road used by vehicles heading to Sagamore Camp. Sagamore Lodge is reached in just over 3 miles. If you have time, check out the tours of this great Adirondack camp.

From the Sagamore, pedal past the parking area, bearing right to a junction in .2 mile. Two barricades block 2 routes. Proceed past the barricade to the right. Don't worry, it is state land; the road is just off-limits to vehicles. The left route proceeds into private land.

The road continues southwest, climbs one hill and then the contours of another, and reaches a fork in 1.6 miles from the Sagamore. Bear right. The left route leads to private land and Moheggan Lake, the site of nineteenth-century Camp Uncas. Camp Uncas was the summer homes of J. P. Morgan and Alfred G. Vanderbilt. The road you just traveled was built to connect Sagamore and Uncas Camps. Continue on the main dirt road for about 2 miles out of Sagamore and encounter a pile of bulldozed debris. Continue straight ahead. The route to your left leads down to the southern shore of Moheggan Lake.

Continue past the debris onto old, abandoned Uncas Road. The road leads gently downhill for over 2.5 miles to NY 28. At NY 28, make a right and a quick left and you have returned to the Eighth Lake Public Campground. An exciting circuit has been completed!

RIDE 80 *THE LIMEKILN LOOP*

Despite all the sleek frames, scientifically designed suspension systems, and technically enriched accessories (gadgetry), mountain biking is still a low-technology, low-impact, and take-your-time sport. Each push of the pedals expands our universe because we take the time to examine the world through which we pass. In doing so, rediscover just how much fun it is to explore the wilderness and embrace its environment. The Limekiln Loop tour is one such ride you shouldn't be in a hurry to complete. This 13-mile loop combines

RIDE 80 *THE LIMEKILN LOOP*

wide, grassy, compact snowmobile, hiking, and old woods road trails. The riding is moderately challenging and suitable for intermediate beginners to advanced riders.

The tour begins at Limekiln Lake, passing through the woodlands surrounding Limekiln Swamp and Third Lake. Loggers used the terrain around the swamp to stockpile logs. The logs were then tossed into the stream that carried them into the Moose River. The last six miles of the loop travels along the hard-packed, dirt, South Shore Road that skirts the shores of the Fulton Chain Lakes system's Fourth Lake. The trails pass through an area of attractive deciduous and conifer forests, lakes, and streams. Limekiln Lake is a great spot to observe wildlife or stop and have a picnic. I spotted several loons paddling in the lake during one ride. Nearby Limekiln State Campground, located on the shores of this scenic lake, is a good place to set up a base and camp out. Build a campfire, eat under the stars, and watch the moon rise. Wake up early and ride, come back for breakfast, and have coffee by the lake. It's your own piece of paradise.

Thanks to a large federal grant in the 1970s, the town of Inlet constructed and improved a cross-country ski trail system near Limekiln Lake. Currently the cross-country ski trails are off-limits to mountain biking. According to the local word, there is a lobbying effort underway to make these wonderful trails open to mountain biking, and this would expand the Limekiln Loop immensely. Let's keep our fingers crossed.

General location: Near the town of Inlet, in Herkimer County, in the west-central region of Adirondack Park in northeastern New York.

Elevation change: Most of the elevation fluctuations occur at the beginning of the loop. Elevations vary between 1,800' and 2,000'. At 3.5 miles the riding levels out after you come out of the hills. From that point on, the riding follows the level of the land.

Season: You can ride after the wet season ends in April or May. It all depends on the amount of snow and rain from prior months. You can then ride until mid-September, which is when hunting season commences. You may don an orange hunting vest, but it is still risky to be moving through the forest at the speed of a young buck. The fall is a beautiful time to ride through the mixed hardwood and conifer forests.

The black flies can be fierce in late spring and last until late June. Deerflies take over where the black flies leave off and can last into July. They look like miniature F-15 jets with their swept-back wings. Remember to bring bug repellent.

Services: Lodging, food, and other services can be found in Inlet, approximately 1 mile north on NY 28.

Ted Christodaro from the bike store Pedals & Petals in Inlet provides daily and overnight backcountry mountain bike tours throughout this area and is a good source for information on the condition of the trails. The shop provides

Winter beckons the adventurous rider to discover its silent beauty.

repairs, supplies, and mountain bike sales. Call Pedals & Petals for any information on clinics, tours, festivals, and races. The Adirondacks have independent weather systems, and it's hard to determine the condition of trails from faraway cities. It's a good idea to telephone ahead before taking off on the trails.

Mountain bikes can be rented from the Mountainman Outdoor Supply Company on NY 28 in Inlet. There is a state campground at Limekiln Lake if you are interested in camping out and sampling the Limekiln Trail and Moose River Plains Trails.

Hazards: This trail is close to the town of Inlet and is popular with hikers and other mountain bikers. Care should be taken on any blind curves and bends. The section of the route known as the Third Lake Creek Trail passes through wet, swampy areas and can be laden with mosquitoes until the end of June. Bring bug repellent.

Rescue index: The route is only 1 mile from the town of Inlet where help can be found. The well-marked and excellently maintained snowmobile trails are marked with orange circular discs and are easy to follow.

Land status: Old Forge and the central region of Adirondack Park offer a variety of terrain with exceptional natural beauty. The route follows roads and trails in the Wild Forests classification of Adirondack Park. They reside on state public land and are available for mountain biking. Mountain biking is presently prohibited in designated Wilderness areas of Adirondack Park and where signage is posted.

The town of Web has expanded the use of their well-maintained snow-mobile trails and opened the well-marked routes for mountain bikers. The potential use of the diverse Old Forge/Web trail system is limitless and an exciting opportunity for mountain bikers to explore.

Maps: USGS, 7.5 minute series Eagle Bay and Big Moose quadrangles, and USGS, 15 minute series Old Forge quadrangles, provide good detail for this route. The Adirondack West-Central Wilderness Area Map published by Plinth, Quoin & Cornice Associates provides excellent topographical detail of the route and surrounding terrain and can be found at most outdoor-type stores in New York State for approximately $4.95. It is based on the USGS, 15 minute series, at a scale of 1:62,500 and a contour level of 20' where 1 inch = .98 mile.

Finding the trail: Take the New York State Thruway (Interstate 87) north to Exit 24 (Albany). Take I-87 north to Exit 25/Route 8, Chestertown and Hague. At the end of the exit ramp, turn left (west) onto NY 8 toward Loon Lake. After passing through Wevertown, turn right (west) at the stop sign onto NY 28. This scenic highway takes you through the towns of North Creek, Indian Lake, and Blue Mountain Lake. Whitewater rafting on the Hudson River is very popular, and there are many outdoor outfitters in the Indian Lake area. Continue on NY 28 west toward Inlet and Old Forge.

Just before you get to the town of Inlet, you will find signs for Limekiln Road and Moose River Recreation Area. Turn left (south) onto Limekiln Road. Proceed for about 1 mile. Look for the trailhead on the right side of the road. This is the Limekiln Swamp trailhead. There is limited parking along the road near the trailhead.

Sources of additional information:

Pedals & Petals
Route 28, P.O. Box 390
Inlet, New York 13360
(315) 357-3281

Forest Ranger
Limekiln Lake
Inlet, New York 13360
(315) 357-4403

Old Forge Tourist Information Center
P.O. Box 68
Old Forge, New York 13420
(315) 369-6983

New York State Department of Environmental Conservation (Region 6)
317 Washington Street
Watertown, New York 13601
(315) 785-2239

Mountainman Outdoor Supply Company
Route 28, P.O. Box 659
Inlet, New York 13360
(315) 357-6672

Notes on the trail: Pedal along a wide, hard-packed, grassy road and follow the New York State Department of Environmental Conservation's yellow cross-country ski markers. You will pass some trails that lead to your right (north). These connect with the town of Inlet's network of cross-country ski trails. At this writing, these trails were closed to mountain biking. A little farther on you will pass an intersecting snowmobile trail. At 1.5 miles another yellow-marked trail leads left (south) to the Limekiln Lake Public Campground. Continue straight, following the route as it traverses mostly southwest. Pass through some tall conifers and parallel Limekiln Creek and its wetland. The route terminates after 3 miles of riding at the intersection with a trail known as the Limekiln Creek–Third Lake Trail. Turn right (north) and follow this generally level trail along Third Lake Creek almost 3 miles to South Shore Road. The route passes by several beaver meadows and small waterfalls as it follows above the Third Lake Creek. After about 1 mile on this trail, you cross a small bridge that spans the creek. The route traverses some majestic hardwoods and fields of ferns. After another half mile the trail travels over a grassy snowmobile trail. Follow it for about 100' and then turn left. You enter a dark, coniferous forest after another .3 mile, and the trail crosses a bridge that spans the outlet of Limekiln Swamp. After reentering the woods, you pass a ski trail on your right. Continue in a north-westerly direction through a mixed hardwood and coniferous woodland over mostly flat, semiswampy terrain. The route follows a vehicle track on and off through dense conifers. Bear right onto a jeep road past a chain barrier; pedal through a hardwood forest to the end of the trail at South Shore Road. Turn right (east) onto the road. Follow South Shore Road almost 6 miles to its end at NY 28. Turn right on NY 28 and then right again on Limekiln Road. Follow Limekiln Road 1 mile to your parking area.

RIDE 81 *MOOSE RIVER MEDLEY*

In 1963, New York purchased a 50,000-acre tract of remote land from the Gould Paper Company. At the heart of this acreage is the flat floodplain of the South Branch of the Moose River, known as the Moose River Plains. The plains are flat and mostly open, with grass, bushes, and expanses of wetland. They are surrounded by mixed hardwood and pine forests interspersed with many lakes and ponds. Moose River Plains is the largest natural open space in the Adirondack Forest Preserve and has a wide-open look with low hills discernible in the distance. The area was extensively logged before the state purchased it, but you can still find plantations of virgin white pine and balsam fir in areas the state purchased before the logging. The majority of the forest consists of second- and third-growth woodland.

A myriad of well-graded and well-maintained, abandoned logging roads form a maze throughout the plains, leading to ponds and lakes. The routes are not technically demanding, but some endurance is required to cover the vast mileage of the rolling terrain of the Moose River Plains. Over 27 miles of mountain bike trails abound, and in winter the place is a snowmobiler's heaven. An exciting day awaits the energetic rider.

A great way to explore the plains is by establishing a base camp and spending the night, camping at one of the lakes. There are many campsites (all primitive) throughout the area, situated in scenic spots near ponds and lakes. A variety of out-and-back trails can be configured to fill several days of exploration.

General location: Near the town of Inlet in Herkimer County, in the west-central region of Adirondack Park in northeastern New York.

Elevation change: The Moose River Plains Recreation Area has some sizable hills and even a mountain range. Little Moose Mountain tops out at 3,620', and many of the ponds and lakes are at unusually high elevations and claim to be the highest bodies of water in the Adirondacks. Most of the riding is along gently rolling terrain, where the maximum elevation gain or loss is only a few hundred feet.

Season: You can ride after the wet season ends in April or May. It all depends on the amount of snow and rain from prior months. The plains officially open on Memorial Day, and you can then ride until mid-September, when hunting season commences. You may don an orange hunting vest, but it is still risky to be moving through the forest at the speed of a young buck. The fall is a beautiful time to ride through the mixed hardwood and conifer forests.

The black flies can be fierce from late spring until late June or early July. Deerflies take over where the black flies leave off and can last into July. They look like miniature F-15 jets with their swept-back wings. Remember to bring bug repellent.

Services: Lodging, food, and other services can be found in Inlet, approximately 1 mile north on NY 28.

Ted Christodaro from the bike store Pedals & Petals in Inlet provides daily and overnight backcountry mountain bike tours throughout this area and is a good source for information on the condition of the trails. The shop provides repairs, supplies, and mountain bike sales. Call Pedals & Petals for any information on clinics, tours, festivals, and races. The Adirondacks have independent weather systems, and it's hard to determine the condition of trails from faraway cities. It's a good idea to telephone ahead before taking off on the trails.

RIDE 81 *MOOSE RIVER MEDLEY*

To Inlet, 14, and 28

Ranger Headquarters

Limekiln Lake

Moose River Rd.

Mt. Tom 2474

Rock Dam Rd.

4WD

Mitchell Ponds

Ice House Pond

Private

Moose River

Beaver Lake

Squaw Lake

Muskrat

Private

Note: *All snowmobile trails are double-track.*

NY

To Cedar
River Flow

Moose River Rd.

Lost
Ponds

MOOSE RIVER
RECREATION AREA

Helldiver
Pond

Moose River

Otter Brook Rd.

To Little
Moose Lake

N

0   1/2   1

MILES

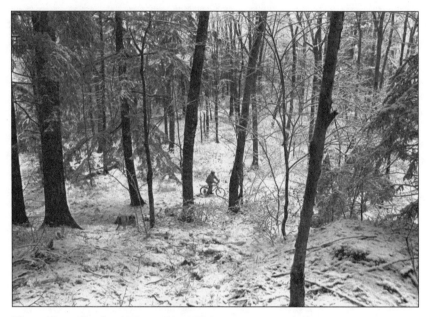

The snowy solitude of Moose River Plains.

Mountain bikes can be rented from the Mountainman Outdoor Supply Company on NY 28 in Inlet. There is a state campground at Limekiln Lake if you are interested in camping out and sampling the Limekiln Trail and Moose River Plains Trails.

Hazards: Be aware of the hunting seasons that begin in mid-September. Call the forest ranger at Limekiln Lake for any further information on hunting season and trail conditions.

Rescue index: The Limekiln forest ranger is on duty usually after Memorial Day weekend. The well-defined roads are excellently maintained, straightforward, and easy to follow, minimizing the chances of getting lost over such a long distance. The route is only 2 miles from the town of Inlet where help can be found. The well-marked and excellently maintained snowmobile trails are marked with orange circular discs and are very easy to follow.

Land status: The trail resides on state public land and is available for mountain biking. Mountain biking is presently prohibited in designated Wilderness areas of Adirondack Park and where signage is posted.

Maps: The Adirondack West-Central Wilderness Area Map published by Plinth, Quoin & Cornice Associates provides excellent topographical detail of the route and surrounding terrain and can be found at most outdoor-type stores in New York for approximately $4.95. It is based on the USGS, 15 minute series, at a scale of 1:62,500 and a contour level of 20' where 1 inch = .98 mile.

Finding the trail: Take the New York State Thruway (Interstate 87) north to Exit 24 (Albany). Take I-87 north to Exit 25/Route 8, Chestertown and Hague. At the end of the exit ramp, turn left (west) onto NY 8 toward Loon Lake. After passing through Wevertown, turn right (west) at the stop sign onto NY 28. This scenic highway takes you through the towns of North Creek, Indian Lake, and Blue Mountain Lake. Whitewater rafting on the Hudson River is very popular, and there are many outdoor outfitters in the Indian Lake area. Continue on NY 28 west toward Inlet and Old Forge.

Just before you get to the town of Inlet, you will see signs for Limekiln Road and Moose River Recreation Area. Turn left (south) onto Limekiln Road. Drive about 3 miles to the recreation area's entrance. The ranger station is at the entrance. You may park here or drive in 10 miles. The trail description here is based on driving in the 10 miles and parking. The plains can also be reached from the east at Cedar River Flow along Cedar River Road, which intersects NY 28/30 near Indian Lake and before Blue Mountain Lake. Follow the town road until its end at Wakely Dam. You must register at either gate.

Sources of additional information:

> Forest Ranger
> Limekiln Lake
> Inlet, New York 13360
> (315) 357-4403

> Pedals & Petals
> Route 28, P.O. Box 390
> Inlet, New York 13360
> (315) 357-3281

> Old Forge Tourist Information Center
> P.O. Box 68
> Old Forge, New York 13420
> (315) 369-6983

> New York State Department of Environmental Conservation (Region 6)
> 317 Washington Street
> Watertown, New York 13601
> (315) 785-2239

> Mountainman Outdoor Supply Company
> Route 28, P.O. Box 659
> Inlet, New York 13360
> (315) 357-6672

Notes on the trail: Drive in about 10 miles until you reach a fork in the main dirt road. Park your car at the intersection of Moose River Road (which you have arrived on from the west gate near Limekiln Lake) and Otter Brook Road. Out-and-back trails lead to Mitchell Ponds, Helldiver Pond, Squaw Lake, and Beaver Lake. If you are camping, an attractive spot to set up camp is along the shores of Mitchell Ponds.

The following ponds and lakes can be accessed from this base point. All these routes are out-and-back, requiring you to return the same way you went in.

Mitchell Ponds: Pedal back (north) on Moose River Road for .3 mile and turn left (west) onto an old double-track road. The trail is unmarked for most of the way, but don't worry; it is very easy to follow. The final approach to the ponds is marked with NYSDEC yellow markers. The trail skirts a rushing stream and comes into a junction in an open, grassy area at about 2 miles. Bear left (west) from the junction and follow the northern contour of Mitchell Pond. The trail terminates at 2.8 miles at the pond's outlet stream.

Helldiver Pond: Head east on Moose River Road for .8 mile and turn right (south) onto a small dirt road. Bear right through an open woodland that soon turns into a dark forest. The pond is reached in .2 mile. It's a short trip, but the woods are exciting to ride through.

Beaver Lake Trail: Pedal south on Otter Brook Road for 1.2 miles. Turn right (west) onto a small dirt road that lies immediately past a small bridge spanning the South Branch of the Moose River. An estate was built down this road in 1904, but all the buildings are long gone. Proceed through a majestic forest of large white pines. These large species of pine were a common sight before logging started in the nineteenth century. Now the state's constitution protects the forest on state land.

After 2 miles and past the pines, you approach a clearing and the site of an old sawmill. Turn down a short road that descends to the shore of the lake. This scenic lake is another great spot to set up a campsite. If you do camp by the lake, stay far enough away from the shore to prevent pollution of the lake's waters. Old camping rule!

Squaw Lake: Pedal south on Otter Brook Road for 1.3 miles and fork right onto Indian River Road just after crossing Otter Brook. Proceed along Indian River Road for 4.9 miles past some small ponds and spur trails. Go past the barrier at the end of the road and head in for another 4.9 miles, whereupon you reach the eastern shore of Squaw Lake.

RIDE 82 *JOURNEY TO STILLWATER RESERVOIR*

The 24-mile, out-and-back (12 miles one-way), gravel Big Moose Road extends from the village of Big Moose to the Stillwater Reservoir. This tour is composed of a wide, hard-pack dirt road with some roller-coaster hills and

Stillwater Reservoir

Beaver River

Optional trailhead accessible by boat only

NY

Big Moose Rd.

Big Moose

To Eagle Bay

Snowmobile Tr.

N

0   1/2   1

MILES

provides fast, easy, nontechnical riding. The Big Moose Road provides a good surface for someone new to off-road riding, allowing beginners to get used to the feel of the bike. More experienced riders should enjoy the fast-paced, cruising track and diverse scenery. The route leaves Big Moose and cuts through the Independence River Wild Forest. It traverses moderately rolling terrain, through forests of conifers and hardwoods, and past spruce-balsam fir swamplands, terminating at the western shore of the Stillwater Reservoir. The reservoir has over 117 miles of shoreline and is a camper's delight. The Stillwater Hotel, which is basically the sole establishment at the reservoir, provides accommodations and a hearty menu. Stay overnight, rent a canoe and cruise the miles of shoreline, and then pedal back.

Two miles to the east of Big Moose, on Big Moose Road, lies Big Moose Lake. The lake was the setting for *An American Tragedy,* Theodore Dreiser's 1924 book about a young man's desire for riches. Big Moose Lake's notoriety was also expanded when Chester Gillette presumably killed his pregnant sweetheart, Grace Bond, in order to marry the boss's daughter. The infamous crime was researched and written about by Craig Brandon in his book, *Murder in the Adirondacks.* Although the names of those involved were changed, the murder has become part of American folklore.

This is a great ride to start in the morning so you can arrive in Stillwater by lunch. The hamlet of Stillwater, population 25, offers boat and canoe rentals. Grab some grub at the Stillwater Hotel and take a boat ride on the Norridgewock Ferry after lunch. The boat tours through the Stillwater Reservoir, passing many of the tiny islands dotting the waters. You can take your bikes on board and disembark at the village of Beaver River. Take a quick jaunt on a six-mile, level gravel road from Beaver River. The riding is easy and the lake scenery is exhilarating. Another option is to pedal and paddle. Pedal to Stillwater, leave your bike at the hotel, and rent a canoe at one of the 46 primitive campsites that dot the reservoir's shoreline.

General location: About 8 miles north of the village of Eagle Bay and near the town of Inlet in Herkimer County, in the west-central region of Adirondack Park in northeastern New York.

Elevation change: Big Moose Road is mostly level and courses through the landscape at an elevation of about 1,600'.

Season: These roads can be ridden throughout the year except after heavy snows. Of course, there are no boat cruises along Stillwater Reservoir in the winter, but Big Moose Road can be fun to ride on with compact snow and bike tire chains. Fall is the prime season to explore Big Moose Road.

Services: Most services can be found in Eagle Bay and Inlet on NY 28, located about 5 miles from the trailhead in Big Moose.

Backcountry mountain bike tours are provided by Ted Christodaro from the bike store Pedals & Petals in Inlet. Daily and overnight tours are a great

The remote Stillwater Reservoir.

way to explore this abundant trail area. Ted is a good source for information on the condition of the trails. The shop provides repairs, supplies, and mountain bike sales. Call Pedals & Petals for any information on clinics, tours, festivals, and races. The Adirondacks have independent weather systems, so it's hard to determine the condition of trails from faraway cities. It's a good idea to telephone ahead before taking off on the trails.

Mountain bikes can be rented from the Mountainman Outdoor Supply Company on NY 28 in Inlet.

The Stillwater Hotel offers seasonal accommodations for the snowmobiler, hunter, fisherman, mountain biker, hiker, and canoeist. The hotel is located along the tranquil shores of the Stillwater Reservoir and provides a cozy atmosphere, a hearty menu, and comfortable lodging. Marian and Joe Romano own this secluded Adirondack lodge and welcome mountain bikers.

Hazards: The ride is strenuous only due to the distance of the route. You should be in reasonable shape to attempt it. Big Moose Road is open to motor vehicles, so watch for them.

Rescue index: Help can be flagged down by passing vehicles or can be found in Stillwater and Eagle Bay.

Land status: Public roads.

Maps: The Adirondack West-Central Wilderness Area Map published by Plinth, Quoin & Cornice Associates provides excellent topographical detail of the route and surrounding terrain and can be found at most outdoor-type stores in New York for approximately $4.95. It is based on the USGS, 15 minute series, at a scale of 1:62,500 and a contour level of 20' where 1 inch = .98 mile.

Finding the trail: Take the New York State Thruway (Interstate 87) north to Exit 24 (Albany). Take I-87 north to Exit 25/Route 8, Chestertown and Hague. At the end of the exit ramp, turn left (west) onto NY 8 toward Loon Lake. After passing through Wevertown, turn right (west) at the stop sign onto NY 28. This scenic highway takes you through the towns of North Creek, Indian Lake, and Blue Mountain Lake. Whitewater rafting on the Hudson River is very popular, and there are many outdoor outfitters in the Indian Lake area. Continue on NY 28 west toward Inlet and Old Forge. In Eagle Bay turn right (north) onto Big Moose Road. In about 6.5 miles the road bears left (west) at a **T** intersection. A road to the right leads east along the northern shores of Big Moose Lake. Continue for another 2 miles into the village of Big Moose. Park at Big Moose station and bear right, heading out of town in a northwest direction along Big Moose Road.

Sources of additional information:

Pedals & Petals
Route 28, P.O. Box 390
Inlet, New York 13360
(315) 357-3281

Old Forge Tourist Information Center
P.O. Box 68
Old Forge, New York 13420
(315) 369-6983

Stillwater Hotel
Star Route Box 258M
Lowville, New York 13367
(315) 376-6470

New York State Department of Environmental Conservation (Region 6)
317 Washington Street
Watertown, New York 13601
(315) 785-2239

Mountainman Outdoor Supply Company
Route 28, P.O. Box 659
Inlet, New York 13360
(315) 357-6672

Notes on the trail: After about 3 miles of pedaling on the moderately hilly Big Moose Road, there will be another dirt road that forks right. Continue straight. Another road is passed after half a mile, on your left. Keep straight, skirting a small hill on your left and passing several streams on your right.

You will pass two more dirt roads on your right and then your left, but continue straight. Birch Creek, the drainage from Polack Swamp, parallels the road. A little over 7 miles from where you started, you will begin to approach the southeastern end of Stillwater Reservoir. From this point the road passes along the eastern shore of the reservoir, and in about 1 mile you'll pass Stillwater Mountain, elevation 3,264', on your left (west). Stillwater is reached in another 2.5 miles. Keep in mind that you must return along the same route you have just traveled.

RIDE 83 *BLOODSUCKER PASSAGE*

A rigorous 18-mile loop passes through attractive forests, meandering streams, sparkling ponds and lakes, and even a small waterfall. The riding is along snowmobile trails that are maintained year-round. During the winter, snowmobile enthusiasts pay a permit fee to ride in the area. The funds are then used to keep the trails in shape, repairing washouts and cutting up blowdowns that block the routes.

The terrain is rugged and not for the faint-hearted. Though not a technical ride, the double-track snowmobile trails will test an intermediate rider's endurance. A strong rider will be challenged by the length of the ride and rolling terrain, but charmed by spectacular woodland scenery. The mixed deciduous and conifer forest provides a dense woodland environment that is a pleasure to ride through. In the nineteenth century, wildlife such as moose, cougars, wolves, and lynx were all hunted to extinction. Fortunately, over the last 100 years, these forests have been given a chance to recover, largely through protections by the state for the Adirondack Forest Preserve. Bald eagles, moose, and peregrine falcons have returned to this unique topography of rivers, lakes, mountains, and forests.

The tour begins just outside of the historic village of Old Forge. The area was known for its rustic hotels, lodges, and private camps built in the late nineteenth century. Hunters and tourists explored the region's waterways in the famous Adirondack guide boat. These boats, an Adirondack creation, resembled a sleeker version of a rowboat. They were fast and light and provided a major industry for Old Forge between 1890 and 1940.

Bloodsucker Passage is a demanding, stimulating, and rewarding trail. The deep, dark, quiet woodlands, streams, and falls provide enough sensory overload for a full day of riding.

General location: Near the town of Old Forge in Herkimer County, in the west-central region of Adirondack Park in northeastern New York. Old Forge is a quiet New England kind of town. It is located at the beginning of

the Fulton Chain of Lakes and is the starting point for the infamous 75-mile canoe trip through the heart of the Adirondack wilderness.

Elevation change: There is one major hill toward the end of the ride near Little Roundtop. The majority of the route traverses a rolling, sometimes hilly terrain. The route levels out for a short distance and then continues to undulate over several short hills.

Season: You can ride after the wet season ends in April or May. It all depends on the amount of snow and rain from prior months. You can then ride until mid-September, which is when hunting season commences. You may don an orange hunting vest, but it is still risky to be moving through the forest at the speed of a young buck. The fall is a beautiful time to ride through the mixed hardwood and conifer forests.

The black flies can be fierce in late spring and last until late June. Deerflies take over where the black flies leave off and can last into July. They look like miniature F-15 jets with their swept-back wings. Remember to bring bug repellent.

Services: Old Forge offers a wide range of accommodations including food, restaurants, hotels, motels, camps, and even homes that can be rented.

Backcountry mountain bike tours are provided by Ted Christodaro from the bike store Pedals & Petals in Inlet. Daily and overnight tours are a great way to explore this abundant trail area. Ted is a good source for information on the condition of the trails. The shop provides repairs, supplies, and mountain bike sales. Call Pedals & Petals for any information on clinics, tours, festivals, and races. The Adirondacks have independent weather systems, and it's hard to determine the condition of trails from faraway cities. It's a good idea to telephone ahead before taking off on the trails.

Mountain bikes can be rented from the Mountainman Outdoor Supply Company on NY 28 in Inlet.

Hazards: This trail is challenging, so be prepared with spare tubes, patches, water, energy bars, and bug repellent.

Rescue index: At its greatest distance the trail is only 6 miles from Old Forge, making this route fairly close to civilization. You can bail out after reaching Nelson Lake on the dirt road that leads down to NY 28. The well-marked and excellently maintained snowmobile trails are marked with orange circular discs, and they are very easy to follow.

Land status: Old Forge and the central region of Adirondack Park offer a variety of terrain with exceptional natural beauty. The route follows roads and trails in the Wild Forests classification of Adirondack Park. They reside on state public land and are available for mountain biking. Mountain biking is presently prohibited in designated Wilderness areas of Adirondack Park and where signage is posted.

The town of Web has expanded the use of their well-maintained snowmobile trails and opened the well-marked routes for mountain bikers. The potential use of the diverse Old Forge/Web trail system is limitless and an exciting opportunity for mountain bikers to explore.

Maps: USGS, 15 minute series McKeever and Old Forge quadrangles provide good detail for this route. The Adirondack West-Central Wilderness Area Map published by Plinth, Quoin & Cornice Associates provides excellent topographical detail of the route and surrounding terrain and can be found at most outdoor-type stores in New York for approximately $4.95. It is based on the USGS, 15 minute series, at a scale of 1:62,500 and a contour level of 20' where 1 inch = .98 mile.

Finding the trail: Take the New York State Thruway (Interstate 87) north to Exit 24 (Albany). Take I-87 north to Exit 25/Route 8, Chestertown and Hague. At the end of the exit ramp, turn left (west) onto NY 8 toward Loon Lake. After passing through Wevertown, turn right (west) at the stop sign onto NY 28. This scenic highway takes you through the towns of North Creek, Indian Lake, and Blue Mountain Lake. Whitewater rafting on the Hudson River is very popular, and there are many outdoor outfitters in the Indian Lake area. Continue on NY 28 west toward Inlet and Old Forge.

After reaching the town of Old Forge, go down Main Street (NY 28) and turn left at the large brick school onto Gilbert Street. Turn right at the next stop sign following the sign for Nicks Lake Public Campground. Bear left at the next stop sign, continuing to follow the signs for the campground. Turn left onto Bisby Road. Park at the second snowmobile trailhead about 100 yards on your right.

Sources of additional information:

Pedals & Petals
Route 28, P.O. Box 390
Inlet, New York 13360
(315) 357-3281

Old Forge Tourist Information Center
P.O. Box 68
Old Forge, New York 13420
(315) 369-6983

New York State Department of Environmental Conservation (Region 6)
3174 Washington Street
Watertown, New York 13601
(315) 785-2239

Mountainman Outdoor Supply Company
Route 28, P.O. Box 659
Inlet, New York 13360
(315) 357-6672

Miles of double-track lie ahead.

Notes on the trail: Pedal southwest on a wide, wooded snowmobile trail. About half a mile southwest of the lake a trail will join the trail you're on. This trail to your left leads east along the north end of Nicks Lake. Continue on the main trail in a southwest direction and in .3 mile you approach a fork. Continue straight for another mile, whereupon you reach an intersection with the snowmobile trail that leads around Nicks Lake. The path straight ahead is known as the Remsen Falls Trail and is the main loop. Taking the snowmobile trail (left), you will soon climb a small hill just south of the lake. As you crest the hill a trail leads off to the left and terminates at the Nicks Lake Campground and beach. Return to the main trail and bear right.

The trail proceeds south, descending and winding closer to Nicks Creek, which drains from Nicks Lake into the South Branch of Moose River. At 4.8 miles, Bloodsucker Pond is passed. Ascend a small hill and descend to Remsen Falls at 6 miles. The falls are created by a natural rock dam across the stream. The falls are on a small spur trail that leads south into the Black Forest Trail system. Continue to bear right (west), paralleling the South Branch of the Moose River. The trail remains mostly in the woods.

Two miles past the falls the trail turns right (north) up a small hill and then down again, crossing a stream. The south shore of Nelson Lake is reached in 2.2 miles (12.2 miles total). A little over a mile past the southern end of Nelson Lake, you reach an intersection with a dirt road that leads west to NY 28. Stay on the snowmobile trail heading east and after .6 mile the trail bears northeast, ascending a large hill. After descending from the hill, pass the snowmobile trail that leads in from the left and bear left at the next fork. This is the same trail you rode on from your parking area. Pedal back along the trail for about 1.8 miles to Bisby Road.

RIDE 84 *BLACK RIVER WILD FOREST*

Over 23 miles of single-track and double-track trails await the energetic intermediate rider in the mood for adventure. An interesting network of snowmobile trails connects three beautiful lakes. Woodhull Lake, shaped like a half-moon, is the largest (with its own island in the middle) and resides at an elevation of 1,875 feet. This lake overflows into and creates Sand Lake at a slightly lower elevation of 1,825 feet. Gulf Lake, which you pass later in the ride, is situated at an elevation of 1,173 feet.

The woodlands are fairly flat with few distant views, but visiting these bodies of water is great fun. Bring some snacks and have a mountain biker picnic along the shores of these remote bodies of water. Toward the end of the eighteenth century, hunters, trappers, and others came through the Black River Valley and discovered its rivers and chains of lakes. The valley provided an easier passage into the west-central Adirondacks and soon became the main passage for many settlers in the Fulton Chain Lakes area. The Oneida Indians occupied the land during this era and ended up selling off over 4 million acres to the white settlers. Logging took hold by 1850, making New York the leading timber-producing state in the nation. After the Civil War, the Adirondacks were popular for recreation, and most of the thoroughfare came through the forested and hilly Black River Valley. As you ride throughout this territory imagine what it must have been like for Native Americans to hunt and fish the land and waters, and think about the trepidation of the first settlers as they traveled through these dense woodlands and the awe inspired by the natural beauty of the lake-riddled landscape. This ride takes you past many such bodies of water. Happy trails.

General location: Near the town of Old Forge in Herkimer County, in the west-central region of Adirondack Park in northeastern New York. The trailhead is located in the town of McKeever, about 10 miles southwest from Old Forge on NY 28.

Elevation change: The ride has hilly ascents on the approach to Woodhull Lake and Sand Lake. One of the trails that leads into the Little Woodhull Lake area is a bit more hilly, and riding varies between 1,800' and 2,000'.

Season: You can ride after the wet season ends in April or May. It all depends on the amount of snow and rain from prior months. You can then ride until

mid-September, which is when hunting season commences. You may don an orange hunting vest, but it is still risky to be moving through the forest at the speed of a young buck. The fall is a beautiful time to ride through the mixed hardwood and conifer forests.

The black flies can be fierce in late spring and last until late June. Deerflies take over where the black flies leave off and can last into July. They look like miniature F-15 jets with their swept-back wings. Remember to bring bug repellent.

Services: Lodging, food, and other services can be found in Old Forge, approximately 10 miles northeast on NY 28.

Ted Christodaro from the bike store Pedals & Petals in Inlet provides daily and overnight backcountry mountain bike tours throughout this area and is a good source for information on the condition of the trails. The shop provides repairs, supplies, and mountain bike sales. Call Pedals & Petals for any information on clinics, tours, festivals, and races. The Adirondacks have independent weather systems, and it's hard to determine the condition of trails from faraway cities. It's a good idea to telephone ahead before taking off on the trails. Mountain bikes can be rented from the Mountainman Outdoor Supply Company on NY 28 in Inlet.

Hazards: This is a long trail. Remember, whatever mileage you cover, you must return along the same route. Bring water, energy bars, first aid, and something that I never go into a forest without: a whistle. It is indispensable if you are injured or lost and need to reach out and grab some attention. The sound is piercing. Not only does it wake up the beavers, but it has a greater impact of attracting human attention than yelling.

Rescue index: The trail's proximity to well-traveled NY 28 at the beginning of the ride should be of some comfort, but as you get further into the ride, you must return the same way you came in. Along NY 28, the towns of McKeever, Otter Lake, and Woodgate are your closest bets for help. Seven miles into the ride, past Woodhull Lake, if you need to bail out, you can take the snowmobile trail out to Woodhull Road. This leads directly into Bear Creek Road and into the town of Woodgate, about 8 miles south on NY 28 from McKeever. The well-marked and excellently maintained snowmobile trails are marked with orange circular discs and are very easy to follow.

Land status: Old Forge and the central region of Adirondack Park offer a variety of terrain with exceptional natural beauty. The route follows roads and trails in the Wild Forests classification of Adirondack Park. They reside on state public land and are available for mountain biking. Mountain biking is presently prohibited in designated Wilderness areas of Adirondack Park and where signage is posted.

The town of Web has expanded the use of their well-maintained snowmobile trails and opened the well-marked routes for mountain bikers. The potential use of the diverse Old Forge/Web trail system is limitless and is an exciting opportunity for mountain bikers to explore.

Maps: USGS, 15 minute series McKeever, North Wilmurt, Ohio, and Old Forge quadrangles provide good detail for this route. The Adirondack West-Central Wilderness Area Map published by Plinth, Quoin & Cornice Associates provides excellent topographical detail of the route and surrounding terrain and can be found at most outdoor-type stores in New York for approximately $4.95. It is based on the USGS, 15 minute series, at a scale of 1:62,500 and a contour level of 20' where 1 inch = .98 mile.

Finding the trail: Take the New York State Thruway (Interstate 87) north to Exit 24 (Albany). Take I-87 north to Exit 25/Route 8, Chestertown and Hague. At the end of the exit ramp, turn left (west) onto NY 8 toward Loon Lake. After passing through Wevertown, turn right (west) at the stop sign onto NY 28. This scenic highway takes you through the towns of North Creek, Indian Lake, and Blue Mountain Lake. Whitewater rafting on the Hudson River is very popular, and there are many outdoor outfitters in the Indian Lake area. Continue on NY 28 west toward Inlet and Old Forge.

From Old Forge proceed another 10 miles to the town of McKeever. Turn left on McKeever Road toward McKeever. Proceed .3 mile and turn left onto a dirt road past the old railroad station. Cross the tracks and park in the first parking area .6 mile from NY 28.

Sources of additional information:

Pedals & Petals
Route 28, P.O. Box 390
Inlet, New York 13360
(315) 357-3281

Old Forge Tourist Information Center
P.O. Box 68
Old Forge, New York 13420
(315) 369-6983

New York State Department of Environmental Conservation (Region 6)
317 Washington Street
Watertown, New York 13601
(315) 785-2239

Mountainman Outdoor Supply Company
Route 28, P.O. Box 659
Inlet, New York 13360
(315) 357-6672

Notes on the trail: There are 2 access points. You can begin in McKeever and follow the Sand Lake Falls snowmobile trail. It leads south into the network. You can also begin in Woodgate and follow the Bear Creek Road to Woodhull Road and follow the trails north to McKeever. The route description below begins at the McKeever–Sand Lake Falls trailhead.

The Moose River passes through the Black River Wild Forest.

The trail heads east and parallels a dirt truck road for about 3 miles and then **T** intersects with another trail. The trail to your left leads to Remsen Falls about 1 mile north. Turn right (south) and cross a small stream. These are some of the drainage streams from Woodhull Lake. They lead farther north into Moose River. The trail begins to ascend and, in 1.3 miles from the last intersection, reaches the shore of Woodhull Lake at Wolf Lake Landing. Continue south and soon another trail leads off to your right in a westerly direction. Ignore this trail and remain on the main trail. After .6 mile, bear right and head southwest. The trail to your left leads back to Woodhull Lake. After 2.2 miles you come to a fork. The small mountain to your right (west) is known as Neejer Hill. The trail to your left leads to a 12-mile loop to Little Woodhull Lake. This loop is optional, and the map clearly describes its passage.

Bearing right will connect you to Woodhull Road. Continuing straight, ignore the next 3 trail intersections, and at 1.3 miles from the fork to Little Woodhull Lake, you'll come to a 4-way intersection. Turning left or right will eventually lead you back to where you are standing. It is a 5.5-mile loop. Turn left and pass by the west shore of Gull Lake. Continue past and you will soon cross the Gull Lake Outlet, a small drainage stream from Gull Lake. You will begin riding on a dirt road. Take that for approximately 1 mile and turn right (north) at the next intersection. Continuing north on the dirt road, the snowmobile trail is picked up again, and you will soon reach the intersection where you started this little loop. To return, proceed north on the snowmobile trail toward Woodhull Lake and back out to McKeever.

RIDE 85 *CEDAR RIVER FLOW*

Cedar River Flow provides the eastern access into the Moose River Plains Recreation Area. A 22-mile, out-and-back (eleven miles one way), double-track dirt road penetrates into the eastern section of the Moose River Plains. The riding is fast and easy, and there is plenty of mileage to take advantage of. Only one steep pitch over the saddle between Sturges Hills at 2,700 feet and Cellar Mountain at 3,447 feet may make your knees wobble, but the rest is all easy to moderate pedaling. At the beginning of the tour, views of Cedar River open up and are then followed by the towering cliffs to the west of Roundtop and then Sugarloaf mountains. The challenging ascent over Sturges Hill is your final obstacle, and the only item remaining is some great cruising on rolling terrain. The terrain is ideal for mountain bikers of all levels, and during the colder months the lack of foliage extends your views to the wide-open surrounding hills and mountains.

Cedar River Road was established to provide access into a popular hunting and fishing region during the latter part of the nineteenth century. W. D. Wakely built a hotel around 1870 near Cedar River Falls and advertised that boats were available for use. They were kept 14 miles farther inland in the Moose River Plains. The hotel burned down, as did so many other of the hotels and camps in the Adirondacks during the late nineteenth and early twentieth centuries.

General location: Near the towns of Blue Mountain Lake and Indian Lake in the west-central Adirondacks.
Elevation change: The old logging road begins a 1.5-mile climb up Sturges Hills from about 2,300' to 2,600', where the route crests at the pass between Cellar Mountain and Sturges Hills. From the pass it's all downhill until you reach the level of the Cedar River Flow at 2,100'.
Season: You can ride after the wet season ends in April or May. It all depends on the amount of snow and rain from prior months. You can then ride until mid-September, which is when hunting season commences. You may don an orange hunting vest, but it is still risky to be moving through the forest at the speed of a young buck. The fall is a beautiful time to ride through the mixed hardwood and conifer forests.

The black flies can be fierce in late spring and last until late June. Deerflies take over where the black flies leave off and can last into July. They look like miniature F-15 jets with their swept-back wings. Remember to bring bug repellent.
Services: Blue Mountain Lake is nearby and offers the nationally acclaimed Adirondack Museum showcasing the region's history. Ted Christodaro from the bike store Pedals & Petals in Inlet provides daily and overnight backcountry

To 28

Wakely Dam

Cedar River Flow

Payne Mtn. 3225

Double-track

Sturges Hills

Cellar Mtn. 3647

Little Moose Lake

To Moose River Medley Trails

Currently Closed to the Public

Double-track

Moose River Rd.

NY

To Moose River Medley Trails

N

MILES
0   1/2   1

mountain bike tours throughout this area and is a good source for information on the condition of the trails. The shop provides repairs, supplies, and mountain bike sales. Call Pedals & Petals for any information on clinics, tours, festivals, and races. The Adirondacks have independent weather systems, and it's hard to determine the condition of trails from faraway cities. It's a good idea to telephone ahead before taking off on the trails.

Hazards: Hunting season begins in mid-September, so if you do venture out on these roads, wear the appropriate hunter-orange colors. Call the Limekiln Ranger for further details on road conditions and the bug index.

Rescue index: Help can be flagged down on the well-traveled NY 28/30 and in Indian Lake.

Land status: New York State park land. The Department of Environmental Conservation manages the forest as a multiple-use area. The well-marked and excellently maintained snowmobile trails are marked with orange circular discs.

Maps: The Adirondack West-Central Wilderness Area Map published by Plinth, Quoin & Cornice Associates provides excellent topographical detail of the route and surrounding terrain and can be found at most outdoor-type stores in New York for approximately $4.95. It is based on the USGS, 15 minute series, at a scale of 1:62,500 and a contour level of 20' where 1 inch = .98 mile.

Finding the trail: Take the New York State Thruway (Interstate 87) north to Exit 24 (Albany). Take I-87 north to Exit 25/Route 8, Chestertown and Hague. At the end of the exit ramp, turn left (west) onto NY 8 toward Loon Lake. After passing through Wevertown, turn right (west) at the stop sign onto NY 28. This scenic highway takes you through the towns of North Creek and Indian Lake. Whitewater rafting on the Hudson River is very popular, and there are many outdoor outfitters in the Indian Lake area. Continue on NY 28 west.

After passing through the village of Indian Lake, turn left onto Cedar River Road, which intersects NY 28/30 near Indian Lake and before Blue Mountain Lake. You may park here or drive in on the town road until its end at Wakely Dam in roughly 12 miles.

Sources of additional information:

Pedals & Petals
Route 28, P.O. Box 390
Inlet, New York 13360
(315) 357-3281

Forest Ranger
Limekiln Lake
Inlet, New York 13420
(315) 357-4403

Cedar River.

The Adirondack Museum
NY 30
Blue Mountain Lake, New York 12812
(518) 352-7311

Notes on the trail: You should register at the cabin near Wakely Dam to go into the plains or if you're just hanging out in the Wakely Dam area, for which currently there is no charge. Pedal past the gate, heading east on the well-defined, hard-packed dirt road. Bear right at a fork in a little over 1 mile and begin your ascent up and over the pass at Sturges Hills. Sturges Hills lie to your south, and Cellar and Payne mountains are to the north. After descending from the pass, bear right at the next fork and just ride to your heart's content. Remember that the distance you ride in on, you must return on, unless of course you are planning to spend the night camping. If you are planning an overnight, you might want to pedal toward Otter Brook Road and Moose River Road; most of the neat campsites are located along the shores of the lakes and ponds. See the Moose River Plains tour description for campsite recommendations.

RIDE 86 *SARGENT PONDS WILD FOREST*

Sargent Ponds Wild Forest offers a four-mile loop of double- and single-track trails with an eight-mile, out-and-back trail (four miles one way) tacked onto the end. The route begins as an eroded single-track and continues along the well-marked snowmobile trails connecting two scenic ponds rimmed with evergreens. The first pond you will arrive at, known as Upper Sargents Pond, is a great spot for camping. The tiny islands in the middle of the lake add great beauty to the scenery. A lean-to can be found on the second pond, Lower Sargents Pond, and makes another great place to camp. From these base camps, you can then set out to explore the eight-mile, out-and-back trip to Tioga Point on Raquette Lake. Tioga Point is located at about the center portion of Raquette Lake. The fairly level ride through a mature woodland of conifer and hardwood makes this out-and-back trail a pleasant and enjoyable trip. There are several lean-tos used for canoe camping, but anyone can camp in them. Reservations must be made ahead of time for the lean-tos by calling the NYSDEC at (800) 456-2267. Fifteen lean-tos and ten campsites are administered from the small DEC office at Tioga Point.

The view from Tioga Point of Raquette Lake is impressive. Although the lake is only 6½ miles long, its many bays and peninsulas give Raquette Lake 99 miles of shoreline.

Lying west of this small jewel of a trail system is the majestic, 3,759-foot Blue Mountain and Blue Mountain Lake. Blue Mountain has a great hiking trail system, and views from the summit are something to seek out. Considered to be one of the most beautiful in the Adirondacks, Blue Mountain Lake is filled with a variety of islands.

This is a great ride and its location is amid great canoeing, camping, and hiking.

General location: Near Blue Mountain and Long Lakes on County Route 3 in the west-central Adirondacks.

Elevation change: There is a minor ascent after leaving CR 3 and then a descent to the level of the ponds. From there it is mostly level riding. The last section of the loop you will take to leave this area requires another small ascent, followed by a short descent back to CR 3.

Season: You can ride after the wet season ends in April or May. It all depends on the amount of snow and rain from prior months. You can then ride until mid-September, which is when hunting season commences. You may don an orange hunting vest, but it is still risky to be moving through the forest at the speed of a young buck. The fall is a beautiful time to ride through the mixed hardwood and conifer forests.

RIDE 86   *SARGENT PONDS WILD FOREST*

The black flies can be fierce in late spring and last until late June. Deerflies take over where the black flies leave off and can last into July. They look like miniature F-15 jets with their swept-back wings. Remember to bring bug repellent.

Services: Blue Mountain Lake is nearby and offers the nationally acclaimed Adirondack Museum showcasing the region's history. Ted Christodaro from the bike store Pedals & Petals in Inlet provides daily and overnight back-country mountain bike tours throughout this area and is a good source for information on the condition of the trails. The shop provides repairs,

Upper Sargent Pond in the Sargent Ponds Wild Forest.

supplies, and mountain bike sales. Call Pedals & Petals for any information on clinics, tours, festivals, and races. The Adirondacks have independent weather systems, and it's hard to determine the condition of trails from far-away cities. It's a good idea to telephone ahead before taking off on the trails.

Hazards: Hunting season begins in mid-September, so if you do venture out on these roads, wear the appropriate hunter-orange color.

Rescue index: Help can be found in Blue Mountain Lake.

Land status: New York State park land. The Department of Environmental Conservation manages the forest as a multiple-use area. The well-marked and excellently maintained snowmobile trails are marked with orange circular discs.

Maps: The Adirondack Central Mountain Area Map published by Plinth, Quoin & Cornice Associates provides excellent topographical detail of the route and surrounding terrain and can be found at most outdoor-type stores in New York for approximately $4.95. It is based on the USGS, 15 minute series, at a scale of 1:62,500 and a contour level of 20' where 1 inch = .98 mile.

Finding the trail: Take the New York State Thruway (Interstate 87) north to Exit 24 (Albany). Take I-87 north to Exit 25/Route 8, Chestertown and Hague. At the end of the exit ramp, turn left (west) onto NY 8 toward Loon Lake. After passing through Wevertown, turn right (west) at the stop sign onto NY 28. This scenic highway takes you through the towns of North Creek and Indian Lake. Whitewater rafting on the Hudson River is very popular, and there are many outdoor outfitters in the Indian Lake area. Continue on NY 28 west.

Turn right (north) at Blue Mountain Lake onto NY 30. Drive about 8 miles to Deerland. Deerland is located at the southern end of Long Lake. Turn left onto North Point Road (CR 3) and park near the NYSDEC trailhead 6.3 miles on your left.

Sources of additional information:

Pedals & Petals
Route 28, P.O. Box 390
Inlet, New York 13360
(315) 357-3281

Forest Ranger
Limekiln Lake
Inlet, New York 13420
(315) 357-4403

The Adirondack Museum
NY 30
Blue Mountain Lake, New York 12812
(518) 352-7311

Notes on the trail: Pedal south over level ground and then ascend a small hill at 1 mile. The trail descends steeply to an intersection. A trail to the left (east) leads to the campsite on the shore of the upper pond.

Bear right (west) at the intersection to continue the ride. The trail meanders along the contours of the hills to your right (north), crossing the stream that connects the upper and lower ponds. In about 1.5 miles the trail **T** intersects with another trail. Turning right (north) will return you to CR 3 (1.5 miles west on CR 3 from where you parked and began riding). This is the loop. To begin the out-and-back, turn left (south). A small, yellow-marked trail leads .4 mile east to the Sargent Pond lean-to on your left.

Continuing on the snowmobile trail, remain straight ahead as the trail hugs the eastern shore of the lower pond.

RIDE 87 *THE OSGOOD/JACKRABBIT RUN*

This tour is great if you come with some people who would like to visit the Adirondack Park Visitor's Interpretive Center at Paul Smiths. They can drop you off at the trailhead and go on ahead to the Interpretive Center. You can meet them there later, after you have completed a nine-mile, moderately level double-track that exits at the doors of the center. Very convenient. The route

RIDE 87 *THE OSGOOD / JACKRABBIT RUN*

To
Malone

Osgood Pond

To
White Pine
Camp

Paul Smiths
Visitor Center

Easy St.

To
30

NY

192

To
Gabriels

30

Double-track

N

0   1/2   1

MILES

Lake Clear

travels over the famed Jackrabbit Cross-Country Ski Trail and passes by the very scenic Osgood Pond. A small detour toward the end of the route, from the Jackrabbit Trail, brings you to an incredible single-track that skirts the shores of Osgood Pond. Several lean-tos dot the shoreline and make for excellent campsites. The route passes over mostly old back roads and logging roads that are wide and well defined.

The Jackrabbit Ski Trail was constructed in 1986 to improve the cross-country skiing in the Lake Placid–Saranac Lake area. It is named in memory of Herman "Jack Rabbit" Johannsen, who laid out many of the trails himself. He was a pioneer of Lake Placid skiing from 1916 to 1928 and died in 1987 at 111. The trail described in this route travels on a small portion of the Jackrabbit Trail system from Lake Clear Junction to the Adirondack Park Interpretive Center at Paul Smiths. You will also pass White Pine Road, which leads to the 1907 White Pine Camp that served as the summer White House for President Calvin Coolidge in 1926. Located on 35 acres of majestic pines and wetlands, this "great camp" is currently undergoing a restoration. It has 3,900 feet of shoreline on Osgood Pond.

The area has an abundance of wildlife. We saw the eastern chipmunk and some loons near Osgood Pond. The forest around Osgood Pond is mostly red pine. This tall conifer reaches heights of 80 feet and has a diameter of 3 feet. The bark is made of diamond-shaped plates. The needles from these majestic trees carpet the single-track that borders the Osgood Pond shoreline.

General location: North of the village of Saranac Lake in Franklin County in the Adirondacks of northeastern New York.

Elevation change: The route follows terrain that is slightly hilly. There is more flat terrain than hills.

Season: The route travels through wetlands and is best ridden during early summer after the black flies have found better things to do with themselves. You can ride well into the winter, providing there is no snow on the ground.

Services: Most services can be found in the village of Saranac Lake, approximately 7 miles from the trailhead on NY 86. The Visitor's Interpretive Center offers rest-room facilities, water, picnic tables, and ranger information. It also has exhibits on the human and natural history of Adirondack Park. Wildlife and ecological processes are described along a network of interpretive nature trails on the 2,800-acre tract.

Hazards: This is a long trail, and in the summer it's quite dry. Bring water and bug repellent.

Rescue index: Vehicles flagged down on the well-traveled NY 30 can be a source of help. Help can also be found at the Adirondack Park Visitor's Center at Paul Smiths.

Land status: New York State Forest Preserve.

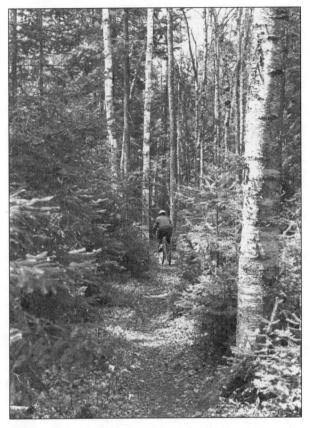

Single-track surrounded by dense wilderness on the
Osgood/Jackrabbit Trail.

Maps: The Adirondack Canoe Map published by Plinth, Quoin & Cornice
Associates provides detail of the surrounding area and can be found at most
outdoor-type stores in the Adirondacks for approximately $4.95.

Finding the trail: Take the New York State Thruway (Interstate 87) north to
Exit 24 (Albany). Take I-87 north to Exit 30. Pick up NY 9 north and follow it
for 2 miles to NY 73. Continue on NY 73 for 28 miles to the Lake Placid area.
Pass through Lake Placid and continue on NY 86 toward Saranac Lake. Continue on NY 86 through Saranac Lake and past Lake Colby. Turn left (west)
onto County Route 186 toward Lake Clear Junction. At Lake Clear Junction,
turn right (north) onto NY 30. Travel about half a mile north of the junction. A
small parking area and dirt road are directly across the roadway from the Lake
Clear Elementary School. You may park your car here or have someone drop
you off and then continue north for about 9 miles on NY 30 to the Adirondack
Park Visitor's Center at Paul Smiths. You can meet up with them later.

Sources of additional information:

Saranac Lake Area Chamber of Commerce
30 Main Street
Saranac Lake, New York 12983
(800) 347-1992, (518) 891-1990

Placid Planet Bicycles
200 Saranac Avenue
Lake Placid, New York 12946
(518) 523-4128

Adirondack Park Visitor Center
Box 3000
Paul Smiths, New York 12970
(518) 327-3000

Notes on the trail: The hard-packed double-track follows the powerline for .1 mile to a main transmission line. Turn left at the main transmission line. You will then pass over 2 gravel roads. At about 2.8 miles, the Jackrabbit Trail makes a sharp right away from the transmission line. The route now follows a wide lumber road. You reach a gravel pit at 4.2 miles. The Jackrabbit Trail now follows an old woods road for a short distance and goes right on a narrow trail, reaching Montou Clearing at 5 miles. NY 86 is reached in just under 6 miles. Cross NY 86, ascend for a short distance, and descend to Jones Pond Road (CR 31) at 6.7 miles. The trail continues across the road. Continue up a small incline and soon the trail intersects with White Pine Road. White Pine Road leads to the White Pine Camp. Continue on the Jackrabbit Trail, crossing over a small bridge that spans the channel between Little Osgood and Church ponds. The route joins a trail with red paint splashes, known as the Red Dot Trail. Continue straight through a 4-way intersection at 8 miles. In .3 mile, turn right at another intersection and descend to a small open field in .4 mile on the western end of Osgood Pond. Some dirt roads lead to the shore of Osgood Pond. The yellow-blazed Osgood Pond shoreline trail is located along the pond and makes a great intermediate single-track. The trail is carpeted with pine needles and hugs scenic Osgood Pond. The lean-tos along the shore can be reached with this trail.

From the open field, a double-track trail leads to NY 30. Continue for a short distance north on NY 30 to the Interpretive Center at 9 miles.

RIDE 88 *SWEET OSEETAH*

About four miles of interesting beginner and intermediate dirt roads and single-track weave through the dense conifer Saranac Lakes Wild Forest. This small network of interconnecting trails provides an excellent opportunity to sample a combination of single-track and double-track mountain bike trails. Though the mileage only adds up to about four miles in total, the trails provide you with great scenery and a small test of your skills.

The easy-cruising, wide Oseetah Marsh snowmobile trail is .7 mile long. The surface is carpeted with the fallen needles of the tall, dense, red and white pine forest it passes through. The entire forest is filled with evergreens and is well shaded, with shafts of sunlight poking through openings in the canopy. Gliding silently on the bed of pine needles is an enjoyable treat. The trail's easy passage makes this a delight for families with small children and those new to the sport. The Oseetah Marsh Trail leads to the marshy shoreline of Lake Oseetah. Lake Oseetah is attractive with many rocky islands sporting birch and pine trees on their tiny acreage in the lake. A .4-mile, beginner spur trail swings off the marsh trail and descends to another section of Oseetah Lake shoreline. Views of the lake, Ampersand Mountain, and the Sawtooth Range open up. The .4-mile-long, Balsam Spur Trail single-track winds over undulating terrain and requires intermediate skills to maneuver the many twists and turns. A .4-mile, beginner single-track leads off the Oseetah Marsh Trail soon after leaving the parking area. The smooth, mostly flat trail arrives near the shoreline of the small Turtle Pond. This small network of trails offers a great opportunity to sample different types of trail riding for all levels.

General location: Seven miles west of the village of Lake Placid, Essex County, in the Adirondacks of northeastern New York.

Elevation change: There is no appreciable elevation gain or loss. There are perhaps a few minor hills to climb, but the trails undulate over a generally flat terrain.

Season: The trails are open and available for riding throughout the year. Of course, if they are covered with snow, you might consider putting on some cross-country skis and exploring the trails. The dense evergreen forest causes most rains to be quickly absorbed into the porous, peaty soil.

Services: Most services can be found in the village of Saranac Lake.

Hazards: Be careful when crossing busy NY 86.

Rescue index: The trails are all within a mile of NY 86, where help can be obtained from a passing motorist.

Land status: New York State land.

Maps: The Adirondack Canoe Map published by Plinth, Quoin & Cornice Associates provides some detail of the route and nearby vicinity. It can be

RIDE 88 *SWEET OSEETAH*

To Saranac Lake

Jackrabbit Loop

NY

Turtle Pond

Turtle Pond Spur

86

To Lake Placid

Shoreline Spur

Oseetah Marsh Tr.

Oseetah Lake

Balsam Spur

N

0   1/8   1/4
MILES

found at most outdoor-type stores in the Adirondacks for approximately $4.95.

Finding the trail: Take the New York State Thruway (Interstate 87) north to Exit 24 (Albany). Take I-87 north to Exit 30. Pick up NY 9 north and follow it for 2 miles to NY 73. Continue on NY 73 for 28 miles to the Lake Placid area. Pass Lake Placid and continue on NY 86 toward Saranac Lake for approximately 7 miles. Pass over the railroad tracks after Ray Brook and park in the parking area immediately to your left.

Single-track simplicity through the evergreen canyons of the Oseetah Lake Trails.

Sources of additional information:

Saranac Lake Area Chamber of Commerce
30 Main Street
Saranac Lake, New York 12983
(800) 347-1992, (518) 891-1990

Placid Planet Bicycles
200 Saranac Avenue
Lake Placid, New York 12946
(518) 523-4128

Notes on the trail: From the parking area, head south directly into the forest, where you will pick up and follow the orange-marked snowmobile trail. This is the Oseetah Marsh Trail. The route follows a wide, double-track path through a dense pine forest. An unmarked trail soon forks to the right. This is the flat, Turtle Pond single-track spur. It is .4 mile in length, and at the end you must turn around.

After returning from Turtle Pond, continue south on the Oseetah Marsh Trail. At .4 mile, another double-track soon forks to the right in a westerly direction. This path is .4 mile in length also and leads down to the shore of Lake Oseetah. Beginners beware: the wide, inviting double-track deteriorates into an exposed-root single-track as you approach the proximity of the lake's shoreline.

Return from this shoreline trail and continue south along the Oseetah Marsh Trail to its terminus at the marshy shore of Lake Oseetah. During the winter, cross-country skiers and snowmobile enthusiasts continue beyond this point across the lake.

There are 2 options for your return. Beginners ought to head back along the Oseetah Marsh Trail. Intermediate to advanced riders can tackle the Balsam single-track that appears to your right soon after returning from the terminus of Oseetah Marsh Trail. Fork right and ascend the unmarked single-track through a spruce-and-fir woodland. After winding through this attractive forest, you soon reach higher ground. The trail is approximately .8 mile in length and leads back in a northerly direction to the parking area on NY 86.

There is still 1 more small, 1.1-mile trail to sample before leaving Sweet Oseetah. Across from the parking area, to the left of a silver-painted, metal transformer box, is another single-track loop. Cross NY 86 and enter the woods to pick up an orange-marked snowmobile trail. In approximately 500', you may be required to dismount and carry your bike around a small, flooded section of trail. Afterward, the route ascends to higher and drier ground, passing through an attractive pine forest. Continue along the snowmobile trail down a small hill. You will arrive in a red pine woodland. At .3 mile, turn left onto the red-blazed Jackrabbit Trail. Follow this cross-country ski route which soon descends to railroad tracks at .7 mile. Proceed over the tracks and turn left. Pedal along the sandy road back to NY 86 and your parking area.

RIDE 89 *KUSHAQUA LOOP TRAIL*

This tour traverses the rolling country of small mountains and is blessed with a lake-filled landscape. Pedaling along this 13-mile loop over double-track and quiet backcountry dirt roads is recommended for those who wish to spend a leisurely day cruising the countryside. While riding along the scenic shores of Lake Kushaqua, you will be enchanted by the bordering columns of tall, white birch trees that line the route. The hard-packed surface is a pleasure to ride on and makes this trip ideal for families and people seeking a day of easy pedaling. Buck Pond public campground that is part of the tour offers a full day of recreational possibilities. After completing the loop, you may wish to swim at Buck Pond's wide, sandy beach, stay overnight in the campground, or canoe on Lake Kushaqua and paddle to several other nearby ponds and lakes.

The Adirondacks are the middle ground between the northern, largely coniferous forests, mixed with spruces and firs, and the hardwood, deciduous species like beeches, birches, and maples. This mixture of flora is very interesting to ride through. During the autumn, the forests are filled with

RIDE 89 *KUSHAQUA LOOP TRAIL*

brilliant colors accented by the deep, rich, perpetual tones of the evergreens, as seen in the surrounding hillsides. The land was glaciated 10,000 years ago, smoothing out the much larger mountains that long ago eroded away. As you pedal along, take a moment to study the lowland mountains, the sandy soils and beaches, and the many bodies of water that dot the land. These features were carved and deposited by the great Ice Age. As the climate warmed and the glaciers melted, the land was flooded with fast-flowing streams from the retreating glaciers. Sediments were carried and deposited. Lakes and ponds appeared and disappeared. Bike through geologic history

Cruising on the birch-bordered Kushaqua double-track.

and imagine acres of ice a thousand feet thick moving over the land! It did happen.

General location: North of the village of Saranac Lake, Franklin County, in the Adirondacks of northeastern New York.

Elevation change: About 2 miles of level double-track skirt the shoreline of Lake Kushaqua. The remaining dirt roads follow easy grades with no strenuous hill climbs or descents.

Season: You can ride this tour in most seasons. Of course, if the trails are well covered with snow, you might want to choose another time. Black flies come out in strength in late spring, from May to June, and it is advisable to bring bug repellent. Fall is brilliant and shouldn't be missed in any part of the Adirondacks. The campground opens in May and remains open through Labor Day. The registration booth is open daily from 8 A.M. to 9 P.M.

Services: Most services can be found in the village of Saranac Lake. There is a small delicatessen 6 miles away in Gabriels.

Hazards: These backcountry roads occasionally see light traffic, so pay attention while cruising and looking at the scenery.

Rescue index: A facility supervisor is on the premises at all times at Buck Pond public campground. Help can also be found in nearby Gabriels.

Land status: Buck Pond is on New York State land, and the roads are public.

Maps: Loon Lake and Debar Mountain 7.5 minute USGS quadrangles provide good detail of the surrounding countryside. The accompanying map should provide most of the detail needed for completing the loop. Buck Pond campground hands out a general map of the area after you pay a $4 day-use fee.

Finding the trail: Take the New York State Thruway (Interstate 87) north to Exit 24 (Albany). Take I-87 north to Exit 30. Pick up NY 9 north and follow it for 2 miles to NY 73. Continue on NY 73 and pass through Lake Placid. Continue on NY 86 toward Saranac Lake. Follow the signs for NY 86 through Saranac Lake and continue to Gabriels. In Gabriels, take County Route 30, 6 miles to Buck Pond public campground. You can park along the access road or in one of the parking areas in the campground.

Sources of additional information:

> Saranac Lake Area Chamber of Commerce
> 30 Main Street
> Saranac Lake, New York 12983
> (800) 347-1992, (518) 891-1990

> Placid Planet Bicycles
> 200 Saranac Avenue
> Lake Placid, New York 12946
> (518) 523-4128

> Buck Pond Public Campground
> Franklin County Road 30
> Onchiota, New York 12968
> (518) 891-3449

Notes on the trail: Pedal back to CR 30 and turn right (west) toward Onchiota. Turn right (north) onto Kushaqua–Mud Pond Road. You will cross a small bridge at 3 miles. You may at this point return to Buck Pond campground by making a sharp right after the bridge beyond a metal barrier. This is a double-track that skirts the eastern shore of Lake Kushaqua.

Thatcherville Road intersects from the right with the route at 4 miles. You will return along Thatcherville Road later. Continue past Thatcherville Road, and after approximately 1 mile turn right (east) on Blue Spruce Drive into Loon Lake. You will arrive at the intersection with NY 99 at 6.2 miles. Turn right onto this paved road and cruise down a pleasant hill. At the bottom of the hill turn right onto Thatcherville Road. The ride along this dirt road is extremely interesting, as it meanders with and parallel to the north branch of the Saranac River. After about 3.5 miles from the intersection of NY 99, you will arrive back at Kushaqua–Mud Pond Road. Turn left (southwest) and continue for about 1 mile. Just before the small iron bridge, turn left onto the double-track that leads around the eastern shore of Lake Kushaqua and into the Buck Pond public campground.

RIDE 90 *THE GREAT SANTANONI*

The five-mile, hard-packed dirt road to Newcomb Lake in the 12,000-acre Santanoni Preserve is a great one-day adventure. The road is easy to ride. Those new to mountain biking who have not ventured beyond the lower mileage trips will find this tour a pleasure to ride. The well-graded surface, easy pedaling, and scenic assets provide a fun and fulfilling package. The ten-mile (total) out-and-back tour, along the well-maintained road that traverses a mixed deciduous and conifer forest, is a joy to ride. The wide road is not technically challenging and its smoothness, good condition, and gentle, rolling grade facilitate a sort of out-of-saddle experience. On this trail, you do not have to try hard to feel great and ride at one with nature. The preserve was once a very large private estate. The one-way, five-mile route leads you up a gentle grade and near its end descends to the shores of the very scenic and remote Newcomb Lake, surrounded by majestic mountains. The imposing Santanoni Peak at 4,607 feet can be seen beyond the northern shores of the lake. Two smaller mountains, Baldwin and Moose mountains, just under 3,000 feet, fill in the western horizon.

You will pass by the remains of a barn, silo, stone milking house, and great camp that were owned and built by the well-to-do Pruyn family of Albany. Situated amid a cedar grove along the rocky southeastern shores of the lake, their great camp, built in the classic Adirondack architectural style, consisted of an enormous rustic lodge, boathouse, and lakeside studio. Many of the "great camps" constructed during this bygone era were located on some remote lake and were created as family retreats. Increasing affluence toward the end of the nineteenth century and a desire to pursue leisure activities in the wilderness led many wealthy individuals to build rustic inns, lavish hotels, and family retreats in the Adirondacks. Trains and steamboats ferried families spending entire summers in the Adirondacks from New York and Boston. The years from 1870 to 1910 were called the Gilded Years. They represented the burgeoning, socially trendy pursuits of relaxation, adventures in the wilderness, and the quest for spiritual and physical well-being. The idyllic mountain and lake atmosphere and camping, fishing, and boating became vacation pastimes for many New Yorkers and Bostonians.

The sounds and sights of this bygone era have been replaced by the chatter of wildlife, and the overgrown environment is a return to the natural solitude.

RIDE 90 *THE GREAT SANTANONI*

This old forest road provides an opportunity to experience a historical, pristine, and enchanting forest environment.

General location: Just outside the village of Newcomb in the central area of Adirondack Park in northeastern New York.

Elevation change: The route gradually ascends for a little over 3 miles and then gently descends to the shores of Newcomb Lake.

Season: The black flies can be fierce in late spring. I passed by several hikers and canoeists sporting bug netting that covered their heads and arms. One tends to avoid the little buggers cruising on a mountain bike, but when you stop they swarm all over you as if you were sent as a special, alluring bug gift.

Services: The nearby town of Newcomb has some services, but you should stock up on picnic supplies before you set out for the day if you intend to spend time around Newcomb Lake. Camping at one of the lean-tos overlooking the lake is available by obtaining a camping permit from the ranger on duty at the gatehouse.

Hazards: Equestrians, walkers, and bikers gladly share the trails. You will encounter horses and hikers on the same trails, so display a mutual respect and courtesy for each other, and this beautiful preserve will remain a recreation area for all to enjoy. A passing hello has always been met with one in return from equestrians and hikers. They are glad to see you enjoying the preserve too.

Rescue index: You are not far from well-traveled NY 28N. The return route is mostly downhill, making it easy and fast to return to the parking area.

Land status: The preserve was first sold to another family who then sold it to the Nature Conservancy in 1972. In 1973 the land was transferred to New York. The New York State Department of Environmental Conservation now manages the property with special restrictions on fishing, camping, and motorized vehicles, but it's fortunately open to bicyclists.

Maps: The Adirondack High Peaks Region Area Map published by Plinth, Quoin & Cornice Associates provides excellent topographical detail of the route and surrounding terrain and can be found at most outdoor-type stores in New York for approximately $4.95. It is based on the USGS, 15 minute series, at a scale of 1:62,500 and a contour level of 20' where 1 inch = .98 mile.

Finding the trail: Take the New York State Thruway (Interstate 87) north to Exit 24 (Albany). Take I-87 (Adirondack Northway) north to Exit 29. Pick up Blue Ridge Road from the Adirondack Northway and follow it for about 40 minutes. Continue on NY 28N west, passing the Harris Lake Campsite in 3.1 miles and crossing the Hudson River in 3.4 miles. The entrance to the preserve is in Newcomb. A small sign just down from the main road marks the narrow access road. Cross a narrow iron bridge, pass the gatehouse on your right, and proceed to the top of the hill, where you will find a small parking lot. The only small requirement for riding on this property is that you register your name at the kiosk near the parking area.

Sources of additional information:

Placid Planet Bicycles
200 Saranac Avenue
Lake Placid, New York 12946
(518) 523-4128

Adirondack Park Agency
PO Box 99, Route 86
Raybrook, New York 12977
(518) 891-4050

New York State Department of Environmental Conservation
P.O. Box 296
Raybrook, New York 12977
(518) 897-1200

Lake Placid/Essex County Visitors Bureau
Olympic Center
Lake Placid, New York 12946
(800) 2PLACID

Newcomb Lake in the Santanoni Preserve.

Notes on the trail: A forest of large hemlock, spruce, tamarack, cedar, and birch greet you just beyond the gatehouse. The road alternates between flat and gentle grades for .9 mile, to a group of old farm buildings with stone walls edging the fields. You will pass the abandoned homes of the farm families who kept the Pruyn family dairy herd and gardens. An interesting stone building was the milk house, and the smaller stone shed beyond the last cottage was the smokehouse. Proceed past the buildings, swinging left and gradually up to the crest of a hill at 1.1 miles. A 1-mile descent brings you down to a beautiful stone bridge. From the bridge you will climb gently to the intersection with Moose Pond Road. Keep to the right because the Moose Pond Trail, which connects with the Cold River horse trails, is not open to bikes. You will climb gently for another quarter-mile to where the road flattens out and begins to descend to the south shore of Newcomb Lake, to a promontory where a picnic table overlooks the lake. Beyond, the bridge carries you over a narrow neck of the lake. Continue along the road, which turns west, past some numbered campsites for .4 mile to the old estate and boathouse. The massive log architecture of these old buildings, with their wide porches and covered breezeways, represents a bygone era of Adirondack history. Rustic logs geometrically pattern the doors, and enormous fieldstone fireplaces heated the numerous rooms. This was the typical building style of the late-nineteenth- and early-twentieth-century Adirondack retreats. Position yourself at the boathouse where you can see Moose Mountain in the west with Santanoni Mountain. Return along the same route.

RIDE 91 *PERKINS CLEARING*

A combination of snowmobile trails and old forest roads provides access throughout 16,000 acres of New York State and International Paper Company (IP) land. An entire network of logging and forest roads branches to remote, scenic places and encompasses anywhere from 10- to 20-mile trips. The well-conditioned roads are wide and smooth and a joy to ride on. You can spend half to a full day exploring these old logging and forest roads. The riding is moderately challenging as you pedal on hard-packed surfaces and over small hills.

Perkins Clearing was historically known as the place on the way to another place. During the early part of the nineteenth century a state road passed through Perkins Clearing, crossing the southern Adirondacks and connecting Albany to an area navigable by a boat near the St. Lawrence River. The route, called Albany Road, became a state road in 1812. One of the trails described below traverses part of that route and follows the old forest trail from Perkins Clearing to Sled Harbor. The route then continues along Old Military Road and follows through a pass to the north of Pillsbury Mountain. Sled Harbor was the point at which lumber supplies were unloaded from horse-drawn wagons and loaded onto sleds destined for the lumber and hunting camps in the remote wilderness of the West Canadas. The West Canadas are a region of high-altitude lakes and forests favored for their hunting and fishing.

A 1984 land swap between IP and New York State provided access for recreationalists through IP land into state land. The constitutionally approved deal opened up some serious off-road opportunities for the adventure-seeking mountain biker.

General location: Near Indian Lake in Hamilton County, eastern-central region of Adirondack Park in northeastern New York.
Elevation change: The moderately hilly terrain is potentially challenging for an intermediate rider.
Season: The black flies can be fierce in late spring. Avoid Perkins Clearing during hunting season or you may find more excitement than you bargained for.
Services: Services can be found in the town of Speculator, farther south on NY 30.
Hazards: Call the New York State Department of Environmental Conservation for information on hunting regulations. The season begins in mid-September. Pay attention to vehicle traffic that occasionally uses these dirt roads. Your tendency to bomb down some hill should be tempered by an awareness for blind turns. You never know when a car, animal, or other biker could be rounding the bend.

RIDE 91 *PERKINS CLEARING*

0 1/2 1
MILES

Pillsbury
Mtn.
3597

Pillsbury Lake

Sled
Harbor

Perkins
Clearing

To
Indian
Lake

Mason
Lake

30

Jessup River

Carpenter
Hill

Hard Wood
Hill

To
Speculator

NY

Rescue index: There is not a whole lot out here, and the nearest and largest town is Speculator, 7 miles to the south on NY 30. Remember to bring the proper provisions for first aid, food, and water.

Land status: These secondary public dirt roads pass through New York State and IP land.

Maps: The Adirondack Central Wilderness Area Map published by Plinth, Quoin & Cornice Associates provides excellent topographical detail of the route and surrounding terrain and can be found at most outdoor-type stores in New York for approximately $4.95. It is based on the USGS, 15 minute series, at a scale of 1:62,500 and a contour level of 20' where 1 inch = .98 mile.

Finding the trail: Take the New York State Thruway (Interstate 87) north to Exit 24 (Albany). Take I-87 north to the exit for Warrensburg and NY 28. Take NY 9 into NY 28. Follow NY 28 for 10 miles to Weavertown. Turn left (west) onto NY 8 for 30 miles to Speculator. Follow NY 30 north from Speculator and take the dirt road at the north end of Mason Lake. Park anywhere along the road and start to ride.

Source of additional information:

Hamilton County Tourism
County Office Building
White Birch Lane, Box 771
Indian Lake, New York 12842
(518) 648-5239

Notes on the trail: Continue on the dirt road south past Mason Lake for about 3 miles. The dirt road parallels the Mason Lake Outlet Stream. Soon you approach a fork at Perkins Clearing. Bear right (west) onto Forest Trail, past the gate, for 2 miles. You will reach the small hamlet of Sled Harbor. You may continue straight after Sled Harbor and take an optional day-hike to Pillsbury Lake or Pillsbury Mountain at 3,597'.

Turn left (southwest) at Sled Harbor, continuing on the dirt road for 3.5 miles and crossing several streams and the Jessup River; you'll reach a T intersection. An optional dirt road that heads into the wilderness can be your choice by turning right (west) at this intersection. It is a 7-mile, one-way dirt road you must return on, bringing your total distance for this dirt road spur to 14 miles. Turning left at the intersection takes you along another dirt road that runs up and over Carpenter Hill. In 1.6 miles the dirt road ends and you can follow 2 snowmobile trail options, one of which takes you back to Perkins Clearing.

You may turn right and continue south on one snowmobile trail. It meanders for about 6.5 miles into the Jessup River Wild Forest, paralleling the Mossy Vly Brook and eventually reaching Fawn Lake. This route tends to skirt swamp areas and may be extremely wet, so keep that in mind.

Turn left onto the snowmobile trail and continue north for about 2 miles to arrive at an intersection with Perkins Clearing. At this point you may return

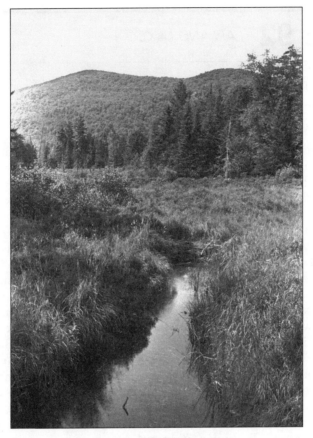

Creeks and bogs near Perkins Clearing.

to your vehicle by turning left to Perkins Clearing, and then right at the Perkins Clearing intersection back to your parking area.

If you are in the mood for some more riding, turn right (southeast) onto the dirt road and proceed up and over Hardwood Hill. Upon descending from Hardwood Hill, notice another dirt road to your right. Turn right onto this dirt road past a gate heading south. This route continues for another 4.5 miles, meandering into the wilderness and paralleling Place Brook. You must return along the same road to get back. If you have completed this dirt road spur, you can now return to Perkins Clearing by turning left after the gate and heading over Hardwood Hill. At Perkins Clearing, turn right to return to your parking area.

RIDE 92 *LAPLAND LAKE*

Lapland Lake, located in the low, rugged mountains and valleys of the southern section of the Adirondack Preserve, is a self-enclosed mountain bike mecca. Over 16 miles of well-maintained, wide, rolling, double-track trails traverse and network through hundreds of pristine, wooded acres of a private resort. During the winter months the Lapland Lake Vacation Center is one of the Northeast's finest cross-country ski centers. During the summer months, the well-configured cross-country ski trail network provides a variety of mountain bike routes that will appeal to all levels and is a work of trail art. Novice riders will enjoy the easy cruising trails and scenic beauty of the countryside, and intermediate riders can test their endurance and skills over the more challenging routes. This oasis of trails is surrounded by vast mountain ranges and accented by a serene, 70-acre, spring-fed wilderness lake. If you decide this is where you want to ride, there is only one requirement. You must stay at the Lapland Lake Resort to utilize their trail system.

This rustic, cozy setting, reminiscent of Finland, combines solitude and relaxation with exciting mountain biking. It is owned and operated by former Olympic skier Olavi Hirvonen and his family. Ann and Olavi Hirvonen are your hosts and the owners of the Lapland Lake Visitor Center and welcome mountain bikers and their families. The experienced staff is eager to help you enjoy your time there.

Stay in one of their tupas, or cottages, with wood burning stoves and screened porches, and ride the trails. These facilities are available exclusively to overnight guests. *Tervetuloa* (Welcome).

General location: Northeastern New York, in the southeastern section of Adirondack Park.
Elevation change: The trails traverse hilly terrain with no appreciable or difficult ascents and descents.
Season: The trails are available for riding after spring thaws, sometime in late May when the land dries out, until late fall. Call the Lapland Visitor Center for more details on the condition of the trails.
Services: Overnight lodging includes free use of rowboats, canoes, beach and swimming facilities, lawn games, hiking, and a Finnish woodburning sauna. There are ten private two-, three-, and four-bedroom tupas. Immaculately maintained, each tupa contains a living room, separate bedrooms, a bathroom with shower, and a fully equipped kitchen. An 1800s farmhouse can also be reserved for large groups and families. Mountain bike rentals and children's bike trailers are also available on the premises. The village of Northville, 9 miles away, offers golf, tennis, antiques, and country stores.

At day's end, cool off your tires and head into the sauna. Afterward, you can say only one thing, *Kiitos saunasta* (Thank you for sauna).

Hazards: The routes are well-maintained, and the only hazard may be that you are enjoying yourself too much and might not return to work on time.

Rescue index: All trails lead back to the visitor center where help can be found.

Land status: Private land.

Maps: The visitor center provides the most detailed map of all the trails. Pick one up before heading out. All trails are marked with the standard cross-country ski trail marking system, and there are trail signs and corresponding numbers at most intersections. Most of the Lapland trails are designated as one way.

Finding the trail: Lapland Lake is just over an hour's drive from Albany and 4 hours from New York City. Take the New York State Thruway (Interstate 87) to Exit 27 at Amsterdam and follow NY 30 north 27 miles. Turn left onto Benson Road for 5.2 miles. Take a right onto Storer Road for the remaining .7 mile, bearing right.

Source of additional information:

Lapland Lake Vacation Center
139 Lapland Lake Road
Northville, New York 12134
(518) 863-4974

Notes on the trail: A large array of trails awaits the energetic mountain biker at Lapland Lake. A tremendous number of riding configurations can be created on the maze of trails and will fill up an entire day of bike riding and exploration. Check in at the office, grab a map, pick a trail, and just begin riding. The routes are well marked and impeccably maintained. The printed map of the trail system will help you to determine and plan which trail to take.

To begin with, you might want to warm up with the easier, flat trail network, consisting of the Lake Trail, Talvi Tie (Winter Road), and Era Polku (Forest Trail). If you wish to head for the more challenging and scenic trails, Sisu (Determination) provides 3 miles of rolling, grass-covered trails that pass along the rocky Grant Stream and through stands of giant pine. Toward the end of Sisu, turn off at the Leilan Latu link, which will connect you to the 3-mile Karhu Polku (Bear Path) loop and the more difficult, black diamond Napa Piiri (Arctic Circle). There are 3 hilly loops that spur off Karhu Polku and are not for the weak of heart. The hills are gruesome, but if you can put up with more than a little physical pain, you're definitely in for the ride of your life. If you're ready for more thrills, at the end of Karhu Polku head up to the Napa Piiri. Make sure you return from the Karhu Polku or Napa Piiri trails along the .6-mile, exhilarating Tuulen Tie (Way of the Wind) Trail that descends and returns you to the ski lodge and bike rental shop.

Note: *All trails are double-track.*

Grant Stream

Era Polku

Private

Cathead Rd.

Talui Tie

Woods Lake

Lake Trail

Tunturi Loop

Lodge

Vasa

NY

Entrance

Storer Rd.

To Benson Rd.
and 30

RIDE 93 *THE INNER CIRCLE*

Many of the best, most exciting trails are shared by the inner circle of cyclists, the esoteric group of riders who know the lay of the land and are obsessed with discovering the best escapes, the most remote routes unknown to the masses. They want these routes left relatively untraveled. They want these routes to themselves.

Garnet Hill Lodge is where you'll find the inner circle. The obsessive ones. But they come to this great riding area even though it's no longer undiscovered. Riders of all abilities and at all levels of commitment to the sport share in the wealth of this mountain biking terrain. Over 25 miles of well-maintained, double- and single-track trails form a maze that winds through the attractive, rolling countryside around the lodge in the southern Adirondacks' North River. In the winter, the lodge area is laced with a network of cross-country ski trails. Once the snow melts, the skiers may be gone, but the trails remain perfect for mountain bikers and have broad enough appeal to meet the requirements of any kind of rider. Novice riders can explore the easy cruising trails and backcountry dirt roads and witness the scenic beauty of the woodland landscape. Expert riders can rough it through some steep, challenging single-track. Indeed, the trails are a mixed bag, beckoning beginning, intermediate, and expert riders. The terrain around the lodge has a seemingly endless network of trails. These vary from flat, wide, and smooth to narrow and steep. Follow the inner circle and explore Garnet Hill Lodge.

General location: Northeastern New York, in the southern section of Adirondack Park.

Elevation change: The hilly terrain provides challenging riding. Trail riding is helped by the skill-level trail markers that designate the wintertime cross-country ski trails.

Season: The trails are available for riding after spring thaws, sometime in late May when the land dries out, until late fall. Call Garnet Hill Lodge for more details on trail conditions.

Services: Overnight lodging is available at Garnet Hill's lovely and attractive inn. Mountain bike rentals and sales are available on the premises. Inquire at Garnet Hill to see if they are running their "bike downhill–ride back" shuttle bus service. Riders can tour the trails and roads at Garnet Hill and eventually ride into North Creek to the pick-up point. The distance is approximately 10 miles and the trip is suitable for all but novice bikers.

Hazards: The routes are well marked and easy to follow. Not all of the cross-country ski trails are suitable for mountain bike riding. As stated in the Garnet Hill mountain bike guide, the novice ski trails are generally the novice bicycle trails, and the expert ski trails become expert-only mountain bike trails. If you are a beginner, it may be wise to attempt the trails at the beginner level. Stop in at the mountain bike center to get the latest update on trail conditions and suggestions.

Rescue index: You are never more than a few miles from the lodge.

Land status: Public land. Many trails at Garnet Hill cross private land. Please do not wander off the trail near houses, barns, or other private buildings.

Maps: The ski center provides the most detailed map of all the trails. Pick one up before heading out. All trails are marked with the standard cross-country ski trail marking system, and there are trail signs and corresponding numbers at most intersections.

Finding the trail: Take the New York State Thruway (Interstate 87) north to Exit 24 (Albany). Take I-87 north to Exit 25/Route 8, Chestertown and Hague. At the end of the exit ramp, turn left (west) onto NY 8 toward Loon Lake. After passing through Wevertown, turn right (west) at the stop sign onto NY 28. This scenic highway takes you through the towns of North Creek and North River. After North River, follow the signs for Garnet Hill Lodge.

Sources of additional information:

Garnet Hill Lodge
13th Lake Road
North River, New York 12856
(518) 251-2821

Gore Mountain Region Chamber of Commerce
P.O. Box 84
North Creek, New York 12853
(518) 251-2612

Notes on the trail: A large array of trails awaits the energetic mountain biker at the Garnet Hill Resort. A tremendous number of riding configurations can be created on the maze of trails and will fill up an entire day of bike riding and exploration. Check in at the office, grab a map, pick a trail, and just begin riding. The routes are well marked, and the printed map of the trail system will help you to determine and plan which trail to take.

The Garnet Hill mountain bike guide provides the following riding advice for the different levels of riders that come and visit the area.

The easiest riding for beginners is on the roads in the area. The best of these rides is the Old Farm Road, returning the same way. (Ride only to the yellow barrier!) 4-H Road and Harvey Road are also easy riding. The Old Faithful Trail connects both these roads and makes for a nice loop.

For intermediate riders, Trapper Trail to Harvey's Tailings is a good route. At Harvey's Tailings, cross the stream to the Cougar Run Trail. Take Cougar Run left past the Sugarhouse Trail, and left at the driveway to Harvey Road.

To 28

Harvey Rd.

Apple Way

Mtn. View

To
Harvey Rd.

Roger's Rd.

Cougar Run

Sugar
House

Coyote Pass

Roger's Rd.
Pickup

Cougar Run

To
Barton Rd.

Harveys
Tailings

Trapper Tr.

Joe Petes Run

NY

Turn left on Harvey Road to 4-H Road and then take the Bobcat/Blue Jay Trail to the lodge. Mountain View and Apple Way Trails are at the end of Cougar Run. These are open field trails with great views of the High Peaks. Another intermediate loop is Sugarhouse Trail and Coyote Pass, both of which branch off Cougar Run after Harvey's Tailings. Sugarhouse Trail ends at Roger's Road. You can ride left on Roger's Road to Harvey Road and left on Harvey Road eventually back to Garnet Hill. This is a very hilly ride.

The expert trails are Bobcat, Matt & Jeff Trail, Joe Pete (open to the ravine only), Solitude, and Duffany's Run.

Afterword

LAND-USE CONTROVERSY

A few years ago I wrote a long piece on this issue for *Sierra* magazine that entailed calling literally dozens of government land managers, game wardens, mountain bikers, and local officials to get a feeling for how riders were being welcomed on the trails. All that I've seen personally since, and heard from my authors, indicates there hasn't been much change. We're still considered the new kid on the block. We have less of a right to the trails than horses and hikers, and we're excluded from many areas, including:

a) wilderness areas
b) national parks (except on roads, and those paths specifically marked "bike path")
c) national monuments (except on roads open to the public)
d) most state parks and monuments (except on roads, and those paths specifically marked "bike path")
e) an increasing number of urban and county parks, especially in California (except on roads, and those paths specifically marked "bike path")

Frankly, I have little difficulty with these exclusions and would, in fact, restrict our presence from some trails I've ridden (one time) due to the environmental damage and chance of blind-siding the many walkers and hikers I met up with along the way. But these are my personal views. The author of this volume and mountain bikers as a group may hold different opinions.

You can do your part in keeping us from being excluded from even more trails by riding responsibly. Many local and national off-road bicycle organizations have been formed with exactly this in mind, and one of the largest—the National Off-Road Bicycle Association (NORBA)—offers the following code of behavior for mountain bikers:

1. I will yield the right of way to other non-motorized recreationists. I realize that people judge all cyclists by my actions.
2. I will slow down and use caution when approaching or overtaking another cyclist and will make my presence known well in advance.
3. I will maintain control of my speed at all times and will approach turns in anticipation of someone around the bend.
4. I will stay on designated trails to avoid trampling native vegetation and minimize potential erosion to trails by not using muddy trails or short-cutting switchbacks.

5. I will not disturb wildlife or livestock.
6. I will not litter. I will pack out what I pack in, and pack out more than my share whenever possible.
7. I will respect public and private property, including trail use signs and no trespassing signs, and I will leave gates as I have found them.
8. I will always be self-sufficient and my destination and travel speed will be determined by my ability, my equipment, the terrain, the present and potential weather conditions.
9. I will not travel solo when bikepacking in remote areas. I will leave word of my destination and when I plan to return.
10. I will observe the practice of minimum impact bicycling by "taking only pictures and memories and leaving only waffle prints."
11. I will always wear a helmet whenever I ride.

Now, I have a problem with some of these—number nine, for instance. The most enjoyable mountain biking I've ever done has been solo. And as for leaving word of destination and time of return, I've enjoyed living in such a way as to say, "I'm off to pedal Colorado. See you in the fall." Of course it's senseless to take needless risks, and I plan a ride and pack my gear with this in mind. But for me number nine smacks too much of the "never-out-of-touch" mentality. And getting away from civilization, deep into the wilds, is, for many people, what mountain biking's all about.

All in all, however, NORBA's is a good list, and surely we mountain bikers would be liked more, and excluded less, if we followed the suggestions. But let me offer a "code of ethics" I much prefer, one given to cyclists by Utah's Wasatch-Cache National Forest office.

Study a Forest Map Before You Ride
Currently, bicycles are permitted on roads and developed trails within the Wasatch-Cache National Forest except in designated Wilderness. If your route crosses private land, it is your responsibility to obtain right of way permission from the landowner.

Keep Groups Small
Riding in large groups degrades the outdoor experience for others, can disturb wildlife, and usually leads to greater resource damage.

Avoid Riding on Wet Trails
Bicycle tires leave ruts in wet trails. These ruts concentrate runoff and accelerate erosion. Postponing a ride when the trails are wet will preserve the trails for future use.

Stay on Roads and Trails
Riding cross-country destroys vegetation and damages the soil.

Always Yield to Others
Trails are shared by hikers, horses, and bicycles. Move off the trail to

allow horses to pass and stop to allow hikers adequate room to share the trail. Simply yelling "Bicycle!" is not acceptable.

Control Your Speed
Excessive speed endangers yourself and other forest users.

Avoid Wheel Lock-up and Spin-out
Steep terrain is especially vulnerable to trail wear. Locking brakes on steep descents or when stopping needlessly damages trails. If a slope is steep enough to require locking wheels and skidding, dismount and walk your bicycle. Likewise, if an ascent is so steep your rear wheel slips and spins, dismount and walk your bicycle.

Protect Waterbars and Switchbacks
Waterbars, the rock and log drains built to direct water off trails, protect trails from erosion. When you encounter a waterbar, ride directly over the top or dismount and walk your bicycle. Riding around the ends of waterbars destroys them and speeds erosion. Skidding around switchback corners shortens trail life. Slow down for switchback corners and keep your wheels rolling.

If You Abuse It, You Lose It
Mountain bikers are relative newcomers to the forest and must prove themselves responsible trail users. By following the guidelines above, and by participating in trail maintenance service projects, bicyclists can help avoid closures which would prevent them from using trails.

I've never seen a better trail-etiquette list for mountain bikers. So have fun. Be careful. And don't screw up things for the next rider.

Dennis Coello

Glossary

This short list of terms does not contain all the words used by mountain bike enthusiasts when discussing their sport. But it should serve as an introduction to the lingo you'll hear on the trails.

ATB	all-terrain bike; this, like "fat-tire bike," is another name for a mountain bike
ATV	all-terrain vehicle; this usually refers to the loud, fume-spewing three- or four-wheeled motorized vehicles you will not enjoy meeting on the trail—except, of course, if you crash and have to hitch a ride out on one
bladed	refers to a dirt road which has been smoothed out by the use of a wide blade on earth-moving equipment; "blading" gets rid of the teeth-chattering, much-cursed washboards found on so many dirt roads after heavy vehicle use
blaze	a mark on a tree made by chipping away a piece of the bark, usually done to designate a trail; such trails are sometimes described as "blazed"
blind corner	a curve in the road or trail that conceals bikers, hikers, equestrians, and other traffic
BLM	Bureau of Land Management, an agency of the federal government
buffed	used to describe a very smooth trail
catching air	taking a jump in such a way that both wheels of the bike are off the ground at the same time
clean	while this may describe what you and your bike *won't* be after following many trails, the term is most often used as a verb to denote the action of pedaling a tough section of trail successfully
deadfall	a tangled mass of fallen trees or branches
diversion ditch	a usually narrow, shallow ditch dug across or around a trail; funneling the water in this manner keeps it from destroying the trail
double-track	the dual tracks made by a jeep or other vehicle, with grass or weeds or rocks between; mountain bikers can

ride in either of the tracks, but you will of course find that whichever one you choose, and no matter how many times you change back and forth, the other track will appear to offer smoother travel

dugway   a steep, unpaved, switchbacked descent

feathering   using a light touch on the brake lever, hitting it lightly many times rather than very hard or locking the brake

four-wheel-drive   this refers to any vehicle with drive-wheel capability on all four wheels (a jeep, for instance, has four-wheel drive as compared with a two-wheel-drive passenger car), or to a rough road or trail that requires four-wheel-drive capability (or a *one*-wheel-drive mountain bike!) to negotiate it

game trail   the usually narrow trail made by deer, elk, or other game

gated   everyone knows what a gate is, and how many variations exist upon this theme; well, if a trail is described as "gated" it simply has a gate across it; don't forget that the rule is if you find a gate closed, close it behind you; if you find one open, leave it that way

Giardia   shorthand for *Giardia lamblia,* and known as the "backpacker's bane" until we mountain bikers expropriated it; this is a waterborne parasite that begins its life cycle when swallowed, and one to four weeks later has its host (you) bloated, vomiting, shivering with chills and living in the bathroom; the disease can be avoided by "treating" (purifying) the water you acquire along the trail (see "Hitting the Trail" in the Introduction)

gnarly   a term thankfully used less and less these days, it refers to tough trails

hammer   to ride very hard

hardpack   a trail in which the dirt surface is packed down hard; such trails make for good and fast riding, and very painful landings; bikers most often use "hardpack" as both a noun and adjective, and "hard-packed" as an adjective only (the grammar lesson will help you when diagramming sentences in camp)

jeep road,
   jeep trail   a rough road or trail passable only with four-wheel-drive capability (or a horse or mountain bike)

kamikaze   while this once referred primarily to those Japanese fliers who quaffed a glass of sake, then flew off as human bombs in suicide missions against U.S. naval vessels, it has more recently been applied to the idiot mountain bikers who, far less honorably, scream down hiking trails, endangering the physical and mental safety of the walking, biking, and equestrian traffic they meet; deck guns were necessary to stop the Japanese kamikaze pilots, but a bike pump or walking staff in the spokes is sufficient for the current-day kamikazes who threaten to get us all kicked off the trails

multi-purpose   a BLM designation of land which is open to many uses; mountain biking is allowed

out-and-back   a ride where you will return on the same trail you pedaled out; while this might sound far more boring than a loop route, many trails look very different when pedaled in the opposite direction

portage   to carry your bike on your person

quads   bikers use this term to refer both to the extensor muscle in the front of the thigh (which is separated into four parts) and to USGS maps; the expression "Nice quads!" refers always to the former, however, except in those instances when the speaker is an engineer

runoff   rainwater or snowmelt

signed   a "signed" trail has signs in place of blazes

single-track   a single, narrow path through grass or brush or over rocky terrain, often created by deer, elk, or backpackers; single-track riding is some of the best fun around

slickrock   the rock-hard, compacted sandstone that is *great* to ride and even prettier to look at; you'll appreciate it even more if you think of it as a petrified sand dune or seabed, and if the rider before you hasn't left tire marks (from unnecessary skidding) or granola bar wrappers behind

snowmelt   runoff produced by the melting of snow

snowpack   unmelted snow accumulated over weeks or months of winter—or over years in high-mountain terrain

spur   a road or trail that intersects the main trail you're following

switchback   a zigzagging road or trail designed to assist in traversing steep terrain: mountain bikers should *not* skid through switchbacks *technical* terrain that is difficult to ride due not to its grade (steepness) but to its obstacles—rocks, logs, ledges, loose soil . . .

topo short for topographical map, the kind that shows both linear distance *and* elevation gain and loss; "topo" is pronounced with both vowels long

trashed a trail that has been destroyed (same term used no matter what has destroyed it . . . cattle, horses, or even mountain bikers riding when the ground was too wet)

two-wheel-drive this refers to any vehicle with drive-wheel capability on only two wheels (a passenger car, for instance, has two-wheel-drive); a two-wheel-drive road is a road or trail easily traveled by an ordinary car

water bar An earth, rock, or wooden structure that funnels water off trails to reduce erosion

washboarded a road that is surfaced with many ridges spaced closely together, like the ripples on a washboard; these make for very rough riding, and even worse driving in a car or jeep

wilderness area land that is officially set aside by the federal government to remain *natural*—pure, pristine, and untrammeled by any vehicle, including mountain bikes; though mountain bikes had not been born in 1964 (when the United States Congress passed the Wilderness Act, establishing the National Wilderness Preservation system), they are considered a "form of mechanical transport" and are thereby excluded; in short, stay out

wind chill a reference to the wind's cooling effect upon exposed flesh; for example, if the temperature is 10 degrees Fahrenheit and the wind is blowing at 20 miles per hour, the wind-chill (that is, the actual temperature to which your skin reacts) is *minus* 32 degrees; if you are riding in wet conditions things are even worse, for the wind-chill would then be *minus 74 degrees!*

windfall anything (trees, limbs, brush, fellow bikers . . .) blown down by the wind

ABOUT THE AUTHOR

MICHAEL MARGULIS and his wife Barbara, his two children, Alize and Chloe, and their Norwegian Elkhound, Shogun, live in Forest Hills, New York. His passion for the outdoors has drawn him to a multitude of state and national parks in the Pacific Northwest, the Southwest, and the Northeast, particularly in New York. His unrelenting drive to explore natural locations has taken him to the French and Swiss Alps, where he led hiking tours.

Michael and his family have a philosophy that life in New York should be balanced by the pursuit of the great outdoors. They camp, hike, bike, or cross-country ski almost every weekend, despite his busy schedule, working as a software engineer for Bergdorf Goodman in Manhattan. He has been a student and teacher of Okinawan Shorin-Ryu Karate-do for 15 years and has earned the rank of second-degree black belt. His other pastimes include photography, carpentry, and piano.

The writing of this book has been a passion fulfilled. It's his way of sharing with other outdoor enthusiasts the challenging and rewarding sport of mountain biking in New York.